Bloom's Modern Critical Views

African American
    Poets: Wheatley–
    Tolson
African American
    Poets: Hayden–
    Dove
Edward Albee
American and
    Canadian Women
    Poets, 1930–present
American Women
    Poets, 1650–1950
Maya Angelou
Asian-American
    Writers
Margaret Atwood
Jane Austen
James Baldwin
Honoré de Balzac
Samuel Beckett
Saul Bellow
The Bible
William Blake
Jorge Luis Borges
Ray Bradbury
The Brontës
Gwendolyn Brooks
Elizabeth Barrett
    Browning
Robert Browning
Italo Calvino
Albert Camus
Truman Capote
Lewis Carroll
Willa Cather
Cervantes
Geoffrey Chaucer
Anton Chekhov
Kate Chopin
Agatha Christie
Samuel Taylor
    Coleridge
Joseph Conrad

Contemporary Poets
Stephen Crane
Dante
Daniel Defoe
Don DeLillo
Charles Dickens
Emily Dickinson
John Donne and the
    17th-Century Poets
Fyodor Dostoevsky
W. E. B. DuBois
George Eliot
T. S. Eliot
Ralph Ellison
Ralph Waldo Emerson
William Faulkner
F. Scott Fitzgerald
Sigmund Freud
Robert Frost
Johann Wolfgang
    von Goethe
George Gordon, Lord
    Byron
Graham Greene
Thomas Hardy
Nathaniel Hawthorne
Ernest Hemingway
Hermann Hesse
Hispanic-American
    Writers
Homer
Langston Hughes
Zora Neale Hurston
Aldous Huxley
Henrik Ibsen
John Irving
Henry James
James Joyce
Franz Kafka
John Keats
Jamaica Kincaid
Stephen King
Rudyard Kipling

Milan Kundera
D. H. Lawrence
Doris Lessing
Ursula K. Le Guin
Sinclair Lewis
Norman Mailer
Bernard Malamud
Christopher Marlowe
Gabriel García
    Márquez
Cormac McCarthy
Carson McCullers
Herman Melville
Arthur Miller
John Milton
Molière
Toni Morrison
Native-American
    Writers
Joyce Carol Oates
Flannery O'Connor
Eugene O'Neill
George Orwell
Octavio Paz
Sylvia Plath
Edgar Allan Poe
Katherine Anne
    Porter
Thomas Pynchon
Philip Roth
Salman Rushdie
J. D. Salinger
Jean-Paul Sartre
William Shakespeare:
    Histories and
    Poems
William Shakespeare:
    Romances
William Shakespeare:
    The Comedies
William Shakespeare:
    The Tragedies
George Bernard Shaw

Bloom's Modern Critical Views

Mary Wollstonecraft
  Shelley
Percy Bysshe Shelley
Alexander
  Solzhenitsyn
Sophocles
John Steinbeck
Tom Stoppard
Jonathan Swift
Amy Tan
Alfred, Lord Tennyson

Henry David Thoreau
J. R. R. Tolkien
Leo Tolstoy
Ivan Turgenev
Mark Twain
John Updike
Kurt Vonnegut
Derek Walcott
Alice Walker
Robert Penn Warren
Eudora Welty

Edith Wharton
Walt Whitman
Oscar Wilde
Tennessee Williams
Thomas Wolfe
Tom Wolfe
Virginia Woolf
William Wordsworth
Richard Wright
William Butler Yeats

Bloom's Modern Critical Views

ROBERT FROST

Edited and with an introduction by
Harold Bloom
Sterling Professor of the Humanities
Yale University

CHELSEA HOUSE
PUBLISHERS
A Haights Cross Communications Company

Philadelphia

©2003 by Chelsea House Publishers, a subsidiary of
Haights Cross Communications.

A Haights Cross Communications ✦ Company

Introduction © 2003 by Harold Bloom.

Printed and bound in the United States of America.
10 9 8 7 6 5 4 3 2 1

Library of Congress Cataloging-in-Publication Data

Robert Frost / edited and with an introduction by Harold Bloom.
    p. cm. -- (Bloom's modern critical views)
Includes bibliographical references (p.) and index.
  ISBN: 0-7910-7443-9
  1. Frost, Robert, 1874-1963--Criticism and interpretation. I. Bloom,
Harold. II. Series.
  PS3511.R94Z9159 2003
  811'.52--dc21

                                        2003000807

Chelsea House Publishers
1974 Sproul Road, Suite 400
Broomall, PA 19008-0914

http://www.chelseahouse.com

Contributing Editor: Jesse Zuba

Cover designed by Terry Mallon

Cover: © E.O. Hoppé/CORBIS

Layout by EJB Publishing Services

Contents

Editor's Note   vii

Introduction   1
    Harold Bloom

Choices   9
    Richard Poirier

Wordsworth, Frost, Stevens and Poetic Vocation   29
    David Bromwich

The Counter-Intelligence of Robert Frost   45
    Herbert Marks

Echoing Eden: Frost and Origins   67
    Charles Berger

The Need of Being Versed: Robert Frost
and the Limits of Rhetoric   87
    Shira Wolosky

The Promethean Frost   109
    George F. Bagby

Robert Frost and the Motives of Poetry   139
    Mark Richardson

The Serpent's Tale   161
    Katherine Kearns

Above the Brim   201
    Seamus Heaney

The Fact Is the Sweetest Dream: Darwin,
    Pragmatism, and Poetic Knowledge   219
    Robert Faggen

The Sense of Sound and the Silent Text   271
    Tyler Hoffman

Chronology   295

Contributors   299

Bibliography   303

Acknowledgments   307

Index   309

Editor's Note

My Introduction explores some elements of Emerson's influence upon Frost, particularly their shared gnosis of "the American Religion."

Richard Poirier traces Frost's early choices that led to his distinctive voice, while David Bromwich contrasts Wordsworth to Frost and to Wallace Stevens as the creator of figures radically other: beggars, vagrants, lost children, grieving women.

Herbert Marks studies displacement and loss in Frost, after which Charles Berger analyzes Frost's fictions of origins.

Shira Wolosky shows how Frost renders rhetorical limitations into creative acts, while George F. Bagby emphasizes the Promethean element in Frost.

Personality, deprecated by the school of T. S. Eliot, is brought forward by Mark Richardson as a prime Frostian motive for metaphor, after which Katherine Kearns pungently explores the nihilism of Frost's sexuality.

The Irish laureate Seamus Heaney celebrates Frost as a poet who could go naked, free of protective ironies, while Robert Faggen gives us a more "philosophical" Frost, responding to Darwin and the Pragmatists.

In a final essay, Tyler Hoffman takes on the difficult task of relating Frost's poetic formalism to the politics of his poetry.

Introduction

I

Frost—at his frequent best—rivals Wallace Stevens as the great American poet of this century. He does not much resemble Stevens, ultimately for reasons that have little to do with the "essential gaudiness" of much early Stevens, or even with the austere clairvoyance of the later Stevens, poet of "The Auroras of Autumn" and "The Rock." Both of those aspects of Stevens rise from a powerful, barely repressed influence-relationship to Whitman, a poet who scarcely affected Frost. Indeed, Frost's uniqueness among modern American poets of real eminence partly stems from his independence of Whitman. Eliot, Stevens, Pound, Hart Crane, W. C. Williams, Roethke—all have complex links to Whitman, covert in Eliot and in Stevens. Frost (in this like Whitman himself) is the son of Emerson, of the harsher Emerson that we begin only now to recover. Any deep reader of Frost understands why the poet of "Two Tramps in Mud Time" and "Directive" seriously judged Emerson's "Uriel" to be "the greatest Western poem yet." "Uriel's voice of cherub scorn," once referred to by Frost as "Emersonian scorn," is the essential mode of irony favored throughout Frost's poetry.

"Uriel" is Emerson's own irreverent allegory of the controversy set off by his "Divinity School Address." There are certainly passages in the poem that seem to have been written by Frost and not by Emerson:

> The young deities discussed
> Laws of form, and metre just,
> Orb, quintessence, and sunbeams,
> What subsisteth, and what seems.
> One, with low tones that decide,
> And doubt and reverend use defied,

With a look that solved the sphere,
And stirred the devils everywhere,
Gave his sentiment divine
Against the being of a line.
"Line in nature is not found;
Unit and universe are round;
In vain produced, all rays return;
Evil will bless, and ice will burn."

At the center of this is Emerson's law of Compensation: "Nothing is got for nothing," as Emerson phrased it later, in the remorseless essay "Power," in his *The Conduct of Life*. The darker Emersonian essays— "Experience," "Power," "Circles," "Fate," "Illusions"—read like manifestos for Frost's poetry. Richard Poirier has demonstrated this in some detail, and I follow him here in emphasizing how pervasive and crucial the affinity between Emerson and Freud tends to be. If there is a particular motto that states the dialectic of Frost's best poems, then it is to be found in a formulation of Emerson's "Self-Reliance."

Life only avails, not the having lived. Power ceases in the instant of repose; it resides in the moment of transition from a past to a new state, in the shooting of the gulf, in the darting to an aim.

One thinks of the extraordinary early poem "The Wood-Pile" (1914), where the poet, "out walking in the frozen swamp one gray day," comes upon "a cord of maple, cut and split / and piled" and then abandoned:

I thought that only
Someone who lived in turning to fresh tasks
Could so forget his handiwork on which
He spent himself, the labor of his ax,
And leave it there far from a useful fireplace
To warm the frozen swamp as best it could
With the slow smokeless burning of decay.

That "slow smokeless burning" is the metaphor for Emerson's "instant of repose," where power ceases. Frost's restless turnings are his most Emersonian moments, American and agonistic. His Job, in *A Masque of Reason*, puzzling over God's Reason, deliberately relates Jehovah's dialectic to that of Emerson's "Uriel":

Yet I suppose what seems to us confusion
Is not confusion, but the form of forms,
The serpent's tail stuck down the serpent's throat,
Which is the symbol of eternity
And also of the way all things come round,
Or of how rays return upon themselves,
To quote the greatest Western poem yet.
Though I hold rays deteriorate to nothing:
First white, then red, then ultrared, then out.

Job's last two lines here mark Frost's characteristic swerve away from
Emerson, except that Emerson is the most difficult of fathers to evade,
having been always so subtly evasive himself. Frost's authentic nihilism is
considerable, but is surpassed by "Fate" in *The Conduct of Life*, and by a grand
more-than-Frostian late entry in Emerson's journals, set down in the autumn
of 1866, when the sage felt burned to the socket by the intensities he had
experienced during the Civil War:

There may be two or three or four steps, according to the genius
of each, but for every seeing soul there are two absorbing facts, *I
and the Abyss.*

Frost's religion, as a poet, was the American religion that Emerson
founded. A latecomer exegete of that religion, I once offered its credo as
Everything that can be broken should be broken, a Gnostic motto that eminently
suits Frost's poetry, where God, whether in *A Masque of Reason*, *A Masque of
Mercy*, or in "Once by the Pacific," is clearly animated neither by reason nor
mercy but only by the blind necessities of being the Demiurge:

It looked as if a night of dark intent
Was coming, and not only a night, an age.
Someone had better be prepared for rage.
There would be more than ocean-water broken
Before God's last *Put out the Light* was spoken.

A God who echoes Othello at his most murderous is himself also
crazed by jealousy. Frost's celebrated negativity is a secularized negative
theology, almost wholly derived from Emerson, insofar as it was not purely
temperamental. Slyly aware of it, Frost used it as the occasion for lovely
jokes, as in the marvelous "Two Tramps in Mud Time":

The water for which we may have to look
In summertime with a witching wand,
In every wheelrut's now a brook,
In every print of a hoof a pond.
Be glad of water, but don't forget
The lurking frost in the earth beneath
That will steal forth after the sun is set
And show on the water its crystal teeth.

"Two Tramps in Mud Time" hymns the Emersonian negativity of refusing to identify yourself with any work, in order instead to achieve the Gnostic identity of the knower with what is known, when the sparks of the Alien God or true Workman stream through you. A shrewd Gnostic, Frost refuses to lament confusion, though he also will not follow Whitman in celebrating it. In Emerson's "Uriel," confusion precedes the dimming of that Miltonic archangel of the sun, who withers from a sad self-knowledge. Uriel-Emerson (for which read Frost) is himself not responsible for engendering the confusion, which results from the failure of nerve suffered by the heavenly powers when they hear Uriel proclaim that "all rays return; Evil will bless, and ice will burn":

As Uriel spoke with piercing eye,
A shudder ran around the sky;
The stern old war-gods shook their heads,
The seraphs frowned from myrtle-beds;
Seemed to the holy festival
The rash word boded ill to all;
The balance-beam of Fate was bent;
The bounds of good and ill were rent;
Strong Hades could not keep his own,
But all slid to confusion.

"Confusion" is a mixing or pouring together of entities that would be better off if kept apart. Whether instinctively or overtly, both Emerson and Frost seem to have known that the Indo-European root of "confusion" originally meant "to pour a libation," as if to the gods. Frost's "form of forms," or confusion which is not confusion, identified by him with the Emersonian rays returning upon themselves, is a kind of libation poured out to the Alien God, as in the trope that concludes his great poem "Directive":

Here are your waters and your watering place.
Drink and be whole again beyond confusion.

II

"Directive" is Frost's poem of poems or form of forms, a meditation whose rays perpetually return upon themselves. "All things come round," even our mental confusion as we blunder morally, since the Demiurge is nothing but a moral blunderer. Frost shares the fine Emersonian wildness or freedom, the savage strength of the essay "Power" that suggests a way of being whole beyond Fate, of arriving at an end to circlings, at a resolution to all the Emersonian turnings that see unity, and yet behold divisions: "The world is mathematical, and has no casualty, in all its vast and flowing curve." "Directive" appears to be the poem in which Frost measures the lot, and forgives himself the lot, and perhaps even casts out remorse. In some sense, it was the poem he always wrote and rewrote, in a revisionary process present already in *A Boy's Will* (1913) but not fully worked out until *Steeple Bush* (1947), where "Directive" was published, when Frost was seventy-three. "The Demiurge's Laugh" in *A Boy's Will* features a mocking demonic derision at the self-realization that "what I hunted was no true god."

North of Boston (1914) has its most memorable poem in the famous "After Apple-Picking," a gracious hymn to the necessity of yielding up the quest, of clambering down from one's "long two-pointed [ladder] sticking through a tree / Toward heaven still." Frost's subtlest of perspectivizings is the true center of the poem:

> I cannot rub the strangeness from my sight
> I got from looking through a pane of glass
> I skimmed this morning from the drinking trough
> And held against the world of hoary grass.
> It melted, and I let it fall and break.

The sheet of ice is a lens upon irreality, but so are Frost's own eyes, or anyone's, in his cosmos. This supposed nature poet represents his harsh landscapes as a full version of the Gnostic *kenoma*, the cosmological emptiness into which we have been thrown by the mocking Demiurge. This is the world of *Mountain Interval* (1916), where "the broken moon" is preferred to the dimmed sun, where the oven bird sings of "that other fall we name the fall," and where the birches:

> shed crystal shells
> Shattering and avalanching on the snow crust
> Such heaps of broken glass to sweep away
> You'd think the inner dome of heaven had fallen.

Mountain Interval abounds in images of the shattering of human ties, and of humans, as in the horrifying "Out, Out—." But it would be redundant to conduct an overview of all Frost's volumes in pursuit of an experiential darkness that never is dispelled. A measurer of stone walls, as Frost names himself in the remarkable "A Star in a Stoneboat," is never going to be surprised that life is a sensible emptiness. The demiurgic pattern of "Design," with its "assorted characters of death and blight," is the rule in Frost. There are a few exceptions, but they give Frost parodies, rather than poems.

Frost wrote the concluding and conclusive Emersonian irony for all his work in the allegorical "A Cabin in the Clearing," the set-piece of *In the Clearing* (1962), published for his eighty-eighth birthday, less than a year before his death. Mist and Smoke, guardian wraiths and counterparts, eavesdrop on the unrest of a human couple, murmuring in their sleep. These guardians haunt us because we are their kindred spirits, for we do not know where we are, since who we are "is too much to believe." We are "too sudden to be credible," and so the accurate image for us is "an inner haze," full kindred to mist and smoke. For all the genial tone, the spirit of "A Cabin in the Clearing" is negative even for Frost. His final letter, dictated just before his death, states an unanswerable question as though it were not a question: "How can we be just in a world that needs mercy and merciful in a world that needs justice." The Demiurge's laugh lurks behind the sentence, though Frost was then in no frame of spirit to indulge a demiurgic imagination.

Frost would have been well content to give his mentor Emerson the last word, though "content" is necessarily an inadequate word in this dark context. Each time I reread the magnificent essay, "Illusions," which concludes and crowns *The Conduct of Life*, I am reminded of the poetry of Robert Frost. The reminder is strongest in two paragraphs near the end that seem to be "Directive" writ large, as though Emerson had been brooding upon his descendant:

We cannot write the order of the variable winds. How can we penetrate the law of our shifting moods and susceptibility? Yet they differ as all and nothing. Instead of the firmament of yesterday, which our eyes require, it is to-day an eggshell which coops us in; we cannot even see what or where our stars of destiny are. From day to day, the capital facts of human life are hidden from our eyes. Suddenly the mist rolls up, and reveals them, and we think how much good time is gone, that might have been saved, had any hint of these things been shown. A sudden rise in the road shows us the system of mountains, and all the summits, which have been just as near us all the year, but quite out of mind. But these alternations are not without their order, and we are parties to our various fortune. If life seem a succession of dreams, yet poetic justice is done in dreams also. The visions of good men are good; it is the undisciplined will that is whipped with bad thoughts and bad fortunes. When we break the laws, we lose our hold on the central reality. Like sick men in hospitals, we change only from bed to bed, from one folly to another; and it cannot signify much what becomes of such castaways,—wailing, stupid, comatose creatures,—lifted from bed to bed, from the nothing of life to the nothing of death.

In this kingdom of illusions we grope eagerly for stays and foundations. There is none but a strict and faithful dealing at home, and a severe barring out of all duplicity or illusion there. Whatever games are played with us, we must play no games with ourselves, but deal in our privacy with the last honesty and truth. I look upon the simple and childish virtues of veracity and honesty as the root of all that is sublime in character. Speak as you think, be what you are, pay your debts of all kinds. I prefer to be owned as sound and solvent, and my word as good as my bond, and to be what cannot be skipped, or dissipated, or undermined, to all the *éclat* in the universe. This reality is the foundation of friendship, religion, poetry, and art. At the top or at the bottom of all illusions, I set the cheat which still leads us to work and live for appearances, in spite of our conviction, in all sane hours, that it is what we really are that avails with friends, with strangers, and with fate or fortune.

RICHARD POIRIER

Choices

Frost could never blame the "age" for anything, or even blame what he did himself at a certain age for what might have happened to him subsequently. This was the virtue of his pride. Moral and literary accomplishment are of a piece in his poetry because of his near-mystical acceptance of responsibility for himself and for whatever happened to him. His biographer misses this entirely. In his harsh, distorted, and personally resentful view of Frost's manipulative, calculating use of other people, Thompson sees only the determinations of a man who wanted fully to control his career and his public image. Unquestionably, that was one of the things he was doing. He was also revealing something wonderful about human life, or, if you wish, about his sense of what it was. He was communicating his conviction that, mysteriously, nothing happens to us in life except what we choose to have happen. A conscious "use" of other people, a conscious exploitation of them in order to be lazy, in order to get work done, or to get good reviews—this was at least making yourself, and others, aware of what you were doing. What is conspicuous about Frost's letters when he is asking for a favor is their uncommon forthrightness. There is in them the relish of self-exposure. He tries to make visible the choices he is making for his life, choices which were there anyway, invisibly at work on himself and on others. What he calls "the trial by existence" in the magnificent Dante-esque poem of that title in *A*

From *Robert Frost: The Work of Knowing* by Richard Poirier. © 1977 by Richard Poirier.

Boy's Will is "the obscuration upon earth" of souls that have chosen to leave heaven and to accept whatever human life might have in store for them. Even after a soul is saved, even after the "bravest that are slain" on earth find themselves in heaven, they discover another opportunity for bravery and choice, an opportunity all the more daring because the choice will not, once taken, even be remembered

> 'Tis of the essence of life here,
>   Though we choose greatly, still to lack
> The lasting memory at all clear,
>   That life has for us on the wrack
> Nothing but what we somehow chose;
>   Thus are we wholly stripped of pride
> In the pain that has but one close,
>   Bearing it crushed and mystified.

There are two kinds of choice here. We "greatly choose" some things and we "somehow chose" all the things that happen to us. The pride we may take in conscious choices is stripped away not by any obvious predominance of the unconscious ones but rather by our being ignorant of how much more inclusive they are. That is, the individual is denied the *privilege* of knowing that in fact no one else has made his life as it is. Frost was always seeking for the restitution of that lost and diminished sense of responsibility even while he was at the same time exalted by the mystery of not being able fully to grasp it. This divided consciousness helps explain the perplexing ways in which a poet who attaches so much value to form, with all the choice that involves, attaches equal value to freedom in the movement of the poem toward a form. The perplexity is not lessened by the fact that within the freedom there are the elements which he also "somehow chose." Thus he will write, in "The Figure a Poem Makes," that a poem "has an outcome that though unforseen was predestined from the first image of the original mood—and indeed from the very mood." For him, life and poems work in much the same way. In both, there is a wondrous emergence into consciousness of those selections, impressions—and choices—that were not available to consciousness when first made.

> The impressions most useful to my purpose seem always those I
> was unaware of and so made no note of at the time when taken,
> and the conclusion is come to that like giants we are always
> hurling experience ahead of us to pave the future with against the

day when we may want to strike a line of purpose across it for somewhere. The line will have the more charm for not being mechanically straight. We enjoy the straight crookedness of a good walking stick. Modern instruments of precision are being used to make things crooked as if by eye and hand in the old days ("The Figure a Poem Makes").

It is not stretching the point to say that this intimation of the peculiar and mysterious workings of choice is what made him so resolute and even ruthless when choice became incumbent or conscious. It was as if the free movement in his life demanded of him that he then do what had to be done either with his career, with a poem, or with a book. Despite differences, he is in this more like Lawrence than like any other writer of the century. And yet it seems apparent that form, for Lawrence as much as for Frost, the more formalistic of the two, by being necessarily to some degree conscious was also, to some degree, imposed, and that what Frost says about "modern instruments of precision" might sometimes apply to his own work on a poem. His claims, again in "The Figure a Poem Makes," to the "wildness of logic" are apt to strike some readers as disingenuous. The "logic" of even some of the best poems, as illustrated by "Spring Pools," does not, as the reader experiences it, appear to be "more felt than seen ahead like prophecy." Some of that, yes—but also a good deal of premeditation and preplotting. Frost is best appreciated if we let him *try* to do the best he can within the drama of form and freedom, and it is in that light that we can understand the design he gave to *A Boy's Will* using some of the poems he then had available. It is a matter of his using "experience," in this case poems, that he had paved "the future with against the day when [he would want] to strike a line of purpose across it for somewhere."

A Boy's Will is an appropriate place for a poem about choices of lives, like "Trial by Existence." The design of the book—what is put in, what is left out, the groupings of the poems, the headnotes—expresses a "choice" about the portrait of man and poet that Frost wanted to present. Or rather what can be inferred from these "choices" of inclusion and exclusion are three portraits whose details sometimes coincide, sometimes blur, sometimes block one another out. One, the cosiest, most availably public, and closest to the glosses, is of a young man who develops a fulfilling relationship to the world after passing through a period of alienation and trial. Another is of a young man trying to shape the complex tension within himself between sexuality and creative powers, between the calls of love and of poetry. This is a more submerged portrait than the first, and its features will remain both more indelible and more obscure all the way through Frost's work. And then there is a darker version of this second portrait, a kind of *pentimento*, a possible portrait later painted over by an author who "repented" and wanted to block out certain features. He kept this portrait hidden, as it were, by the omission of a poem that could have fitted into this volume (bringing with it a darkening of all that would surround it) with at least as much effectiveness as it did into a later group that includes "Never Again Would Bird's Song Be the Same" and "The Most of It" in *A Witness Tree* of 1942. I am referring to "The Subverted Flower," the first draft of which had been written so early, if we are to believe what Frost himself told Thompson, that it could have been published in *A Boy's Will* (Thompson, I, 512).

Taken together these three overlapping portraits, while they do not account for all the poems in the volume—two of the best, "Mowing" and "The Tuft of Flowers," will be discussed in the last chapter—do include most of them and the overall "plot" of the book. In discussing the alternate and interwoven portraits I want above all to insist that none of the features come inadvertently into prominence. Frost knew exactly what he was doing; he was never innocent of what his poems imply. His original omissions and discriminations are the result of his loyalty to the complex and mystifying way in which languages appropriate to sexuality, poetic practice, and nature are, in his consciousness of them, not to be separated one from the other. The elements of intentional disguise in any one of the tracings of the poetic self should not, that is, make anyone think that the other disguises, found beneath the obvious ones, were therefore unconscious. Frost was at once too doggedly responsible for whatever he did about himself and too mistrustful of himself and of his imagination ever to have said more than he knew.

Thompson's discussions of how the book was put together are at the outset too vague to be useful and too simple to be true. "Alone one night, he sorted through the sheaf of manuscripts he had brought with him and could not resist the impulse to see if he had enough to make up a small volume ... [which] would represent his achievement up to the age of thirty-eight" (Thompson, I, 396–97). "Impulse"? For one thing, he had far more than "enough" to make a book, and a better book than the one he put together. For another, what he did pick out for *A Boy's Will* did not begin to represent the variety, much less the size, of his accomplishment up to the age of thirty-eight. Evidence of this is in Thompson's own research into the dates of composition (Thompson, II, 540–42). No dramatic narratives are included in the book, for example, though at least three that were to appear the next year, 1914, in *North of Boston* had been written as early as 1905 and 1906—"The Death of the Hired Man," "The Black Cottage," and "The Housekeeper." In addition, he had on hand over a dozen poems, all written before 1913, and including some of his best. "Bond and Free" was written in the period 1896–1900, and twelve more were written (or at least begun) in Derry between 1900 and 1911, including "An Old Man's Winter Night," "The Telephone," "Pea Brush," "An Encounter," "Range Finding," "Loneliness," "The Line-Gang," "The Flower Boat," and "The Subverted Flower." In addition, some of the great sonnets were written during 1906–7: "The Oven Bird," "Putting in the Seed," and the fifteen-line sonnet variant "Hyla Brook." All these were held until the third book, *Mountain Interval*, in 1916.

Of course Frost may not have "brought with him" (the precise meaning, if any, of Thompson's phrase is never made clear) some of the poems destined for later printing. In that unlikely case, there would be a still stronger indication of some prior decision not to put into his first book works that would presumably fit better into some design of a poetic progress which was to be revealed in subsequent volumes. But there is no evidence that he did not have all of his manuscript poetry with him. Obviously he had to have the poems destined for *North of Boston* since this was printed before he left England. In fact, as soon as *A Boy's Will* was out, he began to play tricks with the whole revered critical notion of chronology and "development," using one of the poems he had had around since 1905–6. His specifically intended victim was also his most renowned admirer, Ezra Pound. Knowing that, when the facts became public, Pound, and the usual cant about newness, would be made to look silly, he gave him "Death of the Hired Man" as a "new poem." After the publication in *Poetry* of his review of *A Boy's Will*, which Frost and his wife found condescending, Pound promised Harriet Monroe, the editor, that he would have something new from Frost "as soon as he has done it." "He has done a 'Death of the Farmhand' since the book [*A Boy's Will*]," he wrote his father on June 3, 1913, and adds with yet another example of his wholly engaging generosity of feeling, that this poem "is to my mind better than anything in it. I shall have that in *The Smart Set* or in *Poetry* before long" (Thompson, I, 437). One thing is sure—that many of the poems held back were incomparably superior to at least three that he chose to publish but would eventually delete from later printings of his poems: "Spoils of the Dead," "In Equal Sacrifice," and "Asking for Roses." The last of these is a fair sample of all three. It is mildly interesting because it offers an early example of Frost's obsession with human dwellings that are impoverished and apparently deserted, and because it is a kind of *Lied* with echoes of Burns and Tom Moore. As the young lovers pass the house, they notice a garden of "old-fashioned roses":

"I wonder," I say, "who the owner of those is."
"Oh, no one you know," she answers me airy,
"But one we must ask if we want any roses."

It is astonishing to learn, if Frost's own testimony is to be believed, that at the time he was willing to see in print this embarrassing poem about a man, a woman, and flowers, he held back "The Subverted Flower" which makes use of the same three items. The complex dramatic interaction between flowers (which are a symptom in the poems of seasonal fertility), sexuality, and poetry is one of the important but uninsistent lines of coherence in the volume. Frost's own awareness of it and of its implications is best indicated by his omission of a poem whose inclusion would have caused a substantial change of emphasis. It would have suggested very dark psychological shadings in the sexual areas which, by the implications of Frost's language in his poetry and in his prose, provide some of the metaphors for artistic creativity. It would also have indicated that he was to some degree victimized by unrequited love and that his career was not as simple an unfolding of self as he wants to suggest.

From the outset "The Subverted Flower" establishes the powerful authority, the psychotic necessity, of its macabre imagery and the relentlessness of its movement. It is the sexual nightmare of an adolescent blankly registering the descent, through sexual repressions, of himself and the girl he desires into different forms of bestiality. The four-beat lines are rhymed in a staggered way that allows sudden accelerations past one fixation, like a nightmare image being recollected, on to the next, where we are suspended as in a trance until a disyllabic rhyme chooses to complete the frame. Except for a few of Meredith's sonnets in "Modern Love" there is little in any poetry before Frost that can approach the direct and graphic sexual terror of this poem, the first lines of which follow:

She drew back; he was calm:
"It is this that had the power."
And he lashed his open palm
With the tender-headed flower.
He smiled for her to smile,
But she was either blind
Or willfully unkind.
He eyed her for a while
For a woman and a puzzle.
He flicked and flung the flower,

And another sort of smile
Caught up like finger tips
The corners of his lips
And cracked his ragged muzzle.

The poem could refer to an incident of so-called indecent exposure in Frost's courtship of Elinor White, but the details make it likely that it is an account of a nightmare in which such an incident was symbolically enacted. This would be a good reason for his wanting to withhold it, and the probability that the poem has *something* to do with Elinor White is advanced by Thompson as the sole reason for Frost's delaying publication until 1942, after her death. The subject, Frost was later to say in his *Paris Review* interview, was "frigidity in women."

There are, however, complicated literary as well as personal reasons for his not having printed the poem in *A Boy's Will*, reasons that become apparent when we see that, except for its style, the poem would not have been out of place, and, oddly enough, would have easily fitted in thematically. The problem would have been that the poem excites a kind of autobiographical speculation that would have materially altered the "portrait of an artist" that Frost wanted to project. To begin with, the strangeness of the poem is considerably lessened once it is placed among those in *A Boy's Will* wherein flowers are a token of either a precarious movement toward sexual, seasonal, and artistic fulfillment or the failure of these. Or perhaps one should say that its strangeness informs and significantly alters these other poems. The volume as a whole begins with landscapes that are barren, even funereal, and in which the young man walks forth conspicuously alone. Following on the barren landscapes of the first three poems, "Into My Own," "Ghost House," and "My November Guest," whose name is Sorrow, we come upon the just-married couple of "Love and a Question." The bride and groom are visited by a tramp in need of shelter. The bridegroom turns him away from the door, and yet is peculiarly equivocal as he "looked at a weary road" while his bride sits behind him at the fire: "But whether or not a man was asked / To mar the love of two / By harboring woe in the bridal house, / The bridegroom wished he knew." Then in the next, or fifth poem, "A Late Walk," there is a faint signal of a new vitality. A "flower" is just barely rescued from the desolation which has dominated the scene up to that point. The young man is still, though married, walking alone amidst "withered weeds," bare trees, except for "a leaf that lingered brown." But his walk ends in a gesture of unification with what little is still alive in the landscape and with the life that awaits him at home: "I end not far from my going forth, / By picking the faded blue / Of the last remaining aster flower / To carry again to you."

From this point on, the isolated "I" who has only begun to express the intimacy of his feeling for "her" is replaced with "we" and "our." But the world continues nevertheless to be found cold and threatening. The next poem is "Stars" with its landscape of snow in which the lovers might be lost "to white rest and a place of rest / Invisible at dawn"—an accent of Emily Dickinson unusual for Frost. In the poem that follows, "Storm Fear," the young man still lies alone in his wakefulness, but he is apparently with his wife and fears not for himself so much as for her and the children. Following on these it is proposed in "Wind and Window Flower" that she is a "flower" and that he is a winter wind "concerned with ice and snow, / Dead weeds and unmated birds, / And little of love could know."

Even before this we have become aware that the threat to love has been gradually internalized by the young poet and that the landscape is an imaginary one of those moods, depressions, and melancholies which threaten their love with devastation and aridity. Only with the next four poems—"To the Thawing Wind" ("Give the buried flower a dream"), "A Prayer in Spring" ("Oh, give us pleasure in the flowers today"), "Flower Gathering," and "Rose Pogonias"—does the young poet escape from "dead weeds and unmated birds." Along with them the poet has himself been seen as a force for frigidity working in conjunction with the most malevolent aspects which he selects or imagines in the natural environment.

Though thematically "The Subverted Flower" could obviously belong to this grouping, it would have materially changed the implication of these poems insofar as they are about the nature of Frost's sexual-poetic imagination. By including it, Frost would have transferred responsibility from the young man to "her," or Elinor. As a result, he would have obscured the fact that the poems in this volume are essentially concerned with the connections between his poetic prowess and his power to find love within a landscape of the mind as well as in relation to another person. The poems trace out the effort to free his imagination so that it might work toward some harmony with natural cycles both of the seasons and of sexuality. With inclusion of "The Subverted Flower," the interest in the volume would have become more psychological than literary; it would have placed greater emphasis on the hazards of sexuality to the confusion of a Wordsworthian subject which more classically includes sexuality: the "Growth of a Poet's Mind." "The Subverted Flower" is not, as are the others, about *his* potentially frigid mind or imagination but about hers. His delicacy about Elinor White Frost was real enough, no doubt, but equally real was the desire to make himself responsible for anything that might have affected his poetry. It was Frost's enormous desire for control, form, design that forbade his including a poem which might imply, even by blaming another, that he was not the master of his literary fates.

The exclusion of this poem helps explain a number of things implied by his also having left out the other poems I have mentioned. First of all, the selection for *A Boy's Will* was not governed in any thoroughgoing way by the novelistic and self-revelatory scheme he himself claimed to have set up: "The psychologist in me," he was to say later on, "ached to call it 'The Record of A Phase of Post Adolescence'" (Thompson, II, xxi, 593). Second, the nature of the volume, and the determination of the order of poems, suggest other reasons for leaving out "The Subverted Flower," reasons having to do with Frost's imagination of a poetic career and with his fierce determination to control the public shaping of his life. He would rather have let at least some people think that part of the structure of *A Boy's Will* was dictated by "the seasons," which is superficially true, than allow most people freely to discover that the seasons are finally only a metaphor for the possible and always threatened perversion or subversion of the poetic imagination by the disasters of love. He would rather have pretended that the volume is about "A Phase of Post Adolescence" than have us ask if the connection in his work between sexuality and the progress of poetry is not far more complicated than he chooses to admit. Which is a way of saying that while he knew everything that was going on in his poetry he was not always anxious that we should know as much as he does.

Many of the early poems, offering some of the psychological and structural sources of all of Frost's poetry, are about this relation of love to poetic making, to making in all other senses of the word. A brief biographical digression might be useful here, a recapitulation of Frost's stormy and passionate courtship of Elinor White, with whom he seems to have fallen in love at first meeting. He was seventeen, she nearly two years older, and they sat next to one another in Lawrence High School (Massachusetts). From the outset, her ability as a poet (she stopped writing poems before she married him and in later life tried to disguise and disown those that had appeared in the *School Bulletin*), her knowledge of literature, her marks in school (they were co-valedictorians, but her average was finally higher), her ability as a painter, her suitors at St. Lawrence University at Canton, New York, all excited his competitive admiration and jealousy. Her attendance at college meant their separation, with Frost going to Dartmouth for a short time, then to teach in the Methuen schools until March 1893, then to act as helper and guardian to Elinor's mother and two of her sisters in Salem, New

Hampshire. Before she left for school and on her vacations in Lawrence he courted her with the help of Shelley's poetry, especially "Epipsychidion," with its inducements to ignore the institution of marriage. And of course he wooed her with poems of his own.

Indeed, his first volume, strictly speaking, was not *A Boy's Will* of 1913, when he was thirty-nine, but *Twilight* in 1894 when he was twenty, the one surviving copy of which is in the Barrett Collection at the University of Virginia. Only two copies were printed, one for Frost and one for Elinor. It included, in addition to "My Butterfly" which was later to appear in *A Boy's Will*, four other poems full of literary echoes ranging from Sidney to Keats, Tennyson to Rossetti, as in the opening lines of the title poem:

> Why am I first in thy so sad regard,
> O twilight gazing from I know not where?
> I fear myself as one more than I guessed!

He carried Elinor's copy on an unannounced trip to her college boarding house in Canton. Surprised, bewildered, prevented by the rules from inviting him in or from going out herself, she accepted her copy in what seemed a casual but was perhaps a merely preoccupied way. She told him to return home at once. He did so, but only to pack a bag and leave for a suicide journey that took him to Virginia and through the Dismal Swamp at night, "into my own," so to speak. The danger was very real. "I was," he later said, "trying to throw my life away" (Thompson, I, 521). Through this and subsequent travails, torments, threats, and melodramatic scenes, he convinced her to marry him before she could finish school and before he had any secure means of support.

Such briefly are the biographical elements probably at play in some of the early poems. But the biographical material does not tell us as much about the man as the poetry does. By that I mean that the poetry does not necessarily come from the experiences of his life; rather, the kind of poetry he wrote, and the kind of experiences to which he was susceptible, both emerge from the same configuration in him, prior to his poems or to his experiences. Sex and an obsession with sound, sexual love and poetic imagination, success in love and success in art—these conspire with one another. A poem is an action, not merely a "made" but a "making" thing, and "the figure a poem makes," one remembers, "is the same as for love." It is as if in talking about the direction laid down by a poem he instinctively uses a language of ongoing sexual action:

No one can really hold that the ecstasy should be static and
stand still in one place. It begins in delight, it inclines to the
impulse, it assumes direction with the first line laid down, it runs
a course of lucky events, and ends in a clarification of life—not
necessarily a great clarification such as sects and cults are founded
on, but in a momentary stay against confusion.... It finds its own
name as it goes and discovers the best waiting for it in some final
phrase at once wise and sad—the happy-sad blend of the drinking
song ("The Figure a Poem Makes").

Three early poems, "Waiting," "In a Vale," and "A Dream Pang,"
coming nearly in the middle of *A Boy's Will*, illustrate the connections,
implicit in the structuring of the whole volume, between sexual love and
poetic making, between the "sounds" of love and a poet's love of sound.
None of the three is in any sense considerable. Frost's investment in them is
relatively slight; they are shy of the complications which, when they emerge
in later poems, are more consciously and subtly managed. And yet the poems
are the stranger for *not* showing very much acknowledgment of their
strangeness. It is as if initially the imagination of the sexual self and of the
poetic self were so naturally, so instinctively identified as not to call for
comment.

The three poems are published in sequence in *A Boy's Will*, always an
important and calculated factor in Frost. They are all what can be called
dream poems, and each suggests a different aspect of the dreamlike
relationship between poetic and sexual prowess. In the first, "Waiting," the
figure of the poet is "specter-like," as he wanders through a "stubble field" of
tall haycocks, a bit like the "stubble-plains" in the last stanza of Keats's ode
"To Autumn"; the "things" about which he has waking dreams are mostly the
surroundings and their noises. From the outset his condition seems
peculiarly vulnerable to sights and sounds, and it is not till the final lines that
one can attribute this to the fact that what means most to him in his dream
is not anything present to his senses but rather "the memory of one absent
most," the girl he loves:

Waiting
Afield at Dusk

What things for dream there are when specter-like,
Moving among tall haycocks lightly piled,
I enter alone upon the stubble field,

From which the laborers' voices late have died,
And in the antiphony of afterglow
And rising full moon, sit me down
Upon the full moon's side of the first haycock
And lose myself amid so many alike.

I dream upon the opposing lights of the hour,
Preventing shadow until the moon prevail;
I dream upon the nighthawks peopling heaven,
Each circling each with vague unearthly cry,
Or plunging headlong with fierce twang afar;
And on the bat's mute antics, who would seem
Dimly to have made out my secret place,
Only to lose it when he pirouettes,
And seek it endlessly with purblind haste;
On the last swallow's sweep; and on the rasp
In the abyss of odor and rustle at my back,
That, silenced by my advent, finds once more,
After an interval, his instrument,
And tries once—twice—and thrice if I be there;
And on the worn book of old-golden song
I brought not here to read, it seems, but hold
And freshen in this air of withering sweetness;
But on the memory of one absent, most,
For whom these lines when they shall greet her eye.

Before the mention of his beloved, in the next to last line, the poem is filled with evocations of natural sounds in the "stubble field" where "the laborers' voices late have died"; there is also the "vague unearthly cry" of the nighthawks who plunge "headlong with fierce twang afar"; there are the "bat's mute antics," the "rasp" of a creature who, "silenced by my advent, finds once more, / After an interval, his instrument." But what is apt to seem most provocative—given its place at the end of the poem and its uniqueness among all the references to natural sound—is an allusion to poetic sound, to the "worn book of old-golden song." It, too, is a carrier of sound, very likely of sound that helped (even more than did the sounds of nature) during his courtship of the one now "absent." But however much our literary-critical dispositions might prompt us to separate this item of sound from others, as being more centrally important, it is necessary to note that the young poet-specter tends merely to put the poetic within the sequence of other items. It is joined to them casually with another of the many "ands" that make up the listing. Apparently he does not intend even to read the book in order to bring her closer to mind. More than that, though the book is "worn" and though the poetry is itself "old," his reasons for holding onto it are that it may "freshen in this air," this Keatsian air "of withering sweetness."

The "old-golden song" is to be freshened, strangely enough, by something that is more apt to dry it, to "wither" it. We are readied by this paradox for the introduction, as in "Pan with Us," of the theme of "new" song, new sounds, something poetic for the future—in short, the very poem we are reading which is destined for her: "for whom these lines when they shall greet her eye." With the vitality of "shall greet her eye" the poet is no longer "specter-like." He has gotten past a number of by-ways: of possible dreams on other sounds, of the invitation to do no more than dream, of losing himself to these sounds—a danger only less intense than that in the later "Stopping by Woods on a Snowy Evening." Past all this, the young lover is able to envision a future in love inseparable from a future in poetry. He has been able to do this because, all the while, as the poem moves along, he has been "making it"; he has been writing "these lines."

One indication of the peculiar nature of Frost's reputation as a poet, when compared to an Eliot or a Yeats, is that few have bothered with poems so clearly not of his best like "Waiting" or the two others grouped with it. His admirers are defensively anxious to show only the favorite things, when some of the lesser ones are often even more revealing of his preoccupations with the plights and pleasures in the life of the poetic self. "In a Vale" is, even more than "Waiting," *fin de siècle* in conception and language. With its "vale," "maidens," "fen," and with words like "wist," "list," "dwelt," there is little going on that predicts the later Frost except the penultimate and best stanza. And yet it is still a most ingratiating poem—like an early picture of someone we have gotten to know only in later years—and it tells us perhaps even more than do more posed sittings:

> When I was young, we dwelt in a vale
>   By a misty fen that rang all night,
> And thus it was the maidens pale
> I knew so well, whose garments trail
>   Across the reeds to a window light.
>
> The fen had every kind of bloom,
>   And for every kind there was a face,
> And a voice that has sounded in my room

Across the sill from the outer gloom.
　　Each came singly unto her place,

But all came every night with the mist;
　　And often they brought so much to say
Of things of moment to which, they wist,
One so lonely was fain to list
　　That the stars were almost faded away

Before the last went, heavy with dew,
　　Back to the place from which she came—
Where the bird was before it flew,
Where the flower was before it grew,
　　Where bird and flower were one and the same.

And thus it is I know so well
　　Why the flower has odor, the bird has song.
You have only to ask me, and I can tell.
No, not vainly there did I dwell,
　　Nor vainly listen all the night long.

　　The time scheme of these poems is importantly suggestive of poetic gestations, of the way past and present provide the nutrients for a poetic future. In "Waiting" we are in the present, witnessing the impressions made upon a young poet who holds the past in his hand—Palgrave's *Golden Treasury*—while composing in his head the "lines" which will in future "greet" his beloved. "In a Vale" is a dream wholly of the past, but it, too, looks ahead to a future wherein the past will have been redeemed by the writing of the poems inspired by it: "You have only to ask me, and I can tell. / No, not vainly there did I dwell, / Nor vainly listen all the night long." The listening, again, is to voices or sounds that he has managed to supersede: "a misty fen that rang all night"; the voices that have "sounded in my room" and that "brought so much to say." The dream is a rather wet one ("the last went, heavy with dew") and it is from these nocturnal experiences that he learns what, in the later daytime of publication, he "can tell." With Lucretius, he can tell that "the bird and flower were one and the same." However, he can also tell a more American and Emersonian story: of a world, again, which reveals itself in forms (odor and song) which have in part been placed there by the human imagination, including human dreams.

　　An absent lover imagined in "Waiting" as a future reader, ghostly lovers or maidens whose sayings "In a Vale" will in some future time allow him to "tell" readers about birds and flowers—these figurations are brought together in the last of the three poems, "A Dream Pang." There the poet is discovered in bed with his lover beside him, her very presence proving that his song has been answered by something more fulfilling than the echoing sounds of nature. This early poem is thereby a prelude to later ones like "Come In" or "A Leaf Treader," where Frost is in danger of succumbing to the call of nature, of losing himself, of having his sound in words absorbed into the sounds made by the natural elements. In this poem he is not learning to "tell" or expecting the "lines" he is writing to be read; here he is already a poet whose song, in his dream, has been endangered by her denials and by his proud withdrawals:

> I had withdrawn in forest, and my song
> Was swallowed up in leaves that blew alway;
> And to the forest edge you came one day
> (This was my dream) and looked and pondered long,
> But did not enter, though the wish was strong:
> You shook your pensive head as who should say,
> "I dare not—too far in his footsteps stray—
> He must seek me would he undo the wrong."
>
> Not far, but near, I stood and saw it all,
> Behind low boughs the trees let down outside;
> And the sweet pang it cost me not to call
> And tell you that I saw does still abide.
> But 'tis not true that thus I dwelt aloof,
> For the wood wakes, and you are here for proof.

Now, as she lies beside him ("this was my dream ... you are here for proof") the poem can come to articulation; before, while they were alienated from one another, "my song / Was swallowed up in leaves." Without her, he and his song are lost to the vagaries of nature and its noises; with her, nature, or the "wood," comes to a more orderly life outside their place: "the wood wakes, and you are here." The implications take us to a variety of poems in which Frost can feel momentarily and terrifyingly included, as he says in "Desert Places," in the loneliness of nature "unawares." Cut off from the communion of human sex and human love, he is answered either by random, accidental, teasing responses, like that of the little bird in "The Wood-Pile," or by evidences of brutish indifference such as greet the speaker of "The Most of It":

> He would cry out on life, that what it wants
> Is not its own love back in copy speech,
> But counter-love, original response.
> And nothing ever came of what he cried
> Unless it was the embodiment that crashed
> In the cliff's talus on the other side....

The failure of love, of love-making, the failure to elicit "counter-love" means, as in "The Subverted Flower," that the young poet cannot finally be joined to that human communication with nature which Emerson promised might be found there. Here as elsewhere Frost's Emersonism is grounded in certain basic actualities, especially the sexual relations of men and women, which Emerson himself tended to pass over with little more than citation. Within this sequence of three poems, "A Dream Pang" looks ahead to the implications of a more considerable sequence of three poems, already mentioned, that includes "The Most of It," "Never Again Would Bird's Song Be the Same," and "The Subverted Flower." The implication, briefly noted also in "The Vantage Point," is that a man alone ("he thought he kept the universe alone") cannot see or hear anything in nature that confirms his existence as human. If he is alone, he cannot "make" the world; he cannot reveal himself to it or in it; he becomes lost to it; it remains alien. He cannot make human sound. In "The Subverted Flower" he can at first hope that the impasse "'has come to us / And not to me alone.'" But even this proposition falls on deaf ears, or essentially deaf ears. It is something "she thought she heard him say; / Though with every word he spoke / His lips were sucked and blown / And the effort made him choke / Like a tiger on a bone."

In the early, as in the later sequence, Frost is concerned in various ways with the possibilities of the sounds of the man-poet-lover in situations where there are competing sounds and where, if he cannot "make it" with his beloved, he cannot "make it" either in competitions with sounds in nature or in other poetry. He cannot "make it" with words so shaped as to reveal his participation in poetry, and—equally important—that such participation is "natural." He is not content to have "*his* song" swallowed up in leaves either of a tree, merely, or of a book, merely. His poetry, his song, must include both.

In the light of this ambition we can best understand Frost's life-long commitment to certain theories of sound and poetic form. The commitment is implicit in all of the poems and in the structural organization of *A Boy's Will*. It was to find theoretical expression somewhat later, in letters written at the time of the publication of the book, and later still in essays and talks. In a letter to the black poet-critic-anthologist William Stanley Braithwaite, on March 22, 1915, for example, Frost said:

> It would seem absurd to say it (and you mustn't quote me as saying it) but I suppose the fact is that my conscious interest in people was at first no more than an almost technical interest in their speech—in what I used to call their sentence sounds—the sound of sense. Whatever these sounds are or aren't (they are certainly not of the vowels and consonants of words nor even of the words themselves but something the words are chiefly a kind of notation for indicating and for fastening to the page) whatever they are, I say, I began to hang on them very young. I was under twenty when I deliberately put it to myself one night after good conversation that there are moments when we actually touch in talk what the best writing can only come near.... We must go into the vernacular for tones that haven't been brought to book. We must write with the ear on the speaking voice. We must imagine the speaking voice (Thompson, *Letters*, pp. 158–59).

"Sentence-sounds" does not refer to the meaning the words give to a sentence but to the meaning the sound of the sentence can give to the words, which is why Frost is so difficult to translate into any other language. It is a matter of stress patterns. Thus, the line "By June our brook's run out of song and speed" is arranged so that the potential of the word "song"—as a possible allusion to "poetry"—is markedly diminished by putting it immediately after the quickly paced vernacular phrase "run out of." The word "song" would be far more potent, but altogether too archly so, if it traded places with the word "speed": "By June our brook's run out of speed and song." Some of these distinctions are clarified in a letter written over a year before, February 22, 1914, to his friend John Bartlett, a newspaper man who was one of his favorite students at Pinkerton Academy:

> I give you a new definition of a sentence:
> A sentence is a sound in itself on which other sounds called words may be strung.
> You may string words together without a sentence-sound to string them on just as you may tie clothes together by sleeves and

stretch them without a clothes line between two trees, but—it is
bad for the clothes.... The sentence sounds are very definite
entities. (This is no literary mysticism I am preaching.) They are
as definite as words. It is not impossible that they could be
collected in a book though I don't at present see on what system
they would be catalogued.

They are apprehended by the ear. They are gathered by the
ear from the vernacular and brought into books. Many of them
are familiar to us in books. I think no writer invents them. The
most original writer only catches them fresh from talk, where
they grow spontaneously.

A man is all a writer if *all* his words are strung on definite
recognizable sentence sounds. The voice of the imagination, the
speaking voice must know certainly how to behave [,] how to
posture in every sentence he offers (Thompson, *Letters*, pp.
110–11).

When Frost refers to the "vocal imagination" (in the essay "The
Constant Symbol") he makes it synonymous with what he calls "images of
the voice speaking." Frost listens for these images as much in nature as in
human dialogue. But there is an important difference in what he wants and
expects to hear from these two different places: only in human dialogue can
such images emerge as "sentence-sounds" rather than as mere echoes, or
vagrant, only potentially significant noises, like "The sweep / Of easy wind
and downy flake," or what Thoreau calls "brute sounds." Furthermore,
Frost's capacity even to find "images of the voice speaking" in nature depends
upon human love; it can be crippled or thwarted by the lack of it. The matter
might be put in a three-part formula: (1) the "artist as a young man," if
doomed to "keep the universe alone," can only call fourth from it alien and
terrifying sounds, and is in danger of becoming either a mere passive receiver
of these sounds or himself a brute; (2) the "artist as a young man" in a
reciprocal relationship of love with another human can, as a result, also find
"images of the voice speaking" in some rudimentary form in nature, though
it is important to know that what he finds is only an image, nothing wholly
equivalent to the human voice speaking: "The Need of Being Versed in
Country Things" is that one is thereby allowed "Not to believe the phoebes
wept." This brings up the third and most important point: (3) that the
clearest, but not only, differentiation of human sound from sounds in nature
is poetry itself, the making of a poem, the capacity literally to be "versed" in
the things of this world. Any falling—of leaves, of snow, of man, of the

garland of roses which Adam is holding when he first sees Eve in her fallen state—can be redeemed by loving, and the sign of this redemption is, for Frost, the sound of the voice working within the sounds of poetry. It could even be said that the proper poetic image of the Fall and of the human will continually to surmount it is—given accentual-syllabism's unique role in the handling of English rhythm—the mounting from unstressed to stressed syllables in the iambic pentameter line. Thus, the oven bird can "frame" the question of "what to make of a diminished thing" in "all but words." The words are at the call of the poet; the "making" is in his power. It consists precisely in his showing how the verse form works with and against mere "saying":

> He sáys | thè eaŕ | lẏ pét | àl fáll | ìs pást,
> When peár | ànd chér | rẏ bloóm | wènt d̀own | ìn shów | eŕs.

The glory of these lines is in the achieved strain between trochaic words like "early" and "petal," "cherry" and "showers," and the iambic pattern which breaks their fall. The meter is a perfect exemplification of what the poem is about, of the creative tension between a persistent rising and a natural falling—a poise of creativity in the face of threatened diminishments.

DAVID BROMWICH

Wordsworth, Frost, Stevens and the Poetic Vocation

The following notes on two modern poems were prompted by some reservations about the recent criticism of Wordsworth. That criticism agrees on the importance of "the image," and shows in detail how the image is fitted to the particular occasions of "the crisis poem."[1] I want to acknowledge these ideas at the outset because I too will be relying on them. But the image has come to stand for two different things: first, a picture which has enduring worth for the poet because it is a fact; and second, an imagining that began as such a picture, has been revolved in the mind, and is prized as a thing of the mind. These two sorts of image are related through the change in meaning by which the first brought forth the second, and we now read Wordsworth with the second ascendant, the first being understood as a distant part of its genealogy. My reservation is that the fact-image had a moral significance for Wordsworth which the mind-image alone can never have. It signalled a connection between the poet and other men; and this was true, no matter what the poet's relation to the object that yielded the image, whether he disturbed its perfect repose, or sent it wandering, or found himself strangely invigorated beside it; whereas for us, the connection has become less and less interesting. We are concerned instead with what the image helps the poet to do for himself.

From *Studies in Romanticism* 21, no. 1 (Spring 1982). © 1982 by the Trustees of Boston University.

This was perhaps inevitable in an age dominated by Yeats, with his thoroughly inward sense of vocation. For us the image has been purged of fact and the crisis poem released from its connection with other men. But Wordsworth himself wished for no such release. He tried to think of poetry in conjunction with other human pursuits, and of the poet as both minister and witness to the needs of others. His eventual failure to meet the conditions of his double office, "by words, / Which speak of nothing more than what we are"—a failure by degrees, of which he left evidence of his own recognition by degrees—produced the poems which at once lament the withdrawal this implies within his vocation, and celebrate the survival of his gift in some form. Wordsworth regarded such poems as a personal response to a personal disappointment. They nevertheless became a pattern to his successors, and one reason why they should have done so is obvious. Wordsworth was the first lyric allegorist of the poetic career. He set the terms in which the whole subject of vocation presents itself to any modern poet. Yet the modern poet as a rule has conceived no Wordsworthian ambitions for the humanizing influence of poetry, and without these nothing compels him to repeat Wordsworth's lament. Looking back at "Tintern Abbey," "Resolution and Independence," the "Ode to Duty" and "Immortality" ode, and "Elegiac Stanzas" on Peele Castle, he may feel a good deal less reluctant than Wordsworth to assert that the poet's sympathy with others is really a bondage.

While alluding to Wordsworth, his successors have thus been able to treat solely as a poetic gain what he described in some measure as a human loss. It will be plain by now that the poem I have most in view is "Resolution and Independence." From its plot the later poet has usually had to abstract a few bold features: what is left out, except in attenuated hints, is the poet's continuing relation to something other than his own mastery. Here, modern commentators on Wordsworth have been guided by modern poetry, in a way that is seldom acknowledged. For those who discuss the poetic crisis solely in poetic terms are interpreting Wordsworth in line with what his successors have made of him. On literary historical grounds one may want to retard this process; it makes Wordsworth's period too neatly continuous with ours. But I believe that more than literary history is at stake. The modern understanding of Wordsworth has fostered great poems, and much thoughtful criticism, but the damage has been great also. What I have to say about two specimens of the Wordsworth tradition is mainly intended to recall the undertone of regret with which an early critic and successor first pronounced him the poet of the egotistical sublime.

Frost's "Two Tramps in Mud Time" and Stevens's "The Course of a Particular" show these poets about as remote from each other as they ever get, in the entire range of their practice, and between the poems themselves no affinity will be claimed, other than their shared descent from "Resolution and Independence." Let me begin by rehearsing in the simplest terms the Wordsworthian situation that all three poems ask us to contemplate. In an unpromising landscape, lit by a change of weather from stormy to fair—a happy change, which nevertheless reminds us of the vicissitudes of all outer and inner weather—a poet filled with unsettling thoughts about his vocation is suddenly brought face to face with a common laborer, or one who suffers the common fate of men and not the uncommon fate of poets. Already I must qualify this, because the poems make the scene visible in different degrees, and the second figure is less clearly realized as we move from Wordsworth to Frost to Stevens. At every step of the way he becomes more strictly a creature of figuration. Indeed, Frost puts his tramps into the title partly to call attention to their absence from the poem, while Stevens reduces the figure to a thing heard but never seen, and that in a negative clause: the "human cry" is one of the things that the cry of leaves is not.

But to return to the meeting of poet and laborer: the important distinction between them seems to be that the laborer has an immediate result to show for his work—a pile of so much wood, a gathering of so many leeches—whereas the poet has none. The poet may be haunted by what he knows of the waste of powers, his own and that of his brother poets, yet he has a place of work to call his own. The laborer, on the other hand, is at home in no place; he may live in constant fear of adversity, yet somehow his spirit remains untroubled. The special nature of the poet's labor apparently needs to be explained, and even justified: this is what the Poem of Resolution and Independence must do, touched all the while by a suspicion that the making of more poems will depend on its success.

Since the link with "Resolution and Independence" will be clear to many readers of "The Course of a Particular," I will give more sustained attention to "Two Tramps in Mud Time." It may help at first to think of Frost's poem as a kind of riddle. At some level he knew all along that he was occupied with another version of Wordsworth's poem, but part of his "fooling" with the reader was to withhold his definitive clue until the middle of the poem, when many other pieces had fallen into place. It comes in the fourth stanza, with the unexpected appearance of a bluebird:

> A bluebird comes tenderly up to alight
> And turns to the wind to unruffle a plume,

> His song so pitched as not to excite
> A single flower as yet to bloom.[2]

To the question, Why this, in a poem about tramps?—the answer is that the
bird, along with the topic it introduces, is entirely within its rights by
authority of the jay, the magpie, the hare, and the "plashy earth" of the
misted sunny moor that occupy the opening stanzas of "Resolution and
Independence." It is of the essence of both poems that they should work hard
to separate landscape from the scene of labor proper: the pleasures of
landscape will belong to the poet alone, and be felt at the intervals of his self-
questioning; to the figure who confronts the poet, on the other hand,
landscape hardly exists; it thus works its way through the poem as a double
counterpoint, always present, but vividly present only to the poet, and much
of the time not even to him.

Looking back, one discovers an earlier touch of craft relevant to the
allusion. This is the modified alexandrine—a pentameter line to vary a
tetrameter base, at the end of the third stanza—which has the look and feel
of the Spenserian stanza one associates with "Resolution and Independence":

> The sun was warm but the wind was chill.
> You know how it is with an April day
> When the sun is out and the wind is still,
> You're one month on in the middle of May.
> But if you so much as dare to speak,
> A cloud comes over the sunlit arch,
> A wind comes off a frozen peak,
> And you're two months back in the middle of March.
>
> (ll. 17-24)

The last line, it could be argued, is really a crowded tetrameter, but against
all objections I would maintain that it is still an alexandrine to the eye, and
so far part of the "in and outdoor schooling" Frost's readers are advised to
have.

Two further clues are at once subtler and more persuasive. First, the
Wordsworthian sentiment of Frost's confession—"That day, giving a loose to
my soul, / I spent on the unimportant wood"—with which one connects such
moments as the "sweet mood" mentioned in "Nutting," when "The heart
luxuriates with indifferent things, / Wasting its kindliness on stocks and
stones." And then, the emergence of a second figure from a ground of
undifferentiated matter, as from a sedimentary deposit: Frost's two strangers

coming "Out of the mud" bring to mind that other stranger whom we first glimpse "As a huge stone is sometimes seen to lie / Couched on the bald top of an eminence," and later, "Like a sea-beast crawled forth."

With these parallels established, one is surprised at a difference that remains. Frost gets through his poem effortlessly, and *without* the tramps. He can do so because in this version of Wordsworth's poem, Frost himself is poet and laborer at once. Imagine now a somewhat modified plot for "Resolution and Independence." Wordsworth looks at the shifting weather, thinks to himself—What a splendid day for a walk!—takes up his staff and sallies out on a lcech-gathering expedition, feeling solid as a rock. On his way he meets an old man, the oldest he ever saw, whose life seems to have been lived on the boundaries of misery, and who offers to do the leech-gathering for him. "He wants my job for pay," Wordsworth mutters, and though he admits that this man's claim to the work outweighs his own, he keeps on with it anyway, exhilarated by thoughts of the different virtues of his two adopted vocations, and how they grow richer by being united. This, with the necessary changes, is Frost's story:

> Nothing on either side was said.
> They knew they had but to stay their stay
> And all their logic would fill my head:
> As that I had no right to play
> With what was another man's work for gain.
> My right might be love but theirs was need.
> And where the two exist in twain
> Theirs was the better right—agreed.
>
> But yield who will to their separation,
> My object in living is to unite
> My avocation and my vocation
> As my two eyes make one in sight.
>
> (II. 57–68)

What a peculiar and original story it is, once we hear "Resolution and Independence" as part of the context Frost evokes. Notice, above all, how completely the sentiment has been altered in the parting gesture, from a widening of sympathy brought on by the recognition of human endurance, to what looks like a rejection of sympathy and charity alike. And yet this cannot be the whole story, if only because we cannot make it tally with the swell and uplift of Frost's concluding lines. Frost has an early poem, also about an experience of charity denied, a poem very roughly parallel to "Two Tramps in Mud Time," called "Love and a Question." There a bridegroom on his wedding night finds a stranger at the door, and though willing to give him a dole of bread and a purse, refuses him shelter for the night: the desire aglow in the "bridal house" is too precious for sharing. In that poem too we have the dismissal of the wanderer, and the moralized closing stanza by Frost, but in a situation more congenial to his point of view. "Love and a Question" is a charming poem. "Two Tramps in Mud Time" is not, nor does it mean to be. Its effect is to limit and qualify the humanizing effect of Wordsworth's poem, and in doing so it involves Frost in a curious drama of self-exposure, of a kind that few poets of his cunning would have wished to trace beyond the first hesitant steps.

Still, one may be mystified by the high spirits Frost discovers at the end, and by the triumphal cadence that goes with them:

> Only when love and need are one,
> And the work is play for mortal stakes,
> Is the deed ever really done
> For Heaven and the future's sakes.
>
> (ll. 69–72)

I think Frost got this tone from Arnold, who was always among his favorite poets. One poem of Arnold's, "Palladium," he seems to have returned to again and again: the soul to the body is as the Palladium, "high 'mid rock and wood," to the soldiers fighting on the battlefield below; so long as it stands. Troy cannot fall; and, with the soul and body it cannot be wholly otherwise. Frost had this in his ear when he wrote "The Trial by Existence," for *A Boy's Will*, and it was with him again for "Two Tramps in Mud Time." I quote the final stanzas of "Palladium" in which Arnold imagines the earthly battles renewed:

> Then we shall rust in shade, or shine in strife,
> And fluctuate 'twixt blind hopes and blind despairs,
> And fancy that we put forth all our life,
> And never know how with the soul it fares.
>
> Still doth the soul, from its lone fastness high,
> Upon our life a ruling effluence send;
> And when it fails, fight as we will, we die,
> And while it lasts, we cannot wholly end.[3]

This need not have appealed to Frost strictly for the poetry, for there was something else, in the cultural predicament of both men, which made him recognize Arnold as a natural ally. Arnold, to himself, was a spirit wandering between two worlds, between, among other things, the world of romanticism, which he conscientiously but never very cheerfully cast into the outer darkness, and the world of utilitarianism, which he could never love or accept. The result for his poetry was that sense of being embattled but deprived of an aim which makes even the end of "Palladium" sound oddly unhappy, for so happy a conceit. Frost, it seems to me, was attracted to the *soldiering* rhetoric because, though from different historical causes, he had the same sense of being embattled without having an enemy properly in sight. The dimensions of the conflict may be suggested by two facts: that Frost was a product of nineteenth-century New England, and that "Two Tramps in Mud Time" is a poem of the New Deal. In the thirties, Richard Poirier writes.

> Frost began to suspect that the metaphors, including that of *laissez-faire*, which governed his thinking and his poetry were being substantially displaced within the national consciousness by two others. On the one hand, there were metaphors of "wasteland," or apocalyptic disillusion, against which individual resistance was presumably useless; and on the other, the metaphor of "planning," of the New Deal, of provision, which, as Frost saw it, was designed to relieve the individual of responsibility for his own fate.
>
> That was the essential problem, and measured against it Frost's lapses of taste, his occasional paranoiac inaccuracies, and his petty complaints should be treated as inessential.[4]

Without treating "Two Tramps in Mud Time" as a lapse of taste one may regard it as a striking instance of his predicament. He has to be both poet and laborer to make the point about his independence; he has to begin with Wordsworth's argument, because Wordsworth's is the great poem in English about the poetic consciousness and its sustaining need of sympathy; the comparison with Wordsworth makes Frost seem colder, as all refusal seems colder than indifference; but he will deal with it how he can, for he is determined to write the poem. Poetry and sympathy are just the matters about which Frost wants to tell us something shocking. "My vocation *and* avocation: let others find theirs if they can; the best help I can give is to tell them so."

Certainly the allusion is a remarkable piece of daring, and could only have been risked by a great poet at the height of his self-confidence. It is that; and yet, in almost any reader's first response to the poem, one impression remains fixed: that Frost has not finally earned his cloquence, that his triumph is a little hollow. The impression remains I think because we have never been shown the distance between Frost's vocation and his asocation, and hence between his nature and that of the tramps. When we see Wordsworth and the leech-gatherer together, we learn to our amazement what different beings they are. Frost too wants to make us feel this, so long as we say afterwards, "But he contains the two tramps; they don't contain him." But we do not say this, because the whole poem has been tipped off balance by a touch of bad faith. At the bottom of it, Poirier believes, is a distrust of poetry. I agree but would add: a disrust of being seen to be a poet. The poem lets us see the two tramps, and a man who we know is a poet because he writes poems, this one among them. But Frost-as-poet is not, so to speak, figured into the poem. To have done so would have been to take on the privilege but also the vulnerability of the poet's situation, and the ambivalence that they imply when taken together. It would not have meant going over to Wordsworth's side on the question of sympathy, even if we could be sure just what that means in a poem like "Resolution and Independence."[5] But the stark improbables of the scene with its two figures, the strange out-feeling that passes from poet to laborer, and the "help and stay secure," or stay against confusion which the poet gets in return: these were the things Frost had to confront. His poem had to be much longer than it is, simply to accommodate the full view of the question to which he pledged himself by alluding to Wordsworth. But he escapes by a trick of foreshortening, in the last stanza, of which the tenor is self-sacrifice, and the vehicle sacrifice of others.

By a full view I mean the dialectic to which we feel Wordsworth has committed himself when he writes:

My whole life I have lived in pleasant thought,
As if life's business were a summer mood;
As if all needful things would come unsought
To genial faith, still rich in genial good;
But how can He expect that others should
Build for him, sow for him, and at his call
Love him, who for himself will take no heed at all.[6]

There Wordsworth steps out of a race humming with labor and vocation, as a special self. After that there was no turning back. Frost, perhaps from an outsize respect for the rhetorical leverage afforded by the style of the ordinary man, never does step forward. Yet he is writing a kind of poem in which this reticence must be fatal. The poet and laborer may indeed be the same person: but we need to see the poet. Frost's reluctance to come to grips with both vocations—a reluctance that really makes us wonder, which is his vocation? which his avocation?—left its stamp on the rousing last stanza. It is a fine enough sort of eloquence that Frost treats us to, a sort that, like Arnold's, can come of an evasion, and cheer us for a while. But it is not quite in earnest. "Two Tramps in Mud Time," could he have gone the whole length and realized the poem that he projected in the shape of an allusion, would have justified Frost's own metaphors of self-reliance more directly than anything else he wrote.

In contrast "The Course of a Particular" may seem to require no supplement at all to assist our understanding. None, at any rate, beyond the assurance that when Stevens writes, "And being part is an exertion that declines," he is making a distant reply to Whitman, whom he had once pictured as the prophet of poetry and life, with his beard of fire, his staff a leaping flame, "singing and chanting the things that are part of him" ("Like Decorations in a Nigger Cemetery," I. 1–6). Besides, so far as the poem refers us to any earlier utterance, it may seem enough to recall "The Snow Man" and "the misery in the sound of the wind, / In the sound of a few leaves," the words that mark the opening chapter of Stevens's life-long effort to subdue the "Ode to the West Wind" to the beauty of innuendoes.[7] The snow man must have been cold a long time not to be moved by the pathos of this particular. In "The Course of a Particular" on the contrary, one "holds off and merely hears the sound": the poet *is* cold, and no longer part of everything; and the exertion once implied by hearing the human appeal in the sound, has now declined. One has grown at last severe enough to be unconcerned, to live "in the absence of fantasia."

The poem's immense dignity and power have much to do with the weight it carries in every feature, the deliberation with which it declares by every step of its forward motion that it is the work of a very old man. In what it asserts, however, this poem is as shocking as "Two Tramps in Mud Time," and as firmly antithetical to the "distress" of the Wordsworthian encounter. So I can offer one strong reason for considering "The Course of a Particular" with Wordsworth instead of Shelley in the background. It is, that while Stevens's largest piece of furniture is evidently Shelley's fiction of the leaves, his motive seems to me Wordsworthian. Again, such constituents as will serve have been abstracted from "Resolution and Independence." The poet, as poet, is brought face to face with life, as life, which—like the man half-rock, half-man, on the lonely moor—goes on without him, in a way that is chastening to regard. Stevens tells us that he can no longer be moved by the particular that has been his, the cry; but still, *that it merely is* appears to be a necessary condition for his poetry; it is the sign of a larger endurance that implies endurance for himself.

As an interpretation of Wordsworth "The Course of a Particular" is reductive but far from absurd. We know that Wordsworth, in composing "Resolution and Independence," originally wrote a substantial monologue for the leech-gatherer; in revising, his aim was to reduce this second human figure to the last bareness of mere being; and he told Sara Hutchinson, who could not see the point of the poem, that his concern had never been with anything about the man but, as it were, simply *that* the man: "What is brought forward? 'A lonely place, a Pond,' 'by which an old man *was*, far from all house and home': not stood, not sat, but *was*."[8] Stevens's poem contains a line that corresponds perfectly to the reading of Wordsworth sanctioned here by Wordsworth himself: "One feels the life of that which gives life as it is." The title, "The Course of a Particular," I take to mean that the sense of one's own engagement with being has run its course throughout one's life: memories of a thing, and the present consciousness of it, have become a spot of time purged of all inessentials; until at last the thing stands "in the most naked simplicity possible," to adapt another phrase of Wordsworth's from the same letter to Sara Hutchinson.[9] The sound concerns no one at all, and yet it still is, and poetry still gets written. Stevens, it is true, had looked forward to this sense of the life of poetry as early as "The Snow Man." But that was a very programmatic poem, and reads comparatively like a manifesto. By the time he wrote, "One feels the life of that which gives life as it is," Stevens knew that he had grown cold enough, without ever ceasing to think of the particular and its wanderings. His composure had become a full fact.

But does not Stevens in his own way suppress one element of his work as a revisionist? The suppression is of course less imposing than Frost's, it has no broad consequences for the shape of the poem, we are made to feel throughout that Stevens has spent a long time working at poetry. Nevertheless there is something—a deflection, a refinement—which by softening the harsher contrasts of the Wordsworth plot, prevents us from seeing clearly what Stevens has done with it, and so works out as irony. I am thinking of the phrase, "One holds off and merely hears the cry." Now, in common speech, one usually holds off from something one will come back to: "Let me hold off on this"; "No, I want to hold off on the parties until I get to know that crowd better." But Stevens does not have it in mind ever to come back to the cry, except as it echoes in the ear. Once gone, it is gone forever. This is in fact an extreme instance of litotes, close in spirit to the withheld denouements which had been proved on the pulses of Stevens's generation by its leading writer of prose: "Well, you better not think about it."[10] Its value for the poem is to make us worry less scrupulously about the closure of all relations effected by Stevens's detachment. We cease to be troubled by it, for it seems in this light a familiar and honorable sort of patience, born of its share of sympathy and of suffering. The poem can imply all this while saying only, with complete honesty, "I have heard the cry; it ran its course; I need it no more." The understatement thus becomes an apology because we are meant to reflect on Stevens's career, and to remember how often, long after "The Snow Man," he had charted the particular's bearings: in "Sad Strains of a Gay Waltz," and "Mozart, 1935" ("The snow is falling / And the streets are full of cries"); in "Like Decorations in a Nigger Cemetery," the coda to "Notes toward a Supreme Fiction," and "Esthétique du Mal" ("Pain is human.... This is a part of the sublime / From which we shrink"). My impression is that the earlier poems or passages are far steadier in tone than the later ones. Stevens would have had reasons of craft as well as temperament for telling us in an ambiguous phrase that his holding-off would be extended indefinitely.

Some differences of concern that separate Frost and Stevens in much of their work ought to emerge from comparing the stances they adopt to "Resolution and Independence." What both try is to internalize the Wordsworthian encounter with the second figure. Frost all but eliminates the figure in favor of the poet, and at the same time he eliminates, the pathos of the poetic vocation itself. This last is the only thing Stevens finds interesting, but he has the advantage that it is the only thing he pretends to find interesting. "Resolution and Independence" addresses itself to the continuity of poetry for the poet, and the justification of poetry to the world. Of those concerns Stevens has to do mainly with the first, the question of continuity, and Frost mainly with the second, the question of justification: the division is writ large throughout their careers. And yet, Wordsworth's comprehensiveness in this respect goes a very small way toward explaining the stature of "Resolution and Independence." He schools our admiration for the poem not only by his movement from one concern to the other, but equally by the way he discloses himself in the process of movement:

The old Man still stood talking by my side;
But now his voice to me was like a stream
Scarce heard; nor word from word could I divide;
And the whole body of the Man did seem
Like one whom I had met with in a dream;
Or like a man from some far region sent,
To give me human strength, by apt admonishment.

                                                    (II. 106–12)

The poem moves from justification to continuity, and Wordsworth displaces
the leech-gatherer's admonishment with his own "killing thoughts." The
familiarity of the stream-as-eloquence topic makes the work of the transition
almost inaudible. Yet Wordsworth marks for us each distinct moment of the
fade-out and usurpation. In the first line the leech-gatherer is wholly present;
in the second he is absorbed into the metonymy of voice; from this follows
the metaphor of the stream; and finally the vision. It is here that the
comparision with Frost and Stevens becomes most telling. For Frost allows
his tramps to lapse from the poem unaccountably. And Stevens begins "The
Course of a Particular" at a point near the end of the fade-out: what he hears
is only voice, unembodied; and to judge by this poem, one would say that in
the past it had concerned him only as *materia poetica*.

Yet elsewhere in his poetry Stevens allows for a more generous
response. In *Notes Toward a Supreme Fiction*, for example, he uses "image" in
a sense entirely consistent with Wordsworth's decision to retain the leech-
gatherer as a distinct presence: "the difficultest rigor is forthwith, / On the
image of what we see, to catch from that / Irrational moment its
unreasoning." About the sort of figure that this effort preserves he says,
"These are not things transformed. / Yet we are shaken by them as if they
were." So too has the leech-gatherer remained untransformed, to repeat his
answer when Wordsworth renews his question. Repetition is here the brute
circumstance that discloses all the intractability of being. The leech-gatherer
is *there*. Only later, as an after-image, when Wordsworth imagines him in his
mind's eye still wandering about the lonely moor, does he begin to be
transformed by the mind.[11] But this final movement of Wordsworth's
imagination gives no more promise of a self-sufficient triumph than does the
hope he confides to Dorothy at the end of "Tintern Abbey," that he may read
his former pleasures in the shooting lights of her eyes. It is an uneasy
compensation, and he risks turning the leech-gatherer, like Dorothy, into a
machine that can be dismissed once it has served its purpose. Since he knows
the risk, "there is a struggle, there is a resistance involved," a scruple about

his actual relation to the leech-gatherer, and about the cost of making him only a thing of the mind's eye. He neither has nor cares to have the pride that Frost and Stevens exhibit in overcoming that resistance.

Now and then in these pages I have used the word "sympathy," always with some hesitation. I am aware how far the criticism of Wordsworth in our time has been associated with a rejection of Arnoldian ideas about him, and with this rejection I agree wholeheartedly. Wordsworth does not seem to me the poet "Of joy in widest commonalty spread." Nor do I believe that it was a joy of communion which passed between Wordsworth and the leech-gatherer, in either direction. Sympathy may therefore be a misleading word for what I mean; "acknowledgement" or "recognition" might be better. But I have stayed with it because its very etymology includes what is central to my argument: a feeling that touches some second figure, and that could not come into being without it. Granted Wordsworth puts such figures to a use which even a liberalism more modest than Arnold's can never endorse. A comment like A. D. Nuttall's on "The Old Cumberland Beggar" suggests in addition that the poems in which he does so are more closely related to "Resolution and Independence" than one cares to remember:

> There is a moralising argument and I had better confess at once that I find it repellent. It turns on an inversion of the normal order of ethical discourse. Instead of saying that charity is good because it relieves distress, Wordsworth is virtually saying that distress is good because it provides stimulus and scope for charity. Thus a sort of meta-ethical realm is introduced. It is important that men should be happy, but it is far more important that charity should *exist*.[12]

But this takes less from the humanity of the poem than it may seem to do. Wordsworth, even on this view, still keeps the beggar wandering, in the belief that he may some day encounter him again. A search of all Stevens's poetry will produce no such figure. One may, on the other hand, find something resembling him in Frost, but never in a poem where the poet also appears as himself. The great difference between Wordsworth and his modern successors, I have begun to think, lies not so much in "the love of man" as in his simple copresence with another figure, radically unassimilable to himself, and the troubling possibilities that this brings. The egotistical sublime could reach its height when it existed in tension with such possibilities.

NOTES

1. See Frank Kermode, *Romantic Image* (London: Routledge and Kegan Paul, 1957), ch. 1; and Harold Bloom, *The Ringers in the Tower* (Chicago: U. of Chicago Press, 1971), pp. 323–37.

2. *The Poetry of Robert Frost*, ed. Edward Connery Latham (New York: Holt, Rinehart and Winston, 1969), ll. 25–28.

3. *The Poetical Works of Matthew Arnold* (London: Oxford U. Press, 1942), ll. 17–24.

4. *Robert Frost: The Work of Knowing* (New York: Oxford U. Press, 1978), pp. 230–31.

5. My aim is to observe the sort of caution that David Ferry argued for in *The Limits of Mortality* (Middletown: Wesleyan U. Press, 1959); especially in his remarks on the "uncouth shape" somewhat akin to the leech-gatherer, who crosses Wordsworth's path in Book IV of *The Prelude*: "His lack of feeling about his own experience ... may be what should be learned from him. This is a figure as close to the border of death as possible, and as far as can be from involvement in 'the ordinary interests of man.' Yet he is an image of that mankind which the love of nature leads us to love" (p. 142).

6. *Poetical Works*, ed. Thomas Hutchinson, rev. Ernest de Selincourt (London: Oxford U. Press, 1936), ll. 36–42.

7. I have drawn on the splendid discussion of Stevens's commerce with the pathetic fallacy, in Harold Bloom, *Wallace Stevens: The Poems of Our Climate* (Ithaca: Cornell U. Press, 1977) pp. 54–63, 354–59. But I prefer not to confine the reference of the particular to "the fiction of the leaves" (p. 354).

8. To Sara Hutchinson, 14 June 1802, *Early Letters of William and Dorothy Wordsworth, 1787–1805*, ed. Ernest de Selincourt (Oxford: Oxford U. Press, 1935). p. 306.

9. Ibid.

10. Last line of "The Killers." Stevens's description of Hemingway is pertinent: "obviously he is a poet and I should say, offhand, the most significant of living poets, so far as the subject of EXTRAORDINARY ACTUALITY is concerned." "To Henry Church," 2 July 1942. *Letters of Wallace Stevens*, ed. Holly Stevens (New York: Knopf, 1970), pp. 411–12.

11. See Geoffrey H. Hartman, *Wordsworth's Poetry* (New Haven: Yale U. Press, 1964). pp.269–71, where the after-image is defined as "a re-cognition that leads to recognition." This seems to me to involve a fully Yeatsian use of the image. It implies a method of internalizing the image, a recognition-scene projected in the mind, and a therapeutic outcome, about all of which Wordsworth is more skeptical than the epigram requires him to be. A true adept of the after-image should be able to report moments when for "twenty minutes more or less / It seemed, so great my happiness, / That I was blessed and could bless." Eventually he may plot such moments in advance. But Wordsworth is always startled by the gift of self-blessing, and never glances at his watch.

12. *A Common Sky: Philosophy and the Literary Imagination* (London: Chatto & Windus 1974), p. 131. Whatever the exaggerations of this judgment, Nuttall reads the poem as Frost is likely to have read it.

HERBERT MARKS

The Counter-Intelligence
of Robert Frost

I. Why the Stars Twinkle

When Robert Frost presents himself to the reader in the late poem
"Directive" as one "who only has at heart your getting lost," or has the
Keeper in *A Masque of Mercy* declare to his fugitive alter ego, "Some people
want you not to understand them. / But I want you to understand me
wrong." he is playing on the interaction of revelation and concealment—a
theological commonplace, consecrated for English literature in Touchstone's
demonstration that "the truest poetry is the most faining...." The problem of
feigning figures prominently in all Frost's work, as a stylistic tendency toward
the gnomic, but also as a theme. Consider a less obvious clue, the preface he
wrote in 1924 to the little-known *Memoirs of the Notorious Stephen Burroughs*,
in which he praises the Massachusetts impostor for his "sophisticated
wickedness, the kind that knows its grounds and can twinkle." Burroughs had
a flair for irony, and Frost, musing toward the end of the essay on his
conversion to Catholicism, appears to have recognized their shared affinities:

> I should like to have heard his reasons for winding up in the
> Catholic Church. I can conceive of their being honest. Probably
> he was tired of his uncharted freedom out of jail and wanted to be

From *The Yale Review* 71, no. 4 (July 1982). © 1982 by Yale University.

moral and a Puritan again as when a child, but this time under a
cover where he couldn't be made fun of by the intellectuals. The
course might commend itself to the modern Puritan (what there
is left of the modern Puritan).

Though couched humorously, two serious notions are here advanced in
defense of Burroughs's "hypocrisy." One is the necessity of concealment, the
other is the flaccidity of unconstrained freedom, and, taken together, they are
among the central articles of Frost's own personal and poetic creed.

The canny style of engagement is characteristic of Frost, who like Bel's
favorite poet in *A Masque of Mercy* seems to have espoused a "doctrine of the
Seven Poses." "We like to talk in parables and in hints and in indirections,"
he explained to an audience at Amherst College, "whether from diffidence or
some other instinct." Perhaps the instinct is self-preservation, or, less starkly,
the desire to rival God, whose glory it is to conceal things, according to the
biblical proverb. Its counterpart, in any case, is the instinct to seek things out,
called by the same proverb the glory of kings; and it is disheartening to
observe that in our less regal moods we tend to relegate each other's evasions
to the realm of confessional hide-and-seek—as when Lawrance Thompson,
in his introduction to Frost's letters, presumes to excuse the poet's "masks"
by reminding us of his "excruciating sensitivities." Three critical dicta are
accordingly in order: that masking is not necessarily a personal symptom;
that poetry can exist only as veiled or elusive meaning—Frost has called it
metaphor; and that these two precepts imply one another. Admittedly, Frost
often provokes some reductive psychologizing even as he reprehends it: one
thinks of his admonition to Sidney Cox, "I have written to keep the over
curious out of the secret places of my mind." But the invitation, "You come
too," at the front of the collected poems is of another, more generous order,
and we misprize it badly if we suppose that poetic masks are something
behind which it is our privilege or duty to peer. As Frost pointedly remarked
in a letter to Thompson, "The right virtue of a natural reader is the nice
ability to tell always when a poem is being figurative....A little of the low-
down on motivation goes a long way."

This is not to deny that personal anxieties, including a fear of exposure,
contributed to the shaping of Frost's personae. Yet his reasons for resisting
biographical criticism go beyond the desire for privacy, and informers
whetted by such seemingly transparent poses as the folksy philosopher or the
good grey poet would do well to pause before exposing themselves. For
Frost, any effort to go behind the masks is finally not only slavish but futile;
for the "true person" is an endlessly receding ideal, valuable as a stimulus or

lure, but proof against definition. A similar premise underlies Frost's resolve to "spoil" his correspondence with Cox "by throwing it into confusion the way God threw the speech of the builders of the tower of Babel into confusion." What sounds like arrogant mystagogy is at bottom a shrewd reminder that the confusion of tongues and the fall of the tower were manifestations of an already extant condition: that given the state of Noah's descendants, our projects for arriving anywhere directly must collapse of their own accord. The cadres at Babel failed to reach heaven by reason of the same law that preserves or isolates the author from his readers, or the friend from his familiars; and these varied restrictions are finally inseparable. When Frost's Jonah confesses, "I think I may have got God wrong entirely," the Keeper only echoes in reply. "All of us get each other pretty wrong."

If the face-to-face vision of God and the poet relieved of his personae are interchangeable fictions, it is their mythical complement, the naked or public muse, who flits through "Paul's Wife," a poem that explores the necessity of concealment from multiple vantage points. Frost's strategy in the poem is clever. His yarning narrator, after posing the problem of Paul's refusal to be questioned about his rumored marriage, first relates a series of anonymous explanations, for the most part based on the self-defeating view that Paul really has no wife, or that "the obscurity's a fraud to cover nothing," to quote Job's words from *A Masque of Reason*. Ideally, such reductiveness should serve as a warning, but the more generous observations of the backwoods magister Murphy elicit a second variety of interpretive shortcuts, this time from the reader.

The story he tells is that Paul took a log the mill had rejected, carved out the pith and carried it to the pond, where it dissolved and reemerged a girl. Recognition followed, and the couple set off for a niche in the mountains, pursued at a distance by Murphy and his gang of spying loggers. There the new bride shone like a star, till shouts of tribute and a flying bottle broke the charm, and the girl vanished. As usual with Frost, the apparently simple report abounds with symbols and mythical echoes. The contrasts between the mill and the jackknife, the empty bottle and the transfiguring pond, trade on familiar Frostian emblems; while the generation of Paul's native Anadyomene from the pithy log corresponds nicely to the birth of Venus in Hesiod. But the serious difficulty, and with it the real interest of the poem, only begins with the conclusion, in which Murphy finally offers his own interpretation of Paul's evasiveness:

> Paul put on all those airs
> About his wife to keep her to himself.
> Paul was what's called a terrible possessor.

Owning a wife with him meant owning her.
She wasn't anybody else's business,
Either to praise her, or so much as name her,
And he'd thank people not to think of her.
Murphy's idea was that a man like Paul
Wouldn't be spoken to about a wife
In any way the world knew how to speak.

At first, these lines seem to echo the arguments from self-preservation and delicacy of feeling suggested by Thompson. Accordingly, they compel two nains of thought: one psychological, about the makeup of the "man like Paul" so leery of intrusion; the second political, about the makeup of the world to which his elusiveness is the fit response. Such readings, like the arguments they would have Murphy echoing, are not so much invalid as incomplete. They allow us to suppose that, given a tougher hide, or a world somehow marter or better mannered, Paul would have been glad to haul his wife back to camp and, like Len the husband in "A Servant to Servants," compel her to cook for the boys. They neglect, in other words, that necessary correspondence between masking and metaphor—the idea that since language is by nature metaphorical, it must inevitably conceal or misrepresent whatever it tries to convey. Ultimately, for Frost, "*any* way the world knew how to speak" to Paul about his wife must have sounded like slander.

I have been suggesting that a basic theme of Frost's work is the paradoxical alliance of truth and concealment. Another, as I shall try to show, speaks to the mutual dependence of freedom and restraint. In a sense, these two antitheses really express a single paradox, the first in epistemological, the second in physical (or ethical) terms. But I prefer to acknowledge the difference between them, and so the power necessary to yoke them together; for it is precisely here, in the fact that Frost's vision spanned both poles, embracing the physical and the mental and making them cohere, that his accomplishment is most impressive.

Perhaps the finest product of this coherence is "The Silken Tent," a poem that conveys both the interdependence of freedom and restraint and, when read allusively, the higher economies of feigning:

She is as in a field a silken tent
At midday when a sunny summer breeze
Has dried the dew and all its ropes relent.
So that in guys it gently sways at ease.

And its supporting central cedar pole.
That is its pinnacle to heavenward
And signifies the sureness of the soul.
Seems to owe naught to any single cord.
But strictly held by none, is loosely bound
By countless silken ties of love and thought
To everything on earth the compass round.
And only by one's going slightly taut
In the capriciousness of summer air
Is of the slightest bondage made aware.

The tent is a figure for poetic incarnation, and the fourteen lines of the poem, which uses the restrictions and compartmentalizations of the Shakespearean sonnet to achieve its single sentence, seem themselves a formal embodiment of the meaning they convey. This correspondence of form to content is reflected in the smallest details: the description of the central pole, for example, which is placed in the central quatrain; or the final couplet, which illustrates its own slight "bondage" to formal restraints by "going taut" as preannounced. On a larger scale, the whole sonnet unfolds within the bounds set by the initial simile, in illustration of the inevitable impingement, restrictive yet sustaining, of metaphor on direct expression. As the momentum of the sentence develops, we are tempted to forget such a flexible parenthesis, just as we tend for the most part to ignore the frames within which our thoughts and feelings run their course. Twice therefore Frost brings us back to the ground of reality by calling attention to the metaphorical relation with deliberate gestures which are themselves "silken ties." In line 7, the central pole is surprised at its work of fictional identification and exposed for what it really is, an index that "signifies." The second time, in line 10, the relation no longer needs to be enforced. So close is the control that it is allowed to dissolve—the fusion the poem sets out to inter diet taking place, by leave, at the very moment its ban resounds most clearly. It is a wonderful moment, the love and thought which are the soul's rarest ornaments merging with the ties that keep the tent erect in a necessarily contingent freedom. The balanced tensions, appropriately, are both erotic and metaphysical. The gracefulness enveloping the figure binds with its earthward pull the virile thrust toward the sublime, so that the complete structure remains at once open toward, yet apt to withstand, the animating breeze as it presides over the conclusion.

Not the least of Frost's triumphs here is his transvaluation of "the earthly tent," a prominent image in ascetic literature used by Paul in his

Second Letter to the Corinthians to figure the temporary abode of the soul. For Paul, the tent suggests the eventuality of being "swallowed up" into a "heavenly dwelling"; in the sonnet, all hint of the provisional is banished. To be sure, Frost preserves the Pauline delight in paradox, but he fosters it for its own sake, unabashedly, rather than in the name of what transcends or resolves it. Where one senses cautious denigration behind Paul's testimony that "we have this treasure in earthen vessels," in Frost's revision, physical embodiment becomes an occasion for pure celebration: not the "earthly" but the "silken" tent.

Especially in Frost's earlier work, the power of such biblical echoes conies from their compression—the layers of connotation through which they are forced to pass. Symbolic locus of the illimitable shekinah in the Pentateuch, figure in John for the indwelling of the Logos, associated with poetic incarnation in *Paradise Regained* and Emerson's "Terminus," the tent is a potentially cumbersome legacy which Frost, by his very reticence, manages to appropriate. In the late poem "Kitty Hawk," by contrast, the economic parallel between poetics and Christology comes to the surface in lines that stand as a sort of creedal summary, a type of the poet's conviction, expressed in "A Constant Symbol," that "the very words of the dictionary are a restriction to make the best of or stay out of and be silent." Frost's claim that "God's own descent / Into flesh" was intended to show the virtue of spending strongly presumes on the strength of sixty years' work, and as often in his last poems, the irony of the reduction borders on persiflage. The ostensibly Platonic description of the soul's birth in "The Trial by Existence" is likewise indebted to the Christic paradox, but less openly and hence to greater effect:

> And from a cliff-top is proclaimed
>   The gathering of the souls for birth.
> The trial by existence named.
>   The obscuration upon earth.

Here, the limitation or misrepresentation Frost considered an essential feature of language is identified by means of a syntactic ambiguity with the act or process of becoming at all. The dodge centers appropriately on the rime-word "named," which may be read either as a predicate of "trial." or, by a Latinate inversion, as qualifying "existence"—the submission to language thus constituting the trial. Emerson too, in Frost's favorite poem "Uriel," likened the career of poetic speech to "the procession of the soul in matter," but Frost, at least in this early piece, makes more of its restrictive or concealing effects—of an "obscuration" derived via tradition from the spending of the preexistent Word.

Perhaps the counterpart to these passages is the vision of Faraway Meadow at the end of "The Last Mowing"—to me, the most poignant lines Frost ever wrote—in which all sense of trial is momentarily laid aside, and a wistful consummation is realized in the obviation of language:

> The place for the moment is ours
> For you, oh tumultuous flowers,
> To go to waste and go wild in,
> All shapes and colors of flowers,
> I needn't call you by name.

The last two lines are an unusual instance of what Richard Poirier has called "negative designation"; of the way Frost's "visionary impulse ... gets affirmed by an act of denial." For the most part. Frost would have agreed with Stevens, "All sorts of flowers. That's the sentimentalist," and it is rare to see him treating his longing—"this limitless trait in the hearts of men"—without irony. Or rather, since even here the poet's imagined moment of intimacy is ironically predicated on hearsay, it is rare to feel that despite all odds it is the longing that has triumphed.

More typical is the parodistic treatment one finds in "An Empty Threat," a deflation of the sublime in the mode of Keats's "A Song About Myself," and Thoreau's "The Old Marlborough Road." Keats, we remember, took "A Book / Full of vowels / And a shirt / With some towels ... / And follow'd his nose to the North"—only to find the ground there as hard as in England. Thoreau, more cautious, recognized before he set out that roving was a spiritual appetite best indulged at home, that one "can get enough gravel / On the Old Marlborough Road"—though the announcement, characteristically, was only to be posted along the Road itself. Like them, Frost knows that the desire to go beyond home, to dispense with the bounds of place or the particular, is apt to confound itself unless tethered to reality. Freedom, communion, transfiguration, the lures that impel the mythical journey, are for him only vapid delusions until embodied in specific forms. His venture north to the realm of "snow and mist / That doesn't exist" in search of a fabulous father figure is thus, as his title tells us, "an empty threat" from the start:

> I stay:
> But it isn't as if ...

The ensuing description of Hudson's Bay, despite the indicative mode, is idle
fantasy, though one senses that in the canvas of Frost's oeuvre such fantasy
works as a vanishing point, imposing its perspective on everything before it.

Like the brilliance of Far-away Meadow, or the mystic's cloud of
unknowing to which it bears a humorous resemblance, the imagined vastness
of Hudson's Bay is unobstructed by language. As a result, thought founders,
and instinctual calls take the place of articulate sound. At times however, our
ears play tricks on us—"The seal yelp / On an ice cake. / It's not men by some
mistake?"—and we fancy ourselves perhaps in the vicinity of an Over-Soul,
or on the ridge of the Alps, our rational, disjunctive light of sense usurped by
the power of Imagination. To be sure, there is always a companion presence,
but even he is an incarnate ambiguity:

> His name's Joe,
> Alias John,
> And between what he doesn't know
> And won't tell
> About where Henry Hudson's gone,
> I can't say he's much help:
> But we get on.

Like the *absconditus* Henry Hudson, whose secret he may or may not share,
this "French Indian Esquimaux" with the double identity is a familiar,
though sadly diminished, figure. As a final comment on the pretensions of
unific intuition, Frost has cast him as a trapper, not of souls, but of furs—"off
setting traps," which, true to tradition, he baits with his own person—"In
one himself perhaps."

In sum, Hudson's Bay is a vacuous happy hunting ground, and Frost is
suspicious of its infinite spaces. "Supreme merit," as he tells us in "Kitty
Hawk," lies "in risking spirit / In substantiation," in sacrificing possibility for
the sake of attainment. Despite the opaqueness of the medium, his ideals
must be embodied and his intuitions expressed; and he leaves it to those he
later labels "monists" to "end up in the universal Whole / As unoriginal as
any rabbit." For the staunch individualist, absorption in this trackless au delà
would constitute a defeat, a surrender to that dream of "easy gold" which he
had already rejected in his early masterpiece "Mowing." There, "Anything
more than the truth would have seemed too weak / To the earnest love that
laid the swale in rows"—where swale is a trope for meaning, and rows for the
formal constraints of language essential to its cultivation.

Nevertheless, Frost is far from impervious to the temptation he derides; for, as Poirier notes, he is at once morally committed to the necessities of form and "congenitally impatient with form and with limits." Thus, the scrupulous reservation in the last lines of "An Empty Threat" only intensifies the impression of sincere regret:

> Better defeat almost,
> If seen clear,
> Than life's victories of doubt
> That need endless talk talk
> To make them out.

It is the dilemma of a professed "anti-Platonist," vacillating between admiration for our daedal embodiments—for the assertion of form upon chaos—and malaise at their speciousness:

> At one extreme agreeing with one Greek
> At the other agreeing with another Greek....
> A baggy figure, equally pathetic
> When sedentary and when peripatetic.   ["The Bear"]

II. THE SERPENT'S TALE

This deep ambivalence toward the status of the Ideal appears most tellingly in Frost's poems about women, many of whom seem to transcend their situations even as they succumb to them. I think it was Williams who once said that he never passed a homely woman without thinking of Helen of Troy. In Frost's case, the fata morgana was Eve. One suspects that at the deepest level he had identified with Milton's Adam and considered himself somehow to blame for her plight. But his fixation has a literary etiology as well; for he found in the myth of the fall the necessary premise and justification for his thoughts on concealment. Once more, one might cite the theologians, who likewise needed a fall from paradise to sustain a doctrine of incarnation.

Fallen man resigns himself with reluctance to the necessity of concealment. Like the lion's carcase, our stubborn refusal to accept dissimilation breeds its swarm of regrets and desires, nourishing the poetic urge to create a language pure enough to present ourselves intact. This urge the myth explains as our residual awareness of an unfallen state. But Frost is no Gnostic, and his work is no post-lapsarian lament for lost perfection. He is willing to embrace his predicament, to entertain with earlier Stoics a notion of design. He even takes pleasure in the opportunity for self-exertion this predicament provides—a frankly pagan attitude which goes against his own Wordsworthian ideas on how poems are conceived, *sola gratia* so to speak, merrily sinning against the systematic logic of the *felix culpa*. But consistency was never Frost's hobgoblin. "You know how I am about chapter and verse," he wrote in a late letter to Victor Reichert, "somewhat irresponsible some would say. I went wielding the phrase *culpa felix* to my own purposes for a long time before I pinned myself down to what it may originally have meant in Church history."

As I have been suggesting, Frost's purposes were metaphysical as well as dramatic, and this equivocacy is reflected in his responses and allusions to the story of Eve—in its Miltonic no less than its biblical form. Since the extraterrestrial was no longer available, however, Frost was forced to localize the cosmic drama within the human part of the story. This he did by adopting the more readily camouflaged topos of the eternal feminine, or consort as muse. His heroines, like Joyce's women, remain unfallen; or rather, like Joyce's women, they remain elusive—now ideal, now vilified.

The clearest expression of this double configuration is to be found in the three "garden of Eden" poems from the section of *A Witness Tree* suggestively entitled "One or Two." The first, "The Most of It," reads like a meditation on Adam's life before Eve's creation. Everything within call is too exactly itself. There is the self, and there is the buck, the utterly other; but there is no mediating term, nothing to initiate the work of analogy and, therewith, the possibility of creative response. "Never Again Would Birds' Song Be the Same," the central leaf of the triptych, testifies to the difference made by Eve's arrival. Here the garden setting is more explicit, though Eve herself, like the ideal she represents, remains a phantasm, visible only through the eyes of the poem's grammatical subject, who is, like the poet or reader of poetry, a descendant of fallen Adam:

> He would declare and could himself believe
> That the birds there in all the garden round
> From having heard the daylong voice of Eve
> Had added to their own an oversound.
> Her tone of meaning but without the words....

In a sense, Frost's Eve is the positive counterpart of the empty threat of Hudson's Bay. As "inarticulate" as Williams's "Beautiful Thing" shimmering through the common fabric of *Paterson*, she moves in a world indifferent to names, made resonant, as the world in "The Most of It" was not, by her ineffable but musical presence. With her transforming power, she resembles too the transcendent creative principle solicited by Milton in his invocation to Urania, "The meaning, not the name, I call," a phrase echoed clearly in the fifth line of the poem. It seems to join there with the more diffused melody of Virgil's first eclogue ("Formosam resonare doces Amaryllida silvas") to mythologize the pathetic fallacy—or perhaps to mock Dr. Johnson's English translation ("And the wood rings with Amarillis' name"), for it is precisely because it is not denominative, not limed in an onomastic net, that Eve's "tone of meaning" is so all-pervasive.

Analogies to this familiar antithesis of pure and embodied meaning from the realm of poetic practice are suggested by Frost's essay, "The Figure a Poem Makes." Though the figuration is different, the alignment of the terms with revelation and concealment, or freedom and restraint, remains the same. To begin with, Frost likens the "sound" of a poem to "the gold in the ore," separable in theory though not in fact from the allegedly "inessential" contextual or verbal meaning. He then splits each of his terms in two and demonstrates the same interdependence between the halves—the conjunction of melody and meter (which recalls Milton's wedding of Voice and Verse in "At a Solemn Musick") standing to the ordering of sounds as the conjunction of "wildness" and "theme" stands to the ordering of ideas: "Just as the first mystery was how a poem could have a tune in such a straightness as meter, so the second mystery is how a poem can have wildness and at the same time a subject that shall be fulfilled." In each case, Frost conceives of the second term as imposing some limitation on the first, and the figures are all potentially metonymic for the relation of meaning and words.

In Frost's version, the fall of Eve, dramatized in the final poem of the group, will thus be represented as a fall into words. Such a development is anticipated at the end of "Never Again," where we see Eve bound for the first time by the notion of design—impressed, as it were, into the service of poetry: "And to do that to birds was why she came." The functional purpose imposed on her is less onerous perhaps than those borne by her literary sisters, but we feel it to be an outrage nonetheless. That Frost himself saw it this way is made clear by the placement of "The Subverted Flower," with its account of an actual, though abortive, impressment. I say placement, because we know from Thompson that the first draft of the poem was composed in Derry, more than thirty years before its inclusion in *A Witness Tree*. However, not only its position in the published sequence, but the parallels within the poem itself to the temptations scenes from Book Nine of *Paradise Lost* invite us to read it as a complement to the idealized vision of Eve presented in the sonnet.

Toward the end of "Never Again," the venue shifts quietly from the garden to the woods—a topographical change that subtly shadows the succession of generations and, by implication, the definitive change of aeons. At the beginning of "The Subverted Flower," Eve has already wandered outside the "garden wall" into the fallen world. The characteristic response of that world is an act of shameful self-exposure—illustrative, as I hope will be clear by now, of that purer enthusiasm, which, whether it neglect the demands of decorum or the astringencies of metaphor, inevitably ends in confusion. As usual, the analogy between sexual and poetic fruition (or frustration) looms closest, and one can trace a probable connection between Frost's attitude toward the exhibitionist in the poem and the suggestion he makes in "The Constant Symbol" that poetry "be judged for whether any original intention it had has been strongly spent or weakly lost.... Strongly spent," he concludes, "is synonymous with kept"—and to keep is to keep concealed.

It is not his will but the progressive overtness of his behavior that finally costs Eve's assailant his human dignity. As initially presented with his command of the past subjunctive, he is not only forceful but controlled, and the courtly trope that signals his desire could as well be his contrivance as the poet's:

> She drew back; he was calm:
> 'It is this that had the power.'
> And he lashed his open palm
> With the tender-headed flower.

Only when he relinquishes these powers of speech and indirection does the impression of crudeness take over. The flower's seed is openly spilt before the girl—and by now the trope is clearly the poet's—till we are left with the naked thing, unaccommodated man at large:

> She looked and saw the worst.
> And the dog or what it was.
> Obeying bestial laws.
> A coward save at night.
> Turned from the place and ran.

> She heard him stumble first
> And use his hands in flight.
> She heard him bark outright.

This sudden revulsion, which expresses itself as flight to cover, is, Frost would suggest, no more than the rigor of natural law against whatever ignores its preservative order—a rigor akin to that which made Milton's Adam, on waking from his first debauch to apprehend his nakedness, and in it the reality of his transgression, cry: "Cover me ye pines / Ye cedars, with innumerable boughs / Hide me...."

In Paradise the admission was consequential; in twentieth-century New England it is simply another instance of a well-established pattern. The question of the girl's role in the episode that brings about this backlash is accordingly the more interesting of the poem's two foci. At the end, of course, the man's degeneracy will redound upon her as well; yet for all the foam on her chin, she remains technically inviolate, like the Anadyomene in "Paul's Wife." In fact, the darkest implications of the poem only become apparent when we recognize that it is precisely her inviolability that brings the episode to its wretched consummation. There is nothing necessarily vicious about the man's original appeal. Rather, like the ambiguous central trope itself, it may be a prelude to fruitfulness. The degradation is gradual; and a closer look suggests that each step is precipitated by her failure to respond:

> He smiled for her to smile,
> But she was either blind
> Or willfully unkind ...
> She was standing to the waist
> In goldenrod and brake,
> Her shining hair displaced.
> He stretched her either arm
> As if she made it ache
> To clasp her—not to harm;
> As if he could not spare
> To touch her neck and hair.
> 'If this has come to us
> And not to me alone—'
> So she thought she heard him say;
> Though with every word he spoke
> His lips were sucked and blown

And the effort made him choke
Like a tiger at a bone.
She had to lean away.

Her uncertainty about his speech is particularly significant, as it seems to
mirror Eve's initial wonder, when flattered by the Serpent in *Paradise Lost*, at
hearing "language of Man pronounc't / By Tongue of Brute." Indeed, the
word "brute" occurs four lines later in Frost; but the image here is inverted,
for it is actually the girl's reception of the broken words that puts their status
as language in question. Likewise, the demeaning description of his manner
of speaking, which we tend to read as her impression, anticipates, rather than
reflects, his dehumanization. Her "shining hair" is sufficient to suggest a
mythical or ideal beauty, which to the man who fails to appreciate its
inaccessibility is potentially pernicious. It is a cold allure, and, though
embodied conventionally in an image of woman, strangely akin in its fatality
to that foreignness that Stevens figured more portentously in his northern
lights. It too can be seen as the serpent's nest, the poetic equivalent of evil's
source, "responsible" for educing what Emerson has called the "tragedy of
incapacity." Thus, the ominous opening words of the poem, "She drew
back," reverberate, once the catastrophe is sure, in indictment of the girl:

A girl could only see
That a flower had marred a man,
But what she could not see
Was that the flower might be
Other than base and fetid:
That the flower had done but part.
And what the flower began
Her own too meager heart
Had terribly completed.

Of course, the very venture beyond the garden wall into the wild field
of flowers was already an invitation to trouble. In Milton's poem. Adam
reproaches Eve with "that strange / Desire of wand'ring," and throughout
Frost's work the same figure is used to signify that "extra-vagant" longing for
perfect freedom which if not restrained brings inevitable calamity. In first-
person poems like "Into My Own," "The Sound of Trees," "An Empty
Threat," "Stopping by Woods," "Come In," and many more, the poet
himself wisely resists this longing—either by subordinating it as contrary to
fact or relegating it to an indefinite future—but the women in the narratives

are often less circumspect. The foreboding that one feels for the wife at the door in "Home Burial" or for the wife in "A Servant to Servants," who could "Drop everything and live out on the ground," is justified by the effect of the fugitive daughter's extravagance in "The Housekeeper," and more terribly by the fate of the woman in "The Hill Wife," who on a sudden "impulse" wanders from the loneliness of a barren marriage to a solitude beyond bound or bourn:

> She rested on a log and tossed
>   The fresh chips,
> With a song only to herself
>   On her lips.
>
> And once she went to break a bough
>   Of black alder.
> She strayed so far she scarcely heard
>   When he called her—
>
> And didn't answer—didn't speak—
>   Or return....

The emphasis on reticence here is typical; for it is their reluctance to compromise themselves with words that gives to so many of Frost's heroines the air of innocence or of nobility incommensurate with the meanness of their lives. By the same token, so long as she keeps silent, the girl in "The Subverted Flower" managers, despite the poet's indictment, to preserve a virginal purity. Unlike the woman in "The Hill Wife," however, she is alert to the call from home—to the repercussions of her absence if not of her presence—and so, in the end, as her passage from pregnant silence to sterile and profane speech makes manifest, her purity perishes while she survives. This passage is carefully anticipated by an awakening of her other senses, corresponding to the simultaneous decline in the man's speech and sight (note that at the end he stumbles and has to "use his hands in flight"). Thus, whereas she begins as if "blind" and with uncertain hearing ("she thought she heard him say"), in the second half of the poem she actively "looks," "sees," or "hears" in five successive sentences before—with Eve, her eyes how opened, and her mind how darkened—she finally accedes to her own voice:

> And oh, for one so young
> The bitter words she spit

Like some tenacious bit
That will not leave the tongue.
She plucked her lips for it,
And still the horror clung.
Her mother wiped the foam
From her chin, picked up her comb
And drew her backward home.

The irony is that this accession is itself a decline. Language here is compared to a "bit"—a restraint unknown to the "tiger at a bone," but alien too to Eve in Paradise. Just as the man's flight and submersion in animality were fit retribution for his presumptive self-exposure, so this figurative curb requites the young Eve for her provocative will to wander. Again, one is reminded of Milton's lines: "restraint she will not brook, / And left to herself, if evil thence ensue, / She first his weak indulgence will accuse." To complete the parallel only two things need be added: that her outburst merits pity as well as reproof, and that the responsibility for the evil wrought is mutual.

In *Paradise Lost*, where the ultimate responsibility for evil—for the struggle between passion and reason (or freedom and restraint) lies outside the human sphere altogether, this second point is less salient. Given the reality of the angelic order, Milton was able to construct a noncommutative chain of influence with Eve, both tempted and tempting, in the center, and the Serpent and Adam at either end (though the fact that Adam initiates their dalliance after the fall doubtless anticipates a new reciprocity). For Frost, however, responsibility is confined to the human sphere, and temptation is thus viciously reciprocal from the start. If Adam is tempted, Eve must be the temptress, *and* vice versa. Although narrative devices and interpolated comments challenging the more obvious reading of the incident both tend to exonerate the man, his culpability is reestablished at a deeper level by the structural parallels between his progress and that of Milton's Tempter: for example, that both prosper through ambiguity until their intentions are realized, or that both then abandon human speech and withdraw. There is Miltonic precedent too for the way Frost aligns perception with speech and uses them to create the chiastic pattern in which the tempter's powers wane as the tempted's revive.

In the end, both masculine and feminine narrative lines circle back on themselves and interlock, until there is no way of telling whether the "subverted flower" of the title is the girl or the man, or simply the prospect of coalescence represented by the nameless flowers of Far-away Meadow. In place of that prospect, we are given a cage of moral ambiguities, reminiscent of the mirrored boxes of Hawthorne or Henry James, whose paradise-lost view of reality Frost shares, as he shares their fascination with emblems and their insistence on craftsmanship. He shares too their respectful impatience with Emerson, of whom he once wrote in criticism that "he could see the 'good of evil born' but he couldn't bring himself to say the evil of good born." If we accept the inaccessible girl with the shining hair as another embodiment of the beautiful thing, then the tale of degradation Frost here tells so powerfully brings that criticism to life.

Admittedly, this sequence of poems shows Frost at his most dialectical. For the most part, the women in the narrative poems have long since been required for their kinship with Eve, and rather than obscure them further, Frost prefers to let them shine as they can. Despite their subject or "fallen" state—generally suggested by the bond of marriage or economic dependence—their speech and vision tend to remain chaste. At its extreme, this chastity threatens to become a cutting-off of all relation, as when the wife in "Home Burial," convinced of her husband's inner blindness, rejects his attempts at rapprochement and, in a line that recalls the conclusion of "Paul's Wife," forbids him to even mention their buried child:

[He:] 'A man can't speak of his own child that's dead.'

[She:] 'You can't because you don't know how to speak.'

But usually it is more benevolent: the granddaughter in "The Generations of Men" simply "using her eyes" to read the true profile of the stranger beside her, or the wife in "West-running Brook" responding with a name to the gay wave in the stream on which her husband discourses. It is as though the poisoned fruit which destroyed their hopes had left their desires still pure, so that they themselves might become a source of nourishment. To be sure, the "sound of meaning" is now all but inaudible. As the wife "with a houseful of hungry men to feed" admits in "A Servant to Servants":

There's nothing but a voice-like left inside
That seems to tell me how I ought to feel.
And would feel if I wasn't all gone wrong

—for she is as tightly confined by life's contingencies as her mad uncle was by his hickory cage. Yet for all their obscurity, they are never devious or indirect, but remain—if only by their passive endurance—priestesses of the Ideal. One might call them hobbled transcendentalists, or remembering their potential balefulness, follow Frost's wrier lead and dub them witches, who though perched between two worlds—as the Pauper Witch of Grafton between her battling towns—must in the end, along with Eve, "come down from everything to nothing."

III. THE LONGEST WAY ROUND

The fall from Eden, like the fall of the tower of Babel, was a fall into conclusion. The late poem "Directive," which ends with an invitation to "Drink and be whole again beyond confusion," has usually been read as Frost's program for a poetic sacrament that would carry us beyond our fallen state. However, the text bristles with warnings that should caution us against accepting its apparent assertions too quickly. Of these, the most striking is the allusion to St. Mark which immediately precedes the conclusion. The symbolic itinerary has been completed, and the poet has brought us to his rustic equivalent of the eternal source or waters of life:

> I have kept hidden in the instep arch
> Of an old cedar at the waterside
> A broken drinking goblet like the Grail
> Under a spell so the wrong ones can't find it,
> So can't get saved, as Saint Mark says they mustn't.

The patent reference is to the lines following the parable of the sower, in which Jesus is represented as expounding the necessity of concealment: "And he said unto them, Unto you it is given to know the mystery of the kingdom of God: but unto them that are without, all these things are done in parables: That seeing they may see, and not perceive; and hearing they may hear, and not understand...." An allusion to the same passage in the roughly contemporaneous essay "A Romantic Chasm" makes it clear that for Frost the outsiders or "wrong ones" are those who lack the patience or dexterity to follow that constant "word-shift by metaphor" which keeps the language of poetry from ever meaning simply what it says.

Elitist postures can be exasperating, and it may be argued that "Directive," like the other blank-verse narratives in which the "I" dissociates itself didactically from the reader ("New Hampshire," "The White-Tailed Hornet"), ends up imposing its purpose rather than "discovering" it the way Frost says a good poem should. Nevertheless, the prerogatives Frost is claiming here are not his own but, as in the tower of Babel letter where he identifies himself with God, those which the mystery of poetry enjoins on its initiates. Moreover, the very flagrance of his posing is our clue that it hides an underlying motive. As should be clear by now, Frost's allusions are far subtler than those flaunted vermiculations to which the "more difficult" modernists have accustomed us. In the case of "Directive," I believe the poetic target is Wordsworth's *Excursion*, and the scriptural stalking-horse is intended simultaneously to publish and to disguise its presence.

This double function begins with the mention of the Grail; for Frost's "broken goblet" is meant to redeem the "useless fragment of a wooden bowl, / Green with the moss of years," which the Wanderer finds by the hidden spring in Book One of Wordsworth's poem. Wordsworth's fragment is "useless" in that the Wanderer will not drink from it. Instead it becomes the focus of the elegiac impulse that dominates this part of the work: a figure, more tentative than the Boy of Winander whom it anticipates, for the poetic self in the obligatory act of dying vicariously in order to be reborn. Echoes of the Wordsworthian dialectic are clearest in the opening lines of Frost's poem, where explicitly elegiac gestures—unless read tongue-in-cheek as the subsequent lapse in diction invites—prepare us for an excursion along the *via negativa*:

> Back out of all this now too much for us,
> Back in a time made simple by the loss
> Of detail, burned, dissolved, and broken off
> Like graveyard marble sculpture in the weather.
> There is a house that is no more a house
> Upon a farm that is no more a farm
> And in a town that is no more a town.

From *Lycidas* to Stevens's dirge for the tropical planter in *Notes Toward a Supreme Fiction*, such secularized paradox is at the heart of the sublime tradition in English and American poetry. Frost, however, is a poet of "counter-love," for whom the supreme fiction has not to be imagined but discovered—and not in ostentatious isolation, but working "whether together or apart" in inevitable league with others. He thus revises the Wordsworthian itinerary by putting the fragment to use. To speak in parables, the bowl outside Wordsworth's ruined cottage resembles the corn of wheat that must die in order to bear; the broken goblet in Frost, like the faithful servant's talent, is a counter for pragmatic exchange.

Like the Gospel parables themselves, "Directive" can be read in two ways. It can be interpreted point for point (allegorically): or it can be construed in its entirety as illustrating a single conviction (the way form criticism insists Jesus' parables were originally meant to be taken). The latter approach suggests an alternative to the sacramental reading of the poem; for search as we may, the only integrating conviction—the only common term between Frost's poem and experience—is the certainty of fragmentation. That is, read as parable, the poem invites us to achieve the only wholeness possible by becoming reconciled to the imperfect. It offers us a road—later called a ladder—that "may seem as if it should have been a quarry," glacial etchings in the rock, cellar holes, a field eroded to the size of a harness gall, and, in its midst, a "children's house of make believe," with some "shattered dishes" and the broken goblet used to draw the water. These analects become more meaningful when read with an eye to their individual histories— especially in Frost's own poems. Thus, if we move to an "allegorical" reading, the "ladder road" recalls the two-pointed ladder of metaphor that points toward heaven in "After Apple Picking"; the glacier "that braced his feet against the Arctic Pole" is a manifestation or emissary of the same elusive unnameable that haunts the polar mind in "An Empty Threat"; and the traces it leaves on the ledges run "southeast northwest" by reason of the same imaginative westering that makes all "zest / To materialize / By on-penetration" run in the same direction in "Kitty Hawk."

This fragmentary style of reference seems especially fitting in a poem that would vindicate process. As Frost writes in "The Prerequisites," "A poem is best read in the light of all the other poems ever written. We read A the better to read B.... Progress is not the aim, but circulation." Moreover, his determination in "The Lesson for Today," to "take [his] incompleteness with the rest," shows that he recognized the limitations of the approach. And yet a close explicator could still argue that the aim of "Directive" is to transcend and so perfect its fragments: that the counterplot I have been tracing is only its *praeparatio evangelica*. The final question is thus whether "the road there," so similar to the dialectical path of the quest romance, leads to some determinate source, or whether our gift at journey's end is just the preacher's vexing wisdom. Does one really come back to the original word or only to another departure?

The answer hinges on our reading of the final phrase, "beyond confusion." The word "confusion" occurs frequently in Frost's work, where it usually connotes disorder and defeat. The reference to the confusion of Babel in Frost's letter to Cox, for example, and the description of "the background in hugeness and confusion shading away from where we stand into black and utter chaos" in his letter to *The Amherst Student* both depend on this usage. If this is the only sense intended in "Directive," then the final line exceeds without question Frost's own definition of a poem's end as "a momentary stay against confusion." The invitation to "drink and be whole again" would be a call to unmediated vision—a call to ascend from Babel not by the two-pointed ladder of metaphor, but directly. But "confusion" may have another meaning, as exemplified in the final line of Frost's early poem "Rose Pogonias:"

> We raised a simple prayer
>   Before we left the spot,
> That in the general mowing
>   That place might be forgot;
> Or if not all so favored,
>   Obtain such grace of hours,
> That none should mow the grass there
>   While so confused with flowers.

Here Frost, the student of Latin poetry, is punning on the etymologically prior sense of blending or fusing together in the manner of Milton, for whom the original sense of a Latinate word often points back toward an unfallen world ("with mazy error," "sapient fruit"). Allowing that the same etymological play is active in the final line of "Directive," Frost's invitation to wholeness is qualified by an antithetical intimation that the only wholeness or health we can know is to be free from the illusory ideal of perfection—to accept, with full knowledge of its inadequacy, the wisdom of concealment and restraint.

A similar ambiguity is active in Job's lines from *A Masque of Reason*, written about the same time:

> Yet I suppose what seems to us confusion
> Is not confusion, but the form of forms.
> The serpent's tail stuck down the serpent's throat,
> Which is the symbol of eternity.

One thinks in reading them of Coleridge's remark to Joseph Cottle (7 March 1815) that "the common end of all *narrative*, nay of *all* Poems, is to convert a series into a *Whole*: to make those events, which in real or imagined History move on a strait Line, assume to our Understandings a *circular* motion—the snake with its Tail in its Mouth." Yet presumably there is an undercurrent in Frost's version that links it to the unconverted and unconverting circles of Emerson's "Uriel," the "greatest Western [i.e., American] poem yet," as Job goes on immediately to say. My own conclusion is that within the context of Frost's poem Job is a weak reader whose word must be completed by that of his wife (Thyatira, after the New Testament city famed for its witches), who knows the world as the "hard place" where man "can try himself / And find out whether he is any good." For Frost, the "tail stuck down the serpent's throat" is the tale Eve swallowed in the garden, the false promise of a prematurely perfected vision. In eternity, perhaps, Uriel's cry will be heard, the series will be converted, and the circle will focus to a single point. In the meantime, that symbol remains a figure; for the fruit that brought the dualities of good and evil to Eve and her descendants also brought duplicity—the coats of skins—and metaphor to bind them together.

"There is throughout nature," wrote Emerson, "something mocking, something that leads us on and on.... We live in a system of approximations. Every end is prospective of some other end." "Directive" is a parable of hermeneutic circulation. True, the search for understanding must begin with our initial faith that some sense is there to be discovered: that *la dive bouteille* when pieced together will not be found empty. But what if we find it half-empty? And if so, should we call it half-empty or half-full? That, to recall a teacher's words, was the oven bird's dilemma—the "diminished thing" and what to make of it. The traditional reading of "Directive" approaches it from the half-full side, as a parable of sufficiency, an affirmation of the power of poetry to embody real meanings in which the properly initiated may happily come to share. It makes the hermeneutical circle a sacramental *temenos*, a magic precinct where source and terminus coalesce. But it misses the critical ambiguity. A reading that achieves its source can only be an icon or an artifact. Frost's sovereign principle of metaphor is, on the contrary, a machine for displacement, and every attained meaning must redeem a correspondent loss.

Late in his career, Frost recounted the history of his own lifelong engagement to this hard truth in a narrative poem, "The Discovery of the Madeiras," and placed it at the end of "One or Two." For all its apparent urbanity, the story of the fugitive lovers has the terrible rigor of a sphinx's riddle; for the interpolated tale of the slave couple sacrificed on the high seas is really a parable of the lovers' own fate. Their responses to the oracle differ, however: she withdraws from its harshness, and, constant to some incommunicable ideal, dies "of thought" on a nameless island; he, more bold, dares to conceive it, and so sails on, having buried her there and written, as marriage lines, an epitaph. In the end, his gesture is naturally misread: the island is named for him, not for her. But that, as Frost tells us, is "neither here nor there"; for history too is a choice of figments.

CHARLES BERGER

Echoing Eden:
Frost and Origins

Of the major modern poets, Frost seems the least driven to create myths or fictions of origin, the least prone to mystify beginnings. He will have nothing to do with the sacred investiture of the past, whether historical or autobiographical. He resembles Stevens in the belief that the sense "of cold and earliness is a daily sense, / Not the predicate of bright origin" ("An Ordinary Evening in New Haven"), but does not share Stevens's obsession with finding first ideas apart from authoritarian first principles. Though Frost is most profoundly an exploratory poet, whose work indeed *is* knowing, as Richard Poirier's title tells us, he would not hymn the search for the ground of such knowing as Stevens does: "To re-create, to use / The cold and earliness and bright origin / Is to search." Frost privileges neither the constructed locus of origin nor the search for it with Stevens' high eloquence. At the same time, one cannot read through Frost's poetry and fail to notice how many of his poems engage, however playfully or skeptically, those issues we group under the figurative heading of "origins," even to the point of his invoking Eden and the Fall to describe ongoing moments in consciousness. In his poems of brooks, pools, and gardens, in his speculations on the wellsprings of sound and song, Frost shows an uncanny ability to approach the formerly sacred source, to broach the beginning of things, without yielding to their hieratic lure. Frost plays upon the prestige of these

---

From *Robert Frost*, ed. Harold Bloom. © 1986 by Charles Berger.

themes, but ends by including or accommodating them within, not outside, the range of lyric discursiveness. His poetic intelligence thrives on the recognition that all beginnings are fictions.

A good example of how Frost can play with the subject of beginnings comes in a little-discussed poem called "The Valley's Singing Day":

> The sound of the closing outside door was all.
> You made no sound in the grass with your footfall,
> As far as you went from the door, which was not far;
> But you had awakened under the morning star
> The first songbird that awakened all the rest.
> He could have slept but a moment more at best.
> Already determined dawn began to lay
> In place across a cloud the slender ray
> For prying beneath and forcing the lids of sight,
> And loosing the pent-up music of overnight.
> But dawn was not to begin their "pearly-pearly"
> (By which they mean the rain is pearls so early,
> Before it changes to diamonds in the sun),
> Neither was song that day to be self-begun.
> You had begun it, and if there needed proof—
> I was asleep still under the dripping roof,
> My window curtain hung over the sill to wet;
> But I should awake to confirm your story yet;
> I should be willing to say and help you say
> That once you had opened the valley's singing day.

This remarkably subtle poem avoids claiming too much for the action it describes, while at the same time showing how easy—how natural—it would be to magnify such an incident. The teasing enjambment of the fourth line makes us first take "awakened" as intransitive (helped in this by the poetical "under the morning star"), accustomed as we are to the heightened rhetoric of beginnings. As we read on, we discover that the action can be explained a little less hyperbolically; something has been jarred from sleep, simply awakened by a nearly inaudible sound. But the initial suggestion roused in us will not entirely disappear and the identification of the bird as "the first" perhaps keeps us within an enlarged sphere of possibility.

But the poem scales down to anecdote, to "story," as if to imply that all accounts of beginnings or awakenings contain their share of arbitrariness or accident. The comedy of disproportion here arises from the gap between effort and effect: so little goes into achieving what might be regarded, in another poem, as so much. Placing oneself at the dawn, inserting oneself at the opening of day so that song would not be "self-begun" but originated by an outside, prevenient presence, this sounds like the plot of a revised hymn to sunrise—but of a different poem, as well. These "larger" themes are echoed playfully throughout this singing day's valley. But it would not be play, as Frost says elsewhere, were it not for mortal stakes.

The dialectical complement of Frost's wary attraction to original sites and sounds may be discovered in his many poems about *echo*. Its obvious associations with pastoralism matter less for the interpreter of Frost than the use of echo as a figure for repetition and reflection (to bring in the visual analogue). Frost's poetry complicates the hierarchical opposition between the fullness of original sound and the faintness of echo. If he does not go all the way toward regarding repetition as mastery or originality, he certainly avoids seeing it as diminution. A central distinction made by John Hollander in *The Figure of Echo* between echo and allusion helps to explain Frost's attitude toward verbal repetition:

> We might, indeed, propose a kind of rhetorical hierarchy for the relationship of allusive modes. Actual *quotation*, the literal presence of a body of text, is represented or replaced by *allusion*, which may be fragmentary or periphrastic. In the case of outright allusion ... the text alluded to is not totally absent, but is part of the portable library shared by the author and his ideal audience. Intention to allude recognizably is essential to the concept.... But then there is echo, which represents or substitutes for allusion as allusion does for quotation.... In contrast with literary allusion, echo is a metaphor of, and for, alluding, and does not depend on conscious intention.

By these criteria, Frost would certainly have to be considered a poet of echo rather than allusion. Echo is less referential and intentional than allusion, while at the same time being more figurative. Rather than calling attention to a particular passage, it makes the reader aware of temporality in its pure state. Echo acknowledges indebtedness by figuratively indicating the temporality of the poet's discourse, but works to free that dependence from association with the notion of poetic property, thereby easing the burden of belatedness. Frost's concept of "sentence sounds," preexisting patterns of sound belonging to the genius of the language, amounts to just such a theory of echoing:

They are apprehended by the ear. They are gathered by the ear from the vernacular and brought into books. Many of them are already familiar to us in books. I think no writer invents them. The most original writer only catches them fresh from talk, where they grow spontaneously.

No critic writing today would have any difficulty exposing the idealizations of this passage, its accordance of priority to speech over writing, or its natural analogues for the process of composition: sounds, which "grow spontaneously" in nature, are gathered (as are crops) or caught (as are animals). Frost himself leaves it an open question as to whether we apprehend sentence sounds from talk or from books. But priority is not really the issue here. What matters for Frost is that the poet capture what Marie Borroff, in her study of Frost's language, terms "native" dialect, the strength of the vernacular. Such a concept seems to fuse origin and echo, insofar as the quest for the vernacular always implies a figurative return to "authentic" language, language at the source, "first" words. But this return also involves a repetition, since the vernacular keeps such language alive and in circulation. It might be said that for Frost the ideal of the native stands in for the stricter sense of the origin that one encounters in other poets. A poem such as "Hyla Brook"—"our brook," as Frost calls it—with its refusal to pursue the stream underground in a quest for the deep source, typifies this attitude. The resonances of native speech represent an accommodated purity, for Frost is not the poet of the still center. Poirier distinguishes Frost from some of the romantics in that he does not regard human consciousness as a burden. I would also add that, as opposed to some of his nearer contemporaries, he does not regard the inherently figurative nature of language to be a burden either, and so does not seek radical cures for the imprecisions of language.

In what follows, I will be considering a series of poems on the subject of origins and echoes. These poems should give a strong sense of the different guises under which this central concern appears in Frost. I hesitate to call it an obsession, since that word does not square with the subtlety of Frost's artistry. Although the sequence I have chosen ends with "Directive"— a poem that ends a number of other essays on Frost—I do not intend that poem to be regarded as a culmination, or summa, of Frost's thinking on the subject. Frost's *oeuvre* is the most decentered of any major, modern poet and for the critic to construct a central poem would be to violate the sceptical integrity of his work. All these poems echo each other, in their strategies of covering and recovering the origin.

I

"The Aim Was Song" begins, "Before man came"—but nothing in Frost's rhetoric suggests that he wishes to capture the accents of this prehistoric, prelinguistic moment. Frost does not mystify the subject of "Before man"; indeed, it remains for him a subject, capable of being declaimed upon along with other subjects. Frost does not try to use language to express the epoch *before* language. Poetic primitivism is not his way:

> Before man came to blow it right
>> The wind once blew itself untaught,
> And did its loudest day and night
>> In any rough place where it caught.
>
> Man came to tell it what was wrong:
>> It hadn't found the place to blow;
> It blew too hard—the aim was song.
>> And listen—how it ought to go!
>
> He took a little in his mouth,
>> And held it long enough for north
> To be converted into south,
>> And then by measure blew it forth.
>
> By measure. It was word and note,
>> The wind the wind had meant to be—
> A little through the lips and throat.
>> The aim was song—the wind could see.

Scattered throughout the poem are teasingly moral terms, such as "right," "wrong," and "ought." The wind itself must be taught. And yet these moral terms have an aesthetic basis to them: "measure" is not so much a moral as an aesthetic category. Learning to measure and order the instrument means learning to play it right, learning to find the smooth as opposed to the rough places. Civilization is a form of measure. Morality might sneak in here in the sense that there is a guiding principle to the search for measure. That is, Frost may be implying that moral systems grow out of a deep-seated, instinctual urge for measure and order, a need on our part to convert things to human scale.

The process of turning undifferentiated wind into the measures of "word and note" involves an act of conversion—"North ... converted into south"—a turning of the wind against itself, so to speak. Wind is drawn in and then returned as the exhalation of song. Insofar as song is composed partly of natural wind, it is mimetic, a point Frost makes through the mirroring of the word in the line, "The wind the wind had meant to be." But nature is also changed by song's superaddition of meaning, even if such a gesture works to restore a sense of natural mimesis by ascribing a similar meaning to nature itself. In his half-jocular way, Frost stands the Wordsworthian model of nature as pedagogue on its head, by having man become the instructor. The lesson learned, "the wind could see."

The conversion of natural wind into song marks a triumph of human scale and meaning. Sound is converted into song through a twisting or a wrenching, a turning of strength inside out. In making of the wind a human song, we thereby create a sense of order: the measures of song precede the measures of law. If the aim is song, then to be wrong is to misaim, to hit the wrong note, the wrong target, to be guilty of *hamartia*.

"Sitting by a Bush in Broad Sunlight" has drawn surprisingly little comment from the critics, as if its underlying complexities were only too readily translated by confident artistry. The poem's tetrameter couplets invoke Emerson's oracular meter, but the trumpeting is muted here, the line more flexible. The poem's overt subject is entropy, the decline from fire to mere warmth, with the specter of winter not far removed:

> When I spread out my hand here today,
> I catch no more than a ray
> To feel of between thumb and fingers;
> No lasting effect of it lingers.
>
> There was one time and only the one
> When dust really took in the sun;
> And from that one intake of fire
> All creatures still warmly suspire.
>
> And if men have watched a long time
> And never seen sun-smitten slime
> Again come to life and crawl off,
> We must not be too ready to scoff.
>
> God once declared He was true
> And then took the veil and withdrew,

And remember how final a hush
Then descended of old on the bush.

God once spoke to people by name.
The sun once imparted its flame.
One impulse persists as our breath;
The other persists as our faith.

Though the poem is startlingly literal in its declaration that "There was one time and only the one," Frost displays little sense of loss, little elegiac lament. To state the terms of decline so baldly is perhaps to expose the impossibility of the original moment—that "one time"—from which we appear to have fallen. Sentences such as "God once spoke to people by name," or "The sun once imparted its flame," are possible only because of "once," the signifier of irrecoverable priority. "Once" marks the precincts of *illo tempore*, the sacred space of story time, of origin conceived as a story. Throughout the poem, Frost threatens to convert these absolute statements into terms of wit, thereby bringing the sacred into the social realm. The act of spreading out "here today" takes priority over the loss of elemental fire. Frost is able both to describe his inability to catch fire, to "take" in the sun, and his inability to mourn the loss of such elemental power.

"Sitting by a Bush in Broad Sunlight" is balanced between scoffing tones and tones of awe, between the coyness of "God ... took the veil and withdrew," and the imagining of a moment when "dust really took in the sun," a moment when it was possible to catch fire from the source of fire. Frost also plays with two creation stories here, one divine, one natural: the spark of genesis comes from God's Word, it comes from the sun's flames. I have deliberately omitted "or" from the last clause, for the two accounts need not be competing ones. Frost has united the images of speech and fire as we find them in the story of the burning bush. God's speech issues in fire: prophetic or pentecostal speech. Frost's poem has no real room for speculation on this kind of speech, nor does Frost do so elsewhere in his poetry, but he gives us a glimpse of such a conjunction in this poem. Frost assumes that we are separated from such fiery speech, just as we are separated from the truth, once declared but now withdrawn, and he does not mourn the loss of such verbal immediacy. The poem's opening line presents an image of the hand as an emblem of artistic technique and Frost chooses it over the burning tongue of prophetic discourse. Along these same lines, he reveals himself to be a watcher, not a seer: "And if men have watched a long time / And never seen.... "

The act of sitting by a bush in broad sunlight is, of course, a pale echo of Moses' stance before the burning bush; Frost's speaker is more like Mordechai before the palace gates. Frostian wit, the power of his epigrammatic style, tempers both the pain of loss and quizzes the reality of the supposed lost object. The last stanza of the poem makes it clear that Frost is interested primarily in what he calls our persistence: this is his strong word for echoing, repetition, continuation. The last lines rhyme "faith" and "breath"—though they are the most pronounced off-rhymes in the poem— but the possibility of chiastic structuring makes it impossible to assign these terms with certainty to either sun or God. Does our breath derive from God's speech or the sun's flame? Fire has been allied with suspiration throughout the poem, so it might be natural to assume that the sun's imparted gift still persists as our breath. God's speech, then, is our faith. But these terms could just as easily be reversed. Is breath stronger than faith? And, if so, is it stronger because it comes from nature and not God?

II

The conjunction of green and gold in "Nothing Gold Can Stay" merges myths of the garden and the golden age, while also introducing, through "gold," an artificial note into the account. *Firstness*, Frost seems to say, has an unnatural cast to it.

> Nature's first green is gold,
> Her hardest hue to hold.
> Her early leaf's a flower;
> But only so an hour.
> Then leaf subsides to leaf.
> So Eden sank to grief,
> So dawn goes down to day.
> Nothing gold can stay.

The ability to distinguish a green that differs from itself, a green that is gold, argues an artificial perspective—the Yeatsian "artifice of eternity"—that can only momentarily be held, whether in Nature or the poet's mind. Such a distinction is doomed to slip away or be elided, a process the poem enacts through the grammatical elision of "Her early leaf's a flower." At the same time, the natural process of growth and expansion is implicated in the loss of earliness to a grosser lateness. What one scale of measurement registers as growth, another sees as loss, diminution, entropic dwindling. The sense of a Fall, made explicit throughout in words such as "sank" and "goes down," is also reinforced by the dominant falling rhythm of the trochaic line. When the word "grief" enters the poem, it has the force of "misery" in Stevens's "The Snow Man," a word which reveals the human reverberations of this apparently impersonal process.

But the loss is not absolute, for the poem proffers a counter-cycle of repetitive restitution. Dawn goes down today but will rise again tomorrow. The hour will again come round. The final line becomes the poem's title and undoes finality by beginning the poem over again. The last line goes down in order to come up again, like the sun. Echoing the title, it takes on the force of a refrain, a daily dirge rather than an epitaph. The first idea, as Stevens says in "Notes toward a Supreme Fiction," comes and goes, comes and goes, all day. Golden vision yields to the day's green going. Art itself is synecdochal, an hour to a day, but an hour that is guaranteed, even as it cannot be prolonged.

"These pools," the emblematic focus of meditation in "Spring Pools," are curiously double in nature: conceived as wellsprings or sources, they nevertheless reflect as well as generate. And in this reflection they do not lose or diminish that which they reflect. If we regard reflection as the visual equivalent of echo, then what is reflected (echoed) is given back nearly in its entirety, or its totality, as Frost puts it: "These pools that, though in forests, still reflect / The total sky almost without defect." So the spring pools, as first idea, as picture of nature in the cleanliness of the first idea, is already a reflection. Derrida might be invoked here, in a comment upon the impossibility of simple unity even at the point or place of origin: "There are no simple origins, for what is reflected is split *in itself* and not only as an addition to itself of its image; the reflection, the image, the double, splits what it doubles." If we privilege the pools as "clear" or "invisible" ink, linked to inner sight, over the darkening scrawl of the summer trees, then we need to remember that the pools are not a transparency but a reflection.

The sense of doubling, or narcissistic reflection culminates in the image of "flowery waters and watery flowers." The doubling of self through reflection is set against the doubling or extension of self through biological propagation, as in the generative power of the trees to produce leaves. It is not a question of poetry being more like one paradigm than the other, more narcissistic than generative; rather, poetry is both at the same time. The poem tricks us into thinking that one phase yields to the other, as early spring to summer, in a mimesis of natural process. Keats said that if poetry comes not as easily as leaves to the tree, it had better not come at all, but poetry also comes as easily as Narcissus to his image. In many poems, Frost is only too willing to align poetry with so-called "natural" generation, but here he reminds us that poetry is also a cold pastoral, fixed on itself, a power not to be used for something else.

The same idea of a cold paradise can be found in "A Winter Eden," another cold pastoral in which the ideal moment proves curiously sexless. The poem combines much of the thinking found in "Nothing Gold Can Stay" and "Spring Pools," but it is a more animated, playful poem. By the calendar of its emblematic setting, "A Winter Eden" takes place earlier than "Spring Pools"; snow remains unmelted, the hibernating trees do not start from their winter sleep:

> A winter garden in an alder swamp,
> Where conies now come out to sun and romp,
> As near a paradise as it can be
> And not melt snow or start a dormant tree.
>
> It lifts existence on a plane of snow
> One level higher than the earth below,
> One level nearer heaven overhead,
> And last year's berries shining scarlet red.
>
> It lifts a gaunt luxuriating beast
> Where he can stretch and hold his highest feast
> On some wild apple-tree's young tender bark,
> What well may prove the year's high girdle mark.

In the great line "So near to paradise all pairing ends," Frost, with the grave whimsy he manages so well, imagines a point at which the marriage-duty ends and, along with it, the duty to be a poet of marriage:

> So near to paradise all pairing ends:
> Here loveless birds now flock as winter friends,
> Content with bud-inspecting. They presume
> To say which buds are leaf and which are bloom.

Whereas "Spring Pools" emphasized a chilly narcissism, "A Winter Eden" plays up the sportiveness of its scene. In both poems the moment itself is valued, as opposed to anything it might induce, even though the "hour of winter day" is shadowed throughout by knowledge of its brevity. The poem's couplets—its "double knock," to use the phrasing of the last stanza—keep this sense of closure before us at all points, culminating in the dirge-like "This Eden day is done at two o'clock." Though such a day is short, we find no sense here that "Eden sank to grief." Not the fruit, but the bark of the "wild apple tree" is eaten; perhaps the absence of marriage sets a limit to disobedience. Frost contrives a language of innocence in "A Winter Eden," in which words such as "romp" and "sport" seem to find their proper place, salvaged from the bin of anachronism by inclusion in a deliberately anachronistic scene, as any return to Eden must be.

III

"The Most of It" presents us with yet another version of the American Adam, our native solitary, willfully establishing himself in a wilderness Eden and echoing Adam's lament over lack of suitable companionship. Poirier is right to point out the absurdity of imagining a dramatic situation here, but surely Frost has nevertheless drawn a recognizable character, however allegorical. And this character, as is often the case in lyric, is a narrower consciousness than its author, distorted through exaggeration. The outrageous presumption of the opening line—"He thought he kept the universe alone"—dwindles into the foibles of an Adamic literalist, one who would go about "recreating" the original story, who would literally place himself in Adam's position in order perhaps to experience the inauguration of a new "counter-love, original response":

> He thought he kept the universe alone;
> For all the voice in answer he could wake
> Was but the mocking echo of his own
> From some tree-hidden cliff across the lake.
> Some morning from the boulder-broken beach
> He would cry out on life, that what it wants
> Is not its own love back in copy speech,
> But counter-love, original response.

Voice calls to voice here, but the solitary receives a debased echo, an echo described as "mocking." This is not a tautological description; other forms of echo abound and the poetic tradition, not to mention Frost's poetry, is filled with them. This echo validates nothing. It issues from a source that remains hidden, a "tree-hidden cliff;" within the cliff, perhaps there is a cave, a hidden mouth. This mocking voice bounces off the cliff-side, not from out of the oracular voice of caves.

The satire here, among numerous possibilities, is that this American Adam should seek an "original response," while remaining himself such a literalist of the original story. A copy himself, he hopes to break the mold. His delusion is to think that by copying Adam he will raise the copy of Eve, another Eve. But though he disclaims any narcissistic motive (and is mocked by Echo), I think that readers can decipher the self-aggrandizing mode of one who thinks he keeps the universe alone. For this character is only self-sponsored; he enters on no colloquy, such as the original Adam. Yet he is also too weak to glory in his solipsism, for perhaps at bottom he realizes that it is indeed derivative. Raising echoes, he himself is an echo. Without the strength either to imagine a fit companion or actually summon the embodiment of his desire, his cry trails off into pathos. The humor in "The Most of It" comes from a weak poet figure placing himself in a situation where impossible strength is required, the strength either to persist in one's own delusion and crown it with the honorific "imagination," or to seduce another into sharing one's solitude. Both solipsism and relationship are equally beyond this crier's powers. Unlike the married solitaries in Frost's earlier narrative poems, he generates no dialogue.

The joke played on him from line ten onwards begins with the qualifier "unless" casting doubt over all that follows. There is no doubt as to the event, but only its connection to the solitary's mating call. Is this a response? Does the solitary recognize it as such? If it is a response, then it belongs to that species of oracular answer in which the supplicant gets what he literally asks for, as if to teach him the necessary deviousness of erotic fulfillment.

> And nothing ever came of what he cried
> Unless it was the embodiment that crashed
> In the cliff's talus on the other side,
> And then in the far-distant water splashed,
> But after a time allowed for it to swim,
> Instead of proving human when it neared
> And someone else additional to him,
> As a great buck it powerfully appeared,
> Pushing the crumpled water up ahead,
> And landed pouring like a waterfall,
> And stumbled through the rocks with horny tread,
> And forced the underbrush—and that was all.

The Adamic parody is heightened by the way in which the buck's coming is described. Frost likens it to a heavenly descent, appropriate to a messenger from the other side: first the creature crashes, then makes its way from the far-distant shore. And when it finally appears, streaming with power, its emblematic significance is hard to avoid, though Frost Americanizes it as a buck, no royal stag, a rough beast standing for nothing other than its own powerful presence—and that was all. By the end of the poem, the solitary is measured against Adam, the namer, and Orpheus, the tamer, of beasts, but neither name nor music issues from his muted lips. Whatever stature he does achieve comes from this muteness at the close, as he and the reader stand witness to a rugged appearance of original power.

Whereas the opening line of "The Most of It" records a delusion—and a weak delusion at that—the beginning of "Never Again Would Birds' Song Be the Same" presents a central figure (less distinguishable from the poet) capable of recognizing a fable strong and apt enough to inspire belief. Once again, as in "The Most of It," Frost undoes specificity of place; the visionary marker "there," as well as the inclusive "in all the garden round," tells us that we are in the region of no place in particular, the region of Utopia:

> He would declare and could himself believe
> That the birds there in all the garden round
> From having heard the daylong voice of Eve
> Had added to their own an oversound,
> Her tone of meaning but without the words.
> Admittedly an eloquence so soft
> Could only have had an influence on birds
> When call or laughter carried it aloft.
> Be that as may be, she was in their song.
> Moreover her voice upon their voices crossed
> Had now persisted in the woods so long
> That probably it never would be lost.
> Never again would birds' song be the same.
> And to do that to birds was why she came.

Access to Edenic origin in this poem is not hedged about by fear or dread; the spot is not ringed by a *cordon sanitaire*. Access to the spot proceeds through the corridors of belief. The declaring and believing poet gets there on his own, gets there "himself." One reason for this relaxation of the rigors of original pursuit is that the origin, the garden, lies all around us, if we can only hear it in the overtone of the birds, those mocking generations. These are the self-same birds who heard, not the sad voice of Ruth, but the laughing voice of Eve. After all these birds seem to pattern themselves on Eve's daylong voice; they are not nighttime warblers, darkling singers. The "daylong voice of Eve" goes back to the sense of day in "Nothing Gold Can Stay," only here the point is precisely that the golden voice of Eve, voice of the golden age, does indeed stay, or persist, in the birds' song about us. The sense of happy mimicry pervading the poem is picked up in the line "Admittedly an eloquence so soft," where Frost's own lines mimic the soft eloquence of Eve—her tone of meaning, but this time with the words. As we repeat the repeating birds, we experience Eve's influence. Here we approach the idea of an originality available through repetition, repetition seen not as curse but as a form of renewal. In line with this emphasis, Frost has little anxiety about the mixing of human and natural orders, little desire to scrutinize the boundaries of contamination. He merely asserts: "she was in their song." There is no effort to separate realms as in Stevens's "The Idea of Order at Key West." Instead, Frost accepts the crossing of voices: "her voice upon their voices crossed." Suspended in the line's final position, "crossed" raises the specter of conflict, as in a crossing of swords, but Frost raises it only to dispel it. He is interested in a creative crossing, a blending, a warp and woof of voice, creating a seamless verbal tapestry.

The nearly hidden ambiguity of "crossed" gets more openly expressed in the way "Never Again" carries elegiac hints only to undo them. The title (especially its first two words) taken alone, seems to indicate loss; the change it augurs appears to be a change for the worse. But the point of the poem is that what we thought was lost has actually persisted—or "probably" has, to use Frost's own qualifier, if only we know how to read that persistence, how to discover its strands of filiation back to the first story. "Persistence" is a virtue Frost also celebrated at the close of "Sitting by a Bush in Broad Sunlight." One of the subtlest ways Frost finds to undo this elegiac impulse comes again by using enjambment to create an undertone. "Moreover her voice upon their voices crossed / Had now persisted in the woods so long," makes us pause at "so long," only to realize as we read on further that the words mean exactly what they say: the phrase does not mean good-by in this context.

"Never Again" tells us that our route back to the garden runs through Eve, not Adam. We follow her verbal trace. Interestingly, Frost associates Eve not only with song, which would square with the Miltonic account, but also with eloquence, a faculty more often associated with Adam. According to this song, eloquence is song, song eloquence; we are not in the realm of the oven bird, who learns in singing not to sing. If Adam appears at all in this poem, it may be in the guise of the "He" who inaugurates the fable. This would be Frost's true version of the American Adam—not someone who forges his own discourse as if made new, but a singer who is also a listener, a repeater of the sounds of originality.

The poignance of this poem might also have something to do with the fact that it was written soon after Elinor Frost's death. As Frost wrote in a letter: "she has been the unspoken half of everything I ever wrote." This might explain the terms of Eve's influence as described here. So "Never Again Would Birds' Song Be the Same" can also be read as a kind of elegy to Elinor which turns out in the end not to be an elegy at all, because her sound still persists in the sound of the birds: "probably it never would be lost."

IV

From the beginning of "Directive" the movement back toward an earlier time is viewed as a return to simplicity, in the root sense of oneness, that which is not compounded or confused, to draw on the poem's last word. To go back behind—or beyond—confusion is to return to the unity of wholeness. This movement, from the beginning, is seen as a fashioned action—"a time made simple"—and a violent one as well. The simple thing, here at the beginning, is seen not so much as totality, but as a synecdoche, a microcosm. Wholeness is not achieved without the violence of prior fragmentation. And the word "simple" of course carries its negative connotations as well, so that the loss of detail could lead to a damning as well as a saving simplicity, could lead to forgetfulness as much as remembrance. Simplicity here is achieved through the loss of what Frost terms "detail," a word that can be taken in a number of contexts, either as richness or as superfluity. How much of a loss *is* the loss of detail.

And this action of burning, dissolving, breaking off—is it a healing violence, a counter-violence aimed against the wounds of the past? Even before Frost reaches the series of famous paradoxes—"a house that is no more a house ... "—the poem is riddled with dark sayings about the nature of this regenerative return to the simple past, filled with the poet's sense of the double nature of what he is doing even as he asserts the triumph of the *simplex*, the single thing that can save us.

Despite its emphasis on wholeness and simplicity, "Directive" also has a kind of division built into it in the form of the split between the narrating guide and his audience. "Let us go then, you and I," goes the poem's implicit beginning; and the poem's action needs an auditor, an interpreter, an other, present at the site, to complete its meaning. One of the poem's many open questions is whether or not narrator and auditor merge at the close in the shared gesture of drinking the waters of the source. The offer is certainly made, but whether or not it is accepted depends upon the reaction of the reader-initiate. Equally unclear is whether the narrator drinks. Is he a guide whose mission is to lead others to a sacred spot he himself is barred from knowing? Or has he already tasted the waters? Poetic tradition certainly offers examples of guides, such as Virgil, or the Ancient Mariner, who can save others but not themselves. One way of saving others is to warn them against the sins of the guide, and in this sense it is worth thinking about the narrator's implication in the scene of ruin he brings us to face. For this site in the woods may also be thought of as a scene of the crime. Indeed, if the allusion to St. Mark's cryptic passage points to the necessity of interpreting parables, then surely one of the poem's prime riddles is what connection can this speaker have to this landscape. To leave the house as merely a generalized example of human decay would seem to solve the riddle too quickly. Why does this speaker take us here? Why is he the only survivor of this house? Where is everyone else? Without joining the biographical debate over Frost's character, I find it perplexing that commentators have not called attention to the ruin of Frost's own "house" in treating the site of "Directive." The grim line "This was no playhouse but a house in earnest" seems to lose all resonance otherwise. Here we have "Home Burial" carried to the extreme: the home, "now slowly closing like a dent in dough," is being buried before our eyes.

Indeed, Frost inscribes himself upon the landscape through a favorite trick: ringing changes on his own name. The spirit of this place is "an enormous Glacier"—"Frost" writ large:

> You must not mind a certain coolness from him
> Still said to haunt this side of Panther Mountain.

As Stevens put it, "Cold is our element," and for Frost there is a kind of mystic attunement, a baptismal bond, between his own name and the waters he calls "Cold as a spring as yet so near its source." To introduce another metaphor, the difficult return to the site resembles the salmon's swim upstream, back to its spawning grounds and its death. Return to the origin can thus itself become the sign of death, death conceived not as alienation but as recognition. Here, the return merges with the great theme of the *nostos*.

As Allen Grossman has pointed out in an essay on Hart Crane and the question of origins, there are two great archetypes of the *nostos* motif:

> One is he return to the remembered place (like Odysseus' return to Ithaka); the other is the return to the unremembered place of origins (like Socrates' return to the Idea, or Shelley's "Die, / If thou woulds't be with that which thou dost seek!"). The return to the remembered place through the good use of time leads to an enhancement of the mortal self, involving an internalization by the voyager of his own past and then its revalidation in the external world (recovery of Ithaka and remarriage with Penelope). The return to the unremembered place is by contrast sacrificial, requiring and justifying the destruction of time and the self at home in it.

Part of the difficulty posed by "Directive" is the way it seems equally poised between the remembered and the unremembered place. The poem is clearly a journey homeward, but to home as remembered place, or to the home that never was? In this sense the real paradox would run: "There is a house that never was a house." The medicinal or healing drink offered at the end of the poem does not appear to cure the wounds of time within time, for the fragmented debris of the past can never be made whole again. The dishes remain shattered, the grail broken, the house slowly closing. These wounds receive the purgatorial waters of tears, not the purifying waters of the origin: "Weep for what little things could make them glad. / Then for the house that is no more a house." Nor does it appear that a return is possible to the mortal world. It is more a question of returning to the Idea that underlies the temporal house, the idea of the pure stream of the origin, "A brook that was the water of the house." Before one calls this the waters of life, it should be noted that the house fed by this brook is now a ghost house. Indeed, the kind of cold Frost associates with the brook has its correlative in poets such as Stevens and Bishop, where it is a kind of deathly cold, an inhuman cold, a cold inhospitable to human life. There is the cold of "The Snow Man": "One must have a mind of winter ... And have been cold a long time." And there is the frigid water of Bishop's "At the Fishhouses": "Cold dark deep and absolutely clear, / element bearable to no mortal." For Bishop, one reason the water is "bearable to no mortal" has to do with the fact that it is *absolutely* clear. She means that adverb with dead seriousness. This absoluteness also underscores the danger of the cold in "The Snow Man" and, I would argue, in "Directive" as well, where absolution is achieved only by contact with the absolute, that which Frost describes as "Too lofty and original to rage." But such absolution signifies death as well as life. Within the Christian matrix of paradoxes, we can accept the idea of dying to the world only to live in a transcendent sphere, but does "Directive" sustain such faith? Though the poem is filled with parodic Christian symbols, best detailed by Marie Borroff, it remains, as Borroff herself writes: "not Christian ... the revelation the poem brings is moral rather than supernatural." Yet this is a hard morality indeed, hard on others, hard on the self.

The question of the poem's tantalizing allusions to New Testament doctrine culminates, of course, in the reference to the passage in Mark on the role of parable:

> And he said unto them, Unto you it is given to know the mystery of the kingdom of God: but unto them that are without, all these things are done in parables:
>
> That seeing they may see, and not perceive; and hearing they may hear, and not understand; lest at any time they should be converted, and their sins should be forgiven them.

Frank Kermode's *The Genesis of Secrecy* takes this passage from Mark as adumbrating the essential condition of interpretive communities:

> In this tradition insiders can hope to achieve correct interpretation, though their hope may be frequently, perhaps always, disappointed; whereas those outside cannot. There is seeing and hearing, which are what naive listeners and readers do; and there is perceiving and understanding, which are in principle reserved to an elect.

It is perhaps this seemingly smug courting of the fit audience, though few, that leads Poirier to complain that the poem's ironies are "consequential" only to those "who have enclosed themselves within the circuit of Frost's own work." There are few other instances of such direct allusion in Frost's poetry, so we have little precedent for how to read such open quotation in his work. "Out, Out—" represents another example and I think interpretation of that poem has suffered for critics taking the allusion with too little sense of its dialectical complexities. The passage from Mark is notoriously "dark" itself and would thus be a strange example to choose in the hope of stabilizing one's meaning. The phrasing of "as Saint Mark says they mustn't," with its prissy tone of smug election, serves to mock rather than enforce any easy distinction between elect and outcast, insider and outsider. And when Frost talks about the "wrong ones," nothing in the poem would lend itself to taking "wrong" as a moral category. After all, the notion of right and wrong is considerably complicated by the fact that the narrator admits to having stolen the goblet.

Poirier asks the crucial question of whether it is *good* to get beyond confusion and surely the answer to this question—if answer is the appropriate response—determines whether one accepts the offered potion. To be "whole" is to return to the unremembered place of origins; it stands in opposition to the remembered place, the slowly closing "hole" of the natural landscape. Such wholeness seems a kind of self-healing, though it cannot reconstitute the ruinous fragments of history or of the self's actions in history. Surveying its own past, the self may stand confused, but this is at least a sign of moral sentience.

The final line of "Directive" will always seem to tear free from context, for what does its action describe if not an escape from the confinement of context and all its confusions? To be untouched by confusion must mean that one is untouched by life and indeed there seems no possibility of return after drinking the potion. Or, if return is possible, it may only be at the cost of becoming confused again. We remain whole only so long as we remain in this spot. Frost brings us to a point where origin and end merge and the story ceases. So does representation: Frost can only call the spring "cold." He has deliberately elided the Keatsian phantasia of the Nightingale Ode, whose magic potion is the wellspring of a gorgeous chain of romance associations, culled from the region of the "warm South," a region not native to Keats and certainly not to Frost. The draught of Keatsian vintage inspires a chain of figurations, whereas Frost's chills language. Keats's flight takes him far away, Frost's to earthward.

For Frost, the enemy of imagination seems to be "confusion," the loss of self in a proliferation of motives, deeds, and events that carry one far from both the remembered place (the home) and the unremembered place of origin. But return to that place of fabricated wholeness can also destroy the imagination. Confronted with the evidence of his actions, the ruins of his historical house, the poet might indeed have given himself up to that "rage" (etymologically, "madness") which it is the presumed power of the spring to cure. As it is, the poem shows us Frost succumbing neither to madness nor to radical cure: the cup is suspended, the spring as yet but "so near" its source. This saving distance from the source is also a form of salvation: the necessary scepticism that keeps one from drowning in one's own fiction.

SHIRA WOLOSKY

The Need of Being Versed:
Robert Frost and the Limits of Rhetoric

Robert Frost's boast about his notable craftsmanship[1] has never quite
been made critically good. Most Frost criticism continues to center upon
issues—thematic, philosophical, religious, historical. Relatively few essays
address formal matters,[2] and those tend to restrict themselves to rhyme
scheme, sound patterns, and above all to prosody—to how natural speech
rhythms, in accordance with Frost's own prosodic discussions, play with and
against traditional meters. As to the significance of form in Frost's work,
most discussions reiterate his definition of poetry as "a stay against
confusion." Form acts to contain chaos: its order both presupposes and
opposes disorder.[3] Rarely is this general rule particularized in pursuit of form
as articulated within specific texts, or as constituting a text's very utterance,
elements, and textuality. Yet there are in Frost's poems events taking place on
the linguistic level beyond such initial formal surfaces as sound and meter,
events which implicate the whole notion of form as a penetrating poetic
concern. An approach to Frost through his language moreover yields a
somewhat different understanding of other thematic concerns more usually
the subject of Frost studies. This is the case most notably for his irony, and
for his place in and relation to a tradition of American poetics and concerns.

Frost's verse is often so apparently paraphrasable as to seem the precis
for some short story: a domination of plot that takes up the slack seemingly

From *Essays in Literature* 18, no. 1 (Spring 1991). © 1991 by Western Illinois University.

left by an overly straightforward, homey, and blunt language. "The Need of Being Versed in Country Things" is in these, as in other ways, prototypical. Comprised of all the expected Frostian elements—the rural setting, the nostalgic or elegiac identification with nature then punctured by the almost equally nostalgic retreat from such identification—the poem even may be said to take Frost's own typical themes as its theme, a metapoem exactly thematizing Frost's usual thematics. And yet the textual life of the poem not only exceeds such stated themes; it significantly complicates them—in their "plot," their conduct, and above all their outcome and implications. Through Frost's exacting craft, the language of the poem enacts a drama of its own that reframes the entire relation to nature and the irony such relation generates, which is the text's explicit subject:

> The house had gone to bring again
> To the midnight sky a sunset glow.
> Now the chimney was all of the house that stood
> Like a pistil after the petals go.
>
> The barn opposed across the way,
> That would have joined the house in flame
> Had it been the will of the wind, was left
> To bear forsaken the place's name.
>
> No more it opened with all one end
> For teams that came by the stony road
> To drum on the floor with scurrying hoofs
> And brush the mow with the summer load.
>
> The birds that came to it through the air
> At broken windows flew out and in,
> Their murmur more like the sigh we sigh
> From too much dwelling on what has been.
>
> Yet for them the lilac renewed its leaf,
> And the aged elm, though touched with fire;
> And the dry pump flung up an awkward arm;
> And the fence post carried a strand of wire.
>
> For them there was really nothing sad.
> But though they rejoiced in the nest they kept,

One had to be versed in country things
Not to believe the phoebes wept.

The compelling aspect of this poem's theme and thematizing is amply registered in its many paraphrases. In these the mistaken anthropomorphism is described, with concomitant moral lessons: "Men may weep to see a home abandoned where there had been so much life, but the birds' springtime duty is nesting and they rejoice in it." "The [birds'] murmuring may sound like weeping to man unless he is versed in the understanding that the task at hand takes all one's energy in country life."[4] "It is up to man himself to comprehend and accept nature on its own terms if he is to achieve any real contact with it.... That the phoebes nesting in the barn are not really lamenting the burning of the house for they are part of the natural world, rather than man's ... [reveals] that nature is independent, self-sufficient, and often brutal: this is what man is to learn from the ironic contrast between his expectations and nature's fulfillment of them."[5] "The birds are oblivious in their homemaking to the destruction of the once productive human household.... We 'need to be versed' for the sake of certain realities that belong specifically to human consciousness, the difference between human love and homemaking and the mating of animals."[6]

Such anthropomorphism on the thematic level in turn functions, on the level of imagery, as pathetic fallacy—a force and concern in so many Frost poems. The poem not only enacts, but also reflects upon the tendency to project onto nature—here the birds—human feelings, concluding with a rejection of or resistance to this tendency, in an ironic move characteristic of Frost. What is masterful in the poem's craft is how this concern with pathetic fallacy informs its linguistic events, and how this linguistic level finally changes if not the nature, then the target of the irony. It does so via the trope of personification. The poem in fact may be read as a study in personification: a trope extending well beyond the birds who are its most explicit subject to include almost every element in the poem in a steady, although various, succession. While personification is without question the poem's governing trope, its power is far from uncontested. As the poem proceeds, the trope not only evolves, but underscores itself, ultimately to question its own claims and finally to reject them.

This process commences in the poem's first line, which contains its first two personifications—albeit almost inaudible ones: "The house had gone" and "to bring again." "Had gone," although somewhat dead as a figure, nevertheless suggests some animate motion. "To bring" similarly need not be more than a sentential complement, equivalent to "and brought." Yet the infinitival form, here and elsewhere in the poem, insinuates a sense of intentionality, carrying within it an implicit purposive: in order to. Here, the two phrases taken together strengthen this impression of both animation and intentionality. "The house had gone to bring again" in its syntax invites an animate subject, and urges joining the first action in purposeful sequence with the second.

These personifications are the opening gestures in a rhetorical strategy conducted throughout the poem, a strategy that distributes different levels and kinds of personification through the text. The poem in fact pursues an exquisite range of personification's possibilities. Often—and this seems to be one of the poem's points—the reader must pause to determine whether or not a personification is even present. Although most of Frost's formal remarks—and certainly those most often cited—underscore prosodic questions, Frost as rhetor is not a surprising figure. As he pointedly remarks in his *Paris Review* interview, he had read "more Latin and Greek than Pound ever did."[7] He had been himself a Latin teacher, and most allusions in his prose are to the classics. In "The Need of Being Versed," Frost accomplishes with personification the "speech with range" he praises in "Education by Poetry" as having "something of overstatement, something of statement, and something of understatement."[8] There are mild personifications, such as those of the opening, and about whose status the reader must hesitate. There are extreme personifications, so extreme that they underscore and make unmistakable their status, but ultimately thereby also call that status into question. And there are hidden personifications. The search for and sensitivity to these different tropological kinds is one of the poem's effects, just as the hesitation regarding whether a personification is even present works to throw attention back onto the whole nature and notion of personification as such.

The first stanza concludes, as it opens, with just such questionable and hidden instances. Is there any personifying force in the assertion that the chimney "stood" or the petals "go"? Or are these dead personifications bereft of force, as perhaps are "had gone" and "to bring" in the first line? The second stanza, however, traces a movement in the opposite direction, toward personifications increasingly unmistakable and yet whose force is also questionable exactly in their being extreme. The barn "opposed" across the way implies nothing more than its spatial placement in relation to the house, with no intentional resistance. That it "would have joined" the house could perhaps also register nothing more than spatial juncture, as when a river joins the sea. The conditional mood, however, with the phrasal complement "in"—"would have joined the house in flame"—nudges the verb in the direction of a sense of choosing to take part, as in the expression "to join in" a country dance. Such encroaching animation then becomes explicit and decisive with "had it been the will of the wind." This near cliche, recalling Frost's first volume title and its echo of Longfellow's "A boy's will is the wind's will," emerges within a context of repeated attributions of intent so subtle as to border on unconscious assumptions, serving in its overtness to bring these to consciousness. But at the very moment the trope achieves clarity it also loses credibility, as do the preceding personificatory gestures of which it is the culmination. The wind simply does not will a barn to decide to join in with a house on fire and burn down too.

The direction and sweep of imagery thus is brought to a momentary halt, as the undercurrent of personificatory projection comes instead to the surface, exposing itself to view and therefore to critical questioning. This is a pattern the poem will repeat. Here it is merely proleptic; and exactly because "the will of the wind" borders on cliche, it is ultimately accepted, allowing the poem to proceed after its discrete pause to pursue descriptions that, however, within the context of encroaching suspicion, vacillate between personification and some possible literal rendering of the scene. Thus the barn as "left / To bear forsaken the place's name" also comes to seem equivocal. The phrase avers that the barn alone remained of the farm. But, following as it does the asserted will of the wind, does "left" acquire an intentional force? Is "forsaken" a predicate adjective describing the barn as simply the last vestige of farmstead, an adverb (colloquially misinflected) expressing the observer's impression of how the sole remaining barn bears the farm's name, or a (direct) adjective indicating the barn's own sense of abandonment? The infinitive especially becomes suspicious in a poem where it repeatedly appears with equivocal functions and whose patterning pursues an escalating personification. "To bear" hovers between sentential complement whose function is merely participial—the barn as left bearing— as against a purposive barn as (purposely) left (in order) to bear—a reading amplified by the object borne: the "place's name," the essential human marker.

The third stanza pursues this pattern of infinitives, no longer with regard to inanimate objects but in terms of animate but unconscious creatures. This stanza is in many ways transitional. The barn is here openly personified, but only as a metonymic substitute for the human agents who open barns for teams: "The more it opened with all one end / For teams." "To drum" and "to brush" are infinitives of habitual action that need impute no intention either to the barn as admitting or to the teams as entering in order to brush or drum. Yet both brushing and druming seem, as activities, to occur at some boundary of the human: each verb originates in actions peculiar to the human sphere, the first to music, the second to cleaning. In descriptions of activity, at least, human categories remain in force. "Scurrying," in contrast, compares one kind of beast to another—the wild forest creatures who perhaps have come to inhabit the abandoned barn, as opposed to the oxen or horses for which the barn was constructed. The farmstead, in being described exactly as depopulated, nonetheless constantly projects a human presence through the poem's categories of description. But the barn is itself a transitional place, situated between the human house now almost completely absent and the wild life of creatures who have come to make the once-farm their home.

It is only in stanza four that these personifying constructions and foci of stanza three fully emerge. Stanza three remains within properly human territory, concerned with domestic animals—albeit absent ones—whose activities are quite properly defined in human terms. Applying to them human categories thus remains plausible, both logically and rhetorically. With stanza four the poem moves expressly out of the human sphere, past the implied "scurrying" creatures to explicit wild birds who now inhabit the barn. Now the crossing of human and non-human involves traversing a much wider distance, so that applying human and sentient terms to the non-human world—as the poem persists in doing—creates a greater and greater rhetorical strain which it is the final act of this poem to snap.

The first step into this different sphere is registered in the "to it" with which the birds, flying through windows, enter the barn (there are presumably no windows left in the house):

> The birds that came to it through the air
> At broken windows flew out and in,
> Their murmur more like the sigh we sigh
> From too much dwelling on what has been.

Like the infinitives threaded through the text, the preposition "to" (and also "for") takes its place within a continuous textual network. And both infinitives and prepositions together constitute in the realm of syntax a corollary to the rhetorical pattern made up by tropes of personification. In this sense, the poem is about—indeed, textually it turns about—the word "to": the "to" of an infinitive; "to" as preposition, and thus as directional; and the differences between these usages, their fields of force as they approach and recede from one another in implication. These differences, as the text probes, exactly mark differences in intentionality—the very intentionality which distinguishes the trope of personification. The preposition "to" implies direction, reference, transfer. But it does so in terms of placement and location without entailing any animation or consciousness. The "to" of an infinitive may similarly be merely a neutral construction for providing a sentence with a verbal form. But the infinitive, at least within this poem's patterns, seems ever to carry with it the purposive construction the infinitive also commands. And the prepositional/directional "to" also becomes infected with suggested purpose. This is the case from the poem's very outset, which offers the first coupling of these two uses of "to." "To bring again / To the midnight sky a sunset glow" plays with an implicit purposive sense of "in order to bring again" that moves toward a trope of personification. This implicitly purposive "to bring" is then matched with a second "to," one no less sly in its running counter to normal syntactic expectations. Completing the infinitive phrase, "To the midnight sky a sunset glow" implies the intentional movement of an object to an intended and specific place. Instead, both object and place dissolve into the near oxymoron of midnight-sunset, so that "to" itself becomes almost figurative. The "midnight sky" is not a circumscribed location to which things may be brought. A "sunset glow" is not a graspable object one may bring.

Within this context of the poem's unfolding rhetorical and grammatical patternings. "The birds that came to it through the air" of stanza four already suggests some intention to the birds' movement. And while the preposition "at" and the adverbs "out" and "in" of "At broken windows flew out and in" reassert the function of pure placement, the detail of broken windows frames the birds' entry and exit in a sense of disruption entirely the property of the human observer. Stanza four's "to it" in fact marks a moment in the poem at cross-purposes: the world of humanized pathos is exactly the domain that, with the wild birds, has been crossed out of. Yet the preposition "to" continues to resist its purely neutral function of placing and locating. The impulse to project the human instead reasserts itself with revitalized and explicit force: "Their murmur more like the sigh we sigh / From too much dwelling on what has been." The poet's identifying with the birds—or rather, his identifying them with himself and assimilating them into the human state—is expressly asserted. Like man, they murmur and sigh. Moreover, like man they dwell—and indeed do so in a specifically figurative and personified sense: not only in constructed shelters, but in the past, for which the current, damaged farmstead is itself merely a figure. For what is this abandoned barn but a sign for the formerly intact, but now absent farmhouse, its surrounding buildings, and the life once lived there? A movement of figuration has overtaken and determined the surviving farmstead, the notion of "dwelling," and also the prepositions "From" (too much dwelling) and "on" (what has been), which indicate relation to "place" only when place represents some non-spatial psychic "territory."

It is precisely this unchecked movement of figuration and personification that it is the task of the following and penultimate stanza to disrupt:

> Yet for them the lilac renewed its leaf,
> And the aged elm, though touched with fire;
> And the dry pump flung up an awkward arm;
> And the fence post carried a strand of wire.

Here, as the poem's turning point, the entire movement of projection, personification, and intentionality is exposed exactly to be such. Until this moment the poem's rhetoric has been realizing and enacting the poem's humanizing point of view. The human mourning for the lost farmstead first infuses the landscape and, in the next stanzas, is shared by nonhuman creatures as well. The very site is seen to mourn—the solitary chimney, the forsaken barn; while the birds in their "murmur" speak with the speaker's voice, their "sigh" like our "sigh," their "dwelling" like our dwelling. But are they indeed like? In a problematic common to much Frost poetry the similarity reveals itself not to be valid. As with the "thrush music" that calls to the poet in "Come In," the poet finally will "not come in ... even if asked, / And I hadn't been." Here too he resists an invitation based upon a likeness which he ultimately sees not to exist. The likeness itself is instead recognized, not as drawn between differing realms but only as based in a humanizing point of view and realized through a personifying rhetoric. This rhetoric now splits open and apart, as the two like things instead prove divergent. From this moment, the poem pursues two paths, speaks with two voices—or rather, shows itself as having done so from the outset. The human voice recognizes itself as representing nature in terms of human categories, as it has done from the poem's start. It equally recognizes that the birds and nature have, and have had, an independent and divergent stance, and wishes somehow to attest to this. But how is it to do so? The scene of desolation, as the poet experiences it, is for the birds another scene altogether. Yet there is an immense difficulty—indeed an impossibility—in rendering this other scene, this scene as "for" the birds. The very preposition "for" carries with it an unfounded attribution, as though the scene either exists teleologically "for" the birds or is being construed intentionally and intelligently by them. Yet neither "for" is within the power of the birds to assert; neither "for" is "for" them. The only legitimate "for" in nature is entirely positional. All others are only "for" the human observer, who however he tries, is unable to extricate himself from human categories—who in the very act of trying to do so only can reassert them.

Nor will this doubling between the human and non-human easily be resolved by yielding to division according to figurative and literal senses. This very difference is called into question. The pun on "dwelling" resolves into a figurative representation of human memory and nostalgia, while the birds from their own point of view may be dwelling only literally. But a problem remains as to how memory and nostalgia can be represented at all except in the spatial imagery of inhabiting or, as in the "nostos" of nostalgia, returning. For memory, there is no literal level—the figurations of space are, for memory, literal. Not literal/figurative distinctions, but levels within figuration are at issue, as is also the case in "Their murmur more like the sigh we sigh." There, the sounds of birds are triply figured. In order to compare it to nostalgic human sighs the speaker must first liken it to a human sigh as such: like the sigh we sigh. "More like" then serves to distinguish a nostalgic human sigh from some other kind. But even "murmur," the supposed ground in nature out of which the figure is built, is figurative. Bird sound murmurs only in likeness to human sound, so that the description of birds is finally only the figuring of three kinds of human utterance.

The poem thus resists its divisions as falling into literal/figurative, natural/human. What emerges instead is a doubling of forces: one personifying, and in counterforce against it, one of depersonification. By the very nature of man and of language, a direct and unmediated presentation of the non-human cannot be accomplished. Inevitably humanized for man through the human categories that mediate it, nature-in-itself as beyond or outside these categories remains inaccessible. Its independent and autonomous status therefore can only be indicated by way of detour—not via an impossible non-personification but rather through a depersonification. Stanza five offers such a detour. The speaker there makes his most concerted effort to adopt and present the birds' experience from the birds' point of view. In this he inevitably fails. "Yet for them the lilac renewed its leaf" raises the problem of "for's" ascriptive powers, both teleological and perceptual, a problem carried through the zeugma in which "for them" constitutes the missing yet controlling phrase of the verse's extended ellipse, a phrase exactly emphasized through its absence. "The aged elm" registers a sense of time, "touched with fire" a sense of space that birds do not possess. The fence post can not traverse for birds the metaphor and personification by which it may be said to "carry" wire. But above all, "The dry pump" could not for them have "flung up its awkward arm."[9] This double personification, ascribing to the pump intent in action and anthropomorphic body can simply not be "for" the birds. And yet its effect in a peculiar way turns back to the birds, exactly in its so impossibly evading them. For the farfetched and almost grotesque quality of the pump's personification is so especially and expressly striking that one cannot help but take note of it. Personification in fact here verges into catachresis—displaying a truncated arm that asserts the human body only in a manner that dismembers and reifies it. And catachresis, rather than convincing us of its illusions, instead forces us to take note of them. By thus underscoring its own rhetoricity, the trope's affect shifts from persuasion to a recognition and consciousness of rhetorical functions, claims, and powers; as a rhetoric that is self-exposing and self-unmasking it is more involved with exploring its own implicit claims than in advancing them.

This technique had in fact made its first appearance earlier in the poem, with the "will of the wind." In taking the attribution of intention to nature too far, there too the trope had drawn attention to itself, forcing the reader toward a consciousness of the claims being made. Such self-betrayal, rather than accomplishing a metaphoric transfer, points to the relation between terms as visibly straining. In so straining, the trope in one sense fails. And yet it is only by such strain that a realm independent of trope can even be indicated. The human language which would ascribe such independence must inevitably compromise it by the very fact that it is in language the attempt is being made. But if language's tropes become so catachrestic as to expose their own effects, these effects can be in a sense negated, leaving open in the space of cancellation a sense not of an extra-linguistic world directly represented without mediation, but of such a world existing where language, in its self-limitation, has withdrawn. "The will of the wind" in this sense so lacks credence that the trope's effect, rather than to personify "wind" by attributing to it intentional "will," is to depersonify "will," making it the wind's random attribute rather than its intentional faculty. Only such space of defiguration—a space not at all equivalent to the "literal"—leaves an opening by which the extra-linguistic world may be indicated.

This will be the strategy controlling the poem's final stanza. "For them there was nothing really sad" is really a very peculiar declaration. It is strangely tautological to say that birds do not experience human emotions when they in fact could not possibly do so. Yet such a denial of a false ascription may perhaps be the most direct and only route of releasing them from the human. The only way to present birds-in-themselves in language may be to release them from the language that has first appropriated them. Releasing the birds from a human emotion only after having ascribed one to them alone can create an affect of extra-human and extra-linguistic bird life. This in no way belittles language; it is still by way of language that the affect of release must be orchestrated. Yet such release remains the sole avenue for indicating what lies without the human world—not through direct apprehension but reflected via retraction.

In this way, "For them there was really nothing sad" offers a tautological doubling which, because empty, serves to retract and negate the human sadness imposed on birds; thus released from pathetic projection, they attain a kind of autonomy. And in so doing, the line constitutes a move into irony characteristic of Frost. The sentimental identification of nature with human feelings, and particularly with elegiac feelings of loss, turns back on itself through self-exposure, the poem itself recognizing that it has been engaged in just such a project of projecting the human onto the non-human world.

Yet the nature of Frost's irony here also shifts. Classical or dramatic irony may be said to consist in a disparity of knowledge: characters or audience each exclusively possess facts denied the others. Romantic irony may be said to consist in a disparity of consciousness: as in a sudden shift from consciousness to self-consciousness, such that, as in Schlegel, the fragmentary and partial status of art becomes itself an object of reflection, or, as in a breaking of illusion, the fictional status of a fiction is exposed.[10] Both of these ironies occur in Frost, the first commonly in dramatic dialogues, and also in lyrics where, however, it is sometimes difficult to locate exactly what knowledge will resolve what problem, or even to determine whether it is knowledge that is lacking at all. The second, romantic irony is perhaps even more prevalent in Frost, and certainly accounts in part for the irony of "The Need of Being Versed in Country Things." The pathetic fallacy with which the poem has proceeded is at last exposed to be just that, the projection onto the things of nature emotions which properly belong to human beings. But there is in the poem a third kind of irony, what might be called an irony of language. In this there is a disparity between the claims implicit in specific linguistic constructions and what these constructions in fact accomplish. This irony need not depend upon a particular acquisition of knowledge or accession to awareness as a narrative event or overt authorial recognition of the nature and status of his art. Rather, such irony explores the implicit assumptions in specific rhetorico-linguistic constructions—grammatical, dictional, tropic—, exposing and exploiting them, making them explicit and thereby inevitably altering their effect. In one sense such linguistic irony recalls the traditional verbal irony that Frost interestingly assimilates to metaphor as such, when in "Education by Poetry" and also "The Constant Symbol" he declares metaphor to be "saying one thing and meaning another."[11] But it is language that says and means otherwise. Yet at issue is not necessarily the kind of aporia implied in Paul de Man's theory of verbal irony, which pits literal against figurative, sign against meaning in an unresolvable structure of mutual negation, such that linguistic claim becomes incompatible with either reference or logic, and linguistic knowledge becomes an impossibility.[12] At issue in Frost seems instead the finer definition of language's powers, not a radical contradiction within its parameters but rather their proper demarcation and limits—as "The Need of Being Versed in Country Things" finally makes evident.

In "The Need of Being Versed in Country Things," all three ironies—classical, romantic, and linguistic—are at play, each augmenting the other. Classical irony is perhaps slightly complicated in that being versed in country things involves not a further knowledge gained, but a false one relinquished. This correlates, on the level of romantic irony, with the self-conscious recognition of pathetic fallacy. And the unmasking of and resistance to pathetic fallacy on the level of romantic irony opens in turn into the unmasking of and resistance to personification on the linguistic and rhetorical level—which, however, introduces its own concerns and its own distinct framework. For, unlike both romantic and classical ironies, exposing the disparity between personification's claims and the existence of a sphere beyond its legitimate reach does not resolve this disparity. The recognition of linguistic projection does not make possible its transcendence. However we try to resist language's personifying tendencies, as through techniques of its exposure, we are ultimately unable to rid our language of personification. A realm without human figuration or fictionalization remains the supreme fiction. Even discussions of language—and this essay's discussion is no exception—cannot escape the tendency to personification, ascribing to language itself human action, intention, volition. However, the shape or boundary of an extra-linguistic realm can be traced by the space left when, having offered a linguistic construction, we then retract it, so that language in a sense is made to retreat from itself: not by impossibly avoiding personification but by exposing it through double or triple figures which dramatize its presence; by the tautologies and double negatives of depersonification which expressly retract the figures they cannot help but obtrude; by self-indicating catachresis; or, at the pole opposite to catachresis, by the hesitation as to whether a figure is personified at all, making us conscious of both the extent and the limits of linguistic claim, as this poem shows us we should be.

The final stanza of the poem offers instances of most of these strategies and serves to recapitulate and repose the issues the poem has hitherto raised. From the opening tautology of "For them there was really nothing sad," it goes on to propose a mildest, most questionable personification, "Though they rejoiced in the nest they kept." Naming the birds' busy activity and full-throated song rejoicing may not represent a projection; but it may. The poem makes us hesitate. And the final two lines then reintroduce the poem's main syntactic features, once again in terms of their rhetorical functions:

> One had to be versed in country things
> Not to believe the phoebes wept.

This poem, with its pathetic fallacies and personifications, had begun not by being versed in, but rather by versing country things. It has been about incorporating the natural into the human—into the verse of the poem, into language, and indeed into the figure of the farmstead that is the poem's subject. It is remarkable that what is taking place here on a linguistic level matches and echoes the struggle that defines both the poem's setting and its narrative action. The effort to domesticate nature is the very activity of farming; and nature's resistance to such effort is the event this poem, in tracing the return of the farmstead to its precultural state, traces.[13] The vicissitudes between nature and culture are felt in the poem through such images as the "stony road," the "dry pump," and the solitary chimney. "Stony road" at first suggests a tautology in the human sphere, where stone is an obvious material out of which farm roads may be made; but it comes to seem an oxymoron in the natural sphere, the yoking together of forces eternally at odds. So "dry pump" is only paradoxical from the standpoint of human technology; and the cold chimney is only the re-sorting of nature and culture into their respective categories as the farmstead resorts to its natural state. But farming is itself a trope for the question that personification enacts as a linguistic activity. It too humanizes reality by incorporating nature into human categories; it too is a kind of personification. At its turn, the poem attempts to pull away from the assimilation of the natural into the human categories of agriculture and linguistic culture. From the pun on "dwelling," with its intrusive insistence that birds live a nostalgic life such as man does, the text becomes one in which the human rage to verse resists itself and reverses itself, in an attempt actively to withdraw in order to leave free some territory not under its hegemony. Just as the birds reclaim the farmstead, so they reclaim their own voice, at least as much as this is possible in a poem humanly uttered: which is to say they speak, but by way of indirection, through the withdrawal and self-negation of utterance as it retreats from an active versing to a grammatically passive being versed.

Such negation is paramount in the poem's close, and is so in a way that resonates and reiterates patterns dominant throughout. "Not to believe" does more than signal a return to the infinitival form with the purposive implications it has carried throughout the poem. It represents in a sense the very archetype of this form: to believe is a specifically human act, and one that entails and asserts the whole question of paradigms and of purpose. Here, moreover, questions of ends, purposes, teleologies especially arise. For it is exactly the belief in and paradigm of conclusion that is at issue here—that has provided the categories for the poet's mis-humanization of the birds and of nature. To him the scene has been an emblem of finality—the finality of the desolate farm engulfed by chaotic natural forces. But in nature itself, the scene instead takes place within a process of continuous reproductivity that exactly confutes such notions of endings by its uninterrupted endlessness. What had been to the speaker a scene of desolation is "for" the birds—and through them as synecdoche, for nature in general—the setting for renewal. What from the human point of view represents an event of finality and closure, from the point of view of nature represents no break in process, no lapse in fertility. The need to be versed in country things is in this sense a need to be versed in country matters, in the sexuality by which nature, through and against whatever traumas, insists on their normalization in an uninterrupted reproductive venture.[14]

The crux of difference between the birds' activity and the human view of it is just this question of closure—a question imposed by human categories, by the human need for categories. Closure is exactly the category governing the discrepancy, misrepresentation, and misinterpretation of the scene, construing it in terms of disruption, finality, and terminus as opposed to a continuous and normal reproductive cycle. And it is exactly this imposition of category that the poem must retract and from which it must retreat—a retreat which in fact shapes the text's movement from first to last. In this regard the poem proceeds inversely. The vision with which it opens is one of radical and even apocalyptic finality—in which not only the human farm is utterly desolate but indeed nature is: sunset at midnight suggests the disorder of the very cosmos, even to an apocalyptic degree. Similarly, the first stanza's comparison of the chimney to "a pistil after the petals go" presents as a simile for the farmstead's depletion toward decline and demise what in nature points in quite other directions. For certain plants at least the petals "go" not merely to their death but as part of the flower's reproductive cycle.[15] The misrepresentation of this dissemination as dissolution registers how fully the human viewpoint intrudes into and distorts the scene that meets its eye, by construing it in accordance with its own preestablished paradigms of conclusion.

From these opening superpositions of human ends on nature's continuities, the poem pursues a way of retraction to arrive at its final "not to believe." And in the end, this locution's force implicates not only the particular belief in pathetic fallacy from which the poet finally withdraws, but the whole intentionality of belief, with its grammar and its rhetoric, and all that this in turn implies regarding human categorization. On the one hand, the negation signals that man cannot simply extricate himself from human experience and human language, to apprehend directly a non-human nature. He can only pursue his linguistic path and then double back on it. Language can indicate the space beyond language only by its self-erasure.

On the other hand, the negation introduces one of the poem's most complicated twists. In this poem, Frost arrives at the sense of difference and distinction from nature which has long been recognized as central to his stance—where, as Robert Penn Warren early described it, poems which seem "to celebrate nature, may really be ... about man defining himself by resisting the pull into nature."[16] Yet, the many discussions of nature as "other" in Frost assume the configuration of difference to be one in which nature is the sphere of disorder and source of "confusion" that it is poetry's task—not least formally—to "stay." And the recognition of difference is itself often described as a regrettable concession on Frost's part, if not a betrayal of a Romantic longing for identity and harmony with the natural world.[17] In "The Need of Being Versed," however, it is not nature that acts as the source of disruption. It is man who does so, with his vision of the scene as desolate. Nor is this quite the ambivalence to imagination that has also been remarked in Frost studies, most fully by Frank Lentricchia. Lentricchia sees Frost as asserting limits for imagination's power; but only in that the artist, first, must respect the "crudity which is rawness" that provides him, as Frost wrote in one letter, with the material from which he then wrests his form. His art must preserve its contact with "the ugly pressures and messiness of the empirical world," a task Lentricchia asserts that Frost accomplishes by countering every assertion of imagination with a skeptical ironic consciousness.[18] Second, imagination is to be distrusted in that it may be "impelled by a disturbed consciousness," when "the fictive is projected by the neurotic and the obsessed."[19]

In "The Need of Being Versed," however, it is not pathological imagination, but imagination in its normative role that is problematic. Not the mind's chaos, but the mind's order, proves to be the disruptive, destructive force, reversing the direction and effect of the relation Lentricchia outlines between imagination and irony. For it is, ironically, irony—the exposure of pathetic fallacy, the retreat of mind—that, instead of deflating, proves to be welcome, salutary. The nostalgic mourning for the lost farmstead seemed, by way of disappointed pathetic fallacy, to give way to a nostalgic mourning for a lost identity with nature. Instead, the release of nature from human identity also releases man. This by no means endorses an independent, innocent nature ordered beyond human experience and human representation: nature is inevitably mediated by and for the human. But it suggests dangers inherent in the activity of mind, especially as mind, in asserting its paradigms for apprehending the world, employs to that purpose a sense of ending. It is not accidental that closure provides the interpretive paradigm for a misreading which is also in this poem a misfortune; for Frost's poem reveals how the interpretive activity itself can imply closure, how the mind's act, closing in on meaning, can involve closure as such. The act of interpretation, that is, carried on and through without limitation, is itself in a sense apocalyptic, and not only when the vision is of apocalypse.

But, with these questions of interpretive paradigms and their consequences, Frost's unobtrusive and unassuming text raises issues whose complexities and enormities shape the American experience throughout its history and the various modes of its several heritages. In personifying nature, in interpreting landscape as his own state, and in projecting the finality of this vision, Frost has not been pursuing a solitary walk on a less travelled road. He has been traversing and tracing one of America's commonest byways, with implications extending beyond this particular and presumably New England farmstead into the general American territory as grasped by American tradition. From the Puritan literalization and historicizing of typology, through the political assertion of identity between American destiny and American territory, and into the economics of settlement and expansion, nature's nation has laid particular claim to the continent it inhabits, in the name of ultimate visions of New Jerusalems attained, paradises regained, and fulfillments of history, sacral and secular. These several and intertwined concerns have been the subject of much scrutiny from various scholarly and critical points of view. Sacvan Bercovitch in a series of studies and collections has explicated the relation within Puritan hermeneutics between what he calls natural theology and federal eschatology, in which the Bible provides not only general insights into spiritual states but the intricate plot, detail by detail, of the Puritan coming to America, which pronounces the realization of the divine promise unfolded in the Bible anew and at last. But this history, with all its millennial import, was no less inscribed for the interpretive gleaning in the Book of Nature, whose every nuance no less encoded an elaborate, and indeed eschatological, significance.[20] Leo Marx, Richard Slotkin, and Myra Jehlen, to name a few, each explores how images of the land impelled, and indeed determined, the social/political forms the nation, as the land's natural expression, came to take.[21] In each case, the confrontation with uncivilized nature—of which, in America, there was so very much—gave rise to an ambivalent response, as at once something to be conquered and something to be obeyed, a world to be imposed upon and yet drawn from. Yet both these impulses are finally forms of possession: identifying the national destiny appropriates the land to human purpose, even if it appears to base the human in the natural. Whether, as Jehlen debates with regard to Emerson, taking nature "as a metaphor for the human mind" curtails or releases man's creative powers, "man is still the focus of all creation," and nature is conceived in man's image. As Emerson himself declares, "Man is placed in the centre of beings, and a ray of relation passes from every other being to him."[22] But to posit reciprocity between mind and nature such that nature provides man with the very basis of his language—as Emerson famously claims in "Nature," calling words the "signs of natural facts"—is still to assume nature-as-construed according to human presuppositions, needs, and above all expectations.[23]

"The land was ours before we were the land's," Frost writes in his perhaps most national poem; but its symmetry of chiasm disguises the asymmetry of possession. And, as Frost shows—in a stance no less familiar to the American tradition—this hermeneutic possession in which the land is ours carries with it an apocalyptic twist. Accounting for everything, appropriating everything into human relevance is ultimately an act of consumption leaving over exactly nothing. As Bercovitch remarks of Emerson's "philology of nature" in which "nature must be the vehicle of his thought," "The real force lies in the relation to ... Emerson's teleology of nature. His exegetical approach is above all prophetic, his Romantic apocalypse of the mind a guide to vaster prospects ahead." Emerson, equating landscape with redemptive history, appeals to the millennium as manifesting itself immediately and at once in Young America.[24] But neither does the dark side of this apocalyptic vision go unnoticed in American letters. Bercovitch cites Melville's *Pierre* as transforming this hermeneutic vision into "an epiphany of the New World landscape as the apocalypse."[25]

The totalization of meaning can take the aspect of madness: apocalyptic, paranoid, violent, possessive. But the irony of "The Need of Being Versed" offers a welcome release from this tyranny of meaning, this tyranny of the human as it appropriates the non-human without end toward its own ends. Divesting of belief, it institutes possibility. Yet this is an astonishing position: the human is supposed to be that which articulates meaning, and endings, since at least Aristotle, to provide a sense of sense. But here it is the release from the human, from human ends, that is liberating; it is the limitation of the human power to mean and to interpret that permits positive assertion. Yet such a positive retreat poses language against itself, against the very categories that constitute it and which it in turn constitutes. Nietzsche, in *The Will To Power*, warns that "all purposes, aims, meaning are only modes of expression and metamorphoses of one will ... the will to power," that they are "only an expression for an order of spheres of power and their interplay." But in this interplay language is far from innocent. Cause and effect, aims and ends in fact find their basis "in language, not in beings outside." And conversely "linguistically we do not know how to rid ourselves of them."[26]

Within Frost's canon, the problem of teleology has long been recognized and debated.[27] But just as his stance toward nature may be less a question of Romantic identifications with nature than of specifically American appropriations of it, so the problem of teleology may be, within his poetic, not generally philosophical and thematic only, but rather specifically placed within the venture of American destiny as enacted within an American hermeneutic—where it in turn implicates language as such. In "Education by Poetry," Frost, in a rhetoric less exotic than Nietzsche's, proposes the metaphoric nature of all knowledge, the radically figural nature of human access to the world. "I have wanted in late years," he remarks, "to go further and further in making metaphor the whole of thinking ... all thinking, except mathematical thinking, is metaphorical." But, he goes on to warn, "unless you are at home in metaphor ... you are not safe anywhere. Because you are not at ease with figurative values: you don't know the metaphor in its strength and its weakness." For "all metaphor breaks down somewhere. That is the beauty of it. It is touch and go with the metaphor."[28] This insistence on the limits of metaphor in no way negates language's power. Rather, it directs toward language's fuller exercise, less appropriating, more appropriate. "The Need of Being Versed in Country Things" thus concludes with an accomplishment that, grammatically, isn't even certainly asserted— "One had to be versed in country things" does not necessarily entail that one is so versed[29]—and with its positive statement of continued rejoicing cast as a negative one: "Not to believe the phoebes wept." But this is not to declare language as limited in the sense of inadequate to its proper tasks. Rather, the self-demarcation of language, in the space it leaves by retraction and its acknowledgment of its own boundaries, releases man from his own foreclosures, his own totalizations, his own tyrannies. Limitation is then a creative act, a recognition of boundaries in order to affirm linguistic power, to engender its possibilities, and properly to embrace them.

NOTES

1. Robert Frost, letter to John Bartlett, 4 July 1913, *Selected Letters of Robert Frost*, ed. Lawrence Thompson (New York: Holt, 1964) 79–81.

2. As John A. Rea remarks, "It is surprising that of well over 2000 items of Frost scholarship, only a handful have set out to treat formal matters despite the poet's own repeated comments on them." "Language and Form in 'Nothing Gold Can Stay,'" *Robert Frost: Studies of the Poetry*, ed. Kathryn Gibbs Harris (Boston: G.K. Hall, 1979) 17.

3. See, for example, James L. Potter, *Robert Frost Handbook* (University Park: Pennsylvania State UP, 1980) 128. Potter describes form as "one means of resisting the confusion of existence." Basing his discussion on Frost letters of 19 Sept. 1929, 21 Mar. 1935, and 7 Mar. 1938, Donald J. Greiner similarly characterizes "form as a resisting the confusion. Confusion is a boundary against which man can act by creating form. Chaos is what you create form out of." "The Difference Made for Prosody," *Robert Frost: Studies of the Poetry* 5. Karen Lane Rood concurs: "Tension between sentence sounds and form ... appears to be a direct reflection of Frost's world view. For if Frost admires freedom or wildness in the rhythms of poetry because wildness mirrors the confusion of this world, he also stresses the need to impose some kind of order upon it." "Robert Frost's Sentence Sounds: Wildness Opposing the Sonnet Form," *Robert Frost: Centennial Essays II*, ed. Jac Tharpe (Oxford, MS: UP of Mississippi, 1976) 196.

4. Kathryn Gibbs Harris, "Lyric Impulses," *Robert Frost: Studies of the Poetry* 146.

5. William H. Pritchard, *Frost: A Literary Life Reconsidered* (New York: Oxford UP, 1984) 168.

6. Potter 62, 77.

7. *Interviews with Robert Frost*, ed. E. C. Lathem (New York: Holt, 1966) 199.

8. Robert Frost, "Education by Poetry," *Selected Prose of Robert Frost*, ed. Hyde Cox and Edward Connery Lathem (New York: Collier, 1966) 36.

9. Potter sees the anthropomorphizing in this stanza as undercutting "by a gentler and more sentimental flavor" Frost's realistic assertion of difference between man and nature (77). In *Robert Frost: Modern Poetics and the Landscapes of the Self* (Durham: Duke UP, 1975). Frank Lentricchia understands the narrative perspective in the line "The dry pump flung up an awkward arm" as "an act of sympathetic

imagination ... which leads the self into the fictive world ... where the precious state of serenity is restored" (83). He therefore sees the anthropomorphizing as a genuine attempt on Frost's part to "link human artifice and nature," but he also argues that the poem finally checks such identification through an ironic consciousness that it exists only in the figures of the poet's language (83–84).

10. Friedrich Schlegel, *Dialogue on Poetry and Literary Aphorisms*, trans. Ernst Behler and Roman Struc (University Park: Pennsylvania State UP, 1968). See, e.g., aphorism No. 108. See also the discussion on Schlegel in Renee Wellek, *History of Modern Criticism* (New Haven: Yale UP, 1955) 2:15.

11. *Selected Prose* 36, 24.

12. For a discussion of Demanian irony, see especially Paul de Man, "The Rhetoric of Temporality," *Interpretation: Theory and Practice*, ed. John S. Singleton (Baltimore: Johns Hopkins UP, 1969) 191 ff.

13. Leo Marx offers a full discussion of the central place that the farm, as the center of an agrarian economy, held in the American conception of itself as a "middle state" of harmony between primitive nature and civilization. *The Machine in the Garden* (New York: Oxford UP, 1964) 100.

14. Richard Poirier notes this Shakespearean pun in *Robert Frost: The Work of Knowing* (New York: Oxford UP, 1977) x.

15. Lentricchia notes the discordance of these images, but sees them as a false projection of nature's rebirth onto "the artificial human enclosure: the house will come back even as the flowers shall bloom again" (84).

16. Robert Penn Warren, "The Themes of Robert Frost," *The Writer and his Craft: The Hopwood Lectures 1932–1952* (Ann Arbor: U of Michigan P, 1954) 223.

17. For an overview of Frost's relation to nature as "other," see Donald J. Greiner, "Robert Frost as Nature Poet," *Robert Frost: The Poet and his Critics* (Chicago: American Library Association, 1974) 207–48.

18. The quotation from Frost appears in *Selected Letters* 465; it is cited in Lentricchia 145–46. This argument adopts terms familiar to Frost criticism. See, for example, Potter's argument that man needs to achieve the right relationship with confusion, one poised between giving in to it and resisting it too much by the artificial imposition of form (157).

19. Lentricchia 157, 163, Cf. Patricia Wallace, who notes in "The Estranged Point of View: The Thematics of Imagination in Frost's Poetry" that "in Frost's poetry characters possessed of imaginative power are often more cursed than blessed." But she sees its curse as inhering in its disruptive, not ordering aspect, as represented in asocial, violent, nightmare figures. *Robert Frost: Centennial Essays II* 177–78. Lentricchia's argument actually vacillates between attributing imagination's dangers to potential pathology and seeing such dangers as inherent in the act of making "monolithic, absolutizing" visions as such, which is closer to my own argument.

20. See in particular Sacvan Vercovitch, "The Myth of America," *Puritan Origins of the American Self* (New Haven: Yale UP, 1975) 136–86. Also Emory Elliott, "From Father to Son: The Evolution of Typology in Puritan New England," *The Literary Uses of Typology*, ed. Earl Miner (Princeton: Princeton UP, 1977) 204–27.

Perry Miller makes the question of nature's religious significance, with the contradictions this entails, a topic in *Nature's Nation* (Cambridge: Harvard UP, 1967) 152–57, 200–04.

21. Marx; Richard Slotkin, *Regeneration Through Violence* (Middletown, CT: Wesleyan UP, 1973); Myra Jehlen, *American Incarnation* (Cambridge: Harvard UP, 1986).

22. Jehlen 106, 110.

23. Jehlen 102; see also Bercovitch 159.

24. Bercovitch 159–60.

25. Bercovitch 162.

26. Frederick Nietzsche, *The Will to Power*, ed. and trans. Walter Kaufman (New York: Vintage, 1967) sections 675, 552, 562, 551.

27. Nina Baym's early "An Approach to Robert Frost's Nature Poetry" asserts that Frost "is consistently uncommitted ... on all such final and teleological questions." *American Quarterly* 17 (1965): 720. George W. Nitchie sees Frost's failure to commit himself as a failure of nerve, a culpable uncertainty. *Human Values in the Poetry of Robert Frost* (New York: Gordian, 1978) 37, 148.

28. *Selected Prose* 37, 41. Compare his remark in his *Paris Review* interview that he could "unsay" just about anything he does say, in an art of "talking contraries." *Writers at Work: Paris Review Interviews*, 2nd Series (New York: Viking, 1963) 28.

29. Pritchard points out that the poem "does not end with positive security, potentially complacent, of being so versed" (168).

GEORGE F. BAGBY

The Promethean Frost

"It is this backward motion toward the source,
Against the stream, that most we see ourselves in,
The tribute of the current to the source.
It is from this in nature we are from.
It is most us." (260)

1.

After the imaginative struggles of the fablelike and prototypical emblem poems, with their occasional defeats and limited victories, the radical assertiveness of the Promethean poems may come almost as a shock. Indeed, the familiar critical view of Frost might lead us to believe that he is anything but Promethean. For this familiar Frost, as one critic puts it, "guarded epiphanies are more than enough"; the familiar Frost practices "resignation to the gravitational pull of a given reality which confines our will" (Bradford 277). While such phrases might adequately characterize the Frost of the fablelike poems, or even of some of the prototypical emblem poems, they scarcely begin to describe the side of Frost which I want to examine in this chapter. This Frost feels a clear and sometimes irresistible Promethean

From *Frost and the Book of Nature* by George F. Bagby. © 1993 by the University of Tennessee Press, Knoxville.

impulse—an impulse to assert the power of the imagination in the face of, and the superiority of the imagination to, natural fact. But surely it is not so surprising to discover a Promethean side of Frost if we think of the central role of the same impulse in poets like Yeats and Stevens.

The relationship of poetic structure to the Promethean impulse in Frost is a bit complicated. For the most part, Frost's Promethean poems overlap with the structural class which I have labeled meditative emblem poems; but, in this case, I hesitate to claim a strict one-to-one equivalence between structure (meditative poems) and vision (Promethean poems). I classify all but one of the meditative emblem poems—all except "On the Heart's Beginning to Cloud the Mind"—as Promethean, but hesitate to insist that all of the Promethean poems are meditative. Unlike fablelike or prototypical emblem poems, the clearly meditative poems—"To a Moth Seen in Winter," "West-Running Brook," "Wild Grapes," and "Birches" are good examples—do not simply, statically juxtapose tenor and vehicle of the synecdoche, emblem and lesson. They are processive: for the first time, the poem itself now acts out the process of natural education, the visionary dynamic of progressing from object or scene to meaning. (Two clear examples: The simple descriptive portion of "Birches" may consist only of its first three lines. That preliminary description of bent trees is followed by speculation about how they got that way—whether from ice storms [lines 5–20] or from a boy's swinging [lines 23–40]—and by a final meditation on the significance of swinging birches. Or, in "Wild Grapes," the speaker tells the story of a traumatic childhood event in the poem's first three sections [lines 1–91] and then—some years later—draws the moral of that experience in the final section [lines 92–103]). The meditative poems are differentiated from the heuristic emblem poems by the fact that in them the movement from emblem to significance is discursive. In terms of the poem's fictions, the natural lesson is not announced directly by the natural messenger, but is arrived at mediately through the poet-observer's contemplation inspired by that messenger or emblem. Here, in short, the natural emblem is not so much a word to be read as a sign to be pondered, a hieroglyph to be deciphered.

Like Wordsworth, Frost explicitly appreciates the potential value of the contemplative means of arriving at the natural lesson, the very indirection of meditative vision. Wordsworth's explicit theory of composition reflects his tacit theory of imaginative perception: natural experience may inspire "powerful feelings," but only in the meditative pause—only when such "emotion" is "recollected in tranquillity" and "contemplated" by the imagination (*Literary Criticism* 27)—can the seer grasp the full meaning of such experience and feelings. This meditative process is acted out in many of Wordsworth's most powerful visionary moments, from "Tintern Abbey" to the climatic Simplon Pass episode in the sixth book of *The Prelude* (itself a remarkably Promethean episode). Natural phenomena are always most meaningful for Wordsworth when they are contemplated in memory, when they "flash upon that inward eye / Which is the bliss of solitude." Frost suggests a similar theory of vision in "Time Out." The Thoreauvian explorer may realize that a mountain is in fact a text albeit done in plant; but "It took that pause to make him" do so. Reading the text seems virtually synonymous with contemplation of it: the "slope" of the seer's "head," the angle of his vision, is "The same for reading as it was for thought." Under all but the most exceptional of circumstances, the perceiving mind "will have its moment to reflect"—to ponder and thus, in one of Frost's favorite puns, in some sense to mirror, the natural scene.

Again in "Carpe Diem," Frost dissents from the traditional suggestion that life should "seize the present." The mind, he insists in Wordsworthian fashion, can come to grips with the meaning of experience only by distancing itself a bit, chiefly through memory and meditation.

> The present
> Is too much for the senses,
> Too crowding, too confusing—
> Too present to imagine.[1]

Virtually all of the dozen Promethean poems which I want to consider in this chapter are clearly meditative. Despite other differences among them—their dates of composition span most of Frost's productive years, from about 1900 to about 1953; their poetic forms represent a good cross section of Frost's whole corpus; their natural emblems vary from habitual to particular, from objects to scenes to incidents; the details of their structure vary widely—all of these poems are characterized by greater or lesser meditative pauses before the speaker reads the lesson implicit in the emblem. Here again it seems clear that there is a link between structure and vision: the introduction of process in the structures of these poems, particularly the discursive movement in which the mind takes up the natural emblem to contemplate it and forge a meaning from it, offer a rich opportunity for the imagination to assert itself, for the mind not only to contemplate but to dominate the natural text.

But not all of these Promethean poems are as unmistakably meditative or contemplative as "West-Running Brook" or "Birches." In three of them—

"Sand Dunes," "On a Tree Fallen Across the Road," and "A Soldier"—the meditative process is telescoped into the narrow span of only fourteen or sixteen lines, so that the poem's processiveness is considerably muted.[2] In any event, whether the meditative pause in these poems is greater or lesser, it clearly *tends* to accompany the remarkably Promethean uprising which they celebrate.

2.

"Kitty Hawk," though not an emblem poem—not, in fact, a nature poem at all in any conventional sense—sheds a great deal of light on the essential vision of the meditative emblem poems. It is a remarkable if not startling poem to have been written by the eighty-year-old Frost: one of his longest poems; one of the dozen or so most important pieces from the last two volumes; surprisingly innovative metrically, working within the tight limitations of the short lines and repeated rhymes of its "three-beat phrases"; and, most remarkably, a radical assertion of the power of mind.

In its fiction, "Kitty Hawk" recounts past and present visits by the poet to the Outer Banks of North Carolina. Part One recalls his first visit to the Kitty Hawk area, in November 1894, when Elinor White had cast the young poet into despair by refusing (temporarily, of course) to marry him. Part Two is set nearly sixty years later, when the speaker returns to Kitty Hawk in 1953 on the fiftieth anniversary of the Wright brothers' flight.[3] Part Two, pondering the historical associations of Kitty Hawk, is an extended, often surprising celebration of western technological thought and achievement—a celebration which, if unexpected in the middle of the twentieth century, nonetheless echoes Emerson's approval of scientific conquest at several points in the 1836 *Nature* and elsewhere.[4] Frost goes so far as to suggest that the Wright brothers' pioneering flight is a synecdoche for the entire history of civilization (lines 258–95), and concludes the poem with a thanksgiving to the "God of the machine, / Peregrine machine." Rewriting Genesis, Frost suggests that God must not altogether condemn the Fall—"Our instinctive venture / Into ... / The material"[5]—since it only parallels, in human terms, the Incarnation:

> God's own descent
> Into flesh was meant
> As a demonstration
> That the supreme merit

> Lay in risking spirit
> In substantiation.

Here again Frost's stance follows Emerson, who notes in *Nature* that "There seems to be a necessity in spirit to manifest itself in material forms" (*Collected Works* 1: 22). Such an argument, which might at first glance seem materialistic, in fact stands simplistic materialism on its head; the celebration of "substantiation" is, on the contrary, a radical assertion of the preeminence of mind or spirit. It assumes, in Blakean or Stevensian fashion, that material nature is barren unless redeemed by human possession: only mind, acting "Like a kitchen spoon / Of a size Titanic," can "keep all things stirred" and thus vital. The homey tropes which Frost uses here, reminiscent of Edward Taylor, underline the domestication of nature by man; but "Titanic" is surely meant to remind us of Prometheus. Without such mental stirring, nature is stagnant and moribund: "Matter mustn't curd, / Separate and settle. / Action is the word." Only mind, here seen primarily in its scientific aspect, can transform the "waste" of infinite space into a human habitation. Through aviation

> We have made a pass
> At the infinite,
> Made it, as it were,
> Rationally ours,
> To the most remote
> Swirl of neon-lit
> Particle afloat.
> Ours was to reclaim
> What had long been faced
> As a fact of waste
> And was waste in name.

To "conquer" nature is not to defeat but to fulfill it. As for Blake and Milton, man is intended to be the ruler over creation; it is his proper task to name the natural world and to order it with mind—"to master Nature / By some nomenclature." Because nature is barren and meaningless in itself, it waits for human intellectual control to transform and fulfill it. Echoing "The Aim Was Song," Frost suggests that technological control clarifies natural purpose and meaning. "Nature's never quite / Sure she hasn't erred / In her vague design" until human beings, by controlling and domesticating space as aviation does, "Undertake to tell her / What in being stellar / She's supposed to mean." The play on "supposed" makes a Blakean or Stevensian point: nature can be expected to mean only what we assume her to mean.

Thus Frost suggests in "Kitty Hawk" that the constant outreach and grasp of the intellect are properly Promethean, and that they both vitalize and fulfill the created world. We ought to fear not a "fall" into contact with the material, but only a sagging into intellectual stagnation, which would also be nature's loss. The most appropriate or (punningly) "becoming fear"

> Is lest habit-ridden
> In the kitchen midden
> Of our dump of earning
> And our dump of learning
> We come nowhere near
> Getting thought expressed.

The importance of getting thought expressed suggests the underlying link between the philosophical assumptions of Part Two and the personal reminiscences of Part One of "Kitty Hawk." The two sections and their widely separated times are held together, not chiefly by the shared location of Kitty Hawk, but by the metaphor of flight: the aeronautical type of the Wright brothers in Part Two, and the aborted poetical flight of the fledgling poet of 1894 ("a young Alastor") in Part One. The poem's subtitle—"A skylark ... in three-beat phrases"—underlines the Shelleyan implications of the flight metaphor. Nor is the metaphor an adventitious link; it is meant to suggest that what is true of technology is also true of poetry. The same claims which Frost is overtly making for science he is implicitly making for art; both represent the triumph of mind or imagination over nature. Physically, he grants, earth can do no more than passively reflect the rays of sun and moon; intellectually, we make our own light.

> All we do's reflect
> From our rocks, and yes,
> From our brains no less.
> And the better part
> Is the ray we dart
> From this head and heart,
> The *mens animi*.

Thus Frost gives his familiar play on "reflecting" a Promethean twist in this poem. Elsewhere, the mind often reflects in the sense of mirroring the natural. Here, while earth's rocks reflect (the sun) in that usual sense, the brain reflects—i.e., meditates—independently and creatively; that intellectual "ray we dart" from our minds, both in science and in poetry, is the central light which orders the universe and gives it meaning.

3.

Before turning to a number of meditative emblem poems which are obviously illuminated by "Kitty Hawk" and its Prometheanism, I want to consider two which seem at first glance to have little to do with the domination of material nature by the mind. One of these is the earliest written of the meditative poems, "To a Moth Seen in Winter," which was composed "Circa 1900" but not published for forty years. The moth, a "Bright-black-eyed silvery creature, brushed with brown," is described only in the first four lines of the poem; in the remaining twenty lines, the poet meditates on the appearance of such a creature in wintertime.

This natural emblem, almost as clearly as the white flower, spider, and moth of "Design," seems a violation of the natural order; yet, despite that fact, there are promising hints of imaginative intimacy between poet and moth. The speaker not only apostrophizes the natural messenger; he reaches out to extend "a gloveless hand warm from my pocket" to touch the moth and provide it "A perch and resting place"; he endows the moth with the implicit ability to respond to his thoughts ("But go. You are right."). Like Thoreau, the poet observes the markings of the moth in some detail; but the first suggestion of imaginative defeat appears in the poem's lone parenthesis: "(Who would you be, I wonder, by those marks / If I had moths to friend as I have flowers?)" This is not incidental information; this insufficiency of Thoreauvian familiarity with moths already suggests a potential barrier between human observer and natural messenger.

In the middle portion of the poem the portrait of the moth becomes increasingly anthropomorphic, and the inescapable lesson which it teaches begins to infiltrate the narrative. The moth is seeking "love of kind," but in doing so it is "lured ... with false hope"; the poet foresees its inevitable fate: "Nor will you find love either, nor love you." Finally the poem's meditation makes the lesson explicit. The moth is a natural exemplum of something essentially tragic in the yearnings of the heart—those yearnings which are the central subject of the Promethean poems as a group: "what I pity in you is something human, / The old incurable untimeliness, / Only begetter of all ills that are." The poet learns from the moth, "more simply wise than I," the

inescapable destruction which that "incurable untimeliness" will bring.
Every creature, whether human being or moth, is irrevocably locked in the
prison of his own yearnings, and none can reach out to touch any other with
life-giving warmth. The barrier between poet and moth—and implicitly
between man and man—which was first hinted at only parenthetically is now
acknowledged openly:

> the hand I stretch impulsively
> Across the gulf of well-nigh everything
> May reach to you, but cannot touch your fate.
> I cannot touch your life, much less can save,
> Who am tasked to save my own a little while.

The peculiar tone of the last line, simultaneously melodramatic, selfpitying,
and hard-headed, is characteristic of Frost's winter moods long after 1900.
The line functions to apply the lesson learned from the moth to the poet's
own situation: human yearning, too, is fatally flawed; human beings, too, are
trapped in isolation.

An even more powerful sense of isolation, and a more direct suggestion
that human enterprise is vulnerable to defeat by external forces, shape "The
Census-Taker," an unusual poem which combines the qualities of a lyric with
those of Frost's dramatic narratives. The natural object of meditation in this
poem, like the moth seen in winter, is an archetypal memento mori in Frost's
world: a deserted house. It is set in the midst of an almost lunar barrenness
and described in extraordinarily spare language. The census-taker comes one
windy autumn evening

> To a slab-built, black-paper-covered house
> Of one room and one window and one door,
> The only dwelling in a waste cut over
> A hundred square miles round it in the mountains ...
> An emptiness flayed to the very stone.

The trees around this rudimentary house are either cut down or rotting and
leafless; inside the cabin, too, all is disuse and decay: "No lamp was lit.
Nothing was on the table. / The stove was cold ... " Everything in the scene,
in short, is bare, dislocated, or nonexistent. Despite the noise made by the
door blowing on its hinges, there are not even any ghosts or skeletons in this
parodic house: "I saw no men there and no bones of men there." The
emptiness and lifelessness of all he sees (and doesn't see) are underlined by

the irony of the errand on which the speaker has come to this "dwelling": "I came as census-taker to the waste / To count the people in it and found none, / None in the hundred miles, none in the house ... "

Clearly Frost relishes describing such a barren scene—partly for the virtuosity of describing something that mostly isn't there, but partly also because the situation ultimately offers him a chance to refuse to accept such nothingness.[6] (In both respects this poem is similar to "Hyla Brook.") The obvious lesson which such a scene might teach is the preliminary object of the poem's closing meditation, apparently a simple lesson of sorrow at the defeat of all human enterprise and vitality:

> I thought what to do that could be done—
> About the house—about the people not there.
> This house in one year fallen to decay
> Filled me with ... sorrow ...

Again, as in "To a Moth Seen in Winter," there appears to be no effective action which the speaker can take to alter or mitigate this forbidding emptiness. All that he can do, in a setting in which, significantly, his voice cannot even raise an echo, is simply to state the fact of lifelessness, to "declare to the cliffs too far for echo, / 'The place is desert.... '"

4.

"To a Moth Seen in Winter" and "The Census-Taker" both describe chiefly the wintry state of the imagination's life, with its sense of isolation and of the fragility, even futility, of human desire and effort in the face of external forces. The latter sense, especially, would seem to be diametrically opposed to the Promethean assertions of imaginative dominance in "Kitty Hawk." I want to return to both of these poems shortly to suggest that this opposition is only apparent—that, even in the wintriest moments of the imaginative stage represented by the meditative emblem poems, the imagination is beginning to stir and to rouse itself from what Blake calls "single vision and Newtons sleep" (693).

The potential for that stirring, awakening, and resistance to massive natural fact is perhaps most famously summarized in the central passage of "West-Running Brook," an unusual emblem poem framed in Frost's narrative-dialogue form. Nature as seen here is chiefly mindless flux or entropy; it threatens not only to isolate human beings ("'It flows between us /

To separate us for a panic moment'") and to overwhelm them ("'it flows over us'"), but also to undo itself: "'even substance lapsing unsubstantial; / The universal cataract of death / That spends to nothingness.'" Poised against the general tendency of natural fact "'To fill the abyss's void with emptiness'" is the natural emblem—a perversely westward-flowing brook and, within it, an equally perverse wave with a contrary eastward impulse. The husband reads the emblem in his long meditation; he insists that even in the great deathward flux of natural fact, this wave hints at, is emblematic of, the counter force of human spirit and will.

> "see how the brook
> In that white wave runs counter to itself.
> It is from that in water we were from
> Long, long before we were from any creature....
> It is this backward motion toward the source,
> Against the stream, that most we see ourselves in,
> The tribute of the current to the source.
> It is from this in nature we are from.
> It is most us."

A number of critics have shown this "'backward motion toward the source'" to be associated with Bergson's *élan vital?* but whether we call it that or mind, spirit, imagination, or will, that "counter" force opposes the entire stream of natural flux, "'The stream of everything that runs away'"; and even nature itself shows that this "'throwing back'" is somehow "'sacred.'" Two of the lines quoted above closely echo each other—"'It is from that in water we were from'" and "'It is from this in nature we are from'"; both seem virtually solecistic in their unnecessarily repeated *froms*. But the near solecisms make a point: we are not *from* nature, but *from from something in nature* (or water); we are far removed from nature, even unnatural.

That unnatural human impulse to resist nature is not only asserted but acted out in a masterful little poem, "Sand Dunes," in which the human is again far removed from water. Like "To a Moth Seen in Winter," "The Census-Taker," and many other of these Promethean pieces, "Sand Dunes" is set at a moment when natural fact threatens to become not just massive but oppressive, even murderous. Here the ocean waves which threaten the land in "Once by the Pacific" are demonically resurrected as dunes: "up from where" the waves "die / Rise others vaster yet, / And those are brown and dry"—clearly associated with death. These demonic waves are determined to assault "the fisher town / And bury in solid sand / The men" whom the ocean "could not drown."

But here, against yet another primal assault of natural fact—seen as more threatening, certainly, than either winter or the depopulation of a mountainous area of New England—Frost asserts a primal faith in the persistence of mind. Speaking still of the sea whose spirit lurks in these dunes, Frost insists with a wonderfully telling verb that "She may know cove and cape, / But she does not know mankind"—after all, only mankind can *know* anything in a more than physical sense—"If by any change of shape / She hopes to cut off mind." Mind is even more Protean than sea:

> Men left her a ship to sink:
> They can leave her a hut as well;
> And be but more free to think
> For the one more cast-off shell.

In this poem, the assault of natural fact clearly does not oppress the human mind or spirit, but strikes a Promethean spark of self-assertiveness from it. This self-assertion is based on a Thoreauvian freedom which derives from the mind's capacity for constant renewal—for repeatedly leaving former shapes (ship or hut) behind in order to save and renew itself. Moreover, that freedom and power, as "Kitty Hawk" would predict, help to transform the natural world at least a bit. Despite the massive threat of sea and dunes, nature recovers a touch of its Thoreauvian friendliness in that last quatrain: it is the hermit crab, like the beautiful bug hatched after sixty years in the applewood tree (*Walden* 333), which serves as model for the mind of how to survive by leaving the past behind, abandoning an outgrown shell and outdoing the sea itself in "changes of shape."

The opposition between man and earth is at least equally stark in a less distinguished poem, "A Soldier," published in the same section of *West-Running Brook*. (The power of this sonnet is vitiated, to my reading, by an overly insistent tone in the final three lines—a tone which I suspect arises from the personal association of this poem with Edward Thomas, who had died a decade before it was first published.) In "A Soldier," natural obstruction appears to be insurmountable, and spirit, at first glance, thoroughly defeated. The soldier—for Frost, as for Stevens at moments, a figure of capable imagination—is a "fallen lance that lies as hurled, / That lies unlifted now, come dew, come rust." The twice-repeated "lies" suggests the finality of the soldier's death; the repeated verb of "come dew, come rust" suggests by contrast that only the natural cycle, corrosive of human effort, goes on. From the apparent futility of the soldier's death the poem's meditation appears to reason outward to the inevitable defeat of all projections of the spirit:

> Our missiles always make too short an arc.
> They fall, they rip the grass, they intersect
> The curve of earth, and striking, break their own;
> They make us cringe for metal-point on stone.

The trajectory of natural process, "The curve of earth," is not only not the same as our "own," the "arc" of human desiring; that natural trajectory is greater than, and destined to defeat, that "too short" arc of our aims. The spirit's desire, if not pointless, is predestined to come up short against natural fact, to be shattered on what Emerson calls "this cropping out in our planted gardens of the core of the world" (*Complete Works* 6: 19).

But even in these first eleven lines the poem has proleptically rejected its own preliminary reading of the soldier's death: "If we" judge it to have been pointless, "It is because like men we look too near." In a larger and more Promethean context we would be able to see the indestructibility of spirit; after all, the fallen lance which is the soldier "still lies pointed as it plowed the dust"—"pointed" with human purpose, having "plowed" the dust in an effort to make it fruitful. The harvest of that sacrifice is the burden of the poem's final straining lines:

> this we know, the obstacle that checked
> And tripped the body, shot the spirit on
> Further than target ever showed or shone.

In some sense not readily apparent to us, the defeat of human effort is not final; as in "Sand Dunes," natural obstruction serves ultimately to strike a spark from the spirit, to "shoot the spirit on" toward some supernatural "target," even as the soldier's body was shot in a different sense. Thus the arc of the soldier's intention turns out not to have been "too short" after all—it was aimed at some invisible and immeasurable goal. And the poem's last word, "shone," recalls the assertion of "Kitty Hawk" that the real sun of our world is not a natural ball of gases but the irrepressible reflection of "The *mens animi*." When Frost says that "we know" all of this, he is not only distinguishing human beings from the sea, which "does not know mankind," but also suggesting that "to know" is, at least in the Promethean poems, chiefly a matter of assertion rather than of passive intellectual acceptance. In these poems, we "know" as much through the imagination or through sheer desire as through intellect.

The ultimate desire, as "A Soldier" intimates, is to live and not die, and that fundamental life wish is central to the Promethean poems. We see it in its purest form, perhaps, in "There Are Roughly Zones." The situation described in the opening lines of that poem—night and winter—is a familiar Frost scene: as in "Storm Fear" or "An Old Man's Winter Night," the domestic center is dramatically opposed to threatening external forces: "We sit indoors and talk of the cold outside"; the winter wind "Is a threat to the house. But the house has long been tried." The struggle between human desires and natural forces here involves a hostage, a peach tree which has been planted "very far north" and may not survive the cold, windy night. In pondering the meaning of the peach tree's plight, the poet asks a pair of questions:

> What comes over a man, is it soul or mind—
> That to no limits and bounds he can stay confined?
> You would say his ambition was to extend the reach
> Clear to the Arctic of every living kind.
> Why is his nature forever so hard to teach
> That though there is no fixed line between wrong and right,
> There are roughly zones whose laws must be obeyed?

Though the peach tree, if it is destroyed, "can blame this limitless trait in the hearts of men," the poem, clearly, is not inclined to do so. It will blame, rather, a kind of natural betrayal: "we can't help feeling more than a little betrayed / That the northwest wind should rise to such a height / Just when the cold went down so many below." Like all of the Promethean poems, this one in fact celebrates the obstinacy of "soul or mind" which refuses to accept the rough zones of natural law, celebrates man's yearnings, "That to no limits and bounds he can stay confined." The positive, Promethean implications of that line are clarified by a parallel passage from "Kitty Hawk," where, using the same antithetical rhyme of "mind" with "confined," Frost notes how surprising it is that humans, of all creatures, can fly:

> That's because though mere
> Lilliputians we're
> What Catullus called
> Somewhat (*aliquid*).

Mind you, we are mind.
We are not the kind
To stay too confined.

Thus the most important lesson of "There Are Roughly Zones" is, paradoxically, the value of refusing to learn the obvious natural lesson of caution. Frost relishes the fact that man's "nature," unlike any other part of nature, is "forever so hard to teach" about natural restrictions, because he is confident that "this limitless trait" is no mere anarchic stubbornness; it is an assertion of life: "You would say his ambition was to extend the reach / Clear to the Arctic of every living kind." The imagination, in true Blakean fashion, wants to transform even the waste of the Arctic into a vital garden; that is the ultimate reason why it struggles against dead nature.

Now, if we look back at the two lyrics with which we began our consideration of meditative emblem poems—two apparently unredeemed visions of autumnal and winter bleakness—we can see the same "limitless trait" lying beneath the somber surface even in those poems. "To a Moth Seen in Winter," though chiefly an account of isolation and destruction, is not without an implicit assertion of the will to life. The moth itself is almost an exemplum of yearning, its "wings not folded in repose, but spread" for flight even in the face of winter cold. When the poet foresees that the moth must "Go till you wet your pinions and are quenched," the latter participle may mean either "extinguished" or "slaked," but whether the moth's yearning is thus implicitly fire or thirst, it is essentially Promethean. And the "old incurable untimeliness" which the poet sees and regrets in the moth might, in other moods, be far from regrettable: as both "Reluctance" and "I Could Give All to Time" make clear, time is one of the great imprisonments of the spirit. That "untimeliness" is in fact an analogue of "this limitless trait in the hearts of men."

Again, looking back at "The Census-Taker," we find beneath the surface of lifelessness and human defeat an unextinguished spark of yearning for life, in the speaker himself. The life-giving force of imagination is not absent even from this barren scene, its presence suggested by the Eolian wind on this "cloud-blowing evening," which "swung a door / Forever off the latch, as if rude men / Passed in ... " With the help of such Eolian activity, "I counted nine I had no right to count / (But this was dreamy unofficial counting)." Though the census-taker "found no people that dared show themselves, / None not in hiding from the outward eye," the inward eye of imagination insists on making its "dreamy unofficial count" of human presences. Its motive, again: "It must be I want life to go on living."

It is accurate to say, in short, that the imagination and its yearning for life and freedom at least partially inform all of these meditative emblem poems. The processive structure of such lyrics reflects the stirring of the imagination, and its Orc-like rebellion (to borrow Blake's terms) against the tyranny of natural "fact."

5.

"There Are Roughly Zones" hints at a surprisingly Promethean use of natural fact which is typical of the poems I am considering: it may educate not only by analogy but also by opposition. One of the poems which most strikingly acts out that process is "On a Tree Fallen Across the Road." This poem, even within the limits of the sonnet, comes close to dramatizing the imagination's struggle with, and the peripeteia in which it overcomes, natural fact. Many of the poems which I am considering hint at a two part movement. "A Soldier," for instance, embodies a kind of double vision: the narrow vision of the soldier as simply defeated in the first eleven lines, counterpoised by the "knowledge" of the last three lines. "On a Tree Fallen Across the Road" acts out this double vision in its very structure and movement: natural fact poses a crucial question in the first five lines, and the imagination emphatically answers it in the last nine.

The opening lines personify natural facts in order to suggest their purposiveness: "the tempest with a crash of wood / Throws down" the tree "in front of us"; or, as the poem's subtitle suggests, the tree has fallen "To hear us talk." The fallen tree is seen, not wholly as an accident, but as a kind of natural challenge: "not to bar / Our passage to our journey's end for good, / But just to ask us who we think we are / Insisting always on our own way so." Thus storm and tree deliberately raise the central question of self-consciousness: "who we think we are."

In the poem's second movement, in lines 6–14, Frost again attributes purpose to the storm: "She likes to halt us in our runner tracks, / And make us get down in a foot of snow / Debating what to do without an ax." The human traveler, as so often in critical moments of American nature writing,[8] is brought up short and forced to deal directly and nakedly with the natural. Out of this direct confrontation, in the second, larger reading of the event's meaning, in the sestet, comes an answer to the crucial question raised earlier. The storm may throw a tree down in front of us;

> And yet she knows obstruction is in vain:
> We will not be put off the final goal

We have it hidden in us to attain,
Not though we have to seize earth by the pole
And, tired of aimless circling in one place,
Steer straight off after something into space.

This is a remarkably Promethean moment—asserted, as in every one of these poems, virtually without any heightening of Frost's usual conversational language, without rising above that "everyday level of diction that even Wordsworth kept above" (*Letters* 83–84).[9] The answer to "who we think we are" has already been implied in the next line of the question: "Insisting always on our own way so." Here that answer is underlined. Human beings are defined by the unbounded yearning of mind, spirit, or imagination—again "this limitless trait in the hearts of men"—which, when it begins to feel its true strength, will not be denied by restrictive natural fact, even if it must titanically "seize earth by the pole" and, like Shelley's skylark or like the Wright brothers, leave earth in its flight, "Steer straight off after something into space." Yet, for all its Prometheanism, this poem suggests that natural opposition to human yearning is only apparent, and that a kind of cooperation underlies the apparent assault of physical forces. The storm here, unlike the sea in "Sand Dunes," finally "knows" something—namely, the intensity of human desire and determination. Natural obstruction "is in vain" only in the immediate sense that it cannot stop the active imagination. In a deeper sense it is not futile: natural barriers can serve, paradoxically, to help make the imagination more aware of its own powers. In a sense, the fallen tree does "bar / Our passage to our journey's end for good"—not permanently, but for our benefit. Obstruction may be instruction, may clarify and intensify the spirit and will. As Emerson puts it: "limitation ... is the meter of the growing man. We stand against Fate, as children stand up against the wall in their father's house and notch their height from year to year" (*Complete Works* 6:30).

Frost tells a more extended story of spiritual growth by opposition to nature in another remarkable poem, "Wild Grapes." In many details of plot—too many, one may suspect, for coincidence—"Wild Grapes" is reminiscent of Wordsworth's fragment called "Nutting," but the poem's lesson is almost the opposite of Wordsworth's.

While "Nutting" begins its recollection with a sense of blessedness, harking back to "One of those heavenly days that cannot die," the remembrance in "Wild Grapes" seems to inspire at first a sense of fear and trauma. The five-year-old heroine of the poem had begun as an active and fearless child, like Wordsworth's young nut-gatherer extra-vagant in nature:

"a little boyish girl / My brother could not always leave at home." But her fearless childhood was apparently brought to an end by an infernal event: "that beginning was wiped out in fear / The day I swung suspended with the grapes, / And was come after like Eurydice."

In the description of that apparently traumatic event, the natural setting is strikingly similar to that of "Nutting." Wordsworth's young nut-gatherer must "force" his way through "tangled thickets" to "A virgin scene!"—"to one dear nook, / Unvisited, where not a broken bough / Drooped with its withered leaves, ungracious sign / Of devastation," but the untouched hazel trees are "with tempting clusters hung." So in Frost's poem the scene is characterized by isolation, peacefulness, and feminine attractiveness: the narrator's brother leads her to "a glade" in which a white birch stands "alone, / Wearing a thin headdress of pointed leaves, / And heavy on her heavy hair behind, / Against her neck, an ornament of grapes."

Soon, however, just as in "Nutting," the tranquility of the virgin scene is disrupted by the human harvester. The girl's brother bends the birch down to the ground to enable her to pluck the wild grapes; but suddenly the appropriation of nature by human is dramatically reversed.

> I said I had the tree. It wasn't true.
> The opposite was true. The tree had me.
> The minute it was left with me alone,
> It caught me up as if I were the fish
> And it the fishpole....

Suddenly the birch snaps back upright, and the terrified little girl finds herself high off the ground, hanging on for dear life. In a preliminary reaction much like the speaker's in "Nutting," this ravishment of human by tree is implicitly seen—at the time—as punishment for violation of the natural order. The brother half-jokingly shouts to the dangling girl not to be afraid of the grapes—"'they won't pick you if you don't them.'" He also tells her that now she knows "'how it feels ... / To be a bunch of fox grapes, ... / That when it thinks it has escaped the fox ... / Just then come you and I to gather it.'" Implicitly, the tree has turned the tables on the human interloper to reprove her assault on the grapes.

If the young Wordsworth's ravishment of nature is a chastening experience, how much more chastening ought this drama to prove—to have been "'run off with by birch trees into space,'" transported like Eurydice to fearful regions of experience. The triumph of "Wild Grapes" is that the experience is finally not chastening at all. In "Nutting," the human assault does not have to be actively reproved: "The silent trees" and "intruding sky" are sufficient to teach the young speaker a lesson in imaginative humility, in restraint of exuberant possessiveness, in "gentleness of heart." In Frost's poem, however, the imagination is in a more Promethean mood. Though the natural emblem would seem clearly to suggest a lesson in humility—though the girl's assault on the grapes has been patently rebuked—the mature woman's meditation on the experience refuses to deduce any such lesson.

In fact, though the plot of "Wild Grapes" is remarkably close to that of "Nutting," both the lesson and the structure of this poem are reminiscent of the climactic Simplon Pass episode of the sixth book of *The Prelude*. There, during the Alpine crossing itself in 1790, Wordsworth is baffled by the natural event, which seems to frustrate his expectations: "I was lost; / Halted without an effort to break through." It is only in retrospect, in a passage added fourteen years after the event, that the poet is able to realize: "But to my conscious soul I now can say— / 'I recognize thy glory'" (lines 596–99). So, in "Wild Grapes," an unusual lapse of time between the natural event, which befalls the five-year-old girl, and the final reading of its significance, retrospectively by the now-grown woman, yields a particularly assertive realization.

Even as early as the opening question of the poem, in the first six lines, it has been suggested that surprising harvests can be found if one knows where to look for them—and the final harvest here is the adult's lesson of the power of desire and imagination. The wild grapes grow high in birches, which always in Frost suggest aspiration, "Mostly as much beyond my lifted hands ... / As the moon used to seem when I was younger." The "lifted hands" of desire, reaching for the moon which is both an extraterrestrial goal and (for Wordsworth as for Coleridge) a sign of imagination, stretch beyond natural limits and in doing so discover, at least retrospectively, the spirit's true strength. This is what the final meditative section of "Wild Grapes" concludes. The immediate lesson of her childhood experience, the mature woman suggests, is that she was ignorant: "It wasn't my not weighing anything / So much as my not knowing anything." Again, as so often in these Promethean poems, knowing and not knowing are crucial issues. But the girl's ignorance is an imaginatively healthy kind of innocence, an ignorance of natural limitation: "I had not taken the first step in knowledge; / I had not learned to let go with the hands." In mature reflection, such ignorance or innocence is seen to be a valuable trait of the spirit; the lesson which this woman finally draws is the opposite of that in "Nutting":

I had not learned to let go with the hands,
As still I have not learned to with the heart,

And have no wish to with the heart—nor need,
That I can see. The mind—is not the heart.
I may yet live, as I know others live,
To wish in vain to let go with the mind—
Of cares, at night, to sleep; but nothing tells me
That I need learn to let go with the heart.

Here again the ultimate lesson, paradoxically, is the importance of *not* learning the obvious natural lesson—of discovering, beyond it, the spirit's own lesson, the power of "this limitless trait in the hearts of men" and girls and women. The little girl's fearful experience may have "wiped out" her intrepid youthful "beginning," but the death of that earlier self was the birth of a second and more triumphant self, "And the life I live now's an extra life." The girl-woman has been "translated" (line 45) to a higher realm of experience, "the upper regions" ruled by the heart's desires.

The final lines of "Wild Grapes" oppose "mind," here the instrument of prudential wisdom, to "heart," here the Promethean force which casts off merely prudential "cares" and limits: it is precisely in "not knowing anything" in the prudential sense about the conventionally accepted limits of desire, in being ignorant in the worldly sense, that the girl discovers the power of the heart and its desires. But such an opposition is atypical of the Promethean poems. Taken as a group, these poems celebrate a rich, powerful, and many-sided force, which Frost variously calls "mind," "heart," "soul," and "spirit," and which clearly includes both imagination and sheer desire as well. Indeed, Frost likes Catullus's phrase *mens animi* because it suggests both heart and intellect—"the thoughts of the heart," in Frost's own rendering (Thompson and Winnick 238). The census-taker's intent is not to add up bodies but "to count souls." Frost asks of the force which "comes over a man" and makes him plant peach trees beyond their natural range, "Is it soul or mind?"

This power which informs the Promethean poems, whether we call it the *mens animi* or the *élan vital* or "this limitless trait in the hearts of men," involves above all the primal desire of the self—not letting go with the heart—and a radical kind of self-assertion—"Insisting always on our own way so." But, as in Emerson, in these poems the self is ultimately not selfish. One of its most insistent desires is for freedom, movement, and newness, signified not only by the flight metaphors of "Kitty Hawk" or the determination to "Steer straight off after something into space," but also by the molting metaphor of "Sand Dunes" (we can cast off our shells and "be but more free to think"). "Mind you, we are mind. / We are not the kind /

To stay too confined"; the human being is by definition that creature who "can stay confined" "to no limits and bounds."

But the radical freedom from any kind of fixity or limits which these poems celebrate is not an end in itself. It is a means, among other things, to dominate and conquer external nature, which is defined, like the sea, as incapable of "knowing" anything, especially mankind, and, like "the Outer Black," as being "heartless" (361). Through mind, both scientific and poetic, and through heart or desire, the Promethean Frost wants to "seize earth by the pole," to make "the infinite" "Rationally ours." The images of illumination in these poems—of "the ray we dart / From this head and heart," of the "artificial light" which we have "taken" "Against the ancient sovereignty of night" (361)—are images of actively seeking out the unknown, probing into it (as in "All Revelation"), knowing it, naming it ("to master Nature / By some nomenclature"), domesticating it, humanizing it. But for Frost, as for Emerson, to conquer nature in this imaginative assault is not to do it ultimate violence, but to give it meaning and so complete it: "Ours was to reclaim" the "waste" of air and space; we appropriately "Undertake to tell" nature what "She's supposed to mean."

The ultimate goals of the imaginative uprisings in these poems, then, are truly Promethean: to humanize nature and, finally, to assert our deepest wish, that life should prove more powerful than death. "A Soldier" asserts almost baldly that war and earth can "check and trip the body," but cannot impede the flight of "the spirit"; the planter risks the peach tree's life, ironically, because "his ambition" is "to extend the reach / Clear to the Arctic of every living kind." For the author of these poems as for the census-taker, "It must be I want life to go on living."

6.

We have for so long thought of Frost as a poet of the "diminished thing" and the "momentary stay against confusion," as an ironist, as a conservative both temperamentally and poetically, as a poet who "almost always ... chooses to counterbalance" "transcendent impulses" (Wyatt 89–91), that it is little short of startling to realize how thoroughly Promethean he can be in certain moods—but then, the Romantic predecessor whom he most often echoes verbally is not Wordsworth or Keats but Shelley, a formidably Promethean writer himself. In poems like "There Are Roughly Zones," "On a Tree Fallen Across the Road," and "Wild Grapes," the imagination rises up "To bathe in the Waters of Life; to wash off the Not Human," as Blake puts it (141). Yet it remains true, of course, that these poems represent an extreme stage in Frost's visionary effort. With such poems we reach the limits, remarkable as they are, of Frost's Prometheanism.

In the final analysis that Prometheanism is less Blakean—central, continuous, and polemical—than Wordsworthian. Like Wordsworth's moments of imaginative self-assertion in the Simplon Pass episode, in his description of "spots of time" (*Prelude* 12: 208–23), and in the closing lines of *The Prelude* (14: 448–54), Frost's Promethean moments are peninsular, outgrowths of a larger body of verse which is more moderate in its claims for the power of imagination vis-à-vis natural fact. We need to recognize more clearly than we have the genuinely Promethean or (in Emerson's sense) Orphic side of Frost's poetry. But that side is, on the whole, outweighted by a more characteristic sense of kinship with the created world.[10] That sense is best dramatized, perhaps, in "Birches," which recognizes a Promethean kind of imaginative yearning but ultimately forgoes it in favor of an earthward return to and acceptance of natural reality.

The first twenty lines of "Birches" clearly hint at Promethean tendencies. The poem is set at that time of the natural year which most suggests imaginative stirrings: the springtime moment in the imagination's life when it begins to rouse itself from winter lethargy. Though immobilized by their wintry covering of ice, as the Eolian "breeze rises" the birches move "and turn many-colored / As the stir cracks and crazes their enamel." "Soon," warmed by the sun, they "shed crystal shells," like the human beings of "Sand Dunes" casting off dead external coverings to take on new shapes and new vitality. The evidences of that spiritual molting, as many have noted, echo the Promethean outreach of *Adonais*: "Such heaps of broken glass to sweep away / You'd think the inner dome of heaven had fallen."[11] And, though the birches are permanently "bowed" by the ice storm, they remain suggestive of aspiration: "You may see their trunks arching in the woods / Years afterwards," still straining toward that inner dome of heaven.

In the poem's central fiction, Frost adroitly converts the birches from emblems of Promethean aspiration to emblems of natural fact conquered by that aspiration. Rather than an ice storm, the poet "should prefer to have some boy bend" the birches; this fictive explanation represents more clearly the central presence of *human* activity, and human domination of the natural ("One by one he subdued his father's trees"). The comparison used to describe the care which the boy takes in climbing to the very "top branches" of the birches—"climbing carefully / With the same pains you use to fill a cup / Up to the brim, and even above the brim"—reminds us that this is not only a poem about trees but a celebration of spiritual thirst.

But, in the last third of the poem, where he explicitly reads in the act of swinging birches a lesson for the governance of one's imaginative life, Frost draws back from the Prometheanism implied earlier in the poem: "I'd like to get away from earth awhile / And then come back to it and begin over." As that latter line suggests, the visionary assertion of "Birches" is ultimately less extreme than that of "Wild Grapes." As Richard Wilbur notes, the echoes of Shelley in this poem are ultimately used to argue against Shelley's Prometheanism: "'Birches,' taken as a whole, is in fact an answer to Shelley's kind of boundless neo-Platonic aspiration" (113). The famous closing lines of the poem clearly move toward a reconciliation of human aspiration and earthly reality. The poet hopes that "no fate" will "willfully misunderstand" him "And half grant what I wish and snatch me away / Not to return. Earth's the right place for love."

> I'd like to go by climbing a birch tree,
> And climb black branches up a snow-white trunk
> *Toward* heaven, till the tree could bear no more,
> But dipped its top and set me down again.
> That would be good both going and coming back.

The proper role of the mind or spirit is seen here, not as a conquest of the natural, not as a transcending of earth or a "steering straight off after something into space," but as an integral part of a larger process of give and take, "launching out" and return. The young girl in "Wild Grapes," because of her "not knowing anything" about "letting go," about accommodating natural fact, is carried off by the birch in that poem like a fish caught by a fish pole. The mature speaker of "Birches," on the other hand, knows how to use natural fact to reach its uppermost limits, to climb "*Toward* heaven, till the tree could bear no more," but then to accept the end of the trip and be returned by the tree in a kind of cooperative effort. The imagination here again asserts its freedom and autonomy by dominating natural fact; but then, refreshed by that flexing of imaginative muscle, it "comes back" to natural fact to "begin over," now willing to accept the different but also "almost incredible freedom," as Frost puts it elsewhere, of being "enslaved to the hard facts of experience" (*Letters* 179).[12]

Such a return or reconciliation would, for Blake or Shelley, amount to surrender. But Frost, like most other American nature writers, does not posit Blake's or Shelley's kind of inevitable struggle to the death between imaginative perception and natural fact. Like Thoreau (with certain exceptions), like Emerson in his more restrained moods, Frost believes that, in the final analysis, the two forces are capable of cooperating to achieve meaning. Even apparent natural obstruction of human desire, as in "A Soldier" or "On a Tree Fallen Across the Road," or apparent natural reproof of human overreaching, as in "Wild Grapes," is part of a larger design: nature impedes the mind in order to clarify and intensify its awareness of its own creative powers. In other words, for Frost, as for Wordsworth,[13] even when the mind learns essentially transcendent lessons about its own strength, those lessons are taught, at least indirectly, by nature.

Frost's final assessment of the balance between imaginative outreach and the return to earthly reality is well summarized in "Bond and Free," the poem immediately preceding "Birches" in *Mountain Interval*. "Thought," with its exploratory flight on "dauntless wings" into the farthest reaches of "the interstellar gloom," is not seen here as unambiguously admirable in the manner of the Wright brothers; it is more nearly an Icarus-like overreacher, returning reluctantly to natural fact "With smell of burning on every plume." "Love," on the other hand, "has earth to which she clings / With hills and circling arms about." Though bound to the natural reality of "snow and sand and turf," however, Love is neither dispirited nor deprived of all revelation:

> some say Love by being thrall
> And simply staying possesses all
> In several beauty that Thought fares far
> To find fused in another star.

In his most characteristic moods, Frost ultimately distrusts that momentary impulse of thought or mind or heart to "steer straight off after something into space"—chiefly, I think, because of the dangers of some kind of solipsism in such flight. Love, in this poem as in the famous line from "Birches" or in "The Silken Tent," ties the spirit to earth and natural fact.

The return to natural fact is ultimately characteristic of Frost—but it *is* a return, and is satisfying to poet and reader alike only because it follows the Promethean flight on "dauntless wings." Poirier is essentially right in speaking of "Frost's congenital distrust of the freedom he liked to extol, his ultimate distrust of an imagination set free as it is in Stevens" (79). But that distrust of unfettered imagination would be neither poetically interesting nor spiritually necessary if Frost did not feel, at least from "Reluctance" to "Kitty Hawk," the attraction of Promethean possibilities.

7.

I want finally to look at an unusual meditative emblem poem, "On the Heart's Beginning to Cloud the Mind." While several of the Promethean poems (like "Sand Dunes") represent only borderline instances of processiveness, this poem is, conversely, the only clearly meditative poem which is not Promethean. It is still, however, an instructive example of what can be accomplished within the processive structure of the meditative and heuristic emblem poems. Its processiveness is unusually clear because it is built, more obviously than any other meditative poem, on a dual movement from synecdochic vehicle to tenor: a preliminary, deathly reading of the natural emblem, followed by an imaginative reversal and triumph.

The poem is set in the diurnal equivalent of midwinter, the season of so many of these meditative poems: the poet looks out of his railroad car "In the desert at midnight." The emblem which he sees involves a contrast between the apparent community of other worlds and the apparent isolation of earthly life: "The sky had here and there a star; / The earth had a single light afar." From this suggestive contrast the poet leaps, in the first movement, to a chilling lesson reminiscent of that in "To a Moth Seen in Winter"; that single, distant earthly light he interprets as

> A flickering, human pathetic light,
> That was maintained against the night,
> It seemed to me, by the people there,
> With a Godforsaken brute despair.
> It would flutter and fall in half an hour
> Like the last petal off a flower.

The apparently human light in this nocturnal landscape is not seen as truly human; it is kept with a "brute" lack of hope and will soon "flutter and fall" like a "petal off a [dying] flower." It seems, in short, to belong to the order of nature—those unthinking, mechanistic cycles which so dismay Frost in the fablelike and in some of the prototypical emblem poems. Like the visibilia in "To a Moth Seen in Winter" and "The Census-Taker," it suggests the inevitable defeat of human effort and inspires only pity.

Significantly, however, this poem is less than a third of the way through its imaginative workings. The poet immediately rejects his preliminary reading of the scene; "my heart," he sees retrospectively, "was beginning to cloud my mind." Here "heart" and "mind" would seem to be used in a sense almost the opposite of that in the closing section of "Wild Grapes." There, "heart" suggests human will and aspiration, "mind" the prudential intelligence; here "heart" suggests the sentimental, weak side of the imagination, which has momentarily obscured the potentially powerful light of the visionary side. But now, in the peripeteia of the last two-thirds of the poem, Frost goes on to a second translation of the same scene, "a tale of a better kind," a more triumphant reading. By imagining that the single light which he can see "flickers because of trees" which he cannot see, and particularly that there may have been other earthly lights which were extinguished earlier in the night, "So lost on me in my surface flight," the poet expands his imaginative perspective in a fashion which we saw foreshadowed in the last chapter. By doing so he is able to envision a healthy social order, rather than the isolation of "To a Moth," "The Census-Taker," and the first reading here. This community is represented not only by the unseen presence of lights from other human dwellings—"They know where another light has been, / And more than one, to theirs akin"—but also by the imagined couple whose light the poet does see. "He is husband, she is wife," Frost speculates in a curiously sing-song passage; "She fears not him, they fear not life." As a result of the community which the lone light paradoxically represents in this new reading, the light itself is transformed. No longer is it the quavering, "pathetic" light for which the poet first mistook it, about to "flutter and fall"; now it is a steady glow of human effort lighting the desert midnight as the wood-pile heats the frozen swamp in that poem:

> The people can burn it as long as they please;
> And when their interests in it end,
> They can leave it to someone else to tend.
> Come back that way a summer hence,
> I should find it no more no less intense.

"On the Heart's Beginning to Cloud the Mind," with its insistent couplets and recurrent tendency to aphorism, is not one of Frost's greatest poetic achievements; but it clearly demonstrates the advantages of a processive structure. Had it been a prototypical emblem poem, it would by definition have been limited to the somber, "pathetic" translation of the first twelve lines. Only the processive nature of the poem makes possible the self-admonition of the thirteenth line; only the meditative "time out" enables the poet's imagination to struggle against, and overcome, its earlier, weaker reading of the lone desert light, and so move to the second, brighter reading.

With that triumphant movement in mind, it is possible to see retrospectively that the descriptive portion of the poem contains hints of the powerful lurking presence of the imagination. In the fourth line, for instance, the poet looks "At moonlit sky and moonlit earth"—the moonlight, again, signalling the presence of the Coleridgean imagination which not only illuminates but also connects sky and earth. The epilogue to the poem suggests more obliquely the same lurking power:

> This I saw when waking late,
> Going by at a railroad rate,
> Looking through wreaths of engine smoke
> Far into the lives of other folk.

"Waking" is a deliberately active adjective, chosen in preference to the more usual but static "awake"; it suggests especially a dawning awareness of human community—shared, as the last line suggests, not only by the imagined inhabitants of the imagined house, but also by the poet.[14] Most importantly, those seemingly workaday "wreaths of engine smoke"—the medium through which the scene of human persistence and community is perceived—are in fact visionary cousins of Wordsworth's trope for the imagination as "an unfathered vapour that enwraps, / At once, some lonely traveller" (*Prelude* 6: 595–96).[15] Unlike Wordsworth's, Frost's imaginative vapors are never unfathered; but they recur in several poems—always as adjuncts to the Coleridgean moonlight—to fill and transform otherwise barren scenes. I noted in the last chapter the "autumn haze" which is the most important physical presence in "The Cocoon"; looking at it in greater detail, we can see how effectively it images the visionary power of the mind:

> this autumn haze
> That spreading in the evening air both ways
> Makes the new moon look anything but new
> And pours the elm-tree meadow full of blue ...

The haze both connects details of the landscape and transforms them. It mingles with the moonlight, not (as it might seem at first glance) to age and yellow it, but to spread its transforming light. Physically, the haze "makes the new moon look anything but new" by diffusing the light to make the moon seem full instead of crescent; imaginatively, it likewise expands the moon's influence, spreading the new light of vision. Moreover, the haze infuses the earthly meadow with the blue of "heaven," as "Fragmentary Blue" puts it. Again in the triumphant vision of "Moon Compasses," though the images are not so carefully detailed, the moon spreads down its measuring and embracing rays "To a cone mountain in the midnight haze."

In all three poems the moonlight illuminates and beautifies, while the vapor fills and transforms, an otherwise bleak landscape into a vision of community (in several senses), of renewal, of acceptance. A kind of human community—of husband and wife in "West-Running Brook," of brother and sister in "Wild Grapes," or of people generally in "On a Tree Fallen Across the Road"—may be implied in many of the Promethean poems; certainly their assertive vision obviates the isolation which dominates "failed" Promethean poems like "To a Moth Seen in Winter" and "The Census-Taker." But, of all the clearly meditative emblem poems, only "On the Heart's Beginning to Cloud the Mind," with its two-part movement and clear triumph of the imagination, foreshadows the central focus of the heuristic emblem poems: not the domination of natural fact by mind or spirit, but the "fellowship" between human beings and, as background for that, between the human and the natural.

To return to the terms used in "Bond and Free," "Thought," or the imagination in its Promethean moods, may seek to assert its power by breaking free from all earthly ties; but Frost instinctively fears the kind of solipsism to which such flight might ultimately lead. As the heuristic emblem poems demonstrate, "Love," or the imagination in its more appreciative and conciliatory moods, not only cherishes the "several beauty" of the created world. By reading the commonplace characters of the vegetable text, "Dwarf cornel, goldthread, and *Maianthemum*," it also discovers the full extent of the relationships between the self and the other, both natural and human.

NOTES

1. Or again, in "The Figure a Poem Makes," Frost writes: "The impressions most useful to my purpose seem always those I was unaware of and so made no note of at the time when taken, and the conclusion is come to that like giants we are always hurling experience ahead of us to pave the future with against the day when we may want to strike a line of purpose across it for somewhere" (*Selected Prose* 19). This distancing of the imagination from the "crowding" present, this retrospective use of experience to pave the progress of the mind, is an important part of what Harry Berger has called Frost's strategy of "revision."

2. I would argue that "Sand Dunes," for instance—one of Frost's best poems, and unmistakably Promethean—is genuinely processive: that Frost describes the dunes in the first quatrain, meditates on their meaning in the second and third quatrains, and deduces their significance in the final quatrain. But it would not be

unreasonable to see the poem's structure as very nearly nonprocessive (the dunes described in the first two stanzas, then their significance immediately read in the last two)—in which case "Sand Dunes" would have to be classified as a fablelike emblem poem, since its emblem is habitual. In other words, while I believe that processiveness, specifically the meditative pause, consistently accompanies Frost's Promethean impulses, I recognize that that claim is arguable. One might reason that the Promethean impulse is sufficiently powerful that it can express itself not only in an unmistakably meditative poem like "Wild Grapes," whose structure offers a clear invitation to imaginative uprising, but even in a nonprocessive, fablelike poem, in which natural fact ought, by structural rights, to have the upper hand.

3. Thompson and Winnick report that Frost began the poem "in 1953 after a visit with his friends the Huntington Cairneses at Kittyhawk" (300).

4. Thus man's contemporary, if not his ideal, "relation to nature, his power over it, is through the understanding; as by manure; the economic use of fire, wind, water, and the mariner's needle; steam, coal, chemical agriculture; the repairs of the human body by the dentist and surgeon" (Emerson, *Collected Works* 1: 43).

5. Fifty years earlier, in "The Trial by Existence," Frost himself (like Blake) had apparently equated creation and birth with a kind of fall, into what he calls "The obscuration upon earth." Here, however, he reverses that attitude.

6. See William Doreski's comments on this and several other "wilderness poems": "The 'confrontation with nothingness,'" he suggests, "usually in Frost's poetry stirs at least a response—usually an affirmative one—from the beholder" (30–31). Or again: Frost's "epiphanies occur to spite nature, to fling humanist values in the face of that monumental indifference" (37). I agree with the latter statement in the case of "The Census-Taker" and the other Promethean poems; but, as I suggest in chapter 7, a number of Frost's most important visions occur with the fictive cooperation of the natural world.

7. See, for instance, Thompson (*The Early Years* 579–81 no. 6; *The Years of Triumph* 300–303) and Poirier (266–67).

8. Compare, for example, the astonishing scene at the end of Part I of "The Bear" in which Isaac McCaslin relinquishes rifle, watch, and compass in order to get lost and thus find the bear.

9. Marie Borroff has written about the simplicity of Frost's language perceptively and in substantial detail (*Language and the Poet* 23–41, "Sound Symbolism"). Indeed, she cites "On a Tree Fallen Across the Road"—an extremely Promethean poem—as a good example of Frost's characteristic "speaking voice," which she distinguishes from his rarer "chanting voice" ("Sound Symbolism" 134–35).

10. For differing views on the balance of these two forces in post Emersonian American poetry, see Bloom (*Ringers* 291–321; *Figures* 67–88) and Yoder (especially chapter 8).

11. Frost's "inner dome of heaven" may also echo "the infinite dome / Of heaven" in "Mont Blanc."

12. See Bacon's comments (especially on 326) on the relationship of "Birches" to "Kitty Hawk."

13. See Hartman, especially 31–69.

14. It is also worth noting that the poem following this one in *A Further Range*, "The Figure in the Doorway," a narrative sequel to it, is about the human ties which may underlie even the most striking apparent isolation. Cf. Thoreau's views on true community in "Solitude" (*Walden* 130–34).

15. See the enlightening discussion of this passage and the vapor image in Hartman (16–18, 39–48); and Bloom's discussion of "the mists of natural imagination" in "Michael" (*Visionary Company* 183).

MARK RICHARDSON

Robert Frost
and the Motives of Poetry

In 1934, Robert Frost's daughter Lesley Frost Francis delivered a lecture on the "New Movement" poetry of the mid-1910s. Apparently at her request Frost wrote her a long letter sketching his own history of the movement and summarizing the aesthetic doctrine of the Movement poets and their successors. He refers to the poet and critic Herbert Read, author of *Form in Modern Poetry* (1932):

> I assume you'll find in Reed [Herbert Read] his [Pound's] latest descendant a full statement of the doctrine of Inner Form, that is to say the form the subject itself takes if left to itself without any considerations of outer form. Everything else is to have two compulsions, an inner and an outer, a spiritual and a social, an individual and a racial. I want to be good, but that is not enough the state says I have got to be good. Every thing has not only formity but conformity. Everything but poetry according to the Pound-Eliot-Richards-Reed school of art. (*Family Letters* 161)

These remarks succinctly frame Frost's interest in the general question of motivation, and in this essay I consider his contribution to the theory of motive and personality in poetry. As I am concerned with it here, a theory of

From *Essays in Literature* 20, no. 2 (Fall 1993). © 1993 by Western Illinois University.

personality in poetry addresses the question of who or what chiefly motivates a work of literary art. Is the controlling discipline (or "compulsion") in a poem the "inner voice" of the writer, his will to expression? Is it the impersonal agencies either of language, form, society, or tradition? Or is it rather a mixture of personal and impersonal motives? In considering Frost's answers to these questions, we confront some of the most important matters addressed in his essays and letters on poetics. Thinking about his theories of personality in poetry also helps us place Frost's work more clearly within the context of his modernist contemporaries. The dismissive force of his reference to the "Pound-Eliot-Richards-Reed" school of art, for example, should not be allowed to obscure what I take to be the deeper sympathy between certain aspects of Frost's thought and T. S. Eliot's.

The letter to Lesley Frost is characteristically concise and informal in its expression. Consider Frost's description of how difficult it is to know where external "compulsion" ends and where inner desire begins: "I want to be good, but that is not enough the state says I have got to be good"—a simple statement of a complex problem. As I take it the idea is that, at least until the state withers away, we simply cannot speak of pure acts of "goodness": there is always an incalculable element of coercion, whether by force or by incentive, since we always act within a texture of constraints and goads ranging from convention to legal imperatives. In view of this, Frost describes a dialectic of necessity and freedom: everything has "two compulsions, an inner and an outer, a spiritual and a social, an individual and a racial.... Every thing has not only formity but conformity."

Kenneth Burke's remarks on a related problem of motivation are illuminating here. He is discussing, in *A Grammar of Motives*, what he calls the "paradox of purity" or of "the absolute":

> [T]he paradox may be implicit in any term for collective motivation, such as a concept of class, nation, the "general will," and the like. Technically it becomes a "pure" motive when matched against some individual locus of motivation. And it may thus be the negation of an individual motive. Yet despite this position as dialectical antithesis of the individual motive, the collective motive may be treated as the source or principle from which the individual motive is familially ... derived in a "like begets like" manner. (37)

The question is whether "collective," external motives exist in antithesis to individual motives, or whether the former "parent" the latter. Frost confronts the paradox implicit in "collective motivation" quite plainly: "I want to be good, but that is not enough the state says I have got to be good." Is his virtue enforced by a "collective" will working against his own "inner form"? Or does his inner desire to "be good" itself derive from his engagement in a collective social enterprise? Collective motives—what Frost would call motives of "conformity"—may be described genetically: they exist in harmony with individual motives as their originating principle. Or they may be described contextually: they work in antithesis to personal motives— what Frost would call the motives of "formity."

Later in the *Grammar*, Burke makes a suggestion that helps bring out the broader implications of Frost's remarks to his daughter. He asks whether or not, strictly speaking, "action" is compatible with "motivation":

> If we quizzically scrutinize the expression, "the motivating of an act," we note that it implicitly contains ... [a] paradox.... Grammatically, if a construction is active, it is not passive; and if it is passive, it is not active. But to consider an *act* in terms of its *grounds* is to consider it in terms of what it is not, namely, in terms of motives that, in acting upon the active, would make it a passive. (40)

Frost asks a similar question in his letter. Does the motivation to conform exercised on us by social forces actually rob individual actors of their agency? Is it possible, again strictly speaking, to perform a "good" action if virtue is enforced? Inner and outer motivation may negate, rather than complement, one another. In the "Afterward" to a recent edition of *Limited Inc* (1988), Jacques Derrida makes much the same point: "A decision can only come into being in a space that exceeds the calculable program that would destroy all responsibility by transforming it into a programmable effect of determinate causes. There can be no moral or political responsibility without this trial and this passage by way of the undecidable" (116). Where Derrida writes "moral responsibility" I read "self-hood" or "agency," since that is really what we are talking about: "agency" and "self-hood" are what exceed calculation and prediction from without.

That true agency exists only beyond the limits of law seemed quite evident to Frost, and here "law" can refer to previous dispositions of the self—a kind of gravitational, constraining inertia—as well as to forces imposed from without. Frost seems to be thinking of this when he offers in his notebooks what must strike some as an odd definition of "sincerity": "There is such a thing as sincerity. It is hard to define but is probably nothing but your highest liveliness escaping from a succession of dead selves" (40). "Sincerity" is not an expression of the deep heart's core; it consists instead in an experience of transition out of previous self-definitions, not in an affirmation or further elaboration of them. To Frost, this held true for corporate agency and "sincerity" as well, as when he writes in an unpublished version of his essay on "The Future of Man" (1959):

> The great challenge, the eternal challenge, is that of man's bursting energy and originality to his own governance. His speed and his traffic police. We become an organized society only as we tell off some of our number to be law-givers and law-enforcers, a blend of general and lawyer, to hold fast the line and turn the rest of us loose for scientists, philosophers, and poets to make the break-through, the revolution, if we can for refreshment.[1]

This is to say, with Derrida, that true agency (bursting energy, originality, refreshment) exists only on the margins of definition and "governance," in a "passage by way of the undecidable." Pure "formity" must be defined against even *self*-conformity. And "making the break-through" means rising, even as an "organized society," to our "highest liveliness escaping from a succession of dead selves." Or, to return to Frost's 1934 letter: there is nothing especially "personal" about good behavior if the state simply compels you so to behave. A "cloistered virtue"—to borrow Milton's phrase in *Areopagitica*—may be derivative or enforced, depending on how you look at it; but in neither case is it properly *intrinsic* to the agent, who is, as Derrida says, merely a "programmable effect of determinate causes."

Another complexity of the problem is that all actions imply further actions, no matter what, or how pure, their originating motivation may have been. All our actions therefore carry within themselves the seeds of necessity, as Emerson recognizes in "Goethe"; "A certain partiality, a headiness, and loss of balance, is the tax which all action must pay. Act, if you like,—but you do it at your peril. Men's actions are too strong for them. Show me a man who has acted, and who has not been the victim and slave of his actions" (749). Frost understood the point well, though he often seems less troubled by it than Emerson. In the talk at Dartmouth College that served as the basis for his essay "The Constant Symbol" (1946), Frost remarks:

> I always test the other man. I suspect him of having gotten lost in his steadily deepening commitments. Everybody does this.... We are all always testing each other's sincerity. I do it when I read

poetry. I do it when I watch the president of the United States as he gets deeper and deeper into commitments. I watch every marriage that way.... In this unfolding of the kept or lost intentions within the deepening commitments is the root and basis of all good writing.

Two aspects of this passage are especially important: the potentially antithetical relationship it establishes between "sincerity" and "commitments," and its paradoxical idea that "intention" is a thing at once "unfolded" (or revealed) *and* "kept." The paradox holds in suspension two very different ideas: (1) that intentions are the grounds or cause of our actions, and (2) that intentions are the products of our actions. Jonathan Culler usefully expresses the point in *On Deconstruction* (1982): "When questioned about the implications of an utterance I may quite routinely include in my intention implications that had never previously occurred to me. My intention is the sum of further explanations I might give when questioned on any point and is thus less an origin than a product, less a delimited context than an open set of discursive possibilities" (127–28). This is essentially what "The Constant Symbol" is about: namely, how the manifold commitments we engage in speaking, in writing a poem, or most generally in acting, produce an intention that we cannot with fidelity say we ever fully or originally possessed. We might describe our actions more accurately as the revelation than as the expression of purpose.

We can see how intention is revealed rather than expressed, Frost suggests, by considering the progress of a career or of a life, or simply by considering the progress of a poem, which is a symbol for each of these larger progressions. "Take the President in the White House," he writes in "The Constant Symbol":

A study of the succession of his intention might have to go clear back to when as a young politician, youthfully step-careless, he made choice between the two parties of our system. He may have stood for a moment wishing he knew of a third party nearer the ideal; but only for a moment, since he was practical. And in fact he may have been so little impressed with the importance of his choice that he left his first commitment to be made for him by his friends and relatives. It was only a small commitment anyway, like a kiss. He can scarcely remember how much credit he deserved personally for the decision it took. Calculation is usually no part in the first step in any walk. And behold him now a statesman so

multifariously closed in on with obligations and answerabilities
that sometimes he loses his august temper. He might as well have
got himself into a sestina royal. (25)

There is an element of satire here. This "youthfully step-careless" politician
probably serves purposes not his own, even if he isn't aware of it. I am
reminded of the clarifications of the President's meaning that inevitably
followed Reagan's press conferences. The mind of the president is not the
same thing as the Presidential Mind. The situation requires that we use the
word "sincerity," for example, a little loosely, since the agent in this particular
economy of motives is larger than a single man: "behold him now a
statesman so multifariously closed in on with obligations and answer-abilities
that sometimes he loses his august temper."

But Frost hardly wants to suggest that self-identical motivation
becomes meaningless only when we describe the progress of "step-careless"
politicians. His satire has a complicated irony, some of it directed at himself
as a writer: the president "might as well have got himself into a sestina royal."
Later in "The Constant Symbol" Frost raises similarly skeptical questions
about Shakespeare's integrity: "What's the use in pretending he was a freer
agent [in writing his sonnets] than he had any ambition to be?" Part of the
irony of Frost's portraits of both president and poet turns upon the question
of what he here calls "temper," which derives from the Latin word *temperare*:
"to regulate" or "to govern." Frost's use of "temper" implies that no pure
regulation or integrity of purpose is ever really there to be lost: we must
speak, not of intention, but of a "succession" or evolution of intention, in
both politics and poetry. All our actions are intemperate.

This "intemperancy" is associated with the dialectic of "formity" and
"conformity" that is featured throughout Frost's work. To appreciate the
range of his concern with it, we need only consider two works that at first
glance seem to have little in common, though these superficial differences
reveal a deeper coherence: his tendency to range all phases of our
experience—no matter how apparently diverse—within the same dialectic of
inner and outer motivation, or "formity" and "conformity." I am thinking of
his sonnet "The Silken Tent" and of his brief, unpublished essay on the
subject of "divine right":

She is as in a field a silken tent
At midday when a sunny summer breeze
Has dried the dew and all its ropes relent,
So that in guys it gently sways at ease,

And its supporting central cedar pole,
That is its pinnacle to heavenward
And signifies the sureness of the soul,
Seems to owe naught to any single cord,
But strictly held by none, is loosely bound
By countless silken ties of love and thought
To everything on earth the compass round,
And only by one's going slightly taut
In the capriciousness of summer air
Is of the slightest bondage made aware.

***

We were talking about the Divine Right of a King or of anyone else who rules. A principle like that may vary in strength but even in a Democracy it never dies out. It is his right first of all to consult the highest in himself. His first answerability must be to the highest in himself, however close a second his answerability may be to his subjects and constituents. He needs the consent of the governed. But he is no sort of leader unless his pride is in providing them with something definite to consent to. Or dissent from! A ruler is distinguished by the proportions in which the two answerabilities are blended in his nature.

"The Silken Tent" strikingly illustrates its idea of freedom-in-bondage by the way Frost sets the single, finely modulated sentence that composes it so comfortably into the strictly answered form of a Shakespearian sonnet. Hardly a "bond" of meter, rhyme, or stanza goes unfulfilled, though in the sonnet form these "silken ties" are especially arresting. And yet in reading "The Silken Tent" we are never "of the slightest bondage made aware." Considered purely as a performance, the poem consummately expresses the "blending of answerabilities" Frost speaks of in the essay on divine right: the answerability to the self (or to the "central cedar pole" of this fourteen line sentence), and the answerability to contractual obligations—whether to voters or to poetic form. As regards the general question of "motivation," the difference between these two works is simply one of emphasis. "The Silken Tent" gives more weight to commitments, the "countless silken ties" of Frost's second answerability; the essay on divine right gives slightly more weight to the first, the "highest" in the self.

However, I would point out that the boundary between the two answerabilities is not definitive: one cannot always tell when the essential motive of his action is the "highest in himself," and when it is the desires of what might be called his "constituents." It is by now a familiar difficulty: "I want to be good, but that is not enough the state says I have got to be good." The term "constituents" is a felicitous (if somewhat inevitable) choice in Frost's brief essay. To an unknowable extent the disciplines from without *constitute* the discipline of the self. It is not possible exactly to know when one is an actor and when one is merely an executive, and in this undecidability lies the mystery of freedom in Frost's work. In this he follows Emerson in "Fate": "We are sure, that, though we know not how, necessity does comport with liberty" (943). Sidney Cox writes in *A Swinger of Birches*: "I recall the relaxed irony in Frost's voice when I divulged in 1924 that I was learning to accept the inevitable. 'If you could tell what *is* inevitable,' he said" (46).

In short, a possibility of indifference and exchange between "external" and "internal" motivation (necessity and freedom) is always implied in the very distinctions Frost draws between them. Think in terms of his metaphor in "The Constant Symbol": "the figure of the will braving alien entanglements," where the "will" is intrinsic and the "entanglements" extrinsic or "alien." This entanglement does not begin at a determinate moment, as an intervention into pure self-realized motivation. Indeed, the entanglement of will reaches back even to its origin—which is, I take it, the inevitable corollary of the sentence: "I want to be good, but that is not enough the state says I have got to be good." John Dewey makes a similar point in *Art as Experience*: "Erroneous views of the nature of the act of expression almost all have their source in the notion that an emotion is complete in itself within, only when uttered having impact upon external material. But, in fact, an emotion is *to* or *from* or *about* something objective, whether in fact or in idea. An emotion is implicated in a situation, the issue of which is in suspense and in which the self that is moved in the emotion is vitally concerned." All emotion, he concludes, must be understood as "an interpenetration of self with objective conditions" (72-73). Read "desire" and "will" where Dewey speaks of "emotion," and "entanglements" where he speaks of "interpenetration," and the analogy to Frost becomes clear. It should be understood, then, that I use the terms "extrinsic" and "intrinsic" with no undue insistence on their rigor.

In his 1934 letter to his daughter, Frost misrepresents the case in linking together Eliot, Pound, and Read as equal advocates of "inner" as against "outer" form. There is much to be said for Frost's and Eliot's similar advocacy of submission to "outer" forms and disciplines. Eliot admiringly quotes Middleton Murry in "The Function of Criticism":

"Catholicism," [Murry] says, "stands for the principle of unquestioned spiritual authority outside the individual; that is also the principle of Classicism in literature." Within the orbit within which Mr. Murry's discussion moves, this seems to me an unimpeachable definition.... Those of us who find ourselves supporting what Mr. Murry calls Classicism believe that men cannot get on without giving allegiance to something outside themselves. (70)

This "something" corresponds to Frost's second "answerability." That he places it second, and Eliot first, is not without importance, but for the moment I simply emphasize the value each assigns to "authority outside the individual"—or to what Frost recognizes as "social" motive to "conform." Later in "The Function of Criticism" Eliot parodies the advocates of the "Inner Voice" in terms that further suggest his affiliation with Frost, and which anticipate Frost's own parody of the "doctrine of Inner Form" in the 1934 letter to his daughter. The English, Eliot objects, "are not, in fact, concerned with literary *perfection* at all—the search for perfection is a sign of pettiness, for it shows that the writer has admitted the existence of an unquestioned spiritual authority outside himself, to which he has attempted to *conform*.... Thus speaks the Inner Voice" (72–73). When speaking in character, of course, Eliot essentially agrees with Frost: "Every thing has not only formity"—the inner voice—"but conformity." Doubtless he would also have approved Frost's remarks in a manuscript draft of "The Constant Symbol": "Poems together maintain the constant symbol of the confluence of the flow of the spirit of one person with the flow of the spirit of the race. The figure of confluence without compromise. Like walking into an escalator and walking with it. Like entering into the traffic to pass and be passed." This figure of the blending of the two answerabilities would have appealed to the author of "Tradition and the Individual Talent." In this respect at least, Frost's and Eliot's projects are one: both value the reconciliation of innovation (originality, difference, idiosyncrasy) with tradition and community. The idea is fundamental to Frost's poetics, whether in "The Constant Symbol," as noted here, or in "The Future of Man," where it is given a new turn: there, the image is of society itself working, almost organically, to resolve and manage the contrary forces of, on the one hand, stability and continuity, and on the other, of "bursting originality" and extravagance.

We begin, then, to see how Frost's scattered writings on form and personality register his participation in a critical debate very much current in the period between the wars: the debate over the constitution and the relative merits of "classicism" and "romanticism." While in England just before the first world war, Frost had discussed poetics with T. E. Hulme, the man who in many ways set the terms of the debate; he watched Eliot closely, of course, and later Herbert Read, whose monograph on *Form in Modern Poetry* (1932) is chiefly concerned with romanticism and classicism in relation to personality in poetry. Romanticism and classicism, as Eliot describes them in "The Function of Criticism," define the two poles (so to speak) in a ratio of *poet* to *poetry*: romanticism emphasizes the motives of the poet, classicism the motives of poetry itself. Romanticism values inner authority as against outer authority, expression and sincerity as against composition; classicism values a subjection of the inner voice to the outer authorities of form. The one emphasizes the personality of the writer, his distinction; the other emphasizes the scene of writing itself, here broadly understood as consisting in the forms of language and poetry, and also of the tradition—each of which acts as a check against the eccentricities, even the desires, of the poet. This is why Eliot, affirming the classicist position, suggests that the romantic is "not in fact interested in art," and why in the same paragraph he quotes with approval Middleton Murry's adage: "The principle of classical leadership is that obeisance is made to the office or to the tradition, never to the man" (72–73).

Today Frost is not often thought of in connection with the classicism here described, but his consistent emphasis on the "harsher discipline from without" (as he puts it in "The Constant Symbol") developed quite naturally in this climate of debate, as did his arguments against expressive theories of poetry. His "classicism" was evident enough to his contemporaries. In a perceptive early study of Frost published in 1927, Gorham Munson argues that "the purest classical poet of America today is Robert Frost" (100). As he sees it, this "should explain why Frost declares that he has written several books against the world in general. For since Rousseau romanticism has been in the ascendancy. A new conception of nature as impulse and temperament has supplanted the old nature as a strict model, a 'return to nature' has come to mean 'letting one's self go.' For imitation has been substituted the self-expression of the spontaneous original genius" (109). There is a sense in which Frost's aphorism in "The Constant Symbol" is impeccably classical, in Eliot's sense of the term: "Strongly spent is synonymous with kept." I would cite also the complex (and strangely Eliotic) idea of "salvation in surrender" underpinning these lines from "The Gift Outright," which essentially transpose the aphorism of "The Constant Symbol" into a new key:

> Something we were withholding made us weak
> Until we found out that it was ourselves
> We were withholding from our land of living,
> And forthwith found salvation in surrender.

Recognition of the value due external motivation—the discipline from without—marks only the first phase of this "classicism." There remains a complementary idea that the "inner voice" of the poet is transformed by the impersonal motives of poetry and language: in a sense, self-surrender is self-realization, self-"salvation." In a moment of insight that seems to me very like some of Frost's own, Eliot writes in "Shakespeare and the Stoicism of Seneca": "Shakespeare, too, was occupied with the struggle—which alone constitutes life for a poet—to transmute his personal and private agonies into something rich and strange, something universal and impersonal" (117). Compare this to Frost's admonition in an April 1932 letter to Sidney Cox:

> A subject has to be held clear outside of me with struts and as it were set up for an object. A subject must be an object.... It would seem soft for instance to look in my life for the sentiments in the Death of the Hired Man. There is nothing in it believe me.... The objective idea is all I ever cared about.... Art and wisdom with the body heat out of it. You speak of Shirley. He is two or three great poems—one very great. He projected, he got, them out of his system and I will not carry them back in to his system.... To be too subjective with what an artist has managed to make objective is to come on him presumptuously and render ungraceful what he in pain of his life had faith he had made graceful. (204)

There is a suggestion here of catharsis: "He projected, he got, them out of his system." The transformation of "subject" to "object" carries this suggestion even more clearly in Eliot's "Three Voices of Poetry": the poet "is oppressed by a burden which he must bring to birth in order to obtain relief. Or, to change the figure, he is haunted by a demon ... and the words, the poem he makes, are a kind of form of exorcism of this demon" (107). Common to these passages is the idea that the poet's personal motives and necessities are transformed, perhaps even exhausted, in the act of writing: in a word, they are made objective. Dewey makes a similar point in *Art as Expression*: "With respect to the physical materials that enter into the formation of a work of art, everyone knows that they undergo change. Marble must be chipped; pigments must be laid on canvas; words must be put together. It is not generally recognized that a similar transformation takes place on the side of 'inner' materials, images, observations, memories and emotions. They are also progressively re-formed; they, too, must be administered" (81). The "inner" and "outer" materials of the artist are thus alike in kind, at least with regard to how they are treated: as objects to be transformed.

In a 1929 letter to Sidney Cox, Frost writes: "There is no greater fallacy going than that art is expression—an undertaking to tell all to the last scrapings of the brain pan" (196). I want now to investigate in detail some of the specific conditions of authorship that justify Frost's dismissal of this "fallacy."

The incompatibility of pure expression and composition issues first of all from the transformation, described by both Eliot and Frost, of the subjective into the objective—the operation of "extrinsic" impersonal motives upon "intrinsic" personal ones. The idea that the "inner" materials of the artist are "re-formed" by the "outer" materials in which he works helps us understand the implications of the reading of "Stopping By Woods on a Snowy Evening" given by Frost himself in "The Constant Symbol." Much commentary on "Stopping By Woods" has suggested that the poem expresses a complicated desire for self-annihilation. The idea is perhaps best handled by Richard Poirier: "The recognition of the power of nature, especially of snow, to obliterate the limits and boundaries of things and of his own being is, in large part, a function here of some furtive impulse toward extinction, an impulse no more predominate in Frost than in nature" (*Robert Frost* 181). Frank Lentricchia makes a similar point about Frost's winter landscapes in general, and quotes an especially apposite passage from Gaston Bachelard's *The Poetics of Space*: "In the outside world, snow covers all tracks, blurs the road, muffles every sound, conceals all colors. As a result of this universal whiteness, we feel a form of cosmic negation in action."

During Frost's own lifetime, however, the matter was often handled much less sensitively. Indeed, critics sometimes set his teeth on edge with intimations about personal themes in the poem, as if it expressed a wish quite literally for suicide, or marked some especially dark passage in the poet's life. Louis Mertins quotes him in conversation (and similar remarks may be found in transcripts of a number of Frost's public readings):

I suppose people think I lie awake nights worrying about what people like [John] Ciardi of the *Saturday Review* write and publish about me [in 1958].... Now Ciardi is a nice fellow—one of those bold, brassy fellows who go ahead and say all sorts of things. He makes my "Stopping By Woods" out a death poem. Well, it would be like this if it were. I'd say, "This is all very lovely, but I must be getting on to heaven." There'd be no absurdity in that. That's all right, but it's hardly a death poem. Just as if I should say here tonight, "This is all very well, but I must be getting on to Phoenix, Arizona, to lecture there." (371)

As does Eliot, Frost often couples suggestions of private sorrows and griefs with statements about their irrelevance. William Pritchard describes the practice well in pointing out how Frost typically "[holds] back any particular reference to his private sorrows while bidding us to respond to the voice of a man who has been acquainted with grief" (230). It is worth bearing in mind that, later in the conversation with Mertins, Frost says: "If you feel it, let's just exchange glances and not say anything about it. There are a lot of things between best friends that're never said, and if you—if they're brought out, right out, too baldly, something's lost" (371–72). To similar effect, he writes in a letter to Sidney Cox: "Poetry ... is a measured amount of all we could say an we would. We shall be judged finally by the delicacy of our feeling for when to stop short. The right people know, and we artists should know better than they know" (196). I think of Eliot in "Tradition and the Individual Talent": "Poetry is not a turning loose of emotion, but an escape from emotion; it is not the expression of personality, but an escape from personality. But, of course, only those who have personality and emotions know what it means to want to escape from these things" (43). He has in mind exactly the sort of readers and writers Frost acknowledges here: "The right people know, and we artists should know better than they know." In any event, Frost's subtle caveat to Mertins is probably meant equally to validate Ciardi's suggestion about "Stopping By Woods" and to lay a polite injunction against it.

But his turning aside of Ciardi's reading is more than an example of tact. He does it in fidelity to his belief that the emotions which give rise to a poem are in some way alienated by it in the result, and his alternative reading of "Stopping By Woods" is worth dwelling on as a roundabout contribution to the theory of personality and motive in poetry. Frost directs our attention not to the poem's theme or content, but to its form: the interlocking pattern of rhyme between the stanzas. He once remarked to an audience at Bread

Loaf, again discouraging biographical or thematic readings of the poem: "if I were reading it for someone else, I'd begin to wonder what he's up to. See. Not what he means but what he's up to" (Cook 81). The emphasis is on the performance of the writer and on the act of writing. Here are Frost's brief comments on it in "The Constant Symbol":

> There's an indulgent smile I get for the recklessness of the unnecessary commitment I made when I came to the first line in the second stanza of a poem in this book called 'Stopping By Woods On a Snowy Evening.' I was riding too high to care what trouble I incurred. And it was all right so long as I didn't suffer deflection.

In emphasizing the lyric's form, Frost really only defers the question of theme or content. It is not that the poem doesn't have a theme, or one worth a reader's consideration; the form simply *is* the theme. If this seems surprising, it is only because Frost's emphasis makes for so complete a reversal in mood. The mood of the poem at this second level of form-as-theme is anything but suggestive of self-annihilation: "I was riding too high to care what trouble I incurred." This is the kind of transformation Poirier has in mind when he remarks, quoting an interview with Frost originally published in the *Paris Review* in 1960: "If [a] poem expresses grief, it also expresses—as an act, as a composition, a performance, a 'making,'—the opposite of grief; it shows or expresses 'what a *hell* of a good time I had writing it'" (*Performing Self* 90). I would point out further that Frost's reading, appearing as it does in "The Constant Symbol," lends the last two lines of "Stopping By Woods" added resonance: "promises" are still the concern, though in "The Constant Symbol" he speaks of them as "commitments" to poetic form. Viewed in these terms "Stopping By Woods" dramatizes the artist's negotiation of the responsibilities of his craft. What may seem to most readers hardly a meta-poetical lyric actually speaks to the central concern of the poet *as a poet* when the form of the poem is taken as its theme.

The question immediately presents itself, however, of a possible disjunction between form and theme, even as they seem to work in tandem. The "unnecessary commitment" that exhilarated Frost—the rhyme scheme—does in fact "suffer deflection" in the last stanza: here there are four matched end-rhymes, not three. Promises are broken, not kept, as Frost relinquishes the pattern he carried through the first three stanzas. Of course, as John Ciardi points out in the *Saturday Review* article alluded to above, this relinquishment is really built into the design itself: the only way not to break the pattern would have been to rhyme the penultimate line of the poem with the first, thereby creating a symmetrical, circular rhyme-scheme. Frost chose not to keep this particular promise, with the result that the progress of the poem illustrates one form of the lassitude that it apparently *resigns* itself to being a stay against—to put the matter somewhat paradoxically.[2] Paradox is only fitting, however, in acknowledging the mixture of motives animating the poem: motives, on the one hand, of self-relinquishment in what Poirier calls Frost's "recognition of the power of nature ... to obliterate the limits and boundaries of things and of his own being"; and motives, on the other hand, of self-assertion and exhilaration in what Frost calls the experience of "riding high." Frost's remark about Robinson's poetry in the introduction to *King Jasper* seems to apply rather well to "Stopping By Woods": "So sad and at the same time so happy in achievement" (67).

One implication of Frost's reading is that any distinction between form and theme must remain flexible and provisional. Relative to readings of "Stopping By Woods" as a poem concerned with possibilities of self-annihilation, Frost's own reading seems rather too exclusively fixed upon form, and doubtless it has struck many readers as evasive. But in the context of the essay in which his reading of the poem appears, "The Constant Symbol," that reading is quite thematic in its concerns, not at all formalistic—as should presently become clear. And in the larger work comprising both the poem and his commentary on it, Frost is in fact interested in destabilizing the oppositions theme/form and content/form.

Three terms concern us: content, theme, form. In approaching some poems it is necessary first to describe the content. Reading Wallace Stevens's poem "The Emperor of Ice Cream," for example, we may say that it describes a funeral—a statement about content. (By contrast, nothing could be plainer than the content of most of Frost's lyrics, especially "Stopping By Woods.") In any event, a critic needs some intelligible ground against which to work in speaking of the theme, or if you prefer, the "concern" of the poem—what it aims to draw our attention to as readers of poetry. What the poem "has in mind" is not to be confused with what it "has in view," though the two categories often overlap. "The Emperor of Ice Cream" may or may not have a funereal theme; "Stopping By Woods" may or may not be "thinking" of a man in a sleigh. Form is still another matter, and to address it a critic usually has to define, and stabilize for purposes of investigation, some notion of theme to work against. Which yields these three (somewhat unstable) concepts: what a poem describes—its content; what it has in mind—its theme; and how it holds together—its form.

Whatever a critic's terminology, it is perhaps inevitable that he rely on each of these concepts. I am suggesting that Frost's critical theory and practice show how they are exchangeable: each term must be considered for its place in a kind of escalation of significance in which theme, form, and content change places. This is, it seems to me, the meaning of Frost's definition in "The Constant Symbol": "Every poem is an epitome of the great predicament; a figure of the will braving alien entanglements." Here is a theme which is not one: that is to say, a theme which stands in no comfortable opposition either to content or form. "Figure" works in three senses here: in the sense of metaphor; in the sense of "subject" or "theme," as when we say that a painting is *of* a human figure; and in the sense of "pattern" or form. The "figure" or pattern a poem makes may "pose" and become either the content or the theme of a particular poem; that is, a poem may either have that pattern "in view" or "in mind." In Frost's reading of "Stopping By Woods," for example, the figure *that* poem makes, its rhyme and stanza scheme, becomes its "figure" or theme. But it is not enough to say that a poem is a "figure"—whether we mean metaphor or theme—of the will braving alien entanglements: it is also an example of it, and this directs our attention to the act of description in a poem rather than to the things it describes. More precisely, it extends the category of "things described" (the content) to include also the act of description. Considered in this light the content of every poem "written regular" (as Frost says) is this "figure of the will braving alien entanglements." His reading plainly undermines the distinction between form and content: the container becomes the thing contained—which brings us to the very heart of the matter.

This exchange and merger of container and contained—of outside and inside, form and content—is central to Frost's understanding of motive. When he writes to Lesley Frost: "I want to be good, but that is not enough the state says I have got to be good," the observation quite naturally occurs to him in connection with a discussion of form in poetry. This suggests the broader implications of the fact that outer motivations become indistinguishable from the inner motivations of the agent—whether he is a poet writing a poem, or a citizen simply endeavoring to be good. It is as impossible to define the essential motive of "Stopping By Woods"— intrinsic? extrinsic? personal? formal?—as it would be to define the essential motive of the desire to be virtuous. In both cases the motive is the *product*, not the antecedent, of engagements with alien entanglements—that is, with the coercive motives, however benign, of form and state.

Since this points to the indissociability of external and internal motivations it naturally bears closely on the question of personality in poetry.

To say that a poet "expresses" himself is to assign priority to intrinsic motives as against extrinsic ones, and to elevate autobiographical impulses above the act of composition. Furthermore, in putting content above form, expressive theories of poetry necessarily assume a stable opposition of message to vehicle, in which the former remains uncontaminated by the latter. Thinking of poetry in terms of expression inevitably engages the battery of assumptions Derrida skeptically describes in "Signature Event Context": "If men write it is: (1) because they have to communicate; (2) because what they have to communicate is their 'thought,' their 'ideas,' their representations. Thought, as representation, precedes and governs communication, which transports the 'idea,' the signified content" (4). In Frost's Derridean-Burkean grammar, the sentence must always read: a poem *is expressed*, which captures the mixture of external and internal motives he finds in himself and in writing. No pure governing intention precedes a poem to be embodied in it. We must speak instead of a "succession" of intention.

This idea of a "successive intention" seems to motivate most of Frost's accounts of the writing experience, and it suggests another respect in which composition is impersonal: poems, in his descriptions, have motives of their own to which the motives of the poet become merely incidental or catalytic. In concluding this discussion I want to look briefly at several of his accounts of what a poem feels like as he writes it.

He remarks in "Before the Beginning and After the End of a Poem," a talk delivered at the Winter Institute of the University of Miami in 1931:

> The subject should emerge as the poem is written. One should not know what to name a poem until he is at least two-thirds through it.... The person who knows the name of his poem or the end of his poem before he writes it ought not to write it. And yet, the thing should emerge as if it had all the enthusiasm of the name, and of the object's being foreknown. When does a person know what he means by a poem? When he draws near the end. (8)

In the lecture delivered at Dartmouth College on "The Constant Symbol," he phrases the idea more succinctly: "A poem is the having of an idea—not an idea put into verse." And he writes to similar effect in "Poetry and School": "Almost everyone should almost have experienced the fact that a poem is a idea caught fresh in the act of dawning." Frost must have agreed with Dewey's remarks in *Art as Experience*: "Even the Almighty took seven days to create the heaven and the earth, and, if the record were complete, we should also learn that it was only at the end of the period that he was aware of just what He set out to do with the raw materials of chaos that confronted Him" (71).

There is a tendency in each of Frost's descriptions to reduce or qualify the agency of the poet, whose actions in part become catalytic and responsive. It is here, I think, that he comes closest to the specific emphases of T. S. Eliot's impersonal theory of poetry. Consider this passage from "The Figure a Poem Makes" (1939):

> I tell how there may be a better wildness of logic than of inconsequence. But the logic is backward, in retrospect, after the act. It must be more felt than seen ahead like prophecy. It must be a revelation, or a series of revelations, as much for the poet as for the reader. For it to be that there must have been the greatest freedom of the material to move about in it and to establish relations in it regardless of time and space. (19)

There is an impersonal quality in the very movement of these sentences—a carefully modulated vagueness that seems quite faithful to the implication that Frost might know as little about the outcome here as we do. Once again he describes the dawning of an idea in poetry: "It must be a revelation." As he does elsewhere in the same essay, Frost leans heavily on the impersonal pronoun "it," a word made all the more strange in this passage because its antecedent seems to remain fluid. Initially "it" refers to "the logic," but in the last sentence the pronoun comes unmoored: "For it [the logic] to be that [a revelation] there must have been the greatest freedom of the material to move about in it [the revelation? the logic? the poem itself?] and to establish relations in it regardless of time and space."

The difficulty is that he is describing the medium in which poetry composes itself. That medium—whatever its qualities—is at least not to be reduced merely to the personality or desire of the writer: there are impersonal exigencies of language, "material," and form to be considered. When Frost curiously speaks of the "freedom of the material to move about in it," I understand him to mean: to move about *in the poem*, in the writing, not simply in the poet. It is exactly as if the poet were a catalyst, a filament of platinum, to recur to Eliot's famous analogy in "Tradition and the Individual Talent" (40); or as if the poet were merely the "fine instrument for transformations" that Eliot finds in Shakespeare (119). I am reminded of Eliot's difficult point in "Tradition and the Individual Talent": "The poet has, not a 'personality' to express, but a particular medium, which is only a medium and not a personality, in which impressions and experiences combine in peculiar and unexpected ways" (9). Frost seems to be have in view something like this "medium": an "it" in which the "materials" of the poem (images? memories? language itself?) move about and recombine.

In closing I recall Dewey's observation in the passage quoted already: A "transformation takes place on the side of 'inner' materials ... they are also progressively re-formed; they, too, must be administered. This modification is the building up of a truly expressive act." In acknowledging this "administrative" complement, Frost sharply distinguishes his own poetics from the poetics of pure expression and personality. For him, the "truly expressive act" is never a mere "undertaking to tell all to the last scrapings of the brain pan." The "truly expressive act" combines and administers disciplines both from within and from without. It marks the confluence of his "two answerabilities," a confluence of the desires and personality of the poet with impersonal forces and commitments.

In "The Poet's Next of Kin in College," Frost makes the point concisely by analogy to the rodeo: "The great pleasure in writing poetry is in having been carried off. It is as if you stood astride of the subject that lay on the ground, and they cut the cord, and the subject gets up under you and you ride it. You adjust yourself to the motion of the thing itself. That is the poem." The athleticism of this analogy is discernable, it seems to me, in Frost's description, in "The Constant Symbol," of his own experience in "Stopping By Woods on a Snowy Evening": "I was riding too high to care what trouble I incurred." And in "The Poet's Next of Kin" Frost is already implicitly concerned with what he would later call the "constant symbol" of poetry. The rodeo artist gives form to the unpredictable and forceful motions of the horse; he expresses them, and is, in a sense, also expressed by them. Frost admires his performance, it seems proper to say, as the "constant symbol" of an artist at once controlling and being controlled by his "subject." The answerabilities to "formity" and to "conformity" merge, becoming all but indistinguishable, as in "The Silken Tent": inner desire and outer coercion form two aspects of a single experience. Every poem "constantly" symbolizes this convergence of necessity and freedom, of the impersonal and the personal, and this is why, according to Frost, motives personal to the poet can never be said to exhaust, or even substantially to define, the motives of the writing itself: "The subject gets up under you and you ride it. You adjust yourself to the motion of the thing itself. That is the poem."

NOTES

1. The manuscript of the essay is held at Dartmouth College Library. It is one of a number of papers associated with Frost's participation in a panel discussion of "The Future of Man" held at the dedication of the Joseph Seagram & Sons Building in New York City in 1959.

2. Allen Tate (citing Cleanth Brooks) notices a similar effect in the fourth stanza: "The external pattern reflects perfectly what we are told; instead of the third unrhymed line, as in the other three stanzas, there is ... one rhyme: deep-keep-sleep-sleep. As one falls asleep it takes too much effort to find a rhyme; so sleep echoes sleep. We may see here what Mr. Cleanth Brooks formerly saw as a paradox: the poet falls asleep as he tells us that he will not" (67).

WORKS CITED

Burke, Kenneth. *A Grammar Of Motives*. New York: Prentice-Hall, 1945.

Ciardi, John. "Robert Frost: The Way to the Poem." *Saturday Review of Literature* 41 (12 April 1958): 13–15, 65.

Cook, Reginald. *Robert Frost: A Living Voice*. Amherst: U of Massachusetts P, 1974.

Cox, Sidney. *A Swinger of Birches: A Portrait of Robert Frost*. New York: New York UP, 1957.

Culler, Jonathan. *On Deconstruction*. Ithaca: Cornell UP, 1982.

Derrida, Jacques. *Limited Inc*. Evanston: Northwestern UP, 1988. [Reprints also Derrida's essay "Signature/Event/Context."]

Dewey, John. *Art As Experience*. Ed. Jo Ann Boydston, et al. Carbondale: Southern Illinois UP, 1987.

Eliot, T.S. "Shakespeare and the Stoicism of Seneca." In *Selected Essays*. New York: Harcourt, 1950.

———. *Selected Prose*. Ed. Frank Kermode. London: Faber, 1975. [Unless otherwise noted, quotations from Eliot's prose are from this edition.]

———. "The Three Voices of Poetry." In *On Poetry and Poets*. New York: Farrar, 1957.

Emerson, Ralph Waldo. *Essays and Lectures*. Ed. Joel Porte. New York: Library of America, 1983.

Evans, William R. *Robert Frost and Sidney Cox*. Hanover: UP of New England, 1981. [A collection of letters.]

Frost, Robert. "Before the Beginning and After the End of a Poem." *The Carrell* 6 (1965): 6–8.

———. *Complete Poems*. New York: Holt, 1949.

———. "The Constant Symbol." Unpublished manuscript. Alderman Library, University of Virginia, Charlottesville.

———. [Talk on "The Constant Symbol."] Reported by Jerry Tallmer in *The Dartmouth*, 22 May 1946.

————. [Essay on "divine right."] Unpublished typescript. Dartmouth College Library, Hanover, New Hampshire.

————., and Elinor White Frost. *The Family Letters of Robert and Elinor Frost*. Ed. Arnold Grade. Albany: State University of New York Press, 1972.

————. "The Future of Man." Unpublished typescript. Dartmouth College Library, Hanover, New Hampshire.

————. "Poetry and School." *Atlantic Monthly* (June 1951): 30–31.

————. "The Poet's Next of Kin in College." *Biblia* 9 (February 1938): 16–18.

————. *Prose Jottings: Selections from His Notebooks*. Ed. Edward Connery Lathem and Hyde Cox. Lunenburg, VT: Northeast-Kingdom, 1982.

————. *The Selected Letters of Robert Frost*. Ed. Lawrance Thompson. New York: Holt, 1964.

————. *Selected Prose of Robert Frost*. Ed. Hyde Cox and Edward Connery Lathem. New York: Holt, 1966.

Lentricchia, Frank. *Robert Frost: Modern Poetics and the Landscapes of Self*. Durham: Duke UP, 1975.

Mertins, Louis. *Robert Frost: Life and Talks-Walking*. Norman: U of Omaha P, 1965.

Munson, Gorham. *Robert Frost*. New York: Doran, 1927.

Poirier, Richard. *The Performing Self*. New York: Oxford UP, 1971.

————. *Robert Frost: The Work of Knowing*. New York: Oxford UP, 1977.

Pritchard, William. *Robert Frost: A Literary Life Reconsidered*. New York: Oxford UP, 1984.

Read, Herbert. *Form In Modern Poetry*. London: Vision, 1948.

Tate, Allen. "Inner Weather: Frost as a Metaphysical Poet." In *Robert Frost: Lectures on the Centennial of His Birth*. Washington: Library of Congress, 1975.

KATHERINE KEARNS

The Serpent's Tail

And if man once thought that straight vision could allow him to escape the opaque barrier that every body presents to the light, now, in his impetuous desire, he is plunged into the darkness that a supposedly enlightened gaze had projected in its very rings and reversals.
—Luce Irigaray, *Speculum of the Other Woman*

At a most fundamental and pervasive level, Frost's poetry documents a man's struggle with his own oppositional impulses of appetite and moderation. Enclosed, tersely resolved against histrionic self-display, a man seeks to keep the battle internal. But desire *will* be made manifest, and so this drama plays itself out correlatively in nature and in women and is enlivened by their natural propensity for capitulation. In the natural world where life rises out of death, fruition out of decay, and light out of darkness, the equivalent downward motion is inevitable: nature and women do not merely accept this gravitational urge but welcome it, inviting men to join them in the fall. Frost's poetry is a heroic assertion of conscious prosodic control placed against his relentlessly subversive awareness of internally derived appetitive impulse. His task is Sisyphean because he cannot remove himself from the source of his desires—enacted by externalities, they are projected from within. And for Frost there are no metaphysical truths to

From *Robert Frost and a Poetics of Appetite* by Katherine Kearns. © 1994 by Cambridge University Press.

counterbalance the appetitive flux: if desire finds its mansion and its grave in an earthy physicality, metaphysics is a rifled and empty crypt ("A Masque of Reason" l. 284). Frost's model of control may be seen then to exceed the specifically Christian or Puritan terms he often chooses to employ, as any external "systematic," religious, political, psychological, or otherwise, lacks the compelling vitality of the desirous self: control has to do more secularly with the violent expense of self through the mechanics of a desire that is self-generating and is both the reward and the punishment of being a man. Frost's concern is the interdependent physical, ethical, and spiritual consequences to the self of that virile and necessary appetite when it is brought to expense.[1] He maintains in "The Constant Symbol" that "Strongly spent is synonymous with kept," but this is true only as long as the energy is poured into a shape, made into a product—a poem, a piece of work, a career.[2] If it is not "kept" within some intact form, however, it is lost. Heautocratic integrity, the internalized deployment of appetite in the service of a virilely informed moderation—or, in poetic terms, the internalized deployment of inspirative "wildness" or delight within the virile containment of a resolute prosodic structure—is a man's best and only goal.[3] The poem reifies that most exquisitely precarious balance, as it arouses the poet to his own powers of control.

For Frost, anything that expends itself in generation necessarily winds down acceleratively to death, but unlike nature and unlike women, men are possessed of the (potential) rationality by which they might imagine themselves to hold this process in abeyance. Frost's implications about "femaleness" extend far beyond gender, as he suggests that women signal a condition of barrierlessness; in this he is no more than strictly traditional.[4] By nature uncontrolled, women are formally compromised in Frost's poetry so that they may, like nature, decompose and reform perpetually: pregnancy, that most singular transformation that begins with the abdomen and extends inexorably to encompass the entire body, is only the first (and frequently the most deferred) metamorphosis in Frost's world, where women emerge as trees, flowers, and fireflics, as dryads and witches and hill wives. Mothers, and mother earth, are possessed of the immense power both to alter and to be altered by what is within them, and one's rootedness to the maternal source remains a conduit through which substance burgeons and subsides. Men, holding themselves as antithetical to this regenerative anarchy, reject the metamorphic capacities that allow for them an eternal recurrence, and it becomes thus all the more essential that they throw up the barriers which, even as they are disintegrating, might slow the inevitable lapse. Women, like seeds or fairy shrimp, may go through periods of quiescence, so that for example the dryad of "Paul's Wife" may remain locked inside her tree as a dry pith until someone should happen to lay that pith beside the pool where it can "drink." Women may, like Paul's wife or like the mother/maple of "Maple," die in one form and be born again in another, so that when the dryad goes out "like a firefly" one can only imagine her reemerging embodied as something else. But men are not formed for transformation, and only a man who rejects some part of his masculinity becomes something other than a man. Thus in "The Subverted Flower" it is not desire alone that brings the male figure to his state of bestial humiliation but also, paradoxically, his sexual ineffectuality. It is his *unmanning* to a state of uncontrol that makes him a beast. Succumbing to a rapacious appetite for a defined "other" while being thwarted in consummation, he is a figure of frustrated impotence. Formal rigor becomes an imperative in this vision where one must be both virile and moderate, for what a man loses is lost forever.

Resonating always with his vision of natural unrest, Frost's poetry articulates this most pervasive irony: that desire itself is circular and self-generating, like the seasons or like the flow of blood in the body, but that succumbing to one's metamorphic, appetitive "femaleness" means an irrevocable loss of self into the shapeless void. Poured into that which is ever-changing, this expense becomes "substance lapsing unsubstantial; / [Into] The universal cataract of death / That spends to nothingness." Desire threatens a most essential violation of the intact system, for while it may be internally generated and with effort safely diverted, it seeks outlets: "Oh, blood will out. It cannot be contained," warns the speaker of "The Flood."[5] Yet most outward manifestations necessitate that autonomy be suspended, if only momentarily, and that there be a dangerous breach in the fortified self. "Eyes seeking the response of eyes" are, in "All Revelation," the apertures that most compromise the global autonomy of the geode.[6] Expent, that which is, as "West-Running Brook" has it, "time, strength, tone, light, life, and love," is felt to "seriously, sadly run [ ] away, / To fill the abyss's void with emptiness." Contained, enclosed, this energy becomes like the brook channeled under the city, a new potency, a radical and even potentially sinister force to keep others from work and sleep, but released, it becomes a movement toward nothingness. For Frost, the poetic structure becomes the tightly sealed receptacle for desire, a formal containment for the witchery of the inspirative possession implicit in the poetic act itself. The figure in "A Servant to Servants" of the madman in his cell of hickory poles, strumming against the bars and talking of love things, resonates throughout the poetry, for within each prosodic cage the drama of appetite against containment is played out.

So it is that for Frost the figure a poem makes is the same for love. It is not insignificant that Frost's famous correlation between love and the poem makes the poetic act virtually inextricable from the sexual, that "love," as the second term, seems the focus of the analogy:

> The figure a poem makes. It begins in delight and ends in wisdom. The figure is the same as for love. No one can really hold that the ecstasy should be static and stand still in one place. It begins in delight, it inclines to the impulse, it assumes direction with the first line laid down, it runs a course of lucky events, and ends in a clarification of life ... in a momentary stay against confusion. (*Prose* 18)

The "ecstasy" of which the analogy speaks remains ambiguously located (is it love or the poem to which he refers?) until "the first line laid down" reveals that the indeterminate "it" is the poem which has reasserted itself. And even here, the line is "laid down," bedded like (instead of?) a lover, and what comes of this is a birth of form, "a clarification of life ... in a momentary stay against confusion." The "poem" becomes, by Frost's semantics, not merely *like* love, but itself a form of virile, controlled loving. One could indeed say that Frost's insistence that metaphor is the whole of thinking might be tropologically too general, nearly a subterfuge, for one comes to feel instead that, for Frost, it is all *metonymy:* that the whole of his thinking about poetry, about women, about nature is felt by him as so many contiguities of his own desirous flesh. "The philosophy of the part for the whole; skirting the hem of the goddess" is not, despite Frost's claim, synecdoche so much as metonymy, extensions of the expanding parameters of self.[7]

The poetic act itself generates that "wonder of unexpected supply" which guarantees that the system of arousal is rheostatic, renewable. "For me the initial delight is in the surprise of remembering something I didn't know I knew," Frost says. "I am in a place, in a situation, as if I had materialized from cloud or risen out of ground. There is a glad recognition of the long lost and the rest follows. Step by step the wonder of unexpected supply keeps growing" (*Prose* 19). Whether the view is Apollonian (materializing from cloud) or chthonic (rising out of ground), such an experience is intensely pleasurable, productive of delight, gladness, and wonder. It makes one feel a giant, making (phallic) order that is like "the straight crookedness of a good walking stick" (*Prose* 19). According to the poet of "How Hard It Is to Keep from Being King When It's in You and in the Situation" (one might substitute "Poet" for "King" and examine the opportunistic overtones of this title), this "perfect moment of unbafflement," the climactic recognition of one's own capacity to exploit the exact affinities of a good simile, comes from some potently energizing place: "It may be wine, but much more likely love—/ Possibly just well-being in the body" (ll. 242–3). One looks for a name for this bodily translation that takes one at once into the clouds and up out of the ground, that makes one feel ten feet tall, that feels like Bacchic wine and like love: that fulfills, in other words, the figure of "love" by a simultaneous spiritual and physical transformation. This is an autonomously derived pleasure that, named after love, comes to generate love's terms, comes, in fact, to seem like love. Tautological, this is the "form of forms," "The serpent's tail stuck down the serpent's throat," indeed.[8] One thing leads to another and on around.

This is a kind of autoerotics, perhaps. Perceiving linguistic pleasure in terms of sex, and sex in terms of the disciplined wildness of the poetic inscription, one performs at a most essential level that unification between discourse and act. Involving a mastery of "wildness," Frost's poetics locates power in the one who can both arouse that wildness and contain it (*Prose* 18). The cunning tongue and the crafty pen come to derive what Foucault describes in *The History of Sexuality* as "pleasure in the truth of pleasure, the pleasure of knowing that truth, of discovering it and exposing it, the fascination of seeing it and telling it, of captivating and capturing others by it, of confiding it in secret, of luring it out in the open—the specific pleasure of the true discourse on pleasure."[9] That Frost began to write poetry just as what Foucault documents as a *Scientia Sexualis* was being codified and disseminated is perhaps not inconsequential to this habit of mind; that he wrote toward the end of an era in which medicine "wove an entire network of sexual causality" to explain every malady and physical disturbance would perhaps explain the sexual etiology implicit in his seemingly nonironic appropriation of the art/love analogy to verify an impulse perceived oppositionally in terms of creation and annihilation.[10] However it may be, Frost may be said to generate his own heat within a self-enclosed system, talking about love, confiding it in secret through his buried allusions to infidelity and arousal, luring it out in the open in his stories of men and the women who leave them, captivating and capturing others by his vision of an earth at once so generative, so dangerous, and so inviting. He is a master of the sexual innuendo, which is always seemingly belied by the hearty voice that utters it. It is not accidental or insignificant that a sexual *metaphor* dominates his vision of nature, for it is in the metaphor-making process that pleasure resides. "The whole thing is performance and prowess and feats of association," he says, as if to suggest that mental gymnastics is exactly that "performance" which may be most lovingly sustained, most tantalizingly obscured, most subtly deployed.[11]

In its most delicate construction the poem is a classical figure of love for Frost, Platonic in its articulation of an erotics deriving from the staunch and upright soul. It becomes, as in "The Silken Tent," a structure of unparalleled harmonic balance whereby the "She" that begins the poem is assimilated to become the body of the text:

> She is as in a field a silken tent
> At midday when a sunny summer breeze
> Has dried the dew and all its ropes relent,
> So that in guys it gently sways at ease,
> And its supporting central cedar pole,
> That is its pinnacle to heavenward
> And signifies the sureness of the soul,
> Seems to owe naught to any single cord,
> But strictly held by none, is loosely bound
> By countless silken ties of love and thought
> To everything on earth to compass round,
> And only by one's going slightly taut
> In the capriciousness of summer air
> Is of the slightest bondage made aware.

It is not the woman, not the tent, but the poetic voice talking this erotically inscribed analogy into being that is foregrounded—as Poirier says, "The elicited suspense waits upon how this voice, with a power of formulation at once flexible, scrupulous, and grand, will conduct itself through the rest of the poem."[12] The female aspect, the silken tissue, is supported interiorly and thus transformed to "tent" by the phallic "central cedar pole" that "signifies the sureness of the soul." As is proper to the classical view, the feminine is realized only through the masculine;[13] without the pole the "tent" would be "silk" or "cloth" but not serviceable as such—not available to be made into something else—in its state as "untent." Such an integral unification of desire and spiritual certitude, where the "female" silk is tethered gently by lines (of poetry and of rope) and at the same time exalted upward by the central pole, is seldom reiterated in Frost's poetry. The poem's extended conceit, a notably "masculine" device of linguistic and intellectual virtuosity, echoes formally the harmonious but clearly contrived tension between intellect, spirit, and flesh.[14] The single, extended, perfectly balanced sentence lasts and does not deflate, even as it embraces itself in interlocking rhymes, even as it proceeds so rhythmically to the delicious double entendre of its final lines, even as it urges the tongue to the rustling virtuosity of "capriciousness" while holding the taut couplet in check.

Yet it is not the tent, which is both yielding and, in its yielding, strong, but the house in stages of disintegration that is the prevailing edifice in Frost's poetry, and for the most part, like the houses that fall, the "soul" may not remain sufficiently upright to counterbalance the gravitational pull. Frost's speakers may yearn upward to heaven for spiritual and intellectual latitude or they may, as in "To Earthward," wish for an earthly love that pulls them down to sensual awareness, but they tend to represent the two directions as antithetical to each other so that spirit and flesh cannot be reconciled. As "Bond and Free" so clearly articulates, Love is in bondage to earth "to which she clings / With hills and circling arms about," while Thought "cleaves the interstellar gloom" toward heaven. The poetic "lines" that join soul to body are seldom so balanced as to remove the sense of bondage to earthly need; another such moment of desire as found in "The Silken Tent" manifests itself instead as "A Line-Storm Song," showing passion as lines of storms—poetic and atmospheric—that destroy equilibrium in a "rout" of wind and rain that bring the sea back to reflood the "ancient lands" long since dry. Such passion not merely silences the lyric birds, conventional singers of love, but obliterates them:

> The birds have less to say for themselves
>   In the wood-world's torn despair
> Than now these numberless years the elves,
>   Although they are no less there:
> All song of the woods is crushed like some
>   Wild, easily shattered rose.
> Come, be my love in the wet woods, come,
>   Where the boughs rain when it blows.

Compared with this orgasmic fantasy—"Come, be my love in the wet woods, come," "Come forth into the storm and rout"—"The Silken Tent" is an unprecedented moment that is not repeated again, and the ephemerality of its vision is reified in the silken tissue it hoists in place of the stolid boards and nails, the heavy doors, and the echoing stairwells erected in other poems to withstand the deluge. Here virility informs moderation, so that the

feminine is penetrated and in fact created by the masculine, making the
poem a rare moment of harmonic *aphrodisia* and of control.

Rare, because however pleasurable such a perpetually renewable source
of *aphrodisia* as is intrinsic to a dialectic of arousal may be, it is also frequently
problematic, as pleasure itself has come to be, through the endless process of
confession to which it has been subjected, almost inevitably productive of
guilt and anxiety.[15] Desire, guiltily perceived, opens a man to abandonment,
violation, and pain, and as Frost discovers and exposes, sees and tells about
it, sexuality is made to confess to its own pathological nature. It may be
projected into egressing women or made to reside in their often-noted
capacities for obsession, hysteria, and lying, so that women become, in effect,
conduits to carry off a form of sexual madness.[16] This leaves men to enact
their desires as husbandmen of the more available earth, but this too emerges
frequently in terms that make pleasure inseparable from and finally
dependent upon pain. The speaker of "The Bonfire," who leans in to rub out
the wildfire and rises, climactically, scorched and ecstatic (and speaks his
delight in a metrical pun as "walking light on air in heavy shoes") is a figure
in this dynamic. The speaker of "To Earthward" assumes the earth as lover,
and he documents the maturation of this love in terms of an increasing desire
for death, a movement from air to earth: "Love at the lips was touch / As
sweet as I could bear; / And once that seemed too much; / I lived on air," he
begins. The speaker recalls the flower- and musk-laden air that once could,
alone and unaided, tantalize and arouse him, crossing his flesh so that he felt
the "swirl and ache," the "sting" of love. This vertigo, these aches and stings,
were in the beginning "strong sweets" enough, but his appetites quickly
become more tangible: "Now no joy but lacks salt, / That is not dashed with
pain / And weariness and fault; / I crave the stain / Of tears, the aftermark /
Of almost too much love." ("One of the greatest changes my nature has
undergone is of record in To Earthward and indeed elsewhere for the
discerning," Frost says; *Letters* 482.)

Indeed, the words "love at the lips" which begin this poem suggest that
the act of speaking out this drama, of saying love outward from the lips
instead of breathing it in, becomes a necessary stimulus. And certainly the
poet must have his listeners: he must indulge in the voyeurism of knowing
that love from his lips, discovered in the "wild space," is bringing others to
pleasure. He must sense that to guarantee pleasure one must, as Barthes says
in *The Pleasure of the Text*, "seek out this reader ... *without knowing where he is.*
A site of bliss is then created. It is not the reader's 'person' that is necessary
... , it is this site: the possibility of a dialectic of desire, of an *unpredictability*
of bliss: the bets are not placed, there can still be a game."[17] Passion arising

from the autonomous self, crossing others autonomously and blurring all conventional heterosexual delimitations for the giving and receiving of erotic pleasure, it proceeds inevitably toward the bittersweet pleasures of masochism, from rose petal to the pungently penetrative "sweet of bitter bark / And burning clove." This figure of "To Earthward" has been so synesthetically alive to nature and to the language that describes his interaction with it that he has needed no human other to awaken desire. This vulnerability proves, as always, to be a problematic bliss, from the beginning described in terms of malaise and pain. The inevitable coital completion of his "love" in its late stages is a fantasy of death in which the speaker is prostrate on the ground: "the earth as rough / To all my length." This speaker who now craves "the stain / Of tears, the aftermark / Of almost too much love" epitomizes the figures throughout Frost's poetry who are informed by a desire that colors and shapes the landscape, for he has become a roué whose engagement with the world's body has been variable but so long-lived that joy must be salted with pain. Invoking a gravity so profound that it will join him to the earth, he is tempted by dissolution.

Telling about desire—"love at the lips"—is itself intrinsically problematic, for confession is imbued with a double sense of power and self-abasement: it is a discourse at once pleasurable and painful, and one becomes dependent on the other. No matter how much the confessing agent knows or has done, or how well he has done it, no matter how subtly or delicately the details are deployed, it is the listener who is felt to be invested with the power to judge and to condemn.[18] Thus Frost's more consistent speaking model of arousal is not a harmonious Platonism in which desire and its articulation rest in perfect balance, but a more volatile dynamic whereby power is always receding from the speaking voice to locate itself elsewhere: the most literal model by which this truth is illustrated is in the husband's final, impotent words in "Home Burial," spoken as his silent wife is about to leave the house yet again. But this paradoxical display—as desire is articulated it undermines itself—is reified consistently throughout Frost's poetry. One sees the pleading man of "The Subverted Flower" reduced in one elided movement to a bestial state of sheer physical dominance, able to "pounce to end it all," and to a position of nondominance, forced to all fours and off the field. At a more subtle level, one sees a persistent image pattern in which a speaker articulates himself in relationship to some vast, wordless power as a figure of impotence. "On Going Unnoticed," in which the speaker is attuned to the mean and pallid coral root clinging to the skirt of a regal and utterly indifferent tree, is a type: variously, speakers take on the forms of a prudent, priggishly self-justifying woodchuck, a flower beaten by the wind, a listless leaf whose ambitions to fly, driven by storm, it admits to be delusory. Speaking, figures are frequently made to confess to their own impotence, to call themselves "too absent-spirited to count" ("Desert Places"), to see themselves as windy-headed and concerned with turbulent "inner" weather ("Tree at My Window"), to announce themselves self-pityingly as "in my life alone" ("Bereft").

Yet it is not merely those lovelorn or depressed speakers succumbing to the confessional impulse who may be found to have subverted themselves through language, for by Frost's terms the power to undermine any speaking voice lies within the venereal force of language itself. True discourse *is* pleasure, like love, and as such it is always threatening barriers, urging one toward lapse, moving one toward promiscuity (*Prose* 39).[19] Thus the symbol of the lyric voice the bird, appears throughout Frost's poetry as at best a compromised figure who "knows in singing not to sing" ("The Oven Bird"). Made to subscribe to Frost's ambivalently declined "sound of sense," it is subsequently burdened, a virtual parody of the romantically conceived lyricist as it consistently represents itself or is represented as powerless, flightless, and lost. As these symbolic birds suggest, it is not ever, in Frost's poetry, within the speakers' scope to seize and hold on to power, which is lost either quite specifically by admission or is taken tacitly by the poet through the more subtle devices of irony. Even the most Apollonian-seeming voices within the poetry may be seen as afflicted. Always subject to ironic subversion, they tend also to betray themselves through their patterns of allusion and imagery. The subtexts frequently reveal darker and far more chthonic preoccupations than the unruffled surfaces would appear to hold, and it comes to seem that utterance for Frost inevitably manifests itself as some version of appetitive impulse. The naked madman upstairs raving about love things, the murdered lover's skeleton sashaying from cellar to attic: these are merely logical extensions of Frost's disabled speakers. Power and control must then reside in form, in sound shaped into prosodic compactness; the bodies within the poem are inevitably compromised while the body of the poem is solid, immune to the hysterias of failed love, tautly disposed in "living lines" so vascularly alive that "they bleed when you cut them" ("but if the body is firm and resistant, if internal space is dense, organized, and solidly heterogeneous in its different regions, the symptoms of hysteria are rare and its effects will remain simple").[20] Thus Frost may be said to come close to having it both ways—talking about pleasure, taking pleasure in the truth of pleasure, while holding himself apart prosodically from pleasure's perceived consequences of anarchy and dissolution.

Frost's is a world where consummation is always productive of conflict and profound ambivalence, however: this is a dynamic fully articulated in (the "war poem") "The Bonfire" by the man who is aroused to put out the deadly and beautiful fire that he himself has set. That the moment of ecstatic triumph comes when the wildfire is rubbed and beaten out—that it is a moment utterly ambiguous in its conflation of orgasm and controlled stoppage—suggests this ambivalence. Marked in the dramas between men and women by childlessness, infidelity, divorce, abandonment, and madness, marriage is that state of consummated "love" which is virtually guaranteed to reify the dissolution of certainties: in "The Thatch" the symbolic value of the abandoned marital house whose thatched roof deteriorates to let rain into the "upper chamber floors" can hardly be underestimated, as it suggests a correlative state of wounded disorientation in the man who has left it. In "Bereft" that "porch's sagging floor" upon which the abandoned speaker stands suggests an equivalent unmanning, for consummation leaves one's footing uncertain. Marked in the dramas between man and nature, there is often that tendency toward abasement one sees in "To Earthward," for if men penetrate the earth, plowing and sowing seeds, they are also brought low by it.

When enacted rather than transfixed as in "The Silken Tent," desire frequently, then, becomes reciprocal with death, contiguously oriented so that the dark and lovely woods simultaneously invite penetration and promise annihilation, equally caseful conditions. It is not fear of death in "Stopping by the Woods" that keeps the man from the woods, but the promises he has to keep. His duty as a man is to resist that generous invitation to nothingness, and yet appetite is felt to extend its seductive invitation even from the grave. Frost so frequently makes this death-desire consummation explicit, he so completely adheres to the synonymity of "husbanding" both women and soil, he so punctuates his landscapes with cellar holes, graves, and tunnel mouths, that he may be said, to paraphrase his own metaphor, to hurl the symbolic value ahead of him "to pave the future with against the day when we may want to strike a line of purpose across it for somewhere" (*Prose* 19). Enriched by love's exceedingly complex terms, Frost's poetry always conforms to his ambiguous disclaimer about "Stopping by the Woods": "It means enough without its being pressed."[21] Thus it is that the husband's plunging spade is said to be felt by the grieving mother of "Home Burial," who cannot herself penetrate the space into which her son has gone, as a brutal conflation of sexual and agricultural terms, the replanting of her husband's seed in the grave (and one who has read "Putting in the Seed" will see the macabre logic here).[22] One who resists the intellectual tyranny of this standard sexual metaphor will greet such a reading first with skepticism—is it this particular spade in this particular grave that is sexually declined or all such digging? But then one sees that the sexual resonance is clearly meant to be there, reinforced internally by, among other things, the explicit sexual frustration the husband articulates, and reinforced canonically again and again.[23]

One may discern the seeds of nihilism within a dynamic in which a problematic, always potentially pathological "love" is the figure a poem makes, for the expense one yearns for is that which is most felt to recapitulate uncertainty and hasten annihilation. If "love" and the poem are the same figure, they share equally in Frost's sense that one can *know* nothing; whether the vicissitudes of love may be said to reify Frost's epistemological skepticism or to cause it (and on this I would not venture to make a guess), love is a figure for Frost of a state of unknowing. One never knows when one will be left, one never knows the beloved loves, and, in that vein, one never knows oneself with absolute certainty as the father or, by upward extension, as the son. Knowing one's mother is to know the very personification of unreason; not knowing one's father, a man cannot, perhaps, know God. In any event, the very figure of love is uncertainty and as such it mimics or mirrors the nihilism implicit in Frost's system of unstable irony. "The Silken Tent," with its Platonic deployment of symbols in a carefully contrived conceit, is a model of love and of poetry impossible to sustain in Frost's restless world of movement and metamorphosis. As it "signifies the sureness of the soul," it is a unique (and artificial) construction in Frost's landscape: as Poirier points out, it brings signification very much to the fore, and this as much as anything else, in the context of Frost's pervasive, unstable ironies, makes it proclaim itself as a poetic tour de force, a declaration of "performance and prowess and feats of association."[24] It is a derivative fantasy predicated on a classical model, and it disguises by its use of the tensile rope and silken cloth the fact that it is so firmly and necessarily staked. It is a vision as static as the figures on Keats's Grecian urn; the tissue, pushed taut by the pole, will nonetheless remain always just before being rent, just as Keats's female remains a "still unravish'd bride." Loosed, the silk would fly away in the summer breeze and the central pole fall. And this more nearly approximates for Frost the consequences of "modern love," which as his references to Meredith's sonnet sequence would suggest, is a complex of pathological appetite, shame, and infidelity: "Love, love. Modern love is different than ancient love," he says with finality. "Anything else?"[25]

Frost's sense that a man must resist that which is irresistible—that the "discipline" he needs most is "to learn his own submission to unreason" ("A

Masque of Reason" l. 210)—rests on a knowledge that the terms by which he must live are mutually exclusive. "Modern love" is merely a (near-comic) "tragic" oxymoron that stands for this state of chronic ambivalence. Modernity, with its satyric bifurcation between soul and body, is better represented by Silenus the satyr than Phaedrus the philosophical lover, and, indeed, the allusion implicit in "The Demiurge's Laugh" articulates Silenus's sardonic nihilism: one who is vouchsafed true knowledge of what is best and most desirable for a man desires nothingness most of all, and the grave is yet another hole toward which one is drawn. As this speaker says, he has heard in the demon's laughter all he needed to hear:

> It was far in the sameness of the wood;
> I was running with joy on the Demon's trail,
> Though I knew what I hunted was no true god.
> It was just as the light was beginning to fail
> That I suddenly heard—all I needed to hear:
> It has lasted me many and many a year.

The Demon who rises from his "wallow" to laugh, brushing dirt from his eyes, is Frost's Silenus, whose act of wallowing in the earth is encoded with information about his wantonly appetitive nature and his association with death and whose refusal to articulate what in other incarnations he so clearly knows suggests that his own nihilism is above all importuning. In Nietzsche's telling of the myth, Silenus, sought out by King Midas for his wisdom, finally laughs and divulges this truth: "Oh, wretched ephemeral race, children of chance and misery, why do you compel me to tell you what it would be most expedient for you not to hear? What is best of all is utterly beyond your reach: not to be born, not to *be*, to be *nothing*. But the second best for you is—to die soon."[26] A man is virilely moderate, rationally controlled or he is nothing, and by the terms of the metaphorical construct to which Frost adheres he must fail these requirements. Aspiring to reason, he finds himself only surrounded by the invitations to unreason whose wildness resonates with his own—Silenus cannot be made to speak but only to laugh, and yet "I knew well what the Demon meant," the speaker says. And because for Frost there are no external systems of reason that similarly resonate, "Passions," as he says, "spin the plot."[27] "Disciplined submission to unreason," yet another of Frost's faux oxymorons whereby the terms are and remain mutually exclusive, suggests oppositional possibilities: the disciplined submission to unreason that is madness or the disciplined submission to unreason that is nihilism.[28] To believe that all ages are equally dark for the

soul is incipient nihilism, and to be bedazzled and misled by that darkness—
to see it as the light of truth—is to be mad. Frost, seeing the difference, puts
his madman to shout in a hickory cage while remaining himself quietly
apprised of Silenus's wisdom, by which death is the logical correlative to
nothingness and, equally so, its antidote.

The immediacy with which a man might capitulate to his own
uncontrol is mirrored by Frost's urgently metamorphic landscape, where a
dry pith becomes of an instant an explicitly seductive woman like Paul's
"wife." ("It slowly rose a person, rose a girl, / Her wet hair heavy on her like
a helmet, / Who, leaning on a log, looked back at Paul.") The predilection
to fall is inherent in every season, in every age, and in both the child and the
man, and the markers of that propensity to capitulation make themselves
inescapably manifest. This is a truth potently synthesized in the crotic image
of the maple/(mother/daughter) of "Maple," who is caught at the very instant
when death and desire are the same figure. "Standing alone with smooth
arms lifted up, / And every leaf of foliage she'd worn / Laid scarlet and pale
pink about her feet," "she"—the dead mother/unfaithful wife reinscribed in
scarlet at the moment of her fall—is at once seductive and cautionary.
"Nothing Gold Can Stay" epitomizes this minimalist, reductionist vision, as
it uses its terms—"gold," "leaf," "Eden"—with the economy of one who sees
mortality as a condition that does not accrue but that comes fully formed in
the very act of generation: "Nature's first green is gold, / Her hardest hue to
hold. / Her early leaf's a flower; / But only so an hour. / Then leaf subsides
to leaf. / So Eden sank to grief, / So dawn goes down to day. / Nothing gold
can stay."[29] When the poet says, "Nature's first green is gold," he could mean
the gold to be a golden flower or even golden pollen—the beginning—or
autumn leaves—the end. It is either way "the hardest hue to hold" in a cycle
whose downward revolution begins at inception. Even such immutable stuff
as gold is predestined to fail—to go green like baser metals—in an appetitive
nature where "leaf subsides to leaf" and golden dawn "goes down to day."
Nature's gold may appear in pre-birth or pre-seed as golden pollen, it may
appear as glorious flowers, or it may appear in miserly sterility in golden fall
leaves, but early or late it represents a moment of capitulation to the
generative instinct that turns flowers to leaves on their way to fall or dawn to
day on its way to night. Conflating humans and their seasonal correlatives,
he analogizes that "So Eden sank to grief" through the death embodied in
its generative nature. "Eden" is that place where nature and human nature
were made inextricably mortal in one appetitive moment. Such a genesis is
the beginning of the book, and it predicts the end, for as "leaf subsides to
leaf" the story is finished before it has begun.

Frost's reduction of the terms leading graveward leaves a gaping vacancy between birth and death, between health and sickness, between being and nothingness: with degenerative "gold" as equally and simultaneously both the pollen and the dead leaf, the middle is excluded, becoming a gravelike gap. The mother of "Home Burial" says angrily, "From the time one is sick to death / One is alone, and he dies more alone." This is a statement whose conviction and impact go far beyond the particulars of infant mortality and far beyond the autobiographical specificities of its source.[30] Born "sick," we are all then sick to death, or sick with death. In this equation, we are born utterly and irrevocably alone and stay that way: the illusion of love as commonalty resolves itself into just such morality plays as Frost transcribes. This is a vision that breeds either stoicism (the man's tack) or hysteria (the domestically confined woman's), and it may be felt to predict the hysterical stoicisms of non-Frostian absurdist characters who articulate quite clearly the nihilism that Frost disguises in homely realisms.[31] One thinks of Pozzo's furious assertions in "Waiting for Godot": "Have you not done tormenting me with your accursed time! It's abominable! ... One day he went dumb, one day I went blind, one day we'll go deaf, one day we were born, one day we shall die, the same day, the same second, is that not enough for you? ... They give birth astride of a grave, the light gleams an instant, then it's night once more."[32] The mother of "Home Burial"—one of the "them" to whom Pozzo refers—is viscerally apprised of her profound isolation and the well of nothingness over which she is suspended. Having given birth astride the grave, she feels a part of herself already interred. She communicates her isolation, however, in a voice that seems, almost literally by virtue of her sudden pronoun change, not her own. The impact of her sibylline pronouncement is to suggest that what she knows, Frost authorizes with equivalent conviction. The movement toward the grave begins at birth and the best one can do in this schema is to be a man about it. Nietzsche predicts as a consequence of the nihilistic sense of meaninglessness a commensurately strengthened faith in moral action.[33] For Frost, heautocratic integrity is the only means by which one might sustain even the illusion of order.

Frost's vision of birth is that it is under sentence of death, and his attitudes toward both maternity and children are infected with the dark sense that one is conceived by and into the very act of falling. If the creative generation of a poem may be stabilized by form, its parturience removes it from the poet's control and gives it its own unpredictable life; like the child, it will either grow (linguistically) beyond the bounds of even the strictest paternalistic order or, like the infant son of "Home Burial," will fail to fill that order. It is not just the anguished mother of "Home Burial" who feels such a parturition as she has endured almost as a form of amputation. In Frost's terms, for a man to expend himself into children is inevitably to lose them—and the part of himself they are—to the mother/earth/grave. They belong, by definition, to the maternal/female camp and become, thus, throughout the poetry markers of an intense ambivalence.[34] A child is proof of a man's sanctioned, domestic virility, yet both its presence, where "motherlove" threatens to supplant the husband for the child, and its absence compromise the model of virile moderation. By implication, it is only children who hold a woman to her domestic life and keep her even nominally to her marital/sexual responsibilities.[35] Without children to keep her home, Estelle of "The Housekeeper" runs away from her childish husband (ll. 170–5), as does the Hill Wife. Her child dead, the woman of "Home Burial" cannot resist the door to the outside while she rejects the door into the bedroom.

Yet for all of his poems about domestic life, Frost seldom envisions children except as flawed products of sin or sadness. Just as his marital relationships are so frequently ambiguous, so too is paternity, where the tenuous nature of the claims a father may make to his sons is reinforced by the theme of cuckolding (this is a potent reification of that "anxiety of influence" which complicates the genealogy of the poem). In at least two of the infrequent poems in which there are children within a marriage, the implication of the wife's infidelity is quite clear—as Frost points out in "New Hampshire," the "dawn people" who furnished Adam's sons with wives were not given to "behaving Puritanly." (Job says, in "A Masque of Reason," "Oh, Lord, let's not go *back* to anything." God answers, snappishly, "Because your wife's past won't bear looking into? –" [ll. 115–16].) In "How Hard It Is to Keep from Being King" King Darius is told that his real father was the cook, a fact the Frostian speaker knows unequivocally by virtue of his command of "quintessences," among them the quintessences of horses, men, and women. While this triad shares traditionally the capacity for lust, presumably it is the quintessence of a woman to be unfaithful and duplicitous: certainly it is the quintessence of romance, for "all romantic comes from the three-cornered love affair.... You had Mars, see, Mars, Aphrodite and Hephaestus. That's a three-cornered love affair, and that comes clear down into all the romantic times of later. Two and one.... "[36] Thus, for Frost the same living artifact— the child—that may stand as proof of a man's (sanctioned) virility always stands simultaneously as potential evidence of his emasculation, just as does the poem stand to testify to a man's dubious status as "poet." Children, hard to come by and hard to keep in Frost's world, are thus thoroughly implicated in the fall.

Not there, children are divisive elements. There, or having been there, they are divisive elements. The son in "The Witch of Coös," for example, may be felt to have caused the death of a man who might have been his father. He is himself quietly mad, and it is unclear whether this visitation of the sins of the father comes from his mother's husband or from her lover, both "fathers" having shown their own corruptive natures through enacted desire with the wanton witch. Though the witch-mother has herself spawned only part of his dementia, she has nurtured and approved it over the years. Ultimately the source of the son's compromised rationality does not matter, for in Frost's poetry almost all male–female bonds are problematic, so that bitterness or lovelessness within wedlock might taint as surely as unlicensed passion. Suggestions of this problematic dynamic infiltrate the poetry at every level, from the most explicit to the most subtle, from the comically rendered story of the son who sells his father into slavery in "How Hard It Is to Keep from Being King," to the allusion to Ahaz, who made a burnt offering of his son, in "New Hampshire."[37] Children may not be born innocent into Frost's fallen world but only unknowing, and they become, thus, vessels in which inevitable corruption may be measured. As Job says in "A Masque of Reason," in all the not-knowing humans must endure—not knowing what we are or who we are, not knowing one another, not knowing God, not even knowing what time it is relative to some illusion of apocalypse or salvation—"It comes down to a doubt about the wisdom / Of having children—after having had them, / So there is nothing we can do about it / But warn the children they perhaps should have none" (ll. 285–94).

Children, most particularly sons, must if possible be reclaimed and salvaged from female/maternal influence. This results in a mild sadism which insists that children lose whatever false sense of (maternally derived) security they may possess. There are moments within the poetry in which children are disabused of their naïveté by paternal figures who speak under the guise of tutelage: "Locked Out; As Told to a Child" and "The Bonfire" each suggest a level at which children are asked by a paternal voice to accommodate a fearful adult vision of violence—intruders who come at dark to try the lock, planes that come at night to rain down fire. Superficially offered in the venerable (always somewhat sadistic) tradition of ghost stories and fairy tales that are simultaneously fascinating and terrifying, the stories that emerge go far toward stimulating a genuinely nightmarish vision, as if to imply that one cannot know too soon about the dark elements within which one lives. The son in "The Witch of Coös" has been taught by his mother to perceive the story of her adultery and the resulting murder of the lover as if it were a ballad, like "The Wild Colonial Boy" her lover used to sing. The apparent causative agent in the murder, he has been encouraged by his mother to tell the story as if it were about strangers—to distance himself from any sense of responsibility, outrage, or fear through the mediating form of narrative.[38] It is significant, then, that only the adult male presence brings the witch momentarily to accountability, so that she instructs her son to "tell the truth for once." Otherwise, he has been allowed to accommodate his mother's appetitive duplicities and his own inheritance in the horror.

Once born into Frost's world, male children bear a great burden about which they must be made aware, and they must be wrested from the protective, enveloping mother so that they may be fully apprised. As if earthly fathers enact their paternal duties by model, Frost envisions God the father inflicting a fearful lesson upon Job in "A Masque of Reason," as he fails to explain, except in terms of a caprice and pridefulness that made Job a pawn in his game with the devil, Job's suffering. And in "A Masque of Mercy" he postulates a retributive God, withholding all certainty, whose "justice" seems so severe and cruel as to amount to injustice. Yet the Father/father enacts a necessary cruelty by Frost's terms, for while the knowledge of impenetrable uncertainty is harsh, it enforces a resolute self-containment. ("You don't have to deserve your mother's love. You have to deserve your father's. He's more particular.")[39] By bringing one to understand that maternal solicitude, mercifully encompassing, is also subversive of that intact manhood which holds itself against all assaults, the father brings the son to self-sufficiency. It is not, then, just the parents of the wounded son in "Out, Out –" who refuse to distinguish between the boy who is a "big boy / Doing a man's work, though a child at heart," and the man, for Frost too sees the urgency of pulling a son into manhood.

The implicit dichotomy Frost establishes between those males who are designated "sons" and those represented as "men" suggests that it is the empowered mother who thwarts manhood with her hysteria, mysticism, and superstition, and with her hunger for men, beginning with her sons. One who remains a "son" becomes prey for all women. "The Housekeeper" is significantly named in the context of Frost's Bachelardian spaces, for the "man's" house is dominated by his lover and, more literally, by her immobilized mother, who is either literally too fat to get through the door or so in possession of the space that she may not be moved (ll. 35–8). He is felt by both of them to be ineffectual in all ways: Estelle "has always held the purse" in the family and her "husband" has not been able to distract her by giving her a child. The "purse" she has held apart is both the generative and the economic one, neither of which the emasculated man has been able to appropriate. The currently resident mother speculates on this fifty-five-year-old's impotence: "He's like a child. / I blame his being brought up by his mother" (ll. 55–6). This pair divests the male of his house, and though he is preoccupied, understandably, with the prize roosters in his chicken yard, he is otherwise incompetent as a husbandman to his land as well, throwing his hoe into the apple tree (instead of penetrating the earth) and leaving the hay in the rain to rot. The middle-aged son of "The Witch of Coös" epitomizes in his impairment the witchery of the mother who would, alternatively, keep her boy locked away and safe; with no access to the outside, he becomes, in effect, inwombed by her. A "son" may then be of any age, from the infant of "Home Burial" to the aging, childlike hired man of "The Death of the Hired Man," who represents for the childless Mary and Warren their prodigal son "come home." Pollen or autumn leaf, they are kept from manhood by a maternal force whose conservational impulse is potent and ultimately degenerative.

In both "Home Burial" and "The Death of the Hired Man," the maternal solicitude that would hold and protect is enacted against the wishes of the adult male figure, who is ready to evict the "son" and move on to other things.[40] Despite Mary's injunction to "Be kind," Warren calls Silas to account for his irresponsibility as regards work. He sees Silas as having chosen a relatively dissolute life, for if Silas has, admirably, rejected the corrupt values implicit in his brother's bank-director status, he has not consistently embraced any more reputable means by which a man may create order. Warren's concerns are economical and his attitude is juridical, and it is only when he is brought to remember that Silas could impose a small but perfect order in building a load of (usable, marketable) hay that he begins to be deterred from anger. He thinks legalistically, in terms of imperatives whose violation would result in some punishment: "Home is the place where, when you go there, / They have to take you in." Mary, whose heart "hurts" for Silas, sees home oppositely as "Something you somehow haven't to deserve."[41]

Such yielding as Mary would awaken in her husband is nonetheless a form of unmanning, almost a kind of bewitchment, as if she would bring Warren to be as ineffectual in worldly terms as the "son" Silas whose case she pleads. She is so tied to nature that she is felt to play "the harplike morning-glory strings, ... / As if she played unheard some tenderness / That wrought on him beside her in the night," and she is felt to hold moonlight in her apron as naturally as a woman might sit with a lap full of apples to peel (or as naturally as the mountain of "The Birthplace" sits, "her lap ... full of trees"). In Frost's landscape of named witches, Coös and Grafton the most notable, she seems to embody a relatively benign form of power, and she occupies a territory neither so pathologically scaled as the Witch of Coös nor so wild as the Witch of Grafton. Her position on the porch suggests a contained, somewhat domesticated form of power, yet she is so much a part of the earth and the night that she brings her husband out the door and shuts it, taking from his arms and setting aside the tokens of socialized domesticity, the "market things" with which he is so concerned. Mysterious, knowing, she is not merely a watcher but one of the elements—"Then there were three there, making a dim row, / The moon, the little silver cloud, and she"—and it is as if she *knows* and is thus potentially implicated in the spell by which the collision of moon with cloud will signal (cause) Silas's death. "The Death of the Hired Man" represents one of the most sustained visions of an apparently noncombative male–female relationship to be found anywhere in Frost's work, and yet implicit in Mary's great power to move Warren toward empathy is an equivalent power to remove him from control. Paradoxically, this poem reveals by its unusual status as a representative of marital harmony the dangers even a "good," domesticated female represents, as she threatens to co-opt rational judgment with emotion.

The maternal impulse that envelops and protects is a dangerously potent distraction from the businesses by which a man subdues female uncontrol, and thus maternity may be seen in quite literally monumental terms. It threatens males with lethargy and even death as it keeps them from autonomy—and therefore from manhood—by encouraging an empathetic openness. "The Birthplace," whose title suggests the earthy femaleness from which twelve children spring, defines the good father's duties on the maternal mountainside: "My father built, enclosed a spring, / Strung chains of wall round everything, / Subdued the growth of earth to grass, / And brought our various lives to pass." The human mother is simply absent from the poem, so that the dozen children seem raised up from the cultivated ground. The mountain is subdued temporarily by the virile man to benignity, but there is "always something in her smile" that suggests a power as sinister as it is safe. This father, who brings the mountain under his control, raises the children to freedom from the mother. The mountain, against whom only the most constant vigilance can enforce and maintain order, pushes these father-oriented children from her knees, "And now her lap is full of trees," the signifiers throughout Frost's poetry of a regal, dangerous power. If allowed, the mother, both desired and terrifying, will keep a boy from becoming a man. Girls and women, ever changeable, may metamorphose into mothers themselves, moving thus toward empowerment. They may, as

"The Birthplace" asserts, change their names, which is to say that they may take husbands for the purpose of being transformed into mothers. But a man may not proceed so deviously against the mother and must instead enforce, as does the father of "The Birthplace," his own powers of control, even unto violence. "I'll follow and bring you back by force. I *will!* –" is a mostly futile battle cry sung by more than just the frenzied husband of "Home Burial."

The mountain/mother of "The Birthplace" holds trees; in "Maple" the dying mother marks her daughter with the name and the nature of "Maple." "She put her finger in your check so hard / It must have made your dimple there, and said / 'Maple,'" the father says. She appropriates the girl to herself by naming aloud that wild, natural part of her daughter which defies paternal control: "Name children some names and see what you do," says the speaker, as if in warning to those who see the girl or her mother as contained and harmless. So apparently genteel, this poem functions, as do many of Frost's stories, at two oppositionally significant levels. Paternal power is illusory, while maternal power evades even patristic authority and seeks assertion. While the father, left alive, has nominal control over his daughter, he has continued to live in the mother's birthplace, and to sleep in his wife's (childhood) bedroom, the place where she has given birth and where she has died. He is possessed of some knowledge of the mother that he withholds, and he unwittingly "sows" in his daughter the desire to know the secret by failing to yield to her that knowledge. These intimations are "Dangerous self-arousing words to sow" in the girl, who begins to repudiate the father in her search for the meaning of her name: like the men who sow fields against the inevitably encroaching forests, this father's husbanding is insufficient to keep either his wife or his daughter from the woods. The subtextual implications, like the house with its two buried stories, are indeed dangerously self-arousing, for by the most oblique of all possible suggestions the mother may have been guilty of marital infidelity in the deep woods. Her secret "may have been / Something a father couldn't tell a daughter / As well as a mother could" (ll. 118–20).[42] The only clue is a maple leaf left inside a Bible, by whom it is not clear.

But the biblical inscription is lost when Maple closes the book without its maple-leaf marker, and only the words "Wave offering" come back much later to her mind. In Exodus, Leviticus, and Numbers there are at least nine mentions of "wave offerings," in which sacrificial offerings are waved in the air, and at its most general and benign level the allusion suggests the waving boughs of the maple tree, a figure of the "good," sanctified maple the father wishfully envisions. But the most extended reference in Numbers 5:12–31 is to a story far darker, as it details the "jealousy offering" made when a woman was thought to have been unfaithful to her husband. Made by priests to drink bitter water, which will cause the impure woman's thigh to rot and her abdomen to swell in a grotesque parody of pregnancy, the accused must prove her purity. After drinking, she is divested by the priest of the poisonous "jealousy offering," which he then waves before the Lord. This gruesome story cannot but be associated with the woman who has died just after childbirth, naming her daughter by the one name that most defies the priestly rebuke. "Maple" consigns the girl to the woods where the queenly maple stands, completely naked, arms raised, surrounded by pink and scarlet fallen foliage. The subtext, then, inescapably suggests a standard scenario, whereby the woman has escaped the bounds of civilization by entering the forest and has copulated with a man or with the devil (this is the empowerment of the witch, countered by a poison contrived by patristic authority). Against this name, "Maple," and against these horrific images is the father's feeble injunction, made despite all evidence, that the name is "some word she left to bid you / Be a good girl—be like a maple tree." Mothers, wives, or daughters—women will rise to stand seductive in the forest, generative, metamorphic, and duplicitous, emblems of desire and death.

The work of manhood is, then, to urge control on the uncontrollable, to impose upon its own "femaleness"—that which embodied in women seems so randomly destructive—moderation and orderliness; "For Once, Then, Something" may in this context be seen to embody Frost's powerful anxiety at the same time that it works to master and overman the fear of the mother by staring obliquely into the keep and narrow watery place that is the source of myths, dreams, and wishes. Here the question of where self stands relative to the "others" is predicated on a prior and submerged interrogation about where it stands relative to femaleness and maternity. In the context of Frost's mother-earth cathexis, a preoccupation that suggests a wishful memory of infantile barrierlessness, his mirror gazing is more than ordinarily problematized. The "mirror stage" marks the moment at which the distinction between self and outside is begun. Narcissism is, as Kristeva calls it, "a screen for emptiness"; it "protects emptiness, causes it to exist, and thus, as lining of that emptiness, insures an elementary separation."[43] It is that crucial moment in which barriers assert themselves, and "without that solidarity between emptiness and narcissism, chaos would sweep away any possibility of distinction, trace, and symbolization, which would in turn confuse the limits of the body, words, the real, and the symbolic."[44] The speaker, defensive and ambivalent about his position on the reflective side of the pool and looking, despite his chosen mirror view, to see beneath the surface as well as above it in the Apollonian heights, is, then, poised precariously between egotism and revelatory insight. He resides in a dangerous medium, for he is triangulated as Narcissus between sky/Apollo/rationality and Telphusa/Pythoness/revelatory "truth." If unable to accept either the narcissistic mirror that discovers and defines emptiness in preparation for the realization of self or the empathetic and temporary barrierlessness of mature insight, he might be left in infantile chaos. To "confuse the limits of the body, words, the real, and the symbolic" is to exist in a true wild space, pre-gendered and unborn, unable to tell the outside from the inside. A failure at this mirror is rife with consequence, for to be left thus is to be incapable of *knowing* form and thus impotent to achieve it.

The speaker defends his right to turn his back to a more demanding, variable nature even as Frost counters his rhetorical stance metaleptically in the Narcissus allusion and figurally in the shallow–deep image of the well.[45] Here the "others" are those who look out too far or in too deep; by implication only this Frostian speaker, witty and articulate, can confer value on a given perspective, which others will miscomprehend. He kneels at the well curb with the light behind him so that he can see reflected "Me myself in the summer heaven, godlike." By conscious choice he is not one who would plumb the depths, looking beyond self for deeper meanings, revealed truths; he would say, with Job in "A Masque of Reason," "Get down into things, / It will be found there's no more given there / Than on the surface." Even so, one time he saw through his reflection to "a something white" underneath, an unsought-for revelation that briefly troubled his narcissistic preoccupation. Like the whiteness of the whale, the whiteness of the thing is enigmatic, illusive, laden with symbolic possibility. But the vision is clouded almost at once by a droplet of dew from above. Water is perceived by the speaker to "rebuke" water, as if neither the narcissistic reflection nor the glimmer of white is a suitable view. The speaker's voice remains more unruffled than the well's surface—he has, after all, been talking hendacasyllabically about himself when "truth" breaks in and then subsides—and his detached tone, which allows the escape route of an ironic reading even as it suggests the validity of his manly egocentricity, commits him emotionally in no way. But beneath his self-congratulatory tone lie deeper anxieties and desires. Even the title, echoed in the last line, predicts an ambivalence that the poem denies tonally, the "for once, then, something" suggesting a more than once rebuked desire to shatter the mirror he professes to erect, and the figure of the well suggests a claustrophobic fantasy of diving, falling, or being thrown deep into a narrow shaft. His well gazing is evocative of childhood fears of falling down a well, and it touches adult fears of finding at the bottom a real body spread like a hapless skydiver and glimmering white, rather than an Apollonian reflection. A well is the source of wishes and of prophetic voices; one must, in this fantasy, be very careful indeed of one's desires.

Even as he sees himself consciously as godlike in the summer sky then, as an empowered Apollonian figure who repudiates the "boy" with his status as a good Greek, transcendent over narcissism and immune (hostile?) to the pull of the mother, he reveals an alternative self. The hendecasyllabic form, the elegantly melodic lines reinforce this association with the musical Apollo, as do the carefully wrought repetitions of words like "curb," "water," and "picture," which give the unrhymed form structural rigor. This Apollo allusion is strengthened by the speaker's ambivalence about penetrating the depths of the pool, for even the most generalized vision of Apollo associates him with sky and air rather than earth and water, elements he rejects almost immediately along with his infantile identity with his mother. Slater analyzes the complex functions of Apollo, showing him to be antithetical to earth and femininity:[46] "He is the personification of anti-matriarchy, the epitome of the sky god, a crusader against Earth deities. He is all sunlight, Olympain, manifest, rational. He opposes all that is hidden, dark, and irrational. Or so, at least, the poets would have us believe."[47] To complicate the Apollonian allusion in this well-centered landscape, Apollo's relationship to water remains complex: to establish the oracle at Delphi, Apollo kills the Python, a giant (female) excrudescence raised from the mud of the flood, as it lies by a clear spring. He even slaughters Telphusa, the spring nymph who lives within the water. Apollo epitomizes apparent autonomy from women and from the earth, but as Slater points out, he must continually win his freedom from the pull of the mother. The Nietzschean dichotomy between the Apollonian and the Dionysian would suggest that this speaker's rational comprehension of the pool is antithetical to the Cybelean/Bacchic apprehension of the geode in "All Revelation."[48] One is urged here to believe in the hendecasyllabic, Apollonian authority of this speaker, who professes his preference for the light over the dark, the sky over the earth, the father over the mother: to believe, in fact, that his is Apollonian poetic "enthusiasm" "taken through the prism of the intellect" (*Prose* 36). One must not forget, however, how elsewhere in the poetry mothers are so crucial, so seductive and fearful: they are pythonesses all.

Yet despite his sense that femaleness and maternity and, by extension, the entire domestic realm are subversive of manliness, Frost suspects that the concept of socially sanctioned growth, of *Bildung*, is equally obviated for an enclosed system wherein a man must enforce his autonomy against

deteriorative conditions. For although the concept of *Bildung* is predicated
on a separation from the mother, it thrusts one into a world that may pretend
to more rational sense but that is equally violative. This sense of an abrasive
externality that eradicates markers of individuality may be felt to reify itself
in the divestment of body parts and the implications of bodily violence that
occur throughout Frost's poetry, as if to suggest that one does not so much
grow by virtue of one's contact with the world's constructions as diminish.[49]
One who eats finds himself eaten. One must "build soil": "Turn the farm in
upon itself / Until it can contain itself no more, / But sweating-full, drips
wine and oil a little" (ll.234–6). He must use his thoughts as fertilizer and
keep his produce to himself: "The thought I have, and my first impulse / Is
to take to market—I will turn it under. / The thought from that thought—I
will turn it under. / And so on to the limit of my nature. / We are too much
out, and if we won't draw in / We shall be driven in" (ll. 239–44).[50] There is
some evidence, in fact, that Frost sees himself sacrificially, as one whose
intrinsic worth not only supersedes the world's constructions but invites
attack from without. He is part Jonah, privy to an alternative vision that is
imagined to be self-endangering, although the modern world might
substitute for his being eaten his being locked away: "the whale you throw
me to / Will be some soulless lunatic asylum," he says to the currently
obdurate crowd ("A Masque of Mercy" ll. 186–7). He is part uncrowned but
inherently regal king, who despite his knowledge of all the "quintessences,"
offers himself up to be sold by his son as a slave ("How Hard It Is to Keep
from Being King" ll. 30–44). He is part Job, lacerated and abused for no
discernible reason, God's "Patient" who remains patient even while made an
experimental subject, to be afflicted with boils until his skin rots ("A Masque
of Reason" ll. 34, 130).[51] He reads in the marked pebble of "A Missive
Missile" two drops of blood and a sacrificial knife: "the sender must have had
to die" ("a meaning ... / I fear entirely mine," he adds).

As "The Lesson for Today" makes clear, Frost specifically mocks those
who pretend to know this "outside" world and who use as an excuse for their
emasculated state the social, artistic, and political "truths" of their age.[52] The
"liberal" speaker, who both is and is not Frost in his opinions, invents a
dialogue with a medieval poet in which he scorns those who claim global and
temporal perspective. One large enough to see epochal truths must "get
outside," a direction antipathetic to the revelatory geodesic interiors of a
poem like "All Revelation." Once outside, "Our muscles never could again
contract: / We never could recover human shape, / But must live out our lives
mentally agape / Or die of philosophical distention." Being "mentally agape"
is a clear perversion of the intact self, an invitation to violation, a dissolution

of the virile tension between appetite and self-control. It also suggests, in the pun on *agape*, the "openmindedness" of liberal, collectivistic love that is nonexclusionary and undisciplined; *agape* becomes another kind of promiscuity.[53] In the context of Frost's conviction that poetry and (erotic) love are the same figure, this pun seems particularly significant: it suggests that the bodily tensions which are reified in poetic form necessitate something beyond *agape*, and that the eroticism of such poetic language may escape the diseases of modernism. If modern love is different from ancient love, so are moderns, he says here, "sick with space," an assertion that reiterates the image of lax formlessness in the above lines.[54] The external correlative for the distended, flaccid "open" mind, space is an infinite void that simultaneously belittles and aggrandizes humankind. The world of metaphysically defined "universals" mirrors this formlessness: Philosophers, "No matter where they stoutly mean to get, / Nor what particulars they reason from, / ... end up in the universal Whole / As unoriginal as any rabbit."[55] To "end up in the universal Whole" is to have fallen into the void, down into Alice's rabbit hole where the "truths" are hallucinatory and "wisdom" is fractured by being institutionalized ("Some violence is always done to the wisdom you build a philosophy out of").[56] Philosophers, poets, the "state" are all rendered to ludicrous sameness when they leave themselves agape to universal truths. They become, not intact, enclosed individuals embraced by natural correlatives of themselves, but, like programmed ants, departmental. Having become part of the whole, they may only proceed programmatically.

Reliance on the external systems by which *Bildung* is traditionally effected is counterproductive, urging one toward formlessness, but philosophical, social, and political despair is prideful folly: "It is immodest of a man to think of himself as going down before the worst forces ever mobilized by God" (*Prose* 105). To induce that despair willingly is to invite intellectual and artistic impotence, "a dilation from which the tissues and the muscles of the mind have never been able to recover natural shape" (*Prose* 106)—but it is also to invite sexual dysfunction. Those so afflicted lose the hands of the lover/artist—"they can't pick up anything delicate or small any more"—and they lose phallic control: "They can't use a pen. They have to use a typewriter. And they gape in agony" (*Prose* 106). Their work becomes uncontrollably ejaculatory, so that they can write only "huge shapeless novels, huge gobs of raw sincerity bellowing with pain" (*Prose* 106). Frost's argument in this paragraph of his letter to *The Amherst Student* reveals again the Scylla and Charybdis of control and release through which he navigates: "Indeed it is as dangerous to try to get outside of anything as large as an age

as it would be to try to engorge a donkey," he says. By implication, the body
that is too self-contained would write, not vast shapeless things, but nothing;
an ass filled to the point of explosion, foundered by its own appetite, the
engorged creature is the monstrous corollary of the "huge gob of raw
sincerity bellowing with pain." Frost's "Lesson," preached first in his letter
to *The Amherst Student* and reiterated later in "The Masque of Reason," is
that one must feel desire in order to contain it and that systematics of any
kind is a cold bedfellow. "Earth's a hard place to save the soul" because, the
"place for love," it is so filled with sensual temptations. As "Fragmentary
Blue" reminds us, even heavenly shards transform as they fall earthward to
become sapphires, bluebirds, butterflies, flowers, and alluringly wide blue
eyes to tempt one from spiritual contemplation. Yet as Frost perpetually
reiterates at every level of his poetics, it is *only* in the struggle for manhood—
called saving "soul," "decency," "integrity"—that there is any meaning;
without "a trial ground where he can try himself / And find out whether he
is any good, / It would be meaningless" ("Masque of Reason" ll. 319–21). If
earth were heaven, one might as well be dead.

Community, with its necessary imposition of public values, threatens to
subvert personal autonomy, and in Frost's vision its systems are transitory
enthusiasms that may well devalue or distort the heautocratic balance: the
will must be left to make its own order. As Poirier points out, Frost places
himself squarely within the American tradition with his sense that
conformity within any system is debilitating, yet his nearphobic distaste for
systems beyond the circulatory exceeds even the most potent American
individualism.[57] He would not favor political revolution, not so much out of
resistance to (political) disorder, but because he sees as its inevitable outcome
a reinstatement of the status quo: as "A Semi-Revolution" says, "The trouble
with a total revolution / ... Is that it brings the same class up on top." He
would "go halfway and stop," tearing up the old order without imposing a
"new" order; a semi-revolution, as it remains perpetually unfinished,
necessarily leaves things in flux. "I'm very much in favor of unfinished
business," he says.[58] This is a vision that recapitulates the instincts among
individual Frostian figures to seek a deconstructing place that makes manifest
their own restless, appetitive changes, and it clearly says as much about
Frost's artistic as about his political leanings. It suggests yet once again the
dangers in that which is stayed or, as "Taking Something Like a Star" puts it,
"staid." Frost is hardly endorsing political anarchy (although this might well
be one of the poems that led *The Masses* to praise Frost's proletariat
sympathies), yet he cannot resist a shot at the systems that keep things and
people in their places.[59] This attitude also explains to some extent his

occasional unashamed endorsements of war and warlike behavior, as a declaration of war "bring[s] to life this old volcano" by being temporarily purgative of static systems ("The Bonfire"). It is the declarative act and not the outcome, of course, that holds potential; war is more valuable metaphorically than politically, as "The Bonfire" suggests in its conflation of world war with the speaker's flagrant and defiant secession from neighborly decorum, for warfare enforces a state in which wildness might prevail over artificial order. Warfare makes a world where the "wild places" infringe upon or take over the systematically ordered edifices of social, political, and religious organizations, and poetry then can play with impunity in the wild space.

One of Frost's rare urban poems, "A Hundred Collars," comically details a Frostian figure (a famous man alienated from his old friends by their awe) who must reluctantly share a hotel room with a stranger: this poem, like "The Lesson for Today" and "The White-Tailed Hornet," works at two distinct levels, one that belittles external systematics and another that questions the poet's own cultural position as a man removed from "democratic" contexts by his intellectuality, his poetic prowess, and his fame. This Ishmael gets only so savage a roommate as a talkative, maternally inclined, sociable traveler: "You can't rest that way. Let me pull your shoes off," he says in a parodically democratized inversion of Queequeg's hiding under the bed to put on his boots. Comically rendered, untattooed but naked above the waist and "creased and shining in the light," the strange bedfellow is nonetheless an equivalent to the civil and charitable "barbarian" who does not recognize the sanctity of the human head: he wants to mail his new friend, the resolutely distant scholar, his hundred outgrown collars, a prospect that offends the decorum of the intellectual beyond all imagining. Frost/Ishmael is also lampooned: "Though a great scholar, he's a democrat, / If not at heart, at least on principle." This figure, it is implied, enhances by his role as a "great scholar" the ways of isolation to which he is prone. He is democratic only in principle, while his heart is tuned autonomously.[60] His roommate, on the other hand, is a genuine, "double-dyed" Democrat, tattooed after all. The typically humorous balance that Frost strikes in "A Hundred Collars" distances one from both men, although the implications are clearly autobiographical as regards the teacher; we become the innkeeper who can say goodnight and go, leaving the (deserving) scholar (who serves as a disguise for the poet) to his own private hell. The tone also makes one dismiss as a primarily ironic and comical device the clear allusive exploitation of *Moby-Dick*. Yet only one judgment is available as to the wearing of another man's collars. Frost would not sanction the democratic switching of heads—

the insight into another's life through the intimacy of the communal collar. If Ishmael were to trade his head for one of Queequeg's, he would end up with a shrunken physiognomy. So too, Frost implies, would any trade he could make shortchange him. The "collar" is explicitly suggestive here of political and social affiliations, as it places the teacher against the salesman and the false democrat against the true, and it is implicitly suggestive of the religious collar as well. Yet this scholar/teacher/(poet) who is and is not Frost is very much an Ishmael at heart, resistant to all methodologies and systems: "And he will be a wild man; his hand will be against every man, and every man's hand against him; and he shall dwell in the presence of all his brethren."[61]

Frost does not subsidize the concept of *Bildung* in his poetry because its assumption of the intrinsic worth of a mediated progress through time and space, of a journey whose value lies in its reciprocity, becomes ludicrous in the face of such vast unknowing as he perceives humankind to endure. For Frost, one's "maturity" lies more in the rejection (or ironic exploitation) of intellectual, spiritual, or political systems and their illusory comforts than in any gradual accommodation to these constructs; as "Bocotian" so succinctly puts it, wisdom must be sought from a position outside systematics: "I love to toy with the Platonic notion / That wisdom need not be of Athens Attic, / But well may be Laconic, even Bocotian. / At least I will not have it systematic." Iconoclastic, the real man will "toy with" notions, even those arising from what is considered a proverbial stupidity, claiming for himself a kind of Nictzschean freedom from any conventional ideology. The Frostian-sounding father and son of "How Hard It Is to Keep from Being King" detail what "freedom" means, and its first premise is that "The only certain freedom is in departure" from any leader's truth, that of Marx or Christ, it makes no difference (I. 194). The most essential freedom, as Frost says here and elsewhere, is the freedom of one's material: the freedom to make intuitive connections that transcend all conventions, all contexts, and all creeds. This is the freedom most circumscribed by adherence to external systems of order, which inevitably short-circuit the simile-making process by suggesting that words are most valuable within the predisposed meanings of their contexts. And the making of a simile—that unexpected coupling of words to produce some brand new thing—is an empowerment that brings one alive. Filled with the energy to generate order out of nothing, to create "the form of forms / The serpent's tail stuck down the serpent's throat," the poet may look to his own tongue for pleasure (ll. 251–3, 339–40).

If the mother co-opts one into a barrierless, empathetic chaos of contradictions, then, encouraging one simultaneously, as mothers always do, to eat everything up and have some more and to remember the starving children elsewhere, the world of more theoretical orders is also co-optive, as it suggests that one might rely on some external system for one's assumptions. What it means to be a "man" is an acceptance of an utter separateness from systems whether emotionally or rationally based. The intact manly dialogue in which desire may be called upon to play its part, arousing the poet to the rigor of his pen, becomes the only available order and the primary source of pleasure. There is no continuity outside the masculine self for Frost, in a world where everything else is constantly metamorphosing, croding, disappearing, with metaphysical "truth" as much as anything else a variable phenomenon. Sexuality per se is merely another system breaking down, and as it is deployed in the recognizable figures of a domestic landscape it takes on a predictable pathology. Frost may even be said to have appropriated without much apparent skepticism or irony a metaphorical construct so ingrained in Western languages and thought as to have become a self-generating "truth," ironically the only one to which he clearly accedes. In this schema, one needs only "mother earth" with all the term implies about female fecundity, beauty, violence, and caprice, and from this comes quite naturally the figure of "To Earthward," talking of the earth as lover. Yet as Frost explores the nuances of the sexual metaphor, focusing on it his full powers of performance, it begins to generate a new dialectic, a stimulating pathology of pleasure against which prosodic bars must be erected and maintained. ("Two things I think about in connection with [(pagan) puritanism]: one is—it is that in you that fears your own pleasure, that distrusts your own pleasure.... I can remember my mother had a way of talking about it when things were going too well, you know—that you were too happy.... You better throw something away that you value and that you better be careful.") [62] The terms—"mother" and "earth"—and all the terms they generate (from "mother" comes father, daughter, son, wife, husband, God; from "earth" comes all the dark chthonic myths against which the Apollonian urge for beautiful form asserts itself) are declined through a poetics of self that first awakens in some Frostian territory outside the boundaries of cultivated intent.

Frost is, finally, a man for whom self-imposed form is quite simply everything: he *feels* the world as metonymous—concentric, contiguous—and this is a terrifying and exhilarating responsibility. Against a "background in hugeness and confusion shading away ... into black and utter chaos" any "figure of order," small and manmade though it be, may concentrate, intensify, and preserve (*Prose* 107). The full significance of Frost's need for formal control cannot be overestimated, for shapeliness is the antithesis of both flaccidity and distension: it is, in other words, the human body holding dissolution in abeyance in the form of a controlled, eternal virility. Frost is preoccupied with spatial organizations that deteriorate, with boundaries that fail, with forms that clide, and these concerns permeate every level of his discourse. His metaphors of making describe the poetic act in terms of molding, sculpting, chiseling, and his worst nightmare is of a world where the artistic artifact, representing the undisciplined and self-indulgent body/mind, has ejaculated itself as a shapeless mass that valorizes by its very formlessness a heautocratically compromised maker (*Prose* 106). He is constantly on guard against that which threatens the structural integrity of manhood, which has enough to do in channeling its own appetitive nature into fruitful and virile order: this is an "individual enterprise" that needs nobody's cooperation; for the making of self-enclosed order, "a basket, a letter, a garden, a room, an idea, a picture, a poem," "we haven't got to get a team together before we can play" (*Prose* 107). And so one finds quite understandably that the first symbolic order of external assault resides very close to home: first mothers, then lovers, wives, and daughters, eat away at the intact self. But the assault is not merely domestic, and in fact those systems perceived traditionally as antithetical to the (niggling and invasive) domestic imperatives of attention to circumstantial detail fare no better. If female ways push one to an explosive turgidity of frustration, abstractions—metaphysics—invite one to a more insidious dissolution, an expansion without barriers into systems that, being large, leave one to swell into grotesque disproportion. It all boils down to the individuated body—to the tissues, the muscles, the blood, the skeleton on their inexorable path toward becoming nothing. For Frost, "home burial" becomes the most complex of all terms, a metonym for the perceived simultaneity of desire and death: earth is the gravitational stuff from which one is made and the most intimate home of all. The place where the demon wallows, the female earth becomes in Frost's poetry the symbolic locus for the penetrative act that signals at once both procreation and burial. Humans are constructed to yield to the downward pull—"we see our images / Reflected in the mud and even dust," laments the speaker of "The White-Tailed Hornet"—and the return to dust is the consequence of rising from it to plow and plant. Thus the body as house, the household as embodiment of domestic love, and the edifice of the poem all stand poised over this grave/cellar hole/abyss into which expent substance lapses.

In a gravitational world, to rise is hard, to stay elevated requires heroic effort, but to fall down is the easiest motion there is. Like Brown's hapless descent down the icy mountain, one can ride fast straight to the bottom like a coasting child, but to get back to the top requires climbing up the long way around. Frost mandates control in a world he designates as rampant with appetite, and he mandates formal order in a world he perceives to be insistently metamorphic. Believing finally, most of all, in the futility of imposing such controlled order on a (human) nature besieged by anarchic impulse, he nonetheless takes the hero's stand. As William James says, "The world thus finds in the heroic man its worthy match and mate; and the effort which he is able to put forth to hold himself erect and keep his heart unshaken is the direct measure of his worth and function in the game of human life."[63] Frost channels virile energy, strongly spent, into poetic order, as a momentary stay against the confusion of appetitive dissolution. Yet his poetry reifies in every nuance the hungry gravity that pulls a man down. Implicit in the imagery of falling and reiterated specifically in the figural iconography of men pulled down to kneeling or prostrate postures, his poetic world suggests that the effort a man "is able to put forth to keep himself erect" is futile and even slightly absurd. As "The Subverted Flower" says, "Obeying bestial laws" one is apt to go down on all fours, where, as "To Earthward" predicts, one is seduced to stretch prone on the fragrant ground as if desire may be immediately conflated into the graveward pull. Implicit in his pervasive imagery of windows, doors, and thresholds is the conviction that the heautocratic dialogue rests on the paradox of assailable points of entry and egression. Implicit at a most essential epistemological level in his pervasive, unstable irony, which casts meaning down as if it might be "thrown out to delay the wolves," is the failure of the word and letter of the law—that which is written and implicitly rational—to hold against gravity. Language is thus brought, through the seriocomic indignities to which irony subjects it, to approximate man fallen in the dust. Everything that falls converges to rise ever so slightly and to fall again, and in a world whose only meaning lies in this comedy of incessant capitulation a man must take his pleasure as he can.

NOTES

1. Michel Foucault, *The Use of Pleasure: The History of Sexuality*, vol. 2, trans. Richard Howard (New York: Pantheon, 1985), documents in detail the heautocratically intent subject as defined in classical Greek terms. By the model of the "good Greek" to which Frost refers in "New Hampshire," a man's heautocratic integrity is his first order of defense against his own and others' dissolution. *Aphrodisia* and other appetitive impulses were categorized by the Greeks as powerful natural conditions that necessitated self-dominance. The active agent is the only truly

moral agent capable of choice, upon whom moderation is incumbent. The passive agent cannot by definition be either moral or moderate since "she" is by nature liable to be filled up to the point of hysteria—with passion, love, anger, maenadic ecstasy, etc. As Aristotle says, one would not apply the term "incontinent" to those in brutish states "any more than one would apply the epithet to women because of the passive part they play in copulation" (*Ethica Nicomachea* 1148, 33). See Lawrance Thompson, *Robert Frost: The Early Years*, 1874–1915 (New York: Holt, Rinehart & Winston, 1966), 239–40, on Frost's interest in James's comments on asceticism.

2. Hyde Cox and Edward Connery Lathem, *Selected Prose of Robert Frost* (New York: Holt, Rinehart & Winston, 1966), 18. All further references will be cited parenthetically as *Prose*.

3. "Heautocratic," a rather cumbersome word, comes from my reading of Foucault's *The Use of Pleasure*, and it is the only term I can discover that locates precisely Frost's instinct for virile moderation, for an enclosed intactness; this is an impulse that, by virtue of its basis in both control and *aphrodisia*, suggests the bipolar energies of Frost's personal and poetic concerns. I have tried to use the word sparingly, but there are moments when nothing else works quite so economically to speak to Frost's subsidies of both chaos ("wildness") and form.

4. See Luce Irigaray's "The Little Girl Is (Only) a Little Boy," in *Speculum of the Other Woman*, trans. Gillian C. Gill (Ithaca, N.Y.: Cornell Univ. Press, 1985), 25–34, for her comments on the Freudian conclusion to a classical philosophy of (male) desire by which women are defined in terms of men: born "masculine," they then must transform themselves by a masochistic process into femininity. This is one essence of the mythology of a transformative femaleness that lacks formal integrity. See too Michel Foucault, *Madness and Civilization: A History of Sanity in the Age of Reason*, trans. Robert Hurley (New York: Pantheon, 1985), 140–54, on the physiology of hysteria. Predicated on the female body as noncompact and prone to upheaval ("slack and therefore feeble, without action or elasticity"; 140), hysteria could run rampant through a barrierless system.

5. *The Poetry of Robert Frost*, ed. Edward Connery Lathem (New York: Holt, Rinehart & Winston, 1975). All further references to Frost's poetry will be cited parenthetically in the text.

6. Consider in this context "Mending Wall," in which the (integumental) barrier, made to seem a living thing nudged by an equally living ground swell, is generative of its own disrepair; it does not take a violent breach of the wall—the apple trees "will never get across / And eat the cones under his pines"—to make gaps.

7. See Donald G. Sheehy, "Refiguring Love: Robert Frost in Crisis, 1938–1942," *New England Quarterly* 63, no. 2 (June 1990); 179–231, for his assessment of the period in which "The Figure a Poem Makes" was produced, at a time when Frost's love affair with Kathleen Morrison was beginning. For more on the Kathleen Morrison story, see Stanley Burnshaw, *Robert Frost Himself* (New York: Braziller, 1986). Richard Poirier's elegant study of Frost, *Robert Frost: The Work of Knowing* (New York: Oxford Univ. Press, 1977), returns often to this inevitable connection in Frost between sex and poetry as a way of "keeping" things from time (see 176–7). We share this crucial central assumption while, I very much hope,

providing two distinct perspectives on its effects and significations throughout the poetry.

8. From "A Masque of Reason," II. 339–40. See Philip E. Slater, *The Glory of Hera: Greek Mythology and the Greek Family* (Boston: Beacon Press, 1968), 75–122, for a discussion of serpents and boundary ambiguity (91), of the serpent's hermaphroditic associations, and of its unifying of dichotomous symbolic values (80–6).

9. Michel Foucault, *The History of Sexuality*, vol. 1: *An Introduction*, trans. Robert Hurley (New York: Pantheon, 1978). 71.

10. Ibid. 65. See too Reginald Cook, *Robert Frost: A Living Voice* (Amherst: Univ. of Massachusetts Press, 1974), 88–99. Frost's preoccupation with the term "Puritanism," which he uses as a metaphor for a concern with sexual continence (thus "pagan puritanism"—"Of course, everything about Diana and Minerva had something to do with chastity and all that—and restraint"; 90), is significant in this context.

11. Edward Connery Lathem, ed., *Interviews with Robert Frost* (New York: Holt, Rinehart & Winston, 1977), xiv.

12. Poirier, *The Work of Knowing*, 234.

13. Foucault, in *The Use of Pleasure*, calls upon many of the classical sources for the designation of "female" as a state antithetical to the compact, muscular body/mind of the virilely moderate man. "Female" becomes the code for shapelessness, passivity, weakness, dissolution, that which in a man is effeminacy. See too K.J. Dover, *Greek Homosexuality* (Cambridge, Mass.: Harvard Univ. Press, 1978). See Aristotle's *Ethica Nicomachea* for an elaboration of this dynamic: "Now the man who is defective in respect of resistance to the things which most men both resist and resist successfully is soft and effeminate; for effeminacy too is a kind of softness" (1150b).

14. For example, we see Eliot in "The Metaphysical Poets" examining the conceit in terms of the rigor it demands from both poet and critic; it "requires considerable agility." This capacity for a "direct sensuous apprehension of thought" requires looking into a "good deal more than the heart. One must look into the cerebral cortex, the nervous system, and the digestive tract."

15. See Foucault, *History of Sexuality*, 1: 17–35, for a discussion of the history of confession, religious, medical, psychoanalytical, etc., to which pleasure has subjected itself and to which it has been subjected. See too Frost's comments, in Cook, *A Living Voice*, 90, on pleasure as "Puritanism" circumscribes it, becoming that "in you that fears your own pleasure, that distrusts your own pleasures."

16. Frank Lentricchia, *Robert Frost: Modern Poetics and the Landscape of Self* (Durham, N.C.: Duke Univ. Press, 1975), 12, calls them "unfortunate female characters, inescapably housed in their obsessions." James M. Cox, "Robert Frost and the Edge of the Clearing," in *Critical Essays on Robert Frost*, ed. Philip L. Gerber (Boston: Hall, 1982), 144–54 says, "[Women] disintegrate into hysteria or slump into depression" (140). See too Patricia Wallace, "The 'Estranged Point of View': The Thematics of Imagination in Frost's Poetry," in *Frost: Centennial Essays II*, ed. Jac Tharpe (Jackson: Univ. Press of Mississippi, 1976), 177–95.

17. Roland Barthes, *The Pleasure of the Text*, trans. Richard Miller (New York: Hill & Wang, 1975), 4.

18. One might locate "To Earthward" in a familiar literary tradition, from Edgar Allan Poe to Gabriele D'Annunzio, of hypersensitive men whose need to *tell* is a source of deep guilt and intense pleasure. Indulging themselves synesthetically, with one locus of pleasure always at the (speaking) lips, they become caught in a spiral that coils inevitably toward masochism. Frost's poem, first published in 1923, seems predicated in part on literary nostalgia. Foucault, in *The Use of Pleasure*, 22–5, locates as a power mechanism the nineteenth-century encouragement of a confessional discourse on sex: "A policing of sex: that is, not the rigor of a taboo, but the necessity of regulating sex through useful and public discourse."

19. See Julia Kristeva, *Tales of Love*, trans. Leon S. Roudiez (New York: Columbia Univ. Press, 1987), 15–16, 267–383, for a discussion of the "amorous dynamics" of symbolic and semiotic systems that are open to one another. See too Paul de Man, "Epistemology of Metaphor," *Critical Inquiry* 5, no. 1 (Autumn 1978): 15–16, as he speaks of cloquence as defined by Locke and as traditionally regarded in precisely these terms: "Like a woman, which it resembles ('like the fair sex'), it is a fine thing as long as it is kept in its proper place. Out of place, among the serious affairs of men ('if we would speak of things as they are'), it is a descriptive scandal—like the appearance of a real woman in a gentleman's club where it would only be tolerated as a picture, preferably naked (like the image of Truth), framed and hung on the wall."

20. Foucault, *Madness and Civilization*, 149. See Cook, *A Living Voice*, 64, for Frost's application of Emerson's praise of Montaigne's prose. "Cut these words and they would bleed; they are vascular and alive; they walk and run": Emerson's journal entry on Montaigne is cited by Frost as applicable to three men—Montaigne, Emerson himself, and Frost.

21. Cook, *A Living Voice*, 52.

22. See Randall Jarrell, "Robert Frost's 'Home Burial,'" in *The Moment of Poetry*, ed. Don Cameron Allen (Baltimore: Johns Hopkins Univ. Press, 1962), 99–132; for his assessment of the sexual overtones of the husband's digging of the grave. One must consider the potential tautology in Jarrell's reading, which, one might argue, imposes a literarily stable (and psychologically prominent) equation on a potentially transparent—nonsymbolically inscribed—action. One who writes on Frost is implicated in the fluid parameters of his language games, so that it is never certain who, critic or poet, brings the metaphor to its breaking point. Or who, in the terms of the sexual analogy, is moving toward prurience.

23. The dangers of imposing what Mary Ellman calls the "intellectual tyranny" of the sexual analogy are omnipresent and, perhaps, inescapable. See *Thinking About Women* (New York: Harcourt, Brace and World, 1968). One can only speculate as scrupulously as possible about how much of this tyranny infiltrates Frost's metaphorical constructs and how much one inevitably reads into Frost's, or any, work.

24. Poirier, *The Work of Knowing*, xiii.

25. See Cook, *A Living Voice*, 169, for Frost's reference to "Modern Love," a poem he quotes in the context of his discussion of tragedy. The entire text of Meredith's sonnet sequence makes an interesting backdrop for Frost's implications about women. See too Lawrance Thompson (ed.), *The Selected Letters of Robert Frost*

(New York: Holt, Rinehart & Winston, 1964), 394. All further references to this text will be cited parenthetically as *Letters*.

26. Friedrich Nietzsche, *The Birth of Tragedy*, trans. Walter Kaufmann (New York: Vintage Books, 1967), 42. Thompson has also noted this allusion, which springs out inescapably as one reads Nietzsche's account. See Thompson, *The Early Years*, 367. Frost himself refers to Silenus, making in near juxtaposition an extended reference to sardonic laughter, in Cook, *A Living Voice*, 93.

27. Cook, *A Living Voice*, 169. This is Frost's quote from Meredith's "Modern Love," an association he makes in the context of talking about tragedy, "women and men, a woman and a man." "George Meredith has a sonnet about that, hasn't he? 'Passions spin the plot,' he says. 'In tragic life, God wot, / No villains need be!' See, he agrees with me. 'Passions spin the plot.'"

28. Frost's frequent pairing of terms that do not yield the doubled meanings of the conventional oxymoron can be found throughout his poetry; just injustice and reasonable unreason are two examples. See Foucault, *Madness and Civilization*, 105–7, for a discussion of madness in which he elaborates upon the term "unreason." Frost's original gloss for this poem was "about science," a reading that adds to questions of reason and nothingness.

29. See de Man, "Epistemology of Metaphor," 18, for his discussion of the Lockean substances. Locke uses "gold" as the first model of a substance, yet cannot hold his own discussion from metaphor. As de Man says, "Not only are tropes, as their name implies, always on the move—more like quicksilver than like flowers or butterflies which one can at least hope to pin down and insert in a neat taxonomy— but they can disappear altogether, or at least appear to disappear." See Judith Oster, *Toward Robert Frost: The Reader and the Poet* (Athens: Georgia Univ. Press, 1991), 224–6, for early versions of this poem.

30. "Home Burial" is informed, according to Thompson in *The Early Years*, 597–8, both by Frost's knowledge of the marital consequences of the death of Leona and Nathaniel Harvey's child and by the death of his own firstborn, Elliott, in 1900.

31. Frost's choices of the autobiographical and historical details he uses in his poetry must be considered part of what Lentricchia, *Modern Poetics*, 4, has called the "primordial ground of Frost's creative acts." In other words, it is not sufficient to assert that Frost was merely reporting on the details of a life that was necessarily afflicted by illness, infant mortality, accident, and death.

32. Samuel Beckett, *Waiting for Godot* (New York: Grove Press, 1954), 58.

33. Friedrich Nietzsche, *The Will to Power*, trans. Walter Kaufmann and R.J. Hollingdale, ed. Walter Kaufmann (New York: Vintage Books, 1968), 16.

34. See Slater's chapter, "The Greek Mother–Son Relationship: Origins and Consequences," in *The Glory of Hera*, 3–74, for a detailed discussion of sources of ambivalence in a classically declined mother–son relationship.

35. A partial list of "marriages" (frequently the legal status is unclear) that are demonstrably or by implication childless: "The Death of the Hired Man," "Home Burial," "A Servant to Servants," "The Housekeeper," "The Fear," "The Hill Wife," "Maple," "Berefit," "The Thatch," "West-Running Brook," and "The Investment."

36. For other suggestions of female infidelity see, e.g., "Maple" and "The Witch of Coös." See too the unpublished "Pride of Ancestry," in Lawrance Thompson, *Robert Frost: The Years of Triumph* (New York: Holt, Rinehart & Winston, 1964), 473: the Deacon's wife "was a bit desirish / And liked her sex relations wild, / So she lay with one of the shanty Irish / and he begot the Deacon's child."

37. That Frost feels the poetic body as almost physical extension is reinforced by Thompson's locating of his poem in the context of Frost's battle to keep E.J. Bernheimer from selling his signed collection of Frost books. See Lawrance Thompson, *Robert Frost: The Later Years* (New York: Holt, Rinehart & Winston, 1976), 187–96. For an alternative account of the creation of this poem see Baird W. Whitlock, "Conversations with Robert Frost," *Xavier Review* 3, no. 2 (1983): 1–3. See too David W. Shaw, "The Poetics of Pragmatism: Robert Frost and William James," *New England Quarterly* 59, no. 2 (June 1986): 165; Shaw sees the poem as a gloss on William James's antideterministic essay, "Great Men and Their Environment."

38. See Jean-François Lyotard, *The Postmodern Condition: A Report on Knowledge*, trans. Geoff Bennington and Brian Massumi (Minneapolis: Univ. of Minnesota Press, 1988), 18–23, on the appropriation of memory into the narrative flow, particularly as it is manifested in the rhythmic cadences of a story like the one the witch and her son tell.

39. *Writers at Work: The "Paris Review" Interviews*, ed. George Plimpton, d ser. (New York, 1963), 25.

40. See Sara Ruddick, "Maternal Thinking," *Feminist Studies* 6 (1980): 342–67, and Margaret Urban Walker, "Moral Understandings: Alternative 'Epistemology' for a Feminist Ethics," *Hypatia* 4, no. 2 (1989): 15–28, for discussions of the epistemological and ethical implications of this maternal solicitude. The allusion to Ahaz in "New Hampshire" seems in these contexts less than circumstantial, since it suggests as the end result of this "father"–"son" competition the sacrifice of the son; "The Witch of Coös" may be said to pose the antithetical triumph of the son over two "fathers." See too Slater, *The Glory of Hera*, on the patterns of violence associated with family dyads; Appendix I, "Aggression in Parent–Child dyads in Apollodorus," 468–9, suggests the classical underpinnings of Frost's dynamics.

41. See Walker, "Moral Understandings," 17–19, for a context within which to place Mary's alternative definition. See too, for the larger implications of an epistemology that valorizes an introspective, perpetually ongoing moral watchfulness over judgmental action, Iris Murdoch, *The Sovereignty of Good* (New York: Ark, 1986). Frost comments on these lines in his *Paris Review* interview (*Writers at Work*, ed. Plimpton), relating the "feminine way" with the New Deal and the Democrats and the masculine, paternal way with the Republicans. Typically, Frost claims the middle ground.

42. Notice the similarity between what the father tells his daughter in "Maple"—"by and by I will tell you"—and what the mother tells her son about the fact that his real father is a cook—"someday I'll tell you, dear"—in "How Hard It Is to Keep from Being King When It's in You and in the Situation."

43. Kristeva, *Tales of Love*, 21–4.

44. Ibid., 24.

45. See John Hollander, *The Figure of Echo: A Mode of Allusion in Milton and After* (Berkeley and Los Angeles: Univ. of California Press, 1981), 113–32, and my discussion of Frost's metalepsis in Chapter 2. Hollander's "figure of echo" is, of course, wonderfully pertinent in this poem predicated in part on the Narcissus/Echo allusion.

46. See the *Homeric Hymn to Apollo*, no. 3, ll. 137–60. Apollo was said to be autonomous almost from birth, never suckling his mother's breast but eating ambrosia from Olympus, casting off his swaddling clothes and talking, and, at four days, assuming the weapons of manhood. Apollo's mother, Leto, was hounded by Hera, who would not allow her to give birth on land; only the rocky island of Delos, a place of "Not-earth," would receive her, and then, in some versions, only after Neptune submerged it in a glaze of water to make it more completely disassociated from earth (defined here implicitly as dirt, where things may grow and be buried).

47. Slater, *The Glory of Hera*, 137.

48. See Friedrich Nietzsche, *The Birth of Tragedy*, trans. Walter Kaufmann (New York: Vintage Books, 1967), for the formulation of this Apollonian–Dionysian distinction.

49. "Two Tramps in Mud-Time," "The Hill Wife," "The Fear," "The Subverted Flower," "The Witch of Coös," "Out, Out–," "The Self-Seeker," "The Bonfire," "The Ax-Helve" all share visions of potential or actual violence; where harm has not been done, it is imagined as imminent, in the ax flying off its handle, the tramps resorting to violence, the man springing like a hungry beast, the irate lover materializing out of the darkness.

50. See Annabel Patterson, "Hard Pastoral: Frost, Wordsworth, and Modernist Poetics," *Criticism: A Quarterly for Literature and the Arts* 29, no. 1 (Winter 1987): 67–87, on Frost's use of "Build Soil" and the pastoral mode to assert autonomy in the face of what would become New Deal policies.

51. This image of rotting skin, which is used further to describe the dissolution of job's tents—"when, as rotten as his skin, / His tents blew all to pieces"—impinges in significant ways on Frost's decaying-house imagery and, more grotesquely, on "The Silken Tent," both used by Frost as correlatives for the body. See Philip Gerber, "Remembering Frost: An Interview with William Jewell," *New England Quarterly* 59, no. 1 (March 1986): Jewell remembers that at Frost's memorial service one of the ministers likened him "quite properly" to Job. See too Poirier, *The Work of Knowing*, 50, as he takes issue with Thompson's reading of Frost and asserts that "Frost would never blame the 'age' for anything.... This was the virtue of his pride."

52. "The Lesson for Today" is one of several poems in which the poet's emasculation within a potentially coercive systematic of some kind is an issue. "The White-Tailed Hornet," with its metonymic stinging wasp as a model of appetitive uncontrol and resultant poetic ineffectuality, is worth consideration in this context. The poem's subtitle, "The Revision of Theories," in *A Further Range* suggests Frost's preoccupation both with Darwinian and with Freudian theories of instinct and appetite; his focus on the ineffectual "stinger" suggests his conflation of pen, sword, and penis in an animal fable in which the wasp *is* the poet bewildered by theoretical considerations. The speaker muses that the wasp might almost be a poet, "comparing

/ Nailhead with fly and fly with huckleberry" and muttering "How like a fly, how very like a fly." Comically, the hornet cannot hit the derisive, mobile fly he hunts for supper, pouncing instead on the look-alike huckleberry, which throws him on his head; that failing, the wasp attacks again, this time mistaking a nailhead for the fly. He quite literally hits the nail on the head, the only problem being that it is the wrong target. In other words, the wasp/poet is in the most essential sense impotent, all stinger but unable to find the target that will accept him; his mistakes are not even particularly legitimate, since the nailhead, flat and not in the least flylike, is fastened down, and the huckleberry is "Wrong shape, wrong color, and wrong scent."

53. One keeps coming back to Frost's definition of the Platonist as "one who believes what we have here is an imperfect copy of what is in heaven. The woman you have is an imperfect copy of some woman in heaven or in someone else's bed" (*Letters*, 462).

54. See Cook, *A Living Voice*, 169.

55. See Shaw, "The Poetics of Pragmatism," 165–6, for his argument that Frost's pragmatism is a mode which, following James's use of "tough-minded" to describe a skeptical, empirical temperament, allows Frost to avoid idealism and metaphysics. I am, myself, not convinced that "pragmatist" is the best term to describe Frost's habits of mind, but as Shaw, and most recently Richard Poirier in *Poetry and Pragmatism* (Cambridge, Mass.: Harvard Univ. Press, 1992) have shown, the conjunction is indeed an interesting one.

56. Guy Rotella, *Reading and Writing Nature* (Boston: Northeastern Univ. Press, 1991), 60.

57. Poirier, *The Work of Knowing*, 264.

58. Rotella, *Reading and Writing Nature*, 60; "I'm less and less for systems and system-building in my old age," says Frost, adding, "I'm afraid of too much structure."

59. Cary Nelson, *Repression and Recovery: Modern American Poetry and the Politics of Cultural Memory, 1910–1945* (Madison: Univ. of Wisconsin Press, 1989), 84.

60. This clear incorporation of biographical detail and of opinions Frost articulates without apparent irony in his prose statements makes the Frostian speaker in longer, issue-oriented poems like "The White-Tailed Hornet," "The Lesson for Today," and "A Hundred Collars" particularly interesting. Their professed liberalism or intellectualism balances against specific biographical detail to create a speaker who is proclaiming himself Frost and not-Frost simultaneously. This tactic continues the Frostian program of undermining abstract terms like "intellectual" and "liberal."

61. *Genesis* 16:12.

62. Thompson, *The Later Years*, 268.

63. See Thompson, *The Later Years*, 238–43, for his speculations on Frost's interest in James.

SEAMUS HEANEY

Above the Brim

Among major poets of the English language in this century, Robert Frost is the one who takes the most punishment. "Like a chimpanzee" is how one friend of mine remembers him in the flesh, but in the afterlife of the text he has been consigned to a far less amiable sector of the bestiary, among the stoats perhaps, or the weasels. Calculating self-publicist, reprehensible egotist, oppressive parent—theories of the death of the author have failed to lay the ghost of this vigorous old contender who beats along undauntedly at the reader's elbow. His immense popular acclaim during his own lifetime; his apotheosis into an idol mutually acceptable to his own and his country's self-esteem, and greatly inflationary of both; his constantly resourceful acclimatization of himself to this condition, as writer and performer—it all generated a critical resistance and fed a punitive strain which is never far to seek in literary circles anyhow.

Still, it would be wrong to see this poet as the unwitting victim of the fashion which he surfed upon for decades. Demonically intelligent, as acute about his own masquerades as he was about others', Frost obeyed the ancient command to know himself. Like Yeats at the end of "Dialogue of Self and Soul," Frost would be "content to live it all again," and be content also to "cast out remorse." Unlike Yeats, however, he would expect neither a flow of sweetness into his breast nor a flash of beatitude upon the world to ensue

From *Homage to Robert Frost* by Joseph Brodsky, Seamus Heaney, and Derek Walcott. © 1996 by the Estate of Joseph Brodsky, Seamus Heaney, and Derek Walcott.

from any such bout of self-exculpation. He made no secret of the prejudice and contrariness at the center of his nature, and never shirked the bleakness of that last place in himself. He was well aware of the abrasiveness of many of his convictions and their unpopular implications in the context of New Deal politics, yet for all his archness, he did not hide those convictions or retreat from them.

Frost's appetite for his own independence was fierce and expressed itself in a reiterated belief in his right to limits: his defenses, his fences, and his freedom were all interdependent. Yet he also recognized that his compulsion to shape his own destiny and to proclaim the virtues of self-containment arose from a terror of immense, unlimited, and undefined chaos. This terror gets expressed melodramatically in a poem like "Design," and obliquely in a poem like "Provide, Provide," but it is also there in many of his more casual pronouncements. Here he is, for example, writing to Amy Bonner in June 1937:

> There are no two things as important to us in life and art as being threatened and being saved. What are ideals of form for if we aren't going to be made to fear for them? All our ingenuity is lavished on getting into danger legitimately so that we may be genuinely rescued.

Frost believed, in other words, that individual venture and vision arose as a creative defense against emptiness, and that it was therefore always possible that a relapse into emptiness would be the ultimate destiny of consciousness. If good fences made good neighbors, if (as Ian Hamilton has suggested) a certain callousness of self-assertion was part of the price of adjusting to reality, Frost was ready to pay that price in terms of exclusiveness and isolation, and in terms also of guardedness and irony (and William Pritchard writes well about this in his deliberately positive study of the poet). The main thing is that Frost was prepared to look without self-deception into the crystal of indifference in himself where his moral and artistic improvisations were both prefigured and scrutinized, and in this essay I shall be concerned to show that his specifically poetic achievement is profoundly guaranteed and resilient because it is "genuinely rescued" from negative recognitions, squarely faced, and abidingly registered.

Frost was always ready to hang those negative recognitions in the balance against his more comfortable imaginings. He made it clear, for example, that there was a cold shadow figure behind the warm-blooded image of his generally beloved horseman in "Stopping by Woods on a Snowy Evening":

> My little horse must think it queer
> To stop without a farmhouse near
> Between the woods and frozen lake
> The darkest evening of the year.
>
> He gives his harness bells a shake
> To ask if there is some mistake.
> The only other sound's the sweep
> Of easy wind and downy flake.

This rider, faring forward against the drift of more than snow, a faithful, self-directed quester with promises to keep and miles to go before he sleeps, this figure finds his counterpart in "Desert Places," a poem of the same length, written in almost the same rhyme scheme. In "Desert Places" Frost implicitly concedes the arbitrariness of the consolations offered by the earlier poem and deliberately undermines its sureties. The social supports that were vestigially present in "promises to keep" have now been pulled away, and the domestic security of woods with owners in the village is rendered insignificant by a vacuous interstellar immensity:

> Snow falling and night falling fast, oh, fast
> In a field I looked into going past,
> And the ground almost covered smooth in snow,
> But a few weeds and stubble showing last.
>
> The woods around it have it—it is theirs.
> All animals are smothered in their lairs.
> I am too absent-spirited to count;
> The loneliness includes me unawares.
>
> And lonely as it is that loneliness
> Will be more lonely ere it will be less—
> A blanker whiteness of benighted snow
> With no expression, nothing to express.
>
> They cannot scare me with their empty spaces
> Between stars—on stars where no human race is.

> I have it in me so much nearer home
> To scare myself with my own desert places.

This poem gives access to the dark side of Frost, which was always there behind the mask of Yankee hominess, a side of him which also became fashionable late in the day, after Lionel Trilling gave it the modernists' blessing in a speech at Frost's eighty-fifth birthday party. Trilling there drew attention to Frost's Sophoclean gift for making the neuter outback of experience scrutable in a way that privileges neither the desolate unknown nor the human desire to shelter from it. I am going to pause with the poem at this early stage, however, not in order to open the vexed question of Frost's dimensions as a philosophical writer or to address the range of his themes or to contextualize his stances, imaginative and civic, within American political and intellectual history. All of these things are worth considering, but I raise them only to salute them dutifully and so pass on to my own particular area of interest.

This arises from a lifetime of pleasure in Frost's poems as events in language, flaunts and vaunts full of projective force and deliquescent backwash, the crestings of a tide that lifts all spirits. Frost may have indeed declared that his whole anxiety was for himself as a performer, but the performance succeeded fully only when it launched itself beyond skill and ego into a run of energy that brimmed up outside the poet's conscious intention and control.

Consider, for example, the conclusion of "Desert Places," which I have just quoted: "I have it in me so much nearer home / To scare myself with my own desert places." However these lines may incline toward patness, whatever risk they run of making the speaker seem to congratulate himself too easily as an initiate of darkness, superior to the deluded common crowd, whatever trace they contain of knowingness that mars other poems by Frost, they still succeed convincingly. They overcome one's incipient misgivings and subsume them into the larger, more impersonal, and undeniable emotional occurrence which the whole poem represents.

I call it an emotional occurrence, yet it is preeminently a rhythmic one, an animation via the ear of the whole nervous apparatus: what Borges called "an almost physical emotion." The tilt of the sound is unmistakable from the beginning. The momentary stay of the stanza is being sifted away from the inside, words are running out from under themselves, and there is no guarantee that form will effect a rescue from danger:

> Snow falling and night falling fast, oh, fast
> In a field I looked into going past ...

This meter is full of the hurry and slant of driven snow, its unstoppable, anxiety-inducing forward rush, all that whispering turmoil of a blizzard. Here the art of the language is like the art of the French farmer in "The Ax-Helve"; what is said in that poem about the lines and grains of a hickory axe shaft applies equally to the lines of "Desert Places." The French farmer

> showed me that the lines of a good helve
> Were native to the grain before the knife
> Expressed them, and its curves were no false curves
> Put on it from without.

The curves and grains of the first two lines of "Desert Places" are correspondingly native to living speech, without any tonal falsity. Who really notices that the letter *f* alliterates five times within thirteen syllables? It is no denigration of Hopkins to say that when such an alliterative cluster happens in his work, the reader is the first to notice it. With Frost, its effect is surely known, like a cold air that steals across a face; but until the lines are deliberately dwelt upon a moment like this, we do not even think of it as an "effect," and the means that produce it remain as unshowy as the grain in the wood:

> Snow falling and night falling fast, oh, fast
> In a field I looked into going past,
> And the ground almost covered smooth in snow,
> But a few weeds and stubble showing last.

This feels like an unpremeditated rush of inspiration, and Frost always declared that he liked to take a poem thus, at a single stroke, when the mood was on him. Yet even if the actual composition of "Desert Places" entailed no such speedy, pell-mell onslaught of perceptions, the finished poem does indeed induce that kind of sensation. There is an urgent, toppling pattern to it all, an urgency created by various minimal but significant verbal delicacies—like, for example, the omission of the relative pronoun from the line "In a field I looked into going past." Compare this with "In a field that I looked into going past" and hear how the inclusion of an extra syllable breaks the slippage toward panic in the line as we have it. Or consider how the end-stopping of the first eight lines does not (as we might expect) add composure to them but contributes instead a tensed-up, pent-up movement:

> The woods around it have it—it is theirs.
> All animals are smothered in their lairs.
> I am too absent-spirited to count;
> The loneliness includes me unawares.

And where does that line about being "too absent-spirited to count" arrive from? Does it mean that the speaker does not matter? Or something else? In the onwardness of a reading, such curiosity registers fleetingly, like something glimpsed from a carriage window. To count what? The animals? The lairs? And what is "it" that the woods have? Is it snow? Is it loneliness? The speaker is so hypnotized by the snow swirl that he doesn't count as consciousness anymore, he is adrift instead, in the dream of smothered lairs. And those triple masculine rhymes of "fast" / "past" / "last," with their monosyllabic stress repeated again in "theirs" / "lairs" / "awares," are like the slowing of the heartbeat in the withdrawn hibernators.

Halfway through the poem, then, the narcotic aspect of the snowfall is predominant, and the vowel music is like a dulled pulse beat: going, covered smooth, stubble showing, smothered. But in the next eight lines we go through the nature barrier, as it were, into the ether of symbolic knowledge. The consolations of being "too absent-spirited to count" are disallowed and the poem suddenly blinks itself out of reverie into vision. The vowels divest themselves of their comfortable roundness, the rhymes go slender first and then go feminine: "loneliness" / "less" / "express"; "spaces" / "race is" / "places." The repetition which at the start was conducive to trance, and included speaker and reader "unawares," now buzzes everybody and everything awake.

Once again, the effect is not "put on from without," not a flourish of craft, but a feat of technique. There is a disconsolateness in the way the word "lonely" keeps rebounding off its image in the word "loneliness"; and the same holds true for the closed-circuit energy of "expression" and "express." Finally, there is a Dantesque starkness about the repetition of the word "stars." Even if these stars are not intended to echo the *stelle* that shine at the end of each of Dante's visions, they still do possess the cold tingle of infinity. So, by such feats of mimesis and orchestration, the speaker's inwardness with all this outward blankness is established long before he declares himself explicitly in the concluding lines. And that is what I meant earlier when I spoke of the excessiveness of the language's own rightness, brimming up beyond the poet's deliberate schemes and performances:

> And lonely as it is that loneliness
> Will be more lonely ere it will be less—
> A blanker whiteness of benighted snow
> With no expression, nothing to express.
>
> They cannot scare me with their empty spaces
> Between stars—on stars where no human race is.
> I have it in me so much nearer home
> To scare myself with my own desert places.

Inevitably, a discussion like this, which concentrates on the poem's musical life, must lead us to take cognizance of Frost's theory of "the sound of sense." This theory, as Frost expressed it in interviews and letters over the years, does fit and complement our experience of what is distinctive about the run of his verse, its posture in the mouth and in the ear, its constant drama of tone and tune. "The sound of sense" presents itself as a technical prescription and serves notice that Frost, even though he broke with the experimental modernists, was still a poet of that critical early-twentieth-century moment, every bit as concerned as the Imagists ever were to heave the art of verse out of its backward drag into nineteenth-century musicality.

A few quotations will suffice to recall the basic convictions which underlay much of Frost's practice; indeed, most of them can be culled from a letter to John T. Bartlett (July 4, 1913), where he begins by distinguishing between the good and bad senses of the word "craft," the bad one applied to those poets whom he calls "mechanics." He goes on then:

> To be perfectly frank with you I am one of the most notable craftsmen of my time ... I am possibly the only person going who works on any but a worn out theory [principle I had better say] of versification ... I alone of English writers have consciously set myself to make music out of what I may call the sound of sense. Now it is possible to have sense without the sound of sense (as in much prose that is supposed to pass muster but makes very dull reading) and the sound of sense without sense (as in Alice in Wonderland which makes anything but dull reading). The best place to get the abstract sound of sense is from voices behind a door that cuts off the words ... It is the abstract vitality of our

speech. It is pure sound—pure form. One who concerns himself
with it more than the subject is an artist ... But if one is to be a
poet he must learn to get cadences by skillfully breaking the
sounds of sense with all their irregularity of accent across the
regular beat of the metre.

This gives the main gist of Frost's poetics. It can be supplemented by many
other declarations about sentence-sounds and tones of voice, all of which are
designed to give an ultimate authority to perfectly pitched natural speech
cadences realized in a written text. Such cadences, Frost is at pains to insist,
re-establish a connection with the original springs of our human being.

Talking of sentence-sounds, for example, which he elsewhere describes
as "the most volatile and at the same time important part of poetry" (the part
we can no longer hear in poems in ancient Greek or Latin), he maintains:

No one makes or adds to them. They are always there, living in
the cave of the mouth ... And they are as definitely things as any
image of sight. The most creative imagination is only their
summoner.

To summon such sounds, therefore, is to recapitulate and refresh a latent
resource of our nature: one might say of them what Frost says of the well at
the end of his poem "Directive": "Here are your waters and your watering
place. / Drink and be whole again beyond confusion." And so it follows that
a poetry which gives access to origin by thus embodying the lineaments of
pristine speech will fulfill, at a level below theme and intention, a definite
social function. As Marjorie Sabin has written:

Frost in 1914 wanted to believe—and wrote poems out of the
belief—that human vitality takes on a supra-personal existence in
the established intonations of speech ... What Frost calls "the
abstract vitality of our speech" ... participates in the verbal forms
through which other people also enact their lives.

When I fixed upon the title for this essay, I had not read Marjorie Sabin's
perceptive comment (included by William Pritchard in *Robert Frost: A
Literary Portrait*). But her observation about the vitality of speech taking on
a supra-personal existence parallels and answers the things I am hoping to
bring into focus through the phrase "above the brim."

This phrase is Frost's own and comes in that heady climbing part of "Birches"—climbing in the musical as much as in the physical sense—where he describes the boy's joyful, expert ascent toward the top of a slender birch tree. Even though the lines that conclude the poem are among some of the most familiar in the canon of twentieth-century verse, I still feel it worthwhile to quote them:

> He always kept his poise
> To the top branches, climbing carefully
> With the same pains you use to fill a cup
> Up to the brim, and even above the brim.
> Then he flung outward, feet first, with a swish,
> Kicking his way down through the air to the ground.
> So was I once myself a swinger of birches.
> And so I dream of going back to be.
> It's when I'm weary of considerations,
> And life is too much like a pathless wood
> Where your face burns and tickles with the cobwebs
> Broken across it, and one eye is weeping
> From a twig's having lashed across it open.
> I'd like to get away from earth awhile
> And then come back to it and begin over.
> May no fate willfully misunderstand me
> And half grant what I wish and snatch me away
> Not to return. Earth's the right place for love:
> I don't know where it's likely to go better.
> I'd like to go by climbing a birch tree,
> And climb black branches up a snow-white trunk
> *Toward* heaven, till the tree could bear no more,
> But dipped its top and set me down again.
> That would be good both going and coming back.
> One could do worse than be a swinger of birches.

This seesawing between earth and heaven nicely represents the principle of redress which I have elsewhere commended. That general inclination to begin a countermove once things go too far in any given direction is enacted by "Birches" with lovely pliant grace. But my main concern here is with the specifically upward waft of Frost's poems, and the different ways in which he releases the feeling, preeminent in the lines just quoted, of airy vernal daring, an overbrimming of invention and of what he once called "supply." The sensation of lucky strike which he describes in his preface to the *Collected Poems* matches very closely the sensation of flourish and plenty which characterizes "Birches." Here are some relevant lines from "The Figure a Poem Makes":

> For me the initial delight is in the surprise of remembering something I didn't know I knew ... There is a glad recognition of the long lost and the rest follows. Step by step the wonder of unexpected supply keeps growing.

The headiness of Frost's poetry has much to do with this revel in artesian energies, as the poet plays eagerly to the top of his bent and then goes over the top and down the other side. But it is not just the sheer happiness of composition that creates a rise of poetic levels. The opposite condition, the sheer unhappiness of the uncomposed world, is even more conducive to the art of the ascending scale. When Frost comes down hard upon the facts of hurt, he still manages to end up gaining poetic altitude. As his intelligence thrusts down, it creates a reactive force capable of raising and carrying the whole burden of our knowledge and experience.

"Home Burial," for example, is a great poem which ends well above the brim of its last line. Its buoyancy is achieved in direct proportion to its pressure upon the ground of the actual. The poem derives from a cruel moment in the married life of the young Robert and Elinor Frost, when their first child, a boy not quite four, died of *cholera infantum* in 1900; and yet "Home Burial" contains no pathos, no Victorian chiaroscuro. It is one of the best of Frost's dramatic eclogues, with all the rigor and dispatch of Greek tragedy.

A husband comes upon a wife, traumatized by grief at the death of their child, keeping a trembly, furious vigil over the grave. The grave is visible through the window of their semi-isolated house, and is the locus around which their drama of recrimination and rebuke exhausts itself. Indeed, the point I want to make is that the entrapment of the couple, their feral involvement with each other as each other's quarry and companion, is not held at a safe narrative distance but interrupts into the space between reader and text. The mixture of anger, panic, and tyranny in the husband's voice at the end of the poem is rendered with a fairness and bareness that presses closure to an extreme where it virtually constitutes a reopening. The top of the reader's head is lifted like the latch of the protagonist's tormented home, and the lifting power resides in the upsurge of language. Both Randall Jarrell and Joseph Brodsky have written magnificently about the poem in line-by-line commentaries which need not be repeated here. Instead, I will quote the final lines where a premature diminuendo is fiercely contradicted. The husband seeks to clear the emotional air too soon and too proprietorially, in a move to suppress the wildness of the wife's sorrow; but when the sound of *her* sense rises in the perfectly pitched anger, he can no longer restrain the note of tyranny:

"There, you have said it all and you feel better.
You won't go now. You're crying. Close the door.
The heart's gone out of it: why keep it up?
Amy! There's someone coming down the road!"
"*You*—oh, you think the talk is all. I must go—
Somewhere out of this house. How can I make you—"

"If—you—do!" She was opening the door wider.
"Where do you mean to go? First tell me that.
I'll follow and bring you back by force. I *will!*—"

This rising note out of the fallen condition is the essential one which Frost achieves in his greatest work. It is the outcry that comes when he follows his early advice to himself, which was to lean hard upon the facts until they hurt. It is writing which is free of Frost's usual emotional protectiveness, and it represents the highest level of his achievement as a poet.

To say this is not to undervalue the mellow resource of Frost's voice at what we might call cruising altitude, or "middle flight," as Milton called it. In that range, the poet draws *indirectly* upon a wisdom which in his greatest poems seems to be wrested *directly* from experience itself. Yet this indirection of his typical level-best work is not an evasion: within its beguiling melodies there is secluded a strong awareness of that unbeguiling world to which the melodies themselves offer a conscious resistance. Indeed, a recurring theme in Frost's work is the way a particular music can actually constitute a meaning. In "The Oven Bird," for example, the bird has the unique gift of knowing how in singing not to sing; and "The question that he frames in all but words / Is what to make of a diminished thing." On the other hand, the song of the phoebes at the end of the poem "The Need of Being Versed in Country Things" is so perfectly matched to human sentiment that it must be resisted because it is a kind of siren song. The birds come flying through the burnt-out ruin of a deserted house, but even so:

For them there was really nothing sad.
But though they rejoiced in the nest they kept,
One had to be versed in country things
Not to believe the phoebes wept.

This mixture of the rejoicing notes and the weeping notes, however, is exactly what Frost achieved in the sonnet "Never Again Would Birds' Song Be the Same," which is, among other things, an oblique dramatic statement of his own poetic creed. What we have here is not quite an allegory and not just an orotundity: we have that sensation of speech in free supply, welling up and riding fluently on the old sounds of sense, moving animatedly and skillfully over and back across the pattern of the verse form. Here, too, birdsong, that most conventional of analogies for poetic utterance, is being presented as something bearing traces of prelapsarian freedom and felicity. To misquote Hopkins slightly, it is the note that man was made for. In Frost's trope, the song of the birds is tuned to the note of Eve's voice in Eden, in much the same way as poetry is tuned to the sound of sense, and to those tones of voice that live in the original cave of the mouth. The choral joys of the mythic garden and the actual resource of the vocal cords are harmonized within a wonderful, seemingly effortless heft of language:

He would declare and could himself believe
That the birds there in all the garden round
From having heard the daylong voice of Eve
Had added to their own an oversound,
Her tone of meaning but without the words.
Admittedly an eloquence so soft
Could only have had an influence on birds
When call or laughter carried it aloft.
Be that as may be, she was in their song.
Moreover her voice upon their voices crossed
Had now persisted in the woods so long
That probably it never would be lost.
Never again would birds' song be the same.
And to do that to birds was why she came.

"He would declare and could himself believe": The first line is in the conditional, optative mood, so all that follows has to be conditional and in part wishful. There is a lovely certitude in the fantasy, but there is a regretful understanding that it is indeed a fantasy; so there is a counterweight in the line "Never again would birds' song be the same" that works against the poem's logical sense. The poem's argument, as I read it, ought to lead to the conclusion that the changed note of the birds' song should be an occasion of joy, since it happened in Paradise and was effected by the paradisial voice of Eve. But that logic is complicated by the actual note of repining that we hear in the line "Never again would birds' song be the same," a note that comes from the fact that we are now beyond Eden, at a great distance of time and space. The Adam figure, the "he" of the poem, has suffered exile from his prelapsarian bliss, so there is a counterweight of heart-break in the statement of what seemed in the beginning a heart-lifting truth.

Memories of Eden-like joys corrected and countered by an acknowledgment of their inevitable passing also underlie Frost's poem "To Earthward." This poem takes us back to Frost at his very strongest. It belongs with "Home Burial," but is intensely lyrical rather than starkly dramatic. The quatrains are like fossils, constrained within their shapes but minutely and energetically expressive of the life that gave them shape:

Love at the lips was touch
As sweet as I could bear;
And once that seemed too much;
I lived on air

That crossed me from sweet things,
The flow of—was it musk
From hidden grapevine springs
Down hill at dusk?

I had the swirl and ache
From sprays of honeysuckle
That when they're gathered shake
Dew on the knuckle.

I craved strong sweets, but those
Seemed strong when I was young;
The petal of the rose
It was that stung.

Now no joy but lacks salt
That is not dashed with pain
And weariness and fault;
I crave the stain

Of tears, the aftermark
Of almost too much love,
The sweet of bitter bark
And burning clove.

When stiff and sore and scarred
I take away my hand
From leaning on it hard
In grass and sand,

The hurt is not enough:
I long for weight and strength
To feel the earth as rough
To all my length.

This poem goes from living and walking on air to living and enduring on earth. It redresses the motion of "Birches," in which the boy climbed in order to be set down. Here the man is sustained even as he seeks to descend. The more he submits himself to the drag of experience and the pull of some moral g-factor, the more a reactive thrust is generated against it. The poetic situation at the end of "To Earthward" is rather different from the pictorial one. Pictorially, we are offered an image of the body hugging the earth, seeking to penetrate to the very *humus* in humility, wishing the ground were a penitential bed. But the paradoxical result of this drive toward abasement is a marvel of levitation: in spite of the physical push to earthward, the psychic direction is skyward. The state of things at the end of the poem is something like that formulated at the end of Frost's sonnet "A Soldier," which deals with the old subject of patriotic death in battle through a beautifully turned conceit. The soldier's body is like a lance in the dust, fallen from its trajectory. Even so, consolation can be found:

But this we know, the obstacle that checked
And tripped the body, shot the spirit on
Further than target ever showed or shone.

The sensation of spirit not so much projected onward as brimming over and above the body is what is thrilling in "To Earthward." There is a wonderful, supple, uningratiating presentation of self going on. The poem does not say "I have faults and deserve to be punished," although it may ruefully admit to this if we put the words in its mouth. Nor does it say "What a good boy am

I, to be so grown up at last." Frost is not running for cover behind cocksureness or blandishment, nor is he exercising that verbal sleight of hand which sometimes furnishes too nifty resolutions to other poems. What this poem advances is all guaranteed. It is neither specter nor sculpture: cut this verse and it will bleed. Compare it, for example, with an equivalent poem by Yeats, "Men Improve with the Years," and you are faced with something unexpected: Frost's is the poem in which he walks naked, Yeats's the one which appears more ironical and protected. The warmth of wanting to feel the earth "as rough / To all my length" contrasts well with Yeats's project of coldness in "Men Improve with the Years":

> But I grow old among dreams,
> A weather-worn, marble triton
> Among the streams.

To emphasize this recurring pattern is to highlight something of distinctive and durable value in Frost's work. It does seem to me that the poems which hold up most strongly embody one or the other of the following movements: a movement which consists of or is analogous to a fullness overflowing, or the corollary of that, a kind of reactive wave, a fullness in the process of rebounding off something or somebody else.

For examples of a fullness overflowing without complication, we need to look no further than his first collection, *A Boy's Will*, where the two acknowledged triumphs are "The Tuft of Flowers" and "Mowing." After all, the flowers which are the occasion of the former poem owe their very survival to what Frost calls "sheer morning gladness at the brim," a gladness which inspired the mower to spare them and so, by a little chain reaction of rapture, inspired the poem. Furthermore, in the sonnet about mowing, where the heart of the poetic matter is the whisper of the scythe, that scythe-whisper is itself presented as a welling up of something out of silence, an expression almost of the silence's own abounding relish of itself:

> There was never a sound beside the wood but one,
> And that was my long scythe whispering to the ground.
> What was it it whispered? I knew not well myself;
> Perhaps it was something about the heat of the sun,
> Something, perhaps, about the lack of sound—
> And that was why it whispered and did not speak.
> It was no dream of the gift of idle hours,
> Or easy gold at the hand of fay or elf:

Anything more than the truth would have seemed too weak
To the earnest love that laid the swale in rows,
Not without feeble-pointed spikes of flowers
(Pale orchises), and scared a bright green snake.
The fact is the sweetest dream that labor knows.
My long scythe whispered and left the hay to make.

This early poem broadcasts a sweetness that we credit easily and that we should set in the balance against the tales of the old poet's vanity and vindictiveness. Its melodies possess a wonderful justifying force, and remind us that Frost is, among other things, one of the most irresistible masters of the sonnet in the English language. (Think of the overbrimming technical joys of "The Silken Tent" or the high tides of mutuality in "Meeting and Passing.")

And yet, the bleaker the recognitions being forced upon Frost, the greater the chance of the absolute poem. I am thinking of a work such as "An Old Man's Winter Night," which expresses what I earlier called "the crystal of indifference" at the core of Frost's being, that which takes in and gives back the signals of a universal solitude. Samuel Beckett would surely incline an appreciative ear to the following lines, where the figure of age, in all its factuality and loneliness, is plainly and strangely rendered:

He stood with barrels round him—at a loss.
And having scared the cellar under him
In clomping here, he scared it once again
In clomping off;—and scared the outer night,
Which has its sounds, familiar, like the roar
Of trees and crack of branches, common things,
But nothing so like beating on a box.
A light he was to no one but himself
Where now he sat, concerned with he knew what,
A quiet light, and then not even that.

To read lines like these is to apprehend fleetingly what Frost means by his compelling if enigmatic declaration in "Mowing" that "The fact is the sweetest dream that labor knows." It certainly would seem that he intends this to be more than a plea for writing as a form of documentary realism. Even though such realism was what Ezra Pound found praiseworthy when he reviewed North of Boston—"Mr. Frost's people are real people"—and even though it contributed vividly to my own original pleasure in his work, it is not what the final sweetest dream is about.

In the beginning, however, I did love coming upon the inner evidence of Frost's credentials as a farmer poet. I admired, for example, the way he could describe (in "The Code") how forkfuls of hay were built upon a wagonload for easy unloading later, when they have to be tossed down from underfoot. And sometimes the evidence was more general but still completely credible, such as that fiercely direct account of a child's hand being cut off by a circular saw and the child's sudden simple death. Coming as I did from a world of farmyard stories about men crushed in quarry machinery or pulled into the drums of threshing mills, I recognized the note of grim accuracy in the poem called "Out, Out—." I was immediately susceptible to its documentary weight and did not mistake the wintry report of what happened at the end for the poet's own callousness.

Nevertheless, the counterweight, the oversound, the sweetest dream within the fact—these things are poetically more rewarding than a record, however faithful, of the data. This is why the imagined hardness of "The Most of It" more than holds its own against the cruel reporting of "Out, Out—," why the extravagance of "The Witch of Coös" excels the pastoral of "The Ax-Helve," and why the mysteriously intuited happenings at the end of "Two Look at Two" are more sustaining than the nostalgic wishfulness in the last line of "Directive":

> Two had seen two, whichever side you spoke from.
> "This *must* be all." It was all. Still they stood,
> A great wave from it going over them,
> As if the earth in one unlooked-for favor
> Had made them certain earth returned their love.

At such moments, and in such poems—if I may repeat my notion one last time—a fullness rebounds back upon itself, or it rebounds off something or someone else and thereby creates a wave capable of lifting the burden of our knowledge and the experience to a new, refreshing plane. Moreover, this bracing lyric power is as dependent on Frost's sense of his own faults as it is on his faultless ear. Implicit in many of the poems I have been praising is a capacity to recognize the shortcomings in himself, and to judge himself for the shortfall between his life and his art. But what is implicit in the poems is explicit in a dialogue which Robert Lowell records and which I wish to quote in conclusion. Here, from Lowell's collection *History*, is part of the sonnet which he calls plainly "Robert Frost":

Robert Frost at midnight, the audience gone
to vapor, the great act laid on the shelf in mothballs,
his voice is musical and raw—he writes in the flyleaf:
For Robert from Robert, his friend in the art.
"Sometimes I feel too full of myself," I say.
And he, misunderstanding, "When I am low,
I stray away ... "

                    [...]

And I, "Sometimes I'm so happy I can't stand myself."
And he, "When I am too full of joy, I think
how little good my health did anyone near me."

ROBERT FAGGEN

The Fact Is the Sweetest Dream: Darwin, Pragmatism, and Poetic Knowledge

The similarities and the crucial differences between Frost and Emerson, Thoreau, and James—the writers with whom he is most often linked—can be understood better in the light of the deeper connections between American romanticism and science. David Porter observed that Frost explored anxieties left unconsidered by Emerson.[1] Jay Parini is correct in observing that in Frost's writing Emerson's "certainty is missing" ... "replaced by a rueful skepticism; the assumed benevolence of the Creator seems missing too—that dogged faith of Emerson's in a mysterious 'unity' underlying nature."[2] But romanticism, in its emphasis on the connection between mind and nature and in its rebellion against religious authority, is deeply connected to the rise of modern natural history and science.

Emerson was himself a great exponent of science and of the progressive powers of the mind to uncover the ultimate design of creation. In the first essay "Nature," Emerson makes clear his alliance with science in the form of natural philosophy. Science was not so much a method or epistemology but, rather, an assertion of an absolute and independent knowledge of the universe liberated from theological dogma:

> Undoubtedly we have no questions to ask which are unanswerable. We must trust the perfection of the creation so far

From *Robert Frost and the Challenge of Darwin* by Robert Faggen. © 1997 by the University of Michigan.

> as to believe that whatever curiosity the order of things has
> awakened in our minds, the order of things can satisfy.... Let us
> inquire, to what end is nature?
>
> All science has one aim, namely to find a theory of nature. We
> have theories of races and of functions, but scarcely yet a remote
> approach to the idea of creation.[3]

As Emerson proceeded in this praise of natural history, he became
increasingly skeptical. The skepticism in both "Fate" and "Experience" does
not represent a reversal of his earlier essays but should be seen as a necessary
consequence of an attempt to ground the self in a reality of flux, yielding only
alienation and nescience.[4] Emerson's adherence to metamorphosis in nature
projects his own ethos of "Cherub scorn," a rebellion from a completed and
determinate history proscribed by theology. Even in his darkest moments
Emerson held that departure from the sepulchers of history into the
liberating subjectivity of nature would still yield progressively higher levels
of transcendent revelation rather than a debilitating solipsism.

Nature in both Emerson and Thoreau became a reliable domain of
escape from the confines of history. In *Walden* Thoreau's self-exile mimed the
deliberateness suggested by nature. Nature was ennobling, ultimately
answering to our questions and our need for a purifying pilgrimage:

> And we are enabled to apprehend at all what is sublime and noble
> only by the perpetual instilling and drenching of the reality which
> surrounds us. The universe constantly and obediently answers to
> our conceptions; we travel fast or slow, the track is laid for us.[5]

Robert Richardson has noted that *Walden* "was a testament to the centrality
and integrity of the individual mind observing nature."[6] But a reader of
Frost's "The Most of It" or "Design" would hardly find those poems
consonant with Thoreau's vision of a reliable nature or the centrality of the
human observer. Frost's dialogue with Thoreau, I will show, reveals
significant dissonances between the two. In an interview in which he praised
Walden Frost called himself "Thorosian."[7] This neologism was a Frostian
joke, acknowledging his debt but also the consequences of "erosion," of both
faith and epistemology, which come from descending into the matter of
natural history.

Thoreau's darker works, *Cape Cod* and *The Maine Woods*, particularly in
"Ktaadn," do place man in a belittled relation to a nature that he sees as, at

times, utterly chaotic. Thoreau's speculations about the French-Canadian Woodchopper in *Walden* and Joe Polis in *The Maine Woods* also reveal an anthropologist skeptical of his own projections. In a fascinating essay "Reflexivity as Evolution in Thoreau's *Walden*" Frederick Turner has argued that Thoreau anticipates Darwin and the birth of American evolutionary anthropology. In his encounters with "contemporary savages," Turner argues, Thoreau intuits the evolution of "civilized man from the savage."[8] Thoreau retained a Rousseauian faith in the virtues and genius of the uncivilized man, in the recovery of a prelapsarian unity of nature and spirit, and in the modern Crusoe's ability to survive independently. Frost became far more skeptical than Thoreau of the exile's ability to find epistemic consonance between inner and outer worlds or to evade severe conflict either in the wilderness or in agriculture.

Thoreau, himself, came to be a great ally of Darwin's thought, particularly on the matter of reproductivity in nature. If in the conclusion to *Walden* Thoreau praised the cypress for being free from the cycles of reproduction, he later came to praise the natural machinery of seed dispersal and reproduction that he found in Darwin. The recent publication of Thoreau's last manuscript, "The Dispersion of Seeds," confirms the extent to which "Wild Fruits," "Wild Apples," "Autumnal Tints," and "The Succession of Forest Trees" were also deeply indebted not only to Darwin's theory of natural selection but to the view that reproduction was nature's highest goal and not to romantic self-sufficiency and independence.[9] Robert Richardson has shown that "Thoreau gradually came to accept the view, for which Darwin was one more confirmation, that any ordering force in the universe must be sought in the developmental principle."[10] That development almost invariably involved a network of interdependencies to make successful propagation possible.

Frost admired the impulse to liberation that Thoreau found in nature, and he regarded Emerson's "Cherub scorn" of theology a figure for the scientific "penetration into matter."[11] But Emerson also embraced the transcendent aspects of Hinduism and the idealism of Platonism, whereas Frost held to the incarnational principle of Christianity and recognized that Western science extended it rather than diverged from it.

It should then be no surprise that Frost would also have been attracted to Darwin's voyage into the wilds of South America and Australia on the *Beagle*, which led to his repudiation of Paleyan natural theology and fundamentalist Christianity. Darwin undertook the voyage at the displeasure of his father, who thought the trip "would be disreputable to my [Charles Darwin's] character as a Clergyman hereafter."[12] Viewing the variety and grandeur of life in South America, Darwin came to doubt special creation and the design argument. His scorn of unreasonable religious authority colored his tense relation with the stubborn Captain Fitzroy, who signed Darwin on as the *Beagle*'s naturalist. Darwin's Whig politics were opposed to Fitzroy's Toryism, and the naturalist hated Fitzroy's advocacy of slavery.[13] Ironically, it was Fitzroy, a religious fundamentalist, who gave Darwin a copy of Lyell's *Geology*, hoping that the young naturalist would be able to find evidence to debunk its challenge to the biblical account of creation. Instead, Lyell's work and his own observations on the *Beagle* went far to undermine Darwin's acceptance of Genesis as literal truth.

Though Lyell's work was crucial to Darwin, only one book accompanied him everywhere during his travels—Milton's poetry, of which his favorite was *Paradise Lost*.[14] Darwin's interest in Milton may have been more than a vestige of faith: admiration of a great heretic who defied accepted theology and boldly reinscribed creation in his attempt at theodicy.[15] In his own distrust of mysticism, and religious and political authority, Milton set his own rationalistic God upon the heavenly throne. Milton the Arminian, Arian, and mortalist abandoned mystical explanations of divine operations; the archangel Raphael (all of Milton's archangels are material beings) warns the inquiring Adam that all earth's creatures, including man, are "one first matter all" (Book 5, l. 473). Advising Adam that he can only explain things heavenly in terms of things earthly, Raphael begins to shift from metaphor to synecdoche when he expresses the material continuum between the angels and man. Milton's ambivalence toward fixed hierarchy found expression in Raphael's organic figure of the possibilities of Adam's development, however circumscribed by the contingencies of choice (see especially Book 5, ll. 468–505) and his adherence to a hierarchy of natures. Darwin's own exploration of God's laws of development reveals an interpenetrating and fluid material world, as though Milton's heaven had finally been brought to earth in a pastoral leveling in which God is finally "all in all."

Milton's vision of the ominpresence of a primordial, material chaos— the primacy of matter—also made an impression on the young Darwin's imagination. In 1832, while traveling in Baiha Blanca, Darwin described the landscape in terms of Milton's chaos: "It was impossible to behold this plain of matter, as it were melted and consuming by heat, without being reminded of Milton's descriptions of the regions of Chaos and Anarchy."[16] In book 2 of *Paradise Lost* Satan leaves for his journey to earth. The passage emphasizes continual instability, potentiality, and warfare in the "womb of nature." Milton drew heavily on Lucretius' *De Rerum Natura* for this vision of primordial nature. Striking references to this passage by Thoreau in "Ktaadn" and by Stevens in "Sunday Morning" bespeak its power as a challenge to the Puritan faith in nature and the American wilderness as a place of salvation:

> the gates wide open stood,
> That with extended wings a bannered host
> Under spread ensigns marching might pass through
> With horse and chariots ranked in loose array;
> So wide they stood, and like a furnace mouth
> Cast forth redounding smoke and ruddy flame.
> Before their eyes in sudden view appear
> The secrets of the hoary deep, a dark
> Illimitable ocean without bound.
> Without dimension; where length, breadth, and highth,
> And time and place are lost; where eldest Night
> And Chaos, ancestors of Nature, hold
> Eternal anarchy, amidst the noise
> Of endless wars, and by confusion stand....
> To whom these most adhere,
> He rules a moment; Chaos umpire sits,
> And by decision more embroils the fray
> By which he reigns; next to him high arbiter
> Chance governs all. Into this wild abyss,
> The womb of Nature and perhaps her grave,
> Of neither sea, nor shore, nor air, nor fire,
> But all these in their pregnant causes mixed
> Confus'dly, and which thus must ever fight,
> Unless th'Almighty Maker them ordain
> His dark materials to create more worlds,
> Into this wild abyss the wary Fiend
> Stood on the brink of hell and looked a while
> Pondering his voyage; for no narrow frith
> He had to cross.[17]

This significant elaboration of the idea of the "tohu-wa-bohu"—formless and void—of Genesis posits the fundamental power of a material world existing outside God. Milton populates this abyss of things with warring factions, most notably governed by "chance." These are God's "dark materials," which reign except when pressed by the maker "to create more worlds." Milton's attempt at theodicy in incorporating the knowledge of science becomes a tragedy of knowledge itself—a battlefield of unreconciled contradictions and a view of the creator and his ways that neither justifies nor exempts Him from evil.

Darwin's recollection of Satan viewing chaos as he viewed Baiha Blanca underscores a parallel. Darwin's own journey, like that of his Miltonic forerunner, ushered a terrible, withering knowledge into a world satisfied with its theology, reanimating—without Paradise and redemption—the power of the idea of original sin. The changing conditions of existence and the literal relations of the human to the rest of the animal kingdom became a moral rebuke to human arrogance: "—the mind of man is no more perfect, than instincts of animals to all & the changing contingencies, or bodies of either.—Our descent, then, is the origin of our evil passions!!—The Devil under form of Baboon is our grandfather!—"[18] The epigraph Freud used for *The Interpretation of Dreams* could well have been the motto for all of Darwin's work: "Flectere si nequeo superos, Acheronta movebo." Darwin's voyage to the nether regions of the world and, metaphorically, into the deep past of the earth gave him the artillery to move the upper regions of civilized life into a troubling awareness of its lowly origins: "with his god-like intellect which has penetrated into the movements and constitution of the solar system—with all these exalted powers—Man still bears in his bodily frame the indelible stamp of his lowly origin."[19]

Frost shares the romantic scientist's forbidden quest into the chaotic underworld as well as the ultimate moral rebuke to the progress and moral and spiritual purity of civilization. Frost, like Darwin and Freud, challenged human narcissism, and science was his weapon of choice. He both feared and enjoyed the struggle and flux, the combat and sexual conflict, implicit in Darwin's vision of survival and renewal. "Every poem," Frost wrote in 1946, "is an epitome of the great predicament, the will braving alien entanglements."[20] This defining statement about poetry and life can be understood better in light of both Darwin and Schopenhauer as far more than an expression of paranoid heroism. The figure of the will braving "entanglements" evokes Darwin's conclusion to *On the Origin of Species*, in which various creatures are pursuing their interests in an "entangled bank":

> It is interesting to contemplate an entangled bank, clothed with
> many plants of many kinds, with birds singing on bushes, with
> various insects flitting about, and with worms crawling through
> the damp earth, and to reflect these elaborately constructed
> forms, so different from each other, and dependent on each other

in so complex a manner, have all been produced by laws acting around us.[21]

These entanglements often enough erupt in warfare for limited supplies or through successful propagation. Both Frost and Darwin were attentive readers of Schopenhauer.[22] And Frost's contemporaries duly noted the importance of Schopenhauer in the development of scientific thought. In his lecture "The Rise of the Doctrine of Evolution," Royce pointed out that "Schopenhauer's view that the longing and struggling will cannot be described apart from experience ... brings him very near the position of most students of modern science. Schopenhauer marks, then, in the history of thought, the transition from romantic idealism to the modern realism, the return to the natural order."[23] Behind Darwin's many kinds and the laws that produce them is Schopenhauer's "will-to-live"—not the individual will but the world's will manifesting itself in individuals: "At bottom, optimism is the unwarranted self-praise of the real author of the world, namely of the will-to-live which complacently mirrors itself in its work." This work is "the continuance of the whole as well as that of every individual being, the conditions are sparingly and scantily given, and nothing beyond these. Therefore the individual life is a ceaseless struggle for existence itself, while at every step it is threatened with destruction."[24]

"Spring Pools" is a stunning meditation on the limits of reflective consciousness born of and struggling among "alien entanglements" in the material world. The pools "still reflect / The total sky," with *still* suggesting both persistence and motionlessness. The mimetic power of reflection is only "*almost* without defect," still imperfect. Aside from that limitation the pools and "the flowers beside them" will be destroyed by other and more powerful life forms, "roots to bring dark foliage on," which demand nourishment and, in doing so, leave the weaker to perish in the inevitable, silent struggle for existing resources of both water and light. (*Dark*, then, in describing the foliage of the trees, is both literal and metaphoric.)

The second stanza expresses the poet's threat against the "trees" and their "pent-up buds," attributing evil to what is merely the inevitable and nonmoral. The "flowery waters" and "watery flowers" of the penultimate line mirror each other but become part of a temporary, oneiric world of consciousness. The final line accepts the inevitability of the change and deflates the anthropic grandeur of the preceding imprecation: "From snow that melted only yesterday" suggests an acceptance of the transformation and ephemerality of all forms in the material world, including those vehicles of "reflection." Most important, the pools owe their existence to prior forms of matter, "snow that melted only yesterday."

DARWIN'S LONG ARGUMENT AND NATURE'S CHAOS

To understand the significance of Darwin for Frost and for pragmatism, it is essential to describe the interplay of fact and metaphor in Darwin's vision, if only to show that it was anything but crudely reductive and does not simply provide a deterministic account of progress with man as the moral and intellectual pinnacle. Philosophies of social, psychological, and spiritual evolution in the late nineteenth and early twentieth centuries reflected the persistence of both Christian and Enlightenment concepts of progress. Some of these reconstructions, however, though often in dialogue with Darwin, had little to do with Darwin himself. Bertrand Russell wrote in 1914: "Evolutionism, in one form or another, is the prevailing creed of our time. It dominates our politics, our literature, and not least our philosophy. Nietzsche, pragmatism, Bergson, are phases in its philosophic development, and their popularity far beyond circles of professional philosophers shows its consonance with the spirit of the age."[25] In America Henry Adams sought a scientific model to save history from chaos and entertained Darwinism as a possible paradigm of development. But he found in it only a limiting methodology and recognized the difference between the implications of Darwin's concept of natural selection and the creed of progressive evolutionism:

> behind the lesson of the day, he [Adams] was conscious that, in geology as in theology, he could prove only Evolution that did not evolve; Uniformity that was not uniform; and Selection that did not select. To other Darwinians—*except Darwin*—Natural selection seemed a dogma to be put in the place of the Athanasian creed; it was a form of religious hope; a promise of ultimate perfection. Adams wished no better; he warmly sympathised with the object; but when he came to ask himself what he truly thought, he felt that he had no Faith; that whenever the next new hobby should be brought out, he should surely drop off from Darwinism like a monkey from a perch; that the idea of form, Law, Order, or Sequence had no more value for him than the idea of none; that what he valued most was Motion, and that what attracted his mind was change.[26]

Adams was suspicious of evolutionary theory turned into a theology, particularly because he became fascinated by historical change. Longing for the medieval order of a completed universe that could not be regained, Adams became fascinated by its opposite: historical change and, ultimately, chaos. He recognized that Darwin's theory, not the creed of progress that some derived from it, was in its implications a fable of mere change and disorder.

Darwin's vision of descent by natural selection contained powerful contradictions that led to the disintegration of any objective conception of nature and that continue to haunt natural science and philosophy. There is a continual dialogue between design and chance, designed laws and a mutability that defies categorization. While emphasizing the deistic view of a creator separated from his creation, which operates according to designed laws, he maintains a sense of providential history and teleology but unknowable from the quotidian contingencies of random events. Asserting the reality of a natural process that governs history, a limited epistemology governed by inference from fact precludes the possibility of reconstructing that history or of knowing its value. Reversing the Enlightenment and romantic privilege accorded to mind, Darwin's epistemology is more cautious about allowing facts to conform to the tyranny of an a priori conception of the whole or of human ideas of purpose. Parts and facts become the primary materials from which we must labor to infer larger contexts.

Natural selection, the mechanism of Darwin's view of evolution, is based on an analogy to the purposive work of animal breeders in picking traits of animals. He acknowledges that breeders participate in the process but points out that they do so in a way that is self-interested. In drawing an analogy between artificial and natural selection, Darwin posits the fact that humans "unconsciously" participate in natural selection. All human choices are ironies, often serving purposes other than those consciously intended. Human fascination with beautiful forms is meaningless except insofar as it serves the interest of procreation.

Nature, in contrast to the artificial, selects but without self-interest. How, then, does nature "select" in any purposive sense? It seems only a mindless process of allowing chance variations from some mysterious source fight it out on the battlefield with the winner left standing, more elimination and waste than choosing. For Darwin the metaphor of selection, with its implied sense of consciousness and purposiveness, still had meaning when transferred to nature. He insisted that nature was an altruistic provider, a maternal laborer choosing variations for the benefit of each of her creatures:

As man can produce and certainly has produced a great result by
his methodical and unconscious means of selection, what may not
nature effect? Man can act only on external and visible characters:
nature cares nothing for appearances, except in so far as they may
be useful to any being. She can act on every internal organ, on
every shade of constitutional difference, on the whole machinery
of life. Man selects only for his own good; Nature only for that of
the being which she tends.[27]

Darwin justifies the imperceptibly slow process of development by
natural selection with profoundly moral rhetoric that echoes I Samuel 16:7:
"For the lord seeth not as man seeth; for man looketh on the outward
appearance, but the lord looketh on the heart." This is the moment when
Samuel selects David to be the future King of Israel. The fact that David is
the youngest of Jesse's sons and the last to be presented represents an
important dramatic instance of biblical pastoralism: God subverts and
overrules human conceptions of primogeniture, hierarchy, and order. The
paradox can be found encapsulated in the Sermon on the Mount or in the
Gospel of St. Mark, that the meek shall inherit the earth and that the first
shall be last. In Darwin's world, the small, minute, and the lowly are revealed
to have great power beyond artificial forms of human control and prediction.
    In addition to being altruistic, natural selection will produce
perfection: "And as natural selection works solely by and for the good of each
being, all corporeal and mental endowments will tend to progress toward
perfection."[28] But perfection, here, is only a tendency and at best a
fulfillment of a certain potential within the limits of an organism and its
internal and external conditions. This maternal altruist-giver may not be
self-interested, but what she gives to each is often part of a general weaponry
for one creature to fight another in self-interest. Darwin's nature is a
provider of supplies and weaponry in warfare in and against environments
that include other creatures: "Thus from the war of nature, from famine and
death, the most exalted object of which we are capable of conceiving, namely,
the production of higher animals, directly follows."[29] Darwin admits,
however, that the valuative term *higher* is empty: "The embryo in the course
of development generally rises in organization: I use this expression, though
I am aware that it is impossible to define clearly what is meant by the
organization being higher or lower."[30]
    Darwin asserts the reality of a temporal hierarchy associated with
"fitness" and that those who are currently alive are actually better by
definition than their predecessors:

There has been much discussion whether recent forms are more highly developed than ancient. I will not here enter on this subject, for naturalists have not as yet defined to each other's satisfaction what is meant by high and low forms. But in one particular sense recent forms must, on my theory, be higher than more ancient; for each new species is formed having had some advantage in the struggle for life over other and preceding forms.[31]

But Darwin's invocation of a principle of "conditions of existence" threatens the teleology implied in this temporal hierarchy. Power resulting from inheritance, the "unity of type," is perpetually unstable because material conditions, internal and external, are always subject to change:

> For natural selection acts by either now adapting the varying parts of each being to its organic and inorganic conditions of life; or by having them adapted during long-past periods of time.... Hence, in fact, the law of Conditions of Existence is the higher law; as it includes, through inheritance of former adaptations, that of Unity of Type.[32]

Natural selection, then, becomes relative, since it acts "chiefly through the competition of the inhabitants one with another, and consequently will produce perfection, or strength in the battle for life, only according to the standard of that country."[33]

Assuming a creature has been "selected," what is it selected for? To make the right sexual selection and produce more of its kind. Successful creatures propagate because that is how they became successful. The purpose of life is to produce more life, and success means no rest or reward but the obligation to continue being successful in the battle of life. Individual creatures manifest life's purposes, with little regard to the individual creature's own sense of purpose. Teleology fades not only in the random process of creating life forms but also in the ultimate aims of life itself. Since no creature can be perfect because of the inevitable variations and conflicts in nature, this process is nonprogressive and nonteleological.

Aside from the tension between providence and chance in his account of natural process, Darwin's other assumptions about ontology threatens the whole of his (or any) epistemology. He was interested in the origins of new species, not in the beginning or original intention of life: "I must premise, that I have nothing to do with the origin of the primary mental powers, any

more than I have with that of life itself."[34] Origin, then, means only
circumstances and conditions that produce variant species, not a course of
progress. Even the species concept, however, is drawn into question.
Linnaean taxonomy and Paleyan concepts of design give way; being becomes
becoming, and Platonic, fixed categories disappear. This makes for a radical
nominalism that precludes the ability to account for any history of
development.[35] Classifications become mere words that attempt but
ultimately fail to grasp the vast complexity of a world of transitional forms
without distinct boundaries:

> Certainly no clear line of demarcation has yet been drawn
> between species and sub-species—that is, the forms which in the
> opinion of some naturalists come very near to, but do not arrive
> at the rank of species; or, again, between sub-species and well-
> marked varieties, or between lesser varieties and individual
> differences. These differences blend into each other in an
> insensible series; and a series impresses the mind with the idea of
> an actual passage.[36]

Evolution, then, is a leap of inference by which individuals are grouped
according to an "insensible series," one which cannot be perceived but must
be intuited. This "series," already a fiction, "impresses the mind," but only
with "the idea of an actual passage." Any narrative of evolution would be a
projection of the mind onto the oceanic multiplicity of forms that do not
submit readily to human naming. The imperfection of the geological record,
which does not reveal the necessary temporal connections of existing and
extinct creatures, threatens always to make the organic world seem an
"inextricable chaos."[37]

The greatest irony in Darwin's thought is the placing of the human
mind within natural history and material descent. He completes the
Enlightenment's decoupling of the mind from divinity; mind has its origins
in matter, matter developed in unpredictable ways by historical process. Not
only is culture historicized, but so is the human mind itself, as it becomes
part of the chaos: "We can understand why a classification founded on any
single character or organ—even an organ so wonderfully complex as the
brain—or the high development of mental faculties, is almost sure to prove
unsatisfactory."[38] The human can be only nominally distinguished from the
rest of the world and becomes an unstable category. Human thought is
brought low and made equal to the survival instruments of other creatures

whose own persistence may be of equal or greater value than human intelligence.

How can mind know the thing of which it is only a tentative and momentary part? Further, how can we be sure that human intelligence is the ultimate reality if the concepts of higher and lower forms are eradicated in a material natural democracy with only temporary dominators? This is, to use Pirandello's phrase, the kick that knocks the whole house apart. Ideas are only temporary instruments in a struggle for survival and control. As Frank Lentricchia has pointed out, what "Kantians describe as the inventive factor in consciousness becomes, after Darwin and the pragmatists, not merely the ground of a cognitively coherent phenomenal experience but a life-preserving response to a hostile, life-denying world."[39] An ongoing battlefield in which hierarchies are made and unmade, in which momentary difference collapses into a leveled equality, is the essence of Darwin's pastoral vision.

Frost often dramatizes the pursuit of verifiable entities, acknowledging their transience and the self-deceptions of a nonobjective observer. Framed by an accentual equivalent of classical, deliberate hendecasyllables, Frost's "For Once, Then, Something" conveys a desire to find a reality beyond the narcissism of human self-reflection while satirizing the futility of that pursuit and the way it is framed by culturally given forms. The poem makes us acutely aware that cognitive conceptions of reflection, surface, and depth are metaphoric and that the pursuit of "truth" is framed by those older constructs, much like the well itself. The "others" of the first line may well be scientists and empiricists who taunt the narrator for looking only at his reflection, which "Gives me back in a shining surface picture / Me myself in the summer heaven godlike / Looking out of a wreath of fern and cloud puffs." Willing to satisfy those who taunt his narcissism, he demonstrates that little else can be known. What he perceives, the "something," is lost when "Water came to rebuke the too clear water," suggesting that the flux of life destroys clear and permanent perception. *Rebuke*, to describe the waves of water, suggests that flux has the moral force of upsetting stagnation and complacency: The title and final line can be taken in two ways: first, *once* and *then* are temporal and suggest a single moment in the past obliterated by time. The same words can be taken as part of an emphatic expression of having found "something." The poem ends with an unresolved tension between loss and gain, mockery and satisfaction. *Something* and *thing* are words which resonate throughout Frost ("The Oven Bird," "Hyla Brook," "Mending Wall," "Design") and should not be taken entirely as a joke. In a late, powerful lyric, "Choose Something Like a Star," the demands for nature to conform to "Fahrenheit" and "Centigrade" terms of measurement are rebuked by a star that says only "I burn." But the star, and the power and force it embodies, "does tell something in the end." The something is a moral rebuke to our narcissism and our demands that the world conform to images, measurements, and metaphors appealing to our sensibilities.

The pursuit of "things," "*res*," "facts" is part of all Frost's poetry and allies him with efforts of science. If Frost is mocking Emerson's view of natural facts as signs of spiritual facts, he is nevertheless fascinated by other kinds of inferences that can be made from facts. Darwin's books *The Voyage of the* Beagle and *On the Origin of Species*, which Frost read as a special student at Harvard, are, as Hayden White has said, "summas of the literature of fact."[40] Involving a variety or cluster of metaphors to describe the process of transformation—"descent," "selection," "struggle for existence," "warfare of nature," "variation," and "Tree of Life"—Darwin's "long argument" remained, by his own admission, open to the challenges of new evidence and new experience and in constant need of recapitulation.[41] These larger metaphors always have for Darwin both a reality and a limitation. The selection of animal breeders is actually part of natural selection. The struggle for existence does actually contain "warfare" of tribe against tribe, although Darwin acknowledges that it also means subsistence on limited resources. The tree of life does literally correspond to a diverging and converging interplay of life forms as well as being a figurative map of lineage. Human selectors do actually participate in natural selection. Aside from its fabric of metaphors, Darwin's *On the Origin of Species* relies heavily on a continual accumulation of facts that, he hopes, will reveal a process. Observations of individual creatures or situations, such as the intercontinental transfer of seeds in the talons of birds, become figures from which a significant part of the machinery of dissemination, instead of special creation, can be inferred. The continual accumulation of these images make them each a synecdoche, a part that does not quite stand for but provides a sample of the totality.

In trying to show that all creatures are descended from common ancestors, Darwin knew he would have to rely on analogies, specifically homologies that would connect all creatures on the plain of the literal. But he also feared analogy as an inadequate proof of the reality he envisioned. In attempting to prove common descent of all creatures, Darwin wrote in his notebooks: "I fear argument must rest upon analogy."[42] But he wrote later in another notebook that analogies produce insights into the real: "experience has shown ... that analogy is a sure guide & my theory explains why it is a sure guide."[43] Darwin's distrust of "analogy" kept him from going to a final step in interpreting facts, to a "belief that all plants and animals are descended from some one prototype,"[44] and he believed that natural history would eventually "cease to be metaphorical and will have plain signification."[45] Like Thoreau, he would like to speak without metaphor. Unlike Thoreau, Darwin's and Frost's desire for "plain signification" does not lead to spirit but, rather, to a completely materialized world that rebukes the observer with its multiplicity and mutability.

Frost believed analogy was the basis of thought, but like the scientist, he felt that analogies must bear the test not only of workability but of reality. "Poets and scientists have in common the biggest thing of all—their metaphors. The poet and the scientist think by metaphor"[46] Facts in Frost serve as momentary points of order, tentative synecdoches for a scheme of coherence. Frost called himself a "synecdochist": "I started calling myself a synecdochist when others called themselves Imagists or Vorticists…. Always, always a larger significance. A little thing touches a larger thing."[47] There is a literal sense of the contiguity of "things" in the plane of the real, which suggests larger connections and processes, not moments of spiritual epiphany. These things are often the irreducible facts in the poems—orchids, walls, ax helves, butterflies—which clarify and order the chaos by revealing aspects of the way things work, "samples." Frost's humility about how much "larger a thing" can be realized is an important characteristic of his thought: "My ambition has been to have it said of me: He made a few connections."[48]

Nature became to Frost and to his contemporaries a vast chaos in an ongoing battle of forms to which the mind contributes additional forms. This has little to do with progress, and in his notebooks Frost was careful to make the distinction between evolution and progress. Progress is nothing more than a projection of recurrent cycles of civilization onto a vast battlefield of imperceptibly slow change:

> Much confusion comes from confusing progress with evolution. Progress goes on visibly around us mounting from savagery to barbarism to civilization to sophistication to decadence and so to destruction. Evolution is a change from form to form invisible, imperceptible and only known if at all by inference like the state of a great battle.[49]

Frost also reveals his unwillingness to regard any civilization as more than a temporary efflorescence, or growth that rises and falls in the immense and chaotic battle of evolution. Frost's use of the word *sophistication* to describe the end point of any civilization betrays some of his own pastoral racialism;

to sophisticate means "to adulterate," and, as I will show, maintenance of clear identity becomes essential to his sense of even temporary survival.

Frost appreciated chaos as a weapon in his war against his collectivity and utopianism. In *Letter to* The Amherst Student the phrase "democratic-socialist-communist-anarchist" describes a "progress" from the individual to the collective and back to the anarchic. We are "born to" and enjoy the anticollective chaos. Form becomes only an "instrument" of temporary control, not the way to perfection or divine reality:

> The background in hugeness and confusion shading away from where we stand into black and utter chaos; and against the background any small man-made figure of order and concentration. What pleasanter than it should be so. Unless we are novelists or economists we don't worry about this confusion; we look out on [it] with an instrument to tackle it to reduce it. It is partly because we are afraid it might prove too much for us and our blend of democratic-socialist-communist-anarchist party. But it is more because we like it, born used to it and have practical reasons for wanting it there. To me any little form I assert upon it is velvet, as the saying is, and to be considered for how much more it is than nothing. If I were a Platonist I should have to consider it, I suppose, for how much less it is than everything.[50]

Though the view that the human mind provides constructs to tackle chaos can be found in pragmatism, Frost stops far short of James's belief that human additions complete reality. But the rejection of Platonism as a determining and controlling reality informs the natural science that gave birth to Darwin, James, and Frost.[51]

Frost's rebuke of Platonism carries with it as much moral force as epistemology. He shares with Aristotle the substantiation of form with matter but extends this to the idea that matter precedes form. Ideas have their roots in the noticing of natural traits, their origin in matter that "comes up from below," "the part of nature not yet human." Neohumanists and Platonists suffer, according to Frost, the pride that positions the human mind and its ideas in a special relation to a divine or ethereal origin. Nature poetry and nature science share the limited process of noticing details, "from the ground up":

> I have a growing suspicion, that might line me up in disloyalty to the humanists, that nothing comes down from above but what has

so long since come up from below that we have forgotten its
origin. All is observation of nature (human nature included),
consciously or unconsciously made by our eyes and minds,
developed from the ground up. We notice traits of nature—that's
all we do. The so-called nature poet, so tiresome to some, toils
not neither does he spin like a natural scientist, but it is to the
natural scientist he is nearest of kin in his fresh noticing of
details.... The proud humanists would be right if they said they
held themselves above the part of nature not yet human. Or
nearer right than when they put on airs of disdain for the praise
of outdoors that, without exclamation of wonderful and beautiful,
pays tribute by reporting details not previously mentioned. That's
nature poetry and nature science.[52]

Darwin makes a very similar dig at Platonism in his own notebooks: "Plato
says in Phaedo that our '*necessary ideas*' arise from the preexistence of the
soul, are not derivable from experience—read monkeys for preexistence."[53]
Frost did not follow the romantic view that the individual found limitless
power from the impulses of nature, and he distrusted the use of analogies by
which the natural serves the spiritual power of the observer.

If Frost accepted the lowly and material origin of our ideas, he also
regarded them as dependent upon and subject to the same laws that govern
nature: growth and decay. In "Education by Poetry" most of Frost's examples
of the possibilities and limitations of metaphor derive from science; one of
the most instructive is his discussion of "evolution," and he recognized—
before Lévi-Straus—the power of metaphor in a culture to structure our
thoughts. The figure, he says, is based on the fact of "the growing plant," or
"growing thing," and is as ancient as Aristotle's discussion of nature in
Physics. Frost deprecates extending this figure beyond its observable basis to
a metaphysical principle of unlimited, progressive development; the vulgar
use of the the term *evolution* has little to do with Darwin's vision of descent
and modification through natural selection:

Another metaphor that has interested us in our time and has done
all our thinking for us is the metaphor of evolution. Never mind
going into the Latin word. The metaphor is simply the metaphor
of the growing plant or the growing thing. And somebody very
brilliantly, quite a while ago, said that the whole universe, the
whole of everything was like unto a growing thing. That is all. I
know the metaphor will break down at some point, but it has not

failed everywhere. It is a very brilliant metaphor, I acknowledge, though I myself get too tired of the kind of essay that talks about the evolution of candy, we will say, or the evolution of elevators—the evolution of this, that, and the other. Everything is evolution. I emancipate myself by simply saying that I didn't get up the metaphor and so am not much interested in it.[54]

The term *evolution* becomes itself a metaphor for logic or thought that reaches too far beyond its limits in observation. In "The Literate Farmer and the Planet Venus," the traveler invokes the world of darkness, night, and the unconscious as a rebuke of progressive tracks of logic:

'We need the interruption of the night
To ease attention off when overtight,
To break our logic in too long a flight,
And ask us if our premises are right.'

The wide variety of "growths" from which we derive figures of thought cannot be readily unified as a linear series; no growth can forget its roots. Frost's concept of nature rejects the monolithic and monometaphorical and embraces a pluralistic and chaotic world barely capable of unified comprehension except as it follows general rules of development:

There are growths. We know no such thing as growth unlimited. All growths we know are toward ends—deaths, whether of persons, trees, or nations. The purpose seems to be rounding off and rounding off and rounding off. Perpetual rounding suggests a rounding off of the whole of existence. That would be evolution by analogy. All analogy breaks down. That means taking too long a view. We can't think of good without evil. Neither can come to an end without the other. The rounding off here could only be in the last of both of them.[55]

The romantic desire to unify historical experience in a vision or image of return fails for Frost, in part, because of his doubts about the sanctity or immortality of the soul. Coleridge and Wordsworth presented myths of reintegration with nature that produced a feeling of being at one with the divine or eternal. Coleridge used the ancient circular figure of the ouroboros to evoke the sense of unity desirable in poetry: "The common end of all narrative, nay, of all Poems is to convert a series into a Whole: to make those events, which in real or imagined history move in a straight line, assume to our understanding a circular motion—the snake with its Tail in its Mouth."[56] In "A Masque of Reason" Frost's Job uses the emblem ouroboros as "the symbol of eternity" or "the form of forms," only to say that in modernity it stands for the circularity of our thought—from matter to form and back again—not mysteriously more but "less than I can understand." Modern science, in denying the grounds of any formal causes, of Platonic form, of the divine or ontological realm, becomes merely circular reasoning. Hypotheses reflect their own operating limitations and have no foundations other than the limited observations from which they grow. Frost quotes a metaphysical assertion in Emerson's "Uriel" that "line in nature is not found, / Unit and universe are round, / In vain produced all rays return" but substantiates the metaphor with Einstein's views about the limits of light emitted by sources whose life ends in deterioration and extinction:

> I expected more
> Than I could understand and what I get
> Is almost less than I can understand.
> But I don't mind. Let's leave it as it stood.
> The point was it was none of my concern.
> I stick to that. But talk about confusion!
> How is that for a mix-up, Thyatira?
> Yet I suppose what seems to us confusion
> Is not confusion, but the form of forms,
> The serpent's tail stuck down the serpent's throat,
> Which is the symbol of eternity
> And also of the way all things come round,
> Or of how rays return upon themselves,
> To quote the greatest Western poem yet.
> Though I hold rays deteriorate to nothing.
> First white, then red, then ultra red, then out.

Frost was less concerned with the revision of theories and beliefs than with their abandonment or disintegration. Beliefs as well as theories also demand shedding because "any belief you sink into when you should be leaving it behind is an illusion. Reality is the cold feeling on the end of the trout's nose from the stream that runs away."[57] And Frost's reality is presented as a metaphor, in terms of the struggle to swim against an entropic stream. Frost did believe in a reality that he defined ethically by the way it is always chilling to our hopes and passions. Religious understanding for Frost

involves a perception of a reality that is not a construct but, rather, a letting
go of metaphors. There is a distrust of final form: "Our perception of God is
that emotion that throws off the metaphors."[58] Closure in theory, form, or
belief would be tantamount to stagnation and comfort and a betrayal of an
impulse of relentless labor in nature: "Believing in God you believe the
future in, believe it into existence. Belief is the end of the sentence more felt
than seen—the end of the paragraph, the end of the chapter. There is no end
so final, no form so closed that it hasn't an unclosed place that opens into
further form."[59] The scientific distrust of human thought and the pursuit of
reality combine in Frost to emphasize not only the creation of constructs,
feats of association, but their abandonment. Frost did not hold, however, to
Emerson's view that nature or thought produced "*ascension*, or the passage of
the soul into higher forms,"[60] nor to James's view that man creates forms that
complete reality. *Further* in Frost does not have the optimistic and
evolutionary resonance that *higher* does in Emerson; it means "difference"
and not "betterness."[61]

Frost also expressed his criticism of Emerson's monism, his being "too
Platonic about evil," in geometric terms that remind us of the figures so
important to Donne and Marvell in describing the shift from the Ptolemaic
to the Copernican and Keplerian cosmologies.[62] Commenting on Emerson's
line "unit and universe are round," Frost added that "another poem could be
made from that, to the effect that ideally in thought only is a circle round. In
practice in nature, the circle becomes an oval. As a circle it has one center—
Good. As an oval it has two centers—Good and Evil. Thence monism versus
dualism."[63] Frost's dualism did not distinguish between heaven and earth but
described an immanent ongoing conflict. The difference between thought
and practice marked the end of the Ptolemaic and the beginning of the
Copernican cosmology. And Kepler's suprarational assumption of the sun's
power enabled him to go beyond the Copernican assumptions of circular
planetary orbits to the possibility of ovals and eventually of ellipses.[64] Frost
uses the analogy of a shift in thought about planetary revolutions to describe
the moral ambiguities brought about by a scientific revolution which
collapsed the hierarchical assumptions of a perfect, heavenly order.

The concept of endlessly superseding ideas and forms are, of course,
part of an organic vision. Frost compared all life to a tree flourishing in
perished matter, denying the intervention of divine or supernatural forces
and the possibility of escape from the cycle. Frost adheres to the Aristotelian
substantiation of form by matter but understood that, if they depart from the
classical and medieval adherence to the idea of universals, all forms become
malleable and temporary. "The medium in which life alone can flourish is

perished matter. The little organized lines in a bath of broken down organisms—disorganisms. The Tree stands growing in its own waste—the bark it sheds and the branches. There is no evolution—only growth of something in its own waste."[65] Frost's image is remarkably similar to Darwin's "Tree of Life" in *On the Origin of Species*. A tree, a part of the organic world standing for the whole of it, illustrates Darwin's branching conception of descent from a common ancestor. Its literal ramifications are the individual forms of life. These forms have their own figurative ramifications as synecdoches for the overall process of life. The tree is a figure that Darwin describes as "true," not only because it so vividly illustrates his map of descent but because it is a powerful symbol of the interrelatedness of the organic world he is describing.[66] Unlike the chain of being, its great predecessor in cosmology, the tree and all its ramifications break down and cover the earth in an image of overgrowth and entanglement rather than in a fully comprehensible design that would correspond to human artifice and the need for finality. The tree is a form that describes the way all forms or growths break down in the process of change:

> The affinities of all the beings of the same class have sometimes been represented by a great tree. I believe this simile speaks the truth. The green and budding twigs may represent existing species. At each period of growth all the growing twigs have tried to branch out on all sides, and to overtop and kill the surrounding twigs and branches, in the same manner as species and groups of species have tried to overmaster other species in the great battle for life.... As buds give rise by growth to fresh buds, and these, if vigorous, branch out and overtop on all sides many a feebler branch, so by generation I believe it has been with the great Tree of Life, which fills with its dead and broken branches the crust of the earth, and covers the surface with its ever branching ramifications.[67]

Frost stated in "The Constant Symbol" that "every poem is a new metaphor inside or it is nothing. And there is a sense in which all poems are the same old metaphor always."[68] He is describing a Heraclitean paradox of permanence within natural change of the kind embodied in the figure of the Tree of Life; new forms, like branches, are synecdoches of the permanent process of growth and decay. The image of growth and movement (and attempts at knowledge and order) amid decay and waste is an important figure in some of Frost's best poems, including "Mowing," "Birches," "After

Apple-Picking," "The Wood-Pile," "Design," and "The Census-Taker." The
emotional force of many of these poems comes from being excluded from the
thrust of life: "As far as we can see it's material, thrust toward something. Our
grief, our pain, is our feeling of being cast off from this thrust and wasted so
to speak."[69]

DARWIN AND THE RISE OF PRAGMATISM

Frost had significant indoor and outdoor schooling in the practice and
philosophy of science, which made his encounter with Darwin
unavoidable.[70] Carl Burrell, a close friend and mentor of Frost in his teen
years, taught him both botanizing—particularly about orchids—and
farming. Burrell was also fascinated by the problems of evolution and its
conflict with religion; he had a large collection of works on the subject,
which he shared and discussed with Frost and which included Darwin,
Huxley, Spencer, Edward Clodd, Grant Allen, Henry Drummond, and
Richard Proctor.[71]

When Frost studied at Harvard from 1898 to 1900, he came into
contact with intellectuals who were the direct inheritors of the post-
Darwinian controversies. At Harvard Asa Gray had been defending Darwin
as having restored teleology to natural phenomena by his transmutation
hypothesis, while Louis Agassiz condemned it as tantamount to undermining
special creation and divine authority. Frost's favorite hobby, botany, was the
focus of many of those debates. Some theologians equated Darwin with
progressive evolutionism and, therefore, a renewal of the Christian idea of
redemption, while others welcomed its erosion of sentimentalism and
certainty in religious thought. Frost studied evolutionary geology under
Nathaniel Southgate Shaler, reading Lyell and Darwin's major works. In his
own writing Shaler posited an evolutionary argument for Christianity,
stating that "Christ is the summit and crown of the organic series. It
expresses the final result of that directed striving which began hundreds and
millions of years ago, and through infinite toil and pains has led to this
supreme accomplishment. It offers the natural line of escape from the evils
of hedonism, and the curse which self-consciousness brought upon
mankind."[72] Shaler's position reflects a justification for suffering in history
similar to Romans 8 and reveals the extent to which Protestant intellectuals
saw evolutionary theory as consonant with rather than at odds with
Christianity. Frost's own attempt at reconciling science and religion, as I will
show, reflected far greater conflict.

Frost also studied philosophy under Santayana while James was on leave and in his last semester at Harvard was a student in Josiah Royce's introductory survey of modern philosophy. Royce's lectures on philosophy included "The Rise of the Doctrine of Evolution" and another entitled "Nature and Evolution: The Outer World and Its Paradox." Anxious to reconcile natural science with his idealism, Royce raised a variety of problems that, I will show, remained important to Frost.[73] In Santayana, Frost thought he had a friend who argued for "animal faith" but found Santayana's aestheticism an unappealing form of escape from the pursuit of reality. However, Santayana's reaction against sentimentality in literature and his advocacy of Whitman's "passionate preference" and "barbarity" found an eager ear in the young Frost.[74] "Passionate preference" became Frost's phrase for "sexual selection," the process by which the individual will finds choice in the machinery of life.

The influence of Darwin and evolution on the founders of pragmatism—James, Peirce, Fiske, and Wright—has been documented in Philip Weiner's 1947 study *Evolution and the Founders of Pragmatism*. That influence was far from monolithic—from the muted empiricism of Wright to the religious optimism of Fiske. Weiner's study does not document the anxiety that these philosophers faced in attempting to accommodate psychology and philosophy to the authority of science. In *Science, Community, and the Transformation of American Philosophy, 1860–1930*, Daniel Wilson has argued that James, in *Principles of Psychology*, was not so much "establishing the state of the science as writing the volume that expressed aptly the pluralism, even confusion, of an era slowly and painfully shedding its reliance on theology and philosophy as the touchstones of culture and yet not ready to declare its allegiance to science."[75] The pluralism and confusion in James parallels what many found in Darwin, a world of change and contingency out of which he tried to save the will to believe from becoming, as his detractors complained, the will to make-believe. William James, whom Frost read widely, was trained as a scientist and physiologist and became a great advocate of Darwinian thought.[76] His book *Principles of Psychology*, which Frost read and taught at the New Hampshire State Normal School in Plymouth in 1911–12, argues against the sudden appearance of consciousness in humans and in favor of its natural development from a primordial source of common descent.

Darwin's model of natural selection was adopted by James as a model for the process of encompassing all of the ideas of change, contingency, and fallibility that one finds in the evolutionary productions of nature. A student's notes from James's introductory course in philosophy reveal the extent to which Darwin played a role in his formulation of pragmatism: "Darwin's idea is known as Natural Selection. Those variations which are useful tend to live. Those which are a detriment die out. These useful variations are transmitted to future generations. They are inherited and thus better and better animals."[77]

In the same notes the student records James's principle of selecting ideals and subjecting them to testing. What James saw in Darwin was a scientific principle upon which to ground a liberal philosophy that emphasized process, pluralism, and contingency: "From the world of facts choose some ideal but do not be sure you are the only one who may be right. Give every other system a show. Act as if all the existing will were yours for the present time."[78]

In *Principles of Psychology* James described the core of human consciousness as an activity of selection and elimination which is a direct analogue of Darwin's theory of natural selection:

> The artist notoriously selects his items, rejecting all tones, colors, shapes, which do not harmonize with each other and with the main purpose of his work. That unity, harmony "convergence of characters," as M. Taine calls it, which gives to works of art their superiority over works of nature, is wholly due to *elimination*.[79]

James reverses the hierarchy of nature over art, which is the cornerstone of Darwin's theory of selection. Darwin reconciles nature and man by arguing that they are both participants in the process and that man is thus an unconscious participant in selection. But James does not deny that consciousness is the response of an organism to its environment and describes this in completely empirical terms:

> Every impression which impinges on the incoming nerves produces some discharge down the outgoing ones, *whether we are aware of it or not*. Using sweeping terms and ignoring exceptions, *we might say that every possible feeling produces a movement, and that the movement is the movement of the entire organism, and of each and all its parts*.[80]

Both Darwin and James view nature and human consciousness as an endless succession of experiments to produce organisms better suited to their environment, but the question of whether "fitness" is progressive or not remains open. Though "selection" implies intention and conscious purpose, both Darwin and James depict an experimenter closer to Schopenhauer's idea of a self-expressive blind will. The dependency of the "outgoing nerves" on sensory data from "incoming nerves" severely limits the interpretation of facts except as they correspond to the biological limitations of the observer. In Darwin and Frost the idea of choice and its relation to art comes into play most clearly in the domain of sexual relations, which holds sway over the isolated designs of any individual.

James's justification of religion was also set in evolutionary terms. Human longing for God, religious sentiment, has persisted in a variety of experiences and feelings, indicating the existence of the divine object. Nonetheless, this view rendered religious belief and truth as a process of verification emptied of content: "True is the name for whatever idea starts the verification process, useful is the name for its completed function in experience."[81] Using a more strongly evolutionary and organic metaphor, "Truth grafts itself on previous truth, modifying it in the process, just as idiom grafts itself on previous idiom, and law on previous law," James gives the impression of accretion rather than directionless supersession.[82] There is also a telos and direction in his conception that "reality ... and the truths men gain about it are everlastingly in a process of mutation—mutation towards a definite goal, it may be—but still mutation."[83] James's own radical empiricism, in which all new forms are both made by and alter the existing order, relies on Darwin's natural selection, in which history is contantly subject to uncertain alterations. It is a reality in which divinity has no place and, as he points out, "design," the cornerstone of natural theology, is little more than a "blank cartridge."

Looked at as a model of philosophy, pragmatism follows Darwin in regarding ideas as useful forms that supersede one another depending on the circumstances or environment. Behind the alliance of science and pragmatism is an ideology of change and liberation that destroys the past and unfounds the present. In his seminal essay of 1909, "The Impact of Darwin on Philosophy," Dewey embraced Darwin's method of bringing the idea of transition to all spheres of life. What Dewey meant by the new scientific method is not really a method at all but an ethos of continuous change and transformation, instead:

> prior to Darwin the impact of the new scientific method upon life, mind, and politics, had been arrested, because between these ideal or moral interests and the inorganic world intervened the kingdom of plants and animals.... The influence of Darwin upon

philosophy resides in his having conquered the phenomena of life for the principle of transition, and thereby freed the new logic for application to mind and morals and life. When he said of species what Galileo had said of the earth, *e pur se muove*, he emancipated, once and for all, genetic and experimental ideas as an organon of asking questions and looking for explanations.[84]

Dewey's invocation of Galileo in this context also reveals the extent to which modern science has its roots in a revolt against conceptions of ethereal immutability derived not from fact but, rather, from religious and political authority. The idea of transitional forms that he admires in Darwin reflects as much his disdain for religious authority and his hope in the possibility of perpetual escape from it as it does any knowledge of the nature of matter. James also linked science to Protestant liberation from central metaphysical or religious authority:

> The earth of things, long thrown into shadow by the glories of the upper ether, must resume its rights. To shift the emphasis in this way means that philosophic questions will fall to be treated by minds of a less abstractionist type than heretofore, minds more scientific and individualistic in their tone yet not irreligious either. It will be an alteration in "the seat of authority" that reminds one almost of the protestant reformation.[85]

In both Dewey and James, Darwin's account of the transformation of species is imaginatively connected to the purpose of science itself: rebellion against the tyranny of the past. The question for James is what does it mean to say that such a way of thinking is "not irreligious" when the consequences of its instrumentalism are completely materialistic, if not nihilistic.

In June 1928 Frost wrote a fascinating letter to Louis Untermeyer, which reveals his remarkable vision of the consequences of science as rebellion against metaphysics and the ideas of the past. Every religion or worldview becomes subject to the same rebellion, including science itself. Liberated from the absolute, the Kantian subject is subjected to his own circular thinking. These are "vicious circles," because the self stands only on the shifting ground of historicism; forms of thought, like species, are superseded in a great battle. Echoing Hamlet, Frost despairs over the inadequacy of language and its lack of correspondence with any permanent reality. "Logic" grows and breaks down, leaving its rider, like the swinger of birch trees, back on earth, cast out from his previous flight. Frost reveals the mind of a skeptic who sees all worldviews as systems that are not recognized as such until we are outside them, observing them:

> If I haven't written in a long time, I suppose it is because I haven't found anything very easy to say. My spirit barely moves in letter writing anyway under its burden of laziness and disinclination. The least addition of sorrow or confusion to my load and I stop altogether. That's an amusing one you call Words Words Words. For a cent I would subscribe to the sentiment. The logic of everything lands you outside of it: the logic of poetry outside of poetry (I needn't tell you how); the logic of religion by nice gradations outside of Catholicism in Protestantism, outside of Protestantism in agnosticism, and finally outside of agnosticism in Watsonian behaviorism: the logic of love, outside of love (if it were only by physical exhaustion); the logic of strife, in China. But what leaves the heart of mystery and the sting of death is the fact that when you have eliminated yourself by logic as clear out as Eenie meenie minne moe, then you are as good as in again. Which is one of several things that has led great men to suspect time and space and motion (however directed) and thought, of being vicious circles—vicious. We are what we are by elimination and by deflection from the straight line. Life is a fight we say and deify the prizefighter. We could go further and say life is a night-club and its presiding deity a *retired* prizefighter or Bouncer, bouncing us forever out.[86]

Frost also invoked natural selection when he stated that what we are is from "elimination," deviation from the straight line. He is describing a process of selection that builds edifices of thought even while it eliminates and wastes all that may not be useful. But what, then, are we if life consists only of shedding and taking on new structures of thought and new entanglements? What can allow us to rest in belief?

Frost asserted that belief has limits in a self-consciousness that recognizes the system as self-conceived. Science has moved from Plato's and Aristotle's model of a universe of eternal circles governed by an unmoved mover, to a process of the historical supersession of religions and cosmologies governed by impulses and strife. Frost calls this inevitable circularity a process of "vicious circles." And here we see Frost's departure from the optimism of Emerson's "Circles," in which Emerson claimed "the life of man is a self-evolving circle, which, from a ring imperceptibly small,

rushes, on all sides outwards to new and larger circles, and that without end."
Unlike Emerson's optimistic evolutionism, Frost sees a diminution from
Catholicism to Protestantism to behaviorism and sexual and civil strife. Life
is not a progression but a fight to maintain tentative constructs of belief. All
forms are developments that fight to exist and are supplanted by new forms.
In notebooks and poems Frost amusingly calls Darwin "John L. Darwin,"
after the American prizefighter John L. Sullivan; the Darwinian world was
the "temple of prize-fighter or fight promoter" or "the retired prizefighter."

The metaphors of battle and strife are crucial to understanding Frost's
poetry. In another letter to Untermeyer, Frost describes a shift in culture
from Darwin's metaphors of strife to Marxist utopian ideals of human family
and back again to strife. The battle and strife metaphors prevail over Marx's,
whom Frost contemptuously regards as a "polemical Jew," meaning a
Messianic prophet preaching for heaven on earth. Frost sees "no logical
connection" in the temporal shift from metaphor to metaphor, but the
instability becomes an endless dialogue between war and shelter, chaos and
form:

> isn't it a poetical strangeness that while the world was going full
> blast on the Darwinian metaphors of evolution, survival values
> and devil take the hindmost, a polemical Jew in exile was working
> up the metaphor of the State's being like a family to displace them
> from mind and give us a new figure to live by? Marx had the
> strength not to be overawed by the metaphor in vogue. Life is
> like a battle. But so is it like a shelter. Apparently we are now
> going to die fighting to make it a secure shelter. The model is the
> family at its best. At the height of the Darwinian metaphor,
> writers like Shaw and Butler were found to go the length of
> saying even the family within was strife, and perhaps the worst
> strife of all. We are all toadies to the fashionable metaphor of the
> hour. Great is he who imposes the metaphor. From each
> according to his ability to each according to his need. Except ye
> become as little children under a good father and mother! I'm not
> going to let the shift from one metaphor to another worry me.
> You'll notice the shift has to be made rather abruptly. There are
> no logical steps from one to the other. There is no logical
> connection.[87]

While Frost is mildly contemptuous of being "today to the fashionable
metaphor of the hour," it is the battle metaphor that both recurs and governs

the process of metaphorical shift. The only ones who are not toadies are those "great" enough "to impose the metaphor," a vision that indicates mastery of the battle.

The epistemic corrosion created by the intrusion of ever new and unexpected obstacles is part of the effect of nineteenth- and twentieth-century science in its exploration of other and previous cultures, thought, and life forms. The geographically remote and strange became associated with the temporally remote. Order was possible so long as the observer could order the remote along a temporal axis of history with his own consciousness as the culmination, or telos. Darwin's science of history, however, with its emphasis on variety and multiplicity of fact, vast expanses of time, and continual struggle, displaced the claim any creature might have to being the purpose or end of history. Darwin's science placed the idea of progress in civilization and, ironically, in science in jeopardy or at least within the confines of inescapable laws of limit and extinction. In *Plato and Platonism* Walter Pater captured the crisis that the Darwinian consciousness of change posed to the ascendancy of mind and thought in all areas, including science:

> Darwin and Darwinism, for which "type" itself properly is not but is only always *becoming* ... [and] the idea of development (that, too, developed in the process of reflection) is at last invading one by one, as the secret of their explanation, all the products of mind, the very mind itself, the abstract reason; our certainty for instance, that two and two make four.[88]

With the extreme loss of certainty and finality inherent in Darwin's thought, theories and ideas cower before the immense possibilities of endless change. Consciousness reaches a growth that it cannot transcend. Wisdom, then, is the awareness of law and limit found in the testing of emotion, invention, thought, form. Hardy entertained a remarkably similar view in his own thoughts on consciousness in the Darwinian age: "We have reached a degree of intelligence which nature never contemplated in framing her laws, and for which she has provided no adequate satisfactions."[89]

For all his late-Victorian assumptions about progress culminating in the scientism of his own era, James Frazer's conclusion to *The Golden Bough*, of which Frost owned all twelve volumes, is a powerful statement about the corrosive effects of historicism and evolution on the sanctity of ideas. He recognizes the continuum between magic, religion, and science and admits that the latter may too be one day glimpsed as a passing fable. It is as trenchant a statement as one finds of how evolutionary historicism and pragmatism intersect. Unlike William James, Frazer expresses a humility and uncertainty about such collective projections as "universe," "world," and the human ability to complete reality:

> It is probably not too much to say that the hope of progress—moral and intellectual as well as material—in the future is bound up with the fortunes of science, and that every obstacle placed in the way of scientific discovery is a wrong to humanity.
>
> Yet the history of thought should warn us against concluding that because the scientific theory of the world is the best that has yet been formulated, it is necessarily complete and final. We must remember that at the bottom the generalisations of science or, in common parlance, the laws of nature are merely hypotheses designed to explain that ever-shifting phantasmagoria of thought which we dignify with the high-sounding names of the world and the universe. In the last analysis magic, religion, and science are nothing but theories of thought; and as science has supplanted its predecessors, so it may hereafter be itself superseded by some more perfect hypothesis, perhaps by some totally different way of looking at the phenomenon—of registering the shadows on the screen—of which we in this generation can form no idea. The advance of knowledge is an infinite progression toward a goal that forever recedes.... The dreams of magic may one day be the realities of science.[90]

Frost at times could seem to enjoy these effects of historicism, of the perishing of all thoughts, allowing the unknown to loom larger and more threatening. He loved that science which creates more unknowns and provides neither comfort nor certainty but, instead, greater fear and less knowledge. He dislikes the science that becomes an imperial theory that closes adventure:

> Think of the great abysses opened up by our study of the atom. Think of the strange and unaccountable actions of the hurrying winds experienced by our travelers of the skies. Think of the marvels of marine life lately brought to us by the explorers of the distant oceans, each more wonderfully wrought than ever mermaid or water sprite of which the poets dreamed.
>
> Life has lost none of its mystery and romance. The more we know of it the less we know. Fear has always been a stimulus to

man's imagination. But fear is not the only stimulus. If science has expelled much of our fear, still there are left a thousand things from which to shape our dreams.[91]

Science is worthy when it satisfies our need for the "strange and unaccountable," "great abysses" (a phrase that evokes Milton's chaos), the interstices in continuity that allow for new things to appear rather than a monotonous line of enforced progress. The new forms are "each more wonderfully wrought" and mollify the human mind's conceptions of beauty. Frost's statement echoes the romantic sublimity of the conclusion of *On the Origin of Species*, in which Darwin proclaims, "There is grandeur in this view of life ... that, whilst this planet has gone cycling on according to the fixed laws of gravity, from so simple a beginning endless forms most beautiful and most wonderful have been, and are being evolved." Darwin acknowledges the fixed laws of cyclical process and Newtonian physics. But biology is a principle of noncyclical, unpredictable creation of new forms; life is an indeterminate rebellion against pure mechanism. Frost's "A Star in a Stone-Boat," in this light, becomes a drama of the way unexpected and uncontrolled worlds of life break through the monotony of our walled-in universe of temporary forms and constructs, revealing the limits of what our imagination can "compass." The idea that life can originate by traveling in meteors from other planets (a view once held by Lord Kelvin among others) undoes the dogma of special creation while leaving obscure the actual origins of life and the relations between organic and inorganic forms.

THE MODERN LUCRETIUS

If Darwin functioned as an Epicurus to Frost's Lucretianism, questions remain about the nature and extent of that relationship in the poetry itself. The figure of the stream as representation of flux is a persistent metaphor in Frost, recurring in "Hyla Brook," "West-Running Brook," "The Mountain," and "The Generations of Men." The Frostian stream has obscure origins and moves in unpredictable and unknowable directions. Thompson has noted that Frost "frequently mentioned his admiration for Lucretius" and speculates that Frost admired the Roman poet's attempt to overcome humanity's worst fears.[92] This Lucretian metaphor of a flux out which creation occurs was appropriated by James in his concept of consciousness as a stream and by Bergson in *Creative Evolution*. Frost did not accept Bergson's locating mind in the flux, or stream, of life, finding it, instead, in the process of resisting and surviving flux.[93] Frost's interest in Bergson's *Creative Evolution* has been well documented, but he was not, as I will show, simply accepting of Bergson's vitalistic creed.[94] Frost's views of metrics, which he discussed in England with the Bergsonian T. E. Hulme, counter the idea of fluidity found in free verse. Frost insists on the limit of strict meters to tame and limit the flow of speech.[95] At least as important for Frost as the stream was Lucretius' depiction of nature as consisting of atom and void, a world that is free from the control of masters and gods. Both Frost and Lucretius find appealing a nature that is incompatible with vaunting human ideals of purpose and with theology.

The complexity of Frost's reinterpretation of Lucretius in modern terms is encapsulated in "Too Anxious for Rivers." The title of the poem and its governing metaphor of rivers suggest a desire for consciousness to find and eradicate the mountain "That someone has said is the end of the world," an immovable icon he would like to challenge:

> Look down the long valley and there stands a mountain
> That someone has said is the end of the world.
> Then what of this river that having arisen
> Must find where to pour itself into and empty?
> I never saw so much swift water run cloudless.
> Oh, I have been often too anxious for rivers
> To leave it to them to get out of their valleys.

As rivers become a surprising figure for untamed, swift-running desire, the speaker recognizes an inevitable spilling of its power into a void that, ironically, subverts its own quest for "the truth." The telos of the search becomes the parabolic canyon "Of Ceasing to Question What Doesn't Concern Us," a geological version of God's rebuke to Job or Michael's rebuke to Adam not to dream of other worlds. But our naturally driven search for truth and for origins leaves us "lost," with the dark closing around us "broodingly soon in every direction":

> The truth is the river flows into the canyon
> Of Ceasing to Question What Doesn't Concern Us,
> As sooner or later we have to cease somewhere.
> No place to get lost like too far in the distance.
> It may be a mercy the dark closes round us
> So broodingly soon in every direction.

This inevitable cessation and awareness of the limitations of inquiry render us like Prometheus trembling in the dark not with fire but with a fading candle and becomes, ironically, a mercy saving us from further torture. As in "Desert Places," the speaker retreats from being scared by the vast interstellar spaces "on stars where no human race is" (*race is* also sounds like *races*, underscoring a conception of life as a competition of species). But there is no real solace, as he is left to "scare himself" with the more immediate emptiness, loneliness, and threat of extinction figured in snowdrift "desert places."

In "Too Anxious for Rivers" we find that the beginning and end of consciousness is the impulse of Eros itself, the "essay of love," a transformation of the paean to Venus that begins *De Rerum Natura*. Science discovers only its own desire to know, circling back ultimately to the shifting fables and premises of consciousness, while ends and beginnings remain ungraspable:

> The world as we know is an elephant's howdah;
> The elephant stands on the back of a turtle;
> The turtle in turn on a rock in the ocean.
> And how much longer a story has science
> Before she must put out the light on the children
> And tell them the rest of the story is dreaming?
> 'You children may dream it and tell it tomorrow.'
> Time was we were molten, time was we were vapor.
> What set us on fire and what set us revolving
> Lucretius the Epicurean might tell us
> 'Twas something we knew all about to begin with
> And needn't have fared into space like his master
> To find 'twas the effort, the essay of love.

"The world as we know" is a striking phrase, evading the expected *it* and suggesting a fluid supersession of fables about our ultimate beginnings and ends, such as the ancient analogy of the world as elephant standing on the back of a turtle. Scientific knowledge becomes a circular dream.

Josiah Royce's essay "Nature and the Paradox of Evolution," in his lectures collected in *The Spirit of Modern Philosophy*, describes a similar predicament for modern science, with strikingly similar analogies. If the universe appears to be a victim of entropic "running down," a stream in which all matter is collapsing into a solid mass, then its beginning must have been infinite distance between particles of matter. Royce points out that this incongruity turns our perception of the evolution of the universe, despite spectroscopic evidence, back upon itself as human fiction, "derived from the analogy of a very special and limited experience of ours, to an infinite regress whose ultimate foundation must be a fable like the account of the world resting on an elephant and the elephant on the back of a tortoise":

> But a conception that you can't universalize, that seems to contradict itself, or gives rise to highly suspicious incongruities, so soon as you press it to the limit, so soon as you suppose it to apply *semper et ubique*, is thereby shown to be in all probability a conception of an essentially human character or else of no world-wide objectivity. It may have truth about it, but this truth will in part be due to our limited point of view, to our particular station in the universe. This notion will be, so to speak, a *mortal* conception of things, not a conception of really eternal truth. For example: the notion of the earth as supported by an elephant that stood on a tortoise was such an essentially transient and merely human conception, just because it was derived from the analogy of a very special and limited experience of ours, and was obviously incapable of true universalization.[96]

The scientific search for the origins and destiny of the universe from limited empiricism and assumptions of universal fluidity leads to the collapse of ontology and epistemology, a fundamental contradiction and permanent limitation. In particular, the assumption that we came from matter, were once "molten" and "vapor," and developed through a fluid, contingent process provides an even greater caveat to taking anything we might conceive as "well-founded":

> On the other hand, what more obvious than *if* one conceives man as the product of a physical evolution of the type that we have heretofore been discussing, if one says that a planet-crust, at a particular stage of its history, brought forth man, while the heat of a slowly dying sun sustained his life, as it had done the lives of his countless animal ancestors before him,—if one holds all this to be true, then one must indeed look with equal wonder upon the power of such a creature to conceive at all of the real universe, or of the eternal, and upon the *naïveté* that trusts, without analysis and criticism, his notions of space and time, his natural perceptions of the outer world, as if they were sure to be well-founded.[97]

The intimation is that the idea of human consciousness as derived from a material and fluid source leads to skepticism about all premises, including the premise of evolution itself. Our power and desire to know is left as an unresolvable mystery:

> The marvel of marvels, that this being, evolved from inorganic nature, from the stuff and energy of a cooling solar system,—this mortal bit of mechanism—should after all *know*, should look forwards and backwards to eternity, and learn so much of the nature that gave him birth,—such a marvel surely calls for deeper scrutiny. The world where such things appear is surely not what it seems; and the lesson is that, in critical study of just this *knowing* power of ours, in the scrutiny of our most fundamental ideas, is to be found, if anywhere, the key to these mysteries. We have been so far inquiring into this or that truth. Now, more than ever, we see the need of assailing the problem, What is truth itself? [98]

Frost's answer to this question is the Lucretian love "moving that in all the ardor burns / For generation and their kind's increase." Venus, the goddess in Lucretius, and natural and sexual selection, the parallel gooddesses in Darwin, have as their ultimate aim moving creatures to success in procreation and leaving progeny. We return also to God's command to Adam and Eve in Eden, "Be fruitful and multiply." Thus, the plucking of the fruit of knowledge or the venturing far into the world of matter or of nature by Epicurus and Darwin leads back to the same humbling wisdom of minding the family. "All science," Frost liked to remark, "is domestic science, increasing our hold on the planet." [99] This wisdom informs God's rebuke of novelty in thought or science in *A Masque of Reason*: "Look at how far we've left the current science / Of Genesis behind. The wisdom there though, / Is just as good as when I uttered it." While the "science," or account of creation, in Genesis has changed with Darwin, the wisdom to be gleaned from the new account is the same as the old one.

In "Too Anxious for Rivers" Frost adds an important fact to substantiate the fable of the elephant and turtle—namely, that the turtle stands "in turn *on a rock* in the ocean" (emphasis mine), a sardonic figure of the way the church of modern natural history stands on geology the way the old church of Christianity was founded on Saint Peter's rock. The idea that the beginning of things is like a rock in a vast ocean recalls Darwin's stunning insights about the power of rivers and oceans to change the landscape of the earth. In *The Voyage of the* Beagle Darwin's geological observations enabled him to confirm the uniformity necessary to premise biological continuity and change over vast periods of time. Though mountains appear stable and final, "the end of the world," rivers can threaten even their sublime presence. Instead of seeing the world as either complete and static or the result of sudden catastrophic upheavals, Darwin considered that flowing water can create great geological shifts by eroding mountains until they become rocks in the ocean. The buildup of deposits becomes, over vast periods of time, the beginning of new islands. What was thought of mystically as the end of the world can eventually become, as an island in the ocean, a new beginning. In one powerful meditation Darwin linked the power of the river to erode even the highest mountains to the way species become extinct over eons:

> The rivers which flow in these valleys ought rather to be called mountain-torrents. Their inclination is very great and their water the colour of mud. The roar which the Maypu made, as it rushed over the great rounded fragments, was like that of the sea.... The sound spoke eloquently to the geologist; the thousands and thousands of stones, which, striking against each other, made the one dull uniform sound, were all hurrying in one direction. It was like thinking on time, where the minute that now glides past is irrecoverable. So was it with these stones; the ocean is their eternity, and each note of that wild music told of one more step toward their destiny.
>
> It is not possible for the mind to comprehend, except by slow process, any effect which is produced by a cause repeated so often, that the multiplier itself conveys an idea, not more definite than the savage implies when he points to the hairs of his head. As often as I have seen beds of mud, sand, and shingle, accumulated to thickness of many thousand feet, I have felt inclined to exclaim that causes, such as the present rivers and the present beaches, could never have ground down and produced such masses. But, on the other hand, when listening to the rattling noise of these torrents, and calling to mind that whole races of animals have passed away from the face of the earth, and that during this whole period, night and day, these stones have gone rattling onwards in their course, I have thought to myself, can any mountains, any continent, withstand such waste?[100]

Yet this same theory that allows for the erosion of mountains gives credence to the unmiraculous geological depositing and buildup of life-supporting land elsewhere. Neither a single direction of degradation nor a certain point of beginning can be comprehended. And Darwin draws an analogy between himself and a savage pointing to the hairs of his head in making these speculations. Nevertheless, extinction and transformation can occur while the process lies hidden from ordinary human perceptions except by inferences made from a few observable facts.

Frost's allegiance to the pursuit and love of fact is apparent in "Mowing," his favorite poem from his first book, *A Boy's Will*. The poem resists closure because of the speaker's inability to ascertain the meaning of the sound of his own isolated labor and the few observations he makes in the field. "Mowing" reflects a desire to unify work and play (after all, he only "scares" the snake) but also expresses the frustration of limited revelation. Death, labor, and time also dwell in Arcadia, "beside the wood." This is more a georgic poem than an eclogue; no voice responds to the laborer. Unlike Wordsworth's "Solitary Reaper," in Frost's poem no one is singing, and no one other than the speaker is hearing it. The emphasis is not on song but, instead, on the laborer and his tool and the surrounding environment. The speaker is, to use Thoreau's phrase, the "tool of his tool," and the Frostian pastoral does not escape the demands of technology. What, if not "easy gold at the hand of fay or elf," a magical or mystical understanding, does the "whispering" of his scythe, do the "feeble-pointed spikes of flowers" or "bright green snake" signify? The poem's tentativeness is summarized in acceptance that "the fact is the sweetest dream that labor knows." What can one infer from fact? There are several facts in the poem: the heat of the sun, the snake, the scythe, the hay, the sound all encompassed in the fact of the laborer's activity. Should there be something more? Is fact itself a dream? Does our labor discover something about nature or the world? Is there any knowledge beyond quiet intimations and perceptions? What we see and hear *is* truth, and "anything more than the truth would have seemed too weak," compromises of the reality of earthly labor and "earnest love." That fact is the "sweetest dream" has the force of "fact is the only dream," the most of it, as sweet as it gets, and deeply related to the most visceral experience; "sweetness" is a quality that pertains to almost all of the senses—sound, sight, taste, smell. The dramatic perspective of the poem places the seeker and laborer in matter accepting circumscribed consciousness and uncertain progress. The willingness to dwell in fact can be taken either as a compromise from more revelatory understanding or as a release from the burden of seeking, progress, harvest, theories, and ideas.

Some of the "facts" of "Mowing" are synecdochic and suggest larger processes that haunt the laborer. Frost reserves the small, constrained form of the sonnet—"The Oven Bird," "Design," "Never Again Would Birds' Song Be the Same" along with "Mowing"—to make some of his largest cosmological suggestions. The "pale orchises" and the "bright green snake" are particularly interesting. In addition to making hay, the speaker is a participant in the destruction of life. The snake's color (more than an allusion to Coleridge's "Christabel," in which a dreaming bard is startled by "a bright green snake" [l. 545] is a form of adaptive camouflage, but here it does him little good and even attracts the eye of the mower. The "spikes of flowers" are only "feeble" and do not protect against the blade. The activity of haying participates in a process of destruction and reminds the mower of his own vulnerability beneath the "heat of the sun."

Frost refers to orchises throughout his poetry; they reflect his deep interest in botany, and their iconography is significant.[101] Orchids were the most highly prized examples of exotic beauty sought after by American and English botany enthusiasts and a primary subject of the crucial scientific controversies that eclipsed natural theology.[102] They were also the subject of one of Darwin's most important books, *The Various Contrivances by Which Orchids Are Fertilized by Insects*. The late Victorians found themselves surprised by this book and similar studies, which showed that the color and beauty of flowers served the purpose of reproduction and cross-pollination rather than the pleasure of human observers. Darwin demonstrated that there was no single ideal type of orchid but, rather, many different orchids. Beauty serves sex, and sex serves healthy cross-fertilization. In "Mowing" the pale orchises would ordinarily have a selective advantage in reproduction by reflecting light and attracting cross-pollinating moths. The reproductive power of these orchises suggests part of a process of sexual reproduction different from his solitary labor in the field. But that reproductive power is no match for a scythe. Another poem in *North of Boston*, "Rose Pogonias," is a prayer that the "thousand orchises" should not "in the general mowing" be cut down with the grass. In the pasture there are two kinds of growth: the grass and the flowers. The grass, more uniform and common, is cultivated for utility and food. The flowers serve no purpose other than the love of beauty for its own sake. One also suspects that the highly suggestive sexual appearance of these orchids, known as the "bearded ladies," is significant because it represents a pleasurable and equally vital aspect of life aside from the labor of agriculture. Their beauty serves to remind us of sexuality and reproduction, part of the overall machinery of life.

The object of "right worship" in "Rose Pogonias" is the burning sun, not God, and this conveys a sense of a world materially governed by environment. In "Mowing" the scythe whispers, perhaps, "something about the heat of the sun." This is not only a literary reference to the more metaphoric sunburned mind of the first sonnet of Sidney's *Astrophel and Stella* but also describes the threatening effect of the literal sun, one of many of Frost's stars that has little more to say than—as in "Choose Something Like a Star"—"I burn."[103] The natural "facts" in "Mowing" are not only Emersonian excavations of the laborer turning the world into poetry. The emphasis in these poems on the power of the sun has particular significance in the history of science and the collapse of sacred cosmology. Heliocentrism represents the Copernican and Keplerian shift away from an earth-centered and man-centered universe. Kepler's sun worship, as I mentioned earlier, combined with his belief in the imperfection and mutability of all things, preceded and enabled his efforts to bring the Ptolemaic cosmology to collapse. In this context, "Mowing" also echoes Spenser's final "Unperfite Canto" of "Mutabilitie," written in the early ferment of the Copernican revolution, in which the poet laments " ... this state of life so tickle, / And love of things so vaine to cast away; / Whose flowering pride, so fading and so fickle, / Short *Time* soon cut down with his consuming sickle."[104] Frost's mower appears an agent of time's "consuming sickle"; his steady motion and sound suggest the passage and effects of time on the perception of a variety of facts. Frost's mower accepts the challenge of mutability, the process and fact of "mowing," refusing or perhaps unable to long for Spenser's "Sabaoth's sight."

In "Mowing" the speaker's "earnest love" contains a tone of frustration and some recklessness; it is a driving energy that not only "laid the swale in rows" but also cut down the "pale orchises" and "scared a bright green snake." Unlike the speaker of "Rose Pogonias," whose love might be fulfilled in consonance with the flora, this laborer is left isolated and questioning. I think that the "facts" of the orchises and the green snake suggest something important about the source of his doubt. As a young man, Frost read Carl Burrell's copy of Grant Allen's *Colin Clout's Calendar: A Record of a Summer*. Praised by Darwin and Huxley, it is a series of pastoral meditations about the operations of natural selection in country life. One chapter, "Haymaking Begins," describes the persistence of flowers in hay-fields in a way that makes them weeds to the cultivator. The point is that it is precisely the struggle for life that produces ever more persistent forms of life that can adapt to the cultivated land:

> See here in the pasture, a large part consists of buttercup stems, uncropped by the cows: of plantains, with their ribbed leaves almost rivalling the blades of grasses and little spreading daisies, with their close rosette of foliage pressed hard and tight against the naked ground, so as to prevent the struggling young seedlings of the grass from pushing their way between the tufts. It is just the same way in the meadow: there, in between the haulms of grass, you get a thick and matted undergrowth of Dutch clover, yellow medick, and rusty-red sorrel, besides all the taller meadow flowers—such as buttercups, corn poppies, and ox-eye daisies. These make up a large and curious group, the true weeds of cultivation. They are as purely human in origin in most cases as wheat or barley: they have assumed their existing shapes under the influence of man's handicraft.... And yet they differ in one important particular—that they are dependent upon him involuntarily instead of voluntarily: they are the results of his weakness, not of his strength.[105]

Thus, the flowers in the hayfields develop as they do inadvertently because of the attempt to cultivate grass. As Allen adds the flowers' "only chance of survival is by exactly adapting their own habits to those of the food plants among which they dwell." The bright green snake, of course, would persist in grassland because his color is suited to hiding in that environment.

But the persistence of flowers reminds the mower of his weakness, his inability to control completely the environment and his unwitting participation in the creation of stronger forms. (A similar view is expressed in "A Star in a Stone-Boat," in which a farmer becomes frustrated after the intrusion of a meteor that makes the soil hot "And burning to yield flowers instead of grain, / Flowers fanned and not put out by all the rain / Poured on them by his prayers prayed in vain.") As Allen, following Darwin, stated: "Indeed no form of selection is really so severe as that unconsciously exerted by man."[106] Struggling to make his own environment suitable and cultivate food, man also cannot help participating in a process of selection that mocks his efforts all under the indifferent watch of the "heat of the sun," which makes labor more difficult but also reminds the laborer of the limited time he has "to make hay while the sun shines." Mowing, like pigeon breeding in *On the Origin of Species*, becomes a participant in the machinery of life. This is a more material, less optimistic extension of Emerson's ideal of the pantheistic soul of nature laboring, expressed in his second essay "Nature": "But if, instead of identifying ourselves with the work we feel that the soul of the workman streams through us, we shall find peace of the morning first dwelling in our hearts, and the fathomless powers of gravity and chemistry, and, over them, of life, preexisting within us in their highest form."[107] Frost's laborers—in "Mowing," "After Apple-Picking," "The Self-Seeker"—do not enjoy Emerson's idea of separating the soul of the workman from work because of their inextricable participation in a machinery of effort and waste that diminishes the individual's power.

The "facts" of "Mowing" tell us something more about why the scythe only whispers but does not speak (much less sing). This quietness is in response to a diffidence about the meaning of human pursuits, of the kind mocked in another poem in *North of Boston*, "The Demiurge's Laugh," which I will discuss in the final chapter. The poem that precedes that meditation on science, "Pan with Us," concludes with the pagan god of shepherds throwing away his pipes. This may be an expression of belatedness, but its causes are complex. Frost's Pan laments both Christianity and its children—history and science. As Nicolas Berdayev observed, "'The Great Pan,' who had been revealed to natural man of antiquity, was driven to take refuge in the uttermost depths of nature. A gulf now separated the natural man from the men who had entered upon the path of Redemption. The effect of Christianity was to divorce man from the inner life of nature, which, as a result, became deanimated. This was the reverse side of the Christian liberation of human nature."[108] Berdayev also noted the paradox inherent in the "Christian liberation," one that goes to the heart of Frost's poem, that "Christianity alone made possible positive science and technique.... it was itself the spiritual result of the Christian act of liberating man from elemental nature and its demons."[109]

Something has changed, and the music of poetry can do little more than "the merest aimless breath of air." "Aimless" air works, at least, for the junipers and bluets as a medium for cross-pollination. "A boy's will," Frost's echo of Longfellow reminds us, is but "the wind's will":

Times were changed from what they were:
Such pipes kept less of power to stir
The fruited bough of the juniper
    And the fragile bluets clustered there
    Than the merest aimless breath of air.

They were pipes of pagan mirth,
And the world had found new terms of worth.
He laid him down on the sun-burned earth

> And raveled a flower and looked away—
> Play? Play?—What should he play?

Ending with an unanswerable question, as do many of Frost's best lyrics, the poem's final dissolution stems from doubts about the "new terms of worth." Those new terms could be the Christian world of sin and redemption, which contradicts the world of "pagan mirth." "Play," of any kind, is not as important as the work of purification in a Protestant work ethic (evoking a muted pun of "panning for gold"). The world had also found frightening new terms of worth for the name "Pan." *Pan* became the term used for the genus of apes that included the chimpanzees, those closest to man in physiology and mental ability. Behind this new term was the idea of the half-human, half-animal (the lower half, of course) nature of the old deity as a metaphor for the living creature most like our remote ancestors. *Pan* is no longer a god but an indeterminate creature. The title "Pan with Us" suggests both America and "Us," as the tentative indicator of the human, threatened by loss of special identity by being related so literally to "lower" creatures. A world governed by such materialism is evoked by the phrase "sunburned earth," a nature that is not responsive to the sounds of pipes.

Frost's refusal to claim much in the face of this grand indifference is justified by an unabashed appeal to creaturely and limited consciousness of the processes of life and the demands of survival. Though the speaker in "Acceptance" describes the disappearance of the sun and the onset of darkness in grand and apocalyptic terms, "no voice in nature" cries because of a tacit knowledge that this is part of an inevitable process:

> When the spent sun throws up its rays on cloud
> And goes down burning into the gulf below,
> No voice in nature is heard to cry aloud
> At what has happened. Birds, at least, must know
> It is the change to darkness in the sky.

While one bird but murmurs something elusive and fades to sleep, another recognizes that darkness is time for him to return to the safety of the nest, which he regains just in time. The bird's return is not a triumphant homecoming but, rather, the acceptance of limited knowledge and creaturely safety in the face of a vast and incomprehensible world:

> Murmuring something quiet in her breast,
> One bird begins to close a faded eye;

Or overtaken too far from his nest,
Hurrying low above the grove, some waif
Swoops just in time to his remembered tree.
At most he thinks or twitters softly, 'Safe!
Now let the night be dark for all of me.
Let the night be too dark for me to see
Into the future. Let what will be, be.'

As in "Mowing," in which the scythe but whispers, the bird proclaims only limited knowledge as it "thinks or twitters softly." The bird's hortatory statements reverse God's proclamation of light in Genesis, echoing the same reversal in Job's powerful curse. Combined with the curse here is Job's acceptance after God's terrifying theophany, one that emphasizes man's limited place in a vast world of creaturely struggle.

Poetry might under the weight of science demand adjustments but not radical change. In this way Frost sets himself in opposition to I. A. Richards's argument in *Science and Poetry* for demonstrative poetic change:

> Poetry must correspond to our needs, impulses, attitudes, which did not arise in the same fashion for poets in the past, and criticism must take notice of the contemporary situation. Our attitudes toward man, to nature, and to the universe change with every generation, and have changed with unusual violence in recent years. We cannot leave these changes out of account in judging modern poetry. When attitudes are changing neither criticism nor poetry can remain stationary.[110]

This is a modernist argument that the present is different from the past and requires a radically new art. But Frost's understanding of Darwin is that science reveals a reality in which, in immediate terms, very little is new. Frost's adherence to strict forms and meters places him in a recognizable tradition of English writers, particularly Wordsworth, Coleridge, Tennyson, Landor, and Hardy. This "old-fashioned way of making things new" underscores his distrust of the concept of originality. Progress is not the province of art. Frost recognized that Emerson's concept of an evolution of art and thought into higher (meaning better) achievements was crippling to the artist's sense of worth:

> I must have taken it as a truth accepted that a thing of beauty will never cease to be beautiful. Its beauty will in fact increase. Which

is the opposite doctrine to Emerson's in "Verily know when half gods go the gods arrive": the poets and poems we have loved and ceased to love are to be regarded as stepping stones of our dead selves to higher things. Growth is a distressful change of taste for the better. Taste improving is on the way upward to creation. Nay-nay. It is more likely on the way to dissatisfaction and ineffectuality. A person who has found out young from Aldous Huxley how really bad Poe is will hardly from the superiority of the position this gives him be able to go far with anything he himself attempts.[111]

Frost had great empathy for those small things that survived or created momentary stays without demeaning their value by considering them only stepping stones. As he concluded in "Hyla Brook," a meditation on change in nature and art, "We love the things we love for what they are," even if their "being" is always threatened by "becoming." The poem refers to that ancient pastoral figure of Hylas the singer, Lucretian flux, a brook near Frost's house, and the hyla frogs Darwin writes of in *The Voyage of the* Beagle. What Frost made of our existence in relation to other creatures explores many of the questions raised by the assumption of common descent.

Notes

1. David Porter, *Emerson and Literary Change* (Cambridge: Harvard University Press, 1978), 22–23.

2. Jay Parini, "Emerson and Frost: The Present Act of Vision," *Sewance Review* 89 (1981): 215. Parini adds: "Yet certain key Emersonian notions persist in Frost: the concentration on the individual quest for selfhood, the belief in an occult relationship between man and nature, and the reliance on the natural world for sustenance." I regard Frost as departing from these notions significantly. Individualism in Frost is often countered by great conflicts and crippling irony. The relationship between man and nature is much more visceral than occult. Parini's assertion that Frost shares especially Emerson's faith in vision conflicts with the many doubts about perception that occur in lyrics and especially in the dramatic poems and his emphasis, above all, on voice and sound.

George Monteiro, *Robert Frost and the New England Renaissance* (Lexington: University Press of Kentucky, 1988), reads almost all Frost's poems in reference to works by Emerson, Thoreau, and Dickinson and the tradition of American transcendentalism.

3. Ralph Waldo Emerson, "Nature," in *Selections from Ralph Waldo Emerson*, ed. Stephen E. Whicher (Boston: Houghton Mifflin, 1957), 22.

4. For a comprehensive view of Emerson and science, see David M. Robinson's "Fields of Investigation: Emerson and Natural History," in *American Literature and Science*, ed. Robert J. Scholnick (Lexington: University Press of Kentucky, 1992). Robinson shows how Emerson incorporated Lyell's geology into his own evolutionary thinking, still believing that the end of that progression is the immortality of the soul. I agree with Robinson's view that Emerson came to recognize how "Nature's metamorphic energy leads to a kind of estrangement, in which the individual is distanced from the reality of nature" (105).

5. Henry David Thoreau, *Walden* (Princeton: Princeton University Press, 1973), 97.

6. Robert D. Richardson, *Henry Thoreau: A Life of the Mind* (Berkeley: University of California Press, 1986), 384.

7. Robert Frost, "A Conversation between Robert Frost and Dr. Reginald Cook" (1954), in *Interviews with Robert Frost*, ed. Edward Connery Lathem (New York: Holt, Rinehart and Winston, 1966), 142–46. In the same interview Frost also mentions Darwin's *The Voyage of the* Beagle and Defoe's *Robinson Crusoe* as favorite books. Both, of course, were important to Thoreau's idea of living deliberately in the woods. Cook seems to observe something funny about Frost's coinage: "'Thorosian,' is, I admit, a new word—so new I haven't decided how to spell the second 'o' sound in it—but it is coining even as you and I converse, and so on its way into the dictionary."

8. Frederick Turner, *Natural Classicism: Essays on Literature and Science* (New York: Paragon House, 1985), 171–201. "What I wish to argue is that, however faulty Thoreau's theory of cultural evolution may have been, he is right in assuming the cultural journey cannot properly take place without a personal one. Except ye become as a little child, ye shall not enter the kingdom of another culture" (191).

9. Henry David Thoreau, *Faith in a Seed: The Dispersion of Seeds and Other Late Natural History Writings*, ed. Bradley P. Dean (Washington, D.C.: Island Press, 1993).

10. Richardson, *Thorcan*, 384.

11. Frost played with lines in "Uriel" in a way that shows his difference from Emerson, particularly on the matter of evil. In "Uriel" from "the good of evil born, / Came Uriel's voice of cherub scorn." Uriel's voice is the good coming from the evil of his rebellion. In a 1955 talk at the Bread Loaf writers' conference, Frost quoted the line in the context of a discussion of Puritanism and Milton's *Comus*. Referring to the lines in *Comus* in which good and evil are supposed to separate (594–98), Frost digs at the Puritan hope of separating good from evil, citing Comus's own assertion that we should not live "like Nature's bastards" instead of "her sons." Frost concludes his remarks with a sly alteration of the Emerson line "'Out of good is evil born ... Cherub scorn.' Now that's my part." Frost rejects the Protestant hope that rebellion will result in greater purity or goodness, an aspiration he associated with Marx. See Reginald Cook's transcript of this talk in *Robert Frost: A Living Voice* (Amherst: University of Massachusetts Press, 1974), 95–96.

12. Charles Darwin, *The Autobiography of Charles Darwin*, ed. Nora Barlow (New York: Harcourt Brace, 1958), 228.

13. Darwin wrote to Henslow on 18 May 1832: "The Captain [Fitzroy] does every thing in his power to assist me, & we get on very well.—but I thank my better fortune he has not made me a renegade to Whig principles: I would not be a Tory, if it was merely on account of their cold hearts about that scandal to Christian Nations, Slavery" (*The Correspondence of Charles Darwin*, vol. 1; *1821–1836* [Cambridge: Cambridge University Press, 1985], 238).

14. Darwin, *Autobiography*, 85.

15. Gillian Beer discusses the central debate in Milton's *Comus*, between selfish appropriation of nature's bounty and a more even distribution of plenty, in relation to Darwin's distinction between artificial and natural selection (*Darwin's Plots* [London: Routledge and Kegan Paul, 1983], 34–36).

That the center of *Paradise Lost* is the battle in heaven might also have been imaginatively interesting to Darwin. In one of his letters from the *Beagle* voyage, Darwin describes a volcanic eruption by alluding to the heavenly warfare: "It appeared to be a representation of Milton's battle of the Angels as described in Paradise Lost" (Darwin, *Correspondence*, 1:479).

16. Charles Darwin, *Charles Darwin's Diary of the Voyage of* H.M.S. Beagle, ed. Nora Barlow (Cambridge: Cambridge University Press, 1934), 107.

17. *Paradise Lost* 2:884–920, in John Milton, *Complete Poems and Major Prose*, ed. Merritt Y. Hughes (Indianapolis: Bobbs-Merrill, 1957), 253–54.

18. Charles Darwin, "Notebook M," in *Charles Darwin's Notebooks, 1836–1844*, ed. Paul H. Barrett et al. (Ithaca, N.Y.: Cornell University Press, 1987), 549.

19. Charles Darwin, *The Descent of Man and Selection in Relation to Sex* (Princeton: Princeton University Press, 1981), 405. This edition is a photographic reprint of the 1871 edition.

20. Robert Frost, "The Constant Symbol," in *Selected Prose of Robert Frost*, 24.

21. Darwin, *On the Origin of Species*, 489.

22. Darwin cites Schopenhauer in *The Descent of Man* on the matter of sexual selection, referring to "The Metaphysics of Sexual Love," a supplemental chapter of *The World as Will and Representation* (see chap. 4). For an interesting discussion of the relation of form and function in Schopenhauer and Darwin, see E. S. Russell, "Schopenhauer's Contribution to Biological Theory," in *Science, Medicine, and History*, ed. E. A. Underwood (London: Oxford University Press, 1953), vol. 2.

Frost refers to Schopenhauer in the context of his poem "The Trial by Existence" (see chap. 6). In his notebooks he makes several references to Schopenhauer, including the following: "At least a year on the book's name before reading the book. The World as Will" (Dartmouth College Library, Ms. Frost 001714).

23. Josiah Royce, *The Spirit of Modern Philosophy* (1892; reprint New York: Dover Books, 1983), 266.

24. Arthur Schopenhauer, *The World as Will and Representation*, trans. E. F. J. Payne (Indian Hills, Colo.: Falcon's Wing Press, 1958), 584.

25. Bertrand Russell, *Our Knowledge of the External World as a Field for Scientific Method in Philosophy* (London: Open Court Publishing, 1914), 11.

26. Henry Adams, *The Education of Henry Adams* (Boston: Houghton Mifflin, 1973), 231 (emphasis mine). This appears in the section entitled "Darwinism (1867–1868)," and the concepts of natural selection and evolution continue to trouble Adams throughout his search for a scientific way out of the labyrinth of supersessive history.

27. Darwin, *On the Origin of Species*, 83.

28. Ibid., 489.

29. Ibid., 490.

30. Ibid., 441.

31. Ibid., 336–37.

32. Ibid., 206.

33. Ibid., 205.

34. Ibid., 207.

35. David Hull, *Darwin and His Critics* (Chicago: University of Chicago Press, 1973), 56: "Evolutionary theory had even more devastating consequences for immanent teleology. If essences are static and if the general goal toward which all things strive is to realize their essence, then the wholesale progressive change entailed by evolutionary theory is impossible. If evolution has occurred, then either essences are not static or else things must strive, not to fulfill their own essence, but the essence of some other species."

36. Darwin, *On the Origin of Species*, 51.

37. Ibid., 462.

38. Darwin, *Descent of Man*, 188.

39. Frank Lentricchia, *Robert Frost: Modern Poetics and the Landscapes of Self* (Durham, N.C.: Duke University Press, 1975), 155.

40. Hayden White, *Tropics of Discourse: Essays in Cultural Criticism* (Baltimore: Johns Hopkins University Press, 1978), 131. Harvard University Archives (HUG 304) lists Frost's enrollment in Nathaniel Southgate Shaler's Geology 4 and 5 courses in 1898–99. The syllabus for those courses includes Darwin's major works, *On the Origin of Species* and *The Descent of Man*.

41. Darwin, *On the Origin of Species*, 459: "As this whole volume is one long argument, it may be convenient to the reader to have the leading facts and inferences recapitulated."

42. Darwin, "C Notebook," in *Notebooks*, 294.

43. Darwin, "E Notebook," in *Notebooks*, 434.

44. Darwin, *On the Origin of Species*, 484.

45. Ibid., 485.

46. Louis Mertins, *Robert Frost: Life and Talks—Walking* (Norman: University of Oklahoma Press, 1965), 368.

47. Elizabeth Shepley Sergeant, *Robert Frost: The Trial by Existence* (New York: Holt, Rinehart and Winston, 1960), 325.

48. Robert Frost, *Letters of Robert Frost to Louis Untermeyer*, ed. Louis Untermeyer (New York: Holt, Rinehart and Winston, 1963), 189.

49. Dartmouth College Library, Ms. Frost 001729.

50. Robert Frost, "Letter to the *Amherst Student*," in *Selected Prose of Robert Frost*, 107.

51. See William James, *Pragmatism* (Cambridge: Harvard University Press, 1975), 122–23. James held that the flux of man "engenders truths" and completes reality and that the "universe" is readily "malleable" by human thought:

> We build the flux out inevitably. The great question is: does it, with our additions, *rise or fall in value?* Are the additions *worthy or unworthy?* ...
> Lotze has in several places made a deep suggestion. We naively assume, he says, a relation between reality and our minds which may be the opposite of the true one. Reality, we naturally think, stands ready-made and complete, and our intellects supervene with the one simple duty of describing it as it is already. But may not our descriptions, Lotze asks, be themselves important additions to reality? And may not previous reality itself be there, far less for the purpose of reappearing unaltered in our knowledge, than for the very purpose of stimulating our minds to such additions as shall enhance the universe's total value? ...
> It is identically our pragmatic conception. In our cognitive as well as in our active life we are creative. We *add*, both to the subject and predicate part of reality. The world stands really malleable, waiting to receive its final touches at our hands. Like the kingdom of heaven it suffers our violence willingly. Man *engenders* truths upon it.

In Frost's dramas humans attempt to impose their ideals, always encountering limitations within themselves, from the environment, or from others. There is little completion of anything as grand as "the universe."

52. Dartmouth College Library, Ms. Frost 001275.

53. Darwin, "M Notebook," in *Notebooks*, 551.

54. Robert Frost, "Education by Poetry," in *Selected Prose of Robert Frost*, 38–39.

55. Dartmouth College Library, Ms. Frost 001730.

56. Coleridge to Joseph Cottle, 7 March 1815, in *Collected Letters*, 4:545; quoted in M. H. Abrams, *Natural Supernaturalism* (New York: W. W. Norton, 1971), 271.

57. Dartmouth College Library, Ms. Frost 1720.

58. Ibid., Ms. Frost 928940.1.

59. Ibid., Ms. Frost 001729.

60. Ralph Waldo Emerson, *The Poet*, in *Selections from Ralph Waldo Emerson*, ed. Stephen E. Whicher (Boston: Houghton Mifflin, 1957), 232.

61. Frost made this distinction in a talk at Bread Loaf in 1959 recounted in Reginald Cook's *Robert Frost*, 212.

62. See Marjorie Nicholson's seminal study of the impact of science on the symbolic use of the circle in *The Breaking of the Circle: Studies in the Effect of the "New Science" on Seventeenth-Century Poetry* (New York: Columbia University Press, 1960).

63. Robert Frost, "On Emerson," in *Selected Prose of Robert Frost*, 118.

64. For an excellent discussion of Kepler's religious thought and, in particular, his sun worship see E. J. Dijksterjuis's *The Mechanization of the World Picture*, trans. C. Dikshoorn (Oxford: Oxford University Press, 1961), 305–11.

65. Dartmouth College Library, Ms. Frost 001275.

66. Gillian Beer observes that "Darwin's metaphor of the tree is a formal analogy whose function is purely diagrammatic, describing a shape not an experience. Its initial value for Darwin lay undoubtedly in the fact that the diagram *declared* itself as tree, rather than being foreknowingly designed to represent a tree-like shape for descent. On the page, however, it could as well be interpreted by the eye as shrub, branching coral, or seawood. But Darwin saw not only the explanatory but mythic potentiality of this diagram, its congruity with past orders of descent" (*Darwin's Plots*, 92–93). I would add that Darwin's use of the tree is part of his search for "plain signification," beyond metaphor in which any part of nature can actually represent the whole.

67. Darwin, *On the Origin of Species*, 130.

68. Robert Frost, "The Constant Symbol," in *Selected Prose of Robert Frost*, 24.

69. Dartmouth College Library, Ms. Frost 001275.

70. For a general overview of Frost's early interests in science, see Kathryn Gibbs Harris, "Robert Frost's Early Education in Science," *South Carolina Review* 7, no. 1 (1974): 13–33.

71. Lawrance Thompson, *Robert Frost: The Early Years* (New York: Holt, Rinehart and Winston, 1966), 89. Thompson emphasizes Frost's interest in Proctor's book *Our Place among the Infinities*, which I discuss in chapter 6.

72. Nathaniel Southgate Shaler, *The Interpretation of Nature* (Boston: Houghton Mifflin, 1893), 275.

73. Josiah Royce's introductory lectures on philosophy were published as *The Spirit of Modern Philosophy* (1892; reprint, New York: Dover, 1983).

74. Frost used the phrase "passionate preference" in "Accidentally on Purpose" and elsewhere in his talks and writing including "The Future of Man." It was a psychological form of natural selection similar to James's appropriation of selection as a psychological metaphor. Santayana uses the phrase to discuss Whitman in *The Sense of Beauty* (Cambridge: MIT Press, 1988), 72.

75. Daniel Wilson, *Science, Community and the Transformation of American Philosophy* (Chicago: University of Chicago Press, 1990), 96.

76. See Robert J. Richards, *Darwin and the Emergence of Evolutionary Theories of Mind and Behavior* (Chicago: University of Chicago Press, 1987), chap. 9, "The Personal Equation in Science: William James's Psychological and Moral Vision of Darwinian Theory." See also Morton White, *Science and Sentiment in America* (New York: Oxford University Press, 1972), 170–217.

77. John B. Walker, Notes to Philosophy 3 (1883–84), Harvard University Archives.

78. Ibid.

79. William James, *Psychology*, American Science Series, Briefer Course (New York: Henry Holt, 1892), 170. I cite this edition rather than the full *Principles of Psychology* since that is the edition Frost used in his teaching.

80. James, *Psychology*, 376; emphasis mine.

81. James, *Progmatism*, 98.

82. Ibid., 116.

83. Ibid., 107.

84. John Dewey, "The Influence of Darwin on Philosophy," in *The Influence of Darwin on Philosophy and Other Essays in Contemporary Thought* (New York: Henry Holt, 1910), 46.

85. James, *Pragmatism*, 62.

86. Robert Frost in *Letters of Robert Frost to Louis Untermeyer*, 188–89.

87. Robert Frost, "Letter to Louis Untermeyer, November 25, 1936," ibid., 285.

88. Walter Pater, *Plato and Platonism*, vol. 6 of *The Works of Walter Pater* (London: Macmillan, 1910), 21. See also Philip Appleman, "Darwin, Pater, and a Crisis in Criticism," in *1859: Entering an Age of Crisis*, ed. Philip Applebaum, William A. Madden, and Michael Wolff (Bloomington: Indiana University Press, 1959), 81–95.

89. Florence Hardy, *The Early Years of Thomas Hardy* (London: Macmillan, 1925), 213.

90. James George Frazer, *The Golden Bough*, abridged ed. (New York: Macmillan, 1922), 825–26.

91. Edward Connery Lathem, ed., *Interviews with Robert Frost* (New York: Holt, Rinehart and Winston, 1966), 64.

92. Lawrance Thompson, *Robert Frost: The Years of Triumph* (New York: Holt, Rinehart and Winston, 1970), 624–25. Thompson also speculates that Lucretius' belief that no visible objects perish without contributing to new formations was consonant with the Pauline dualistic view that life perishes to be reborn in imperishable spirit. I would argue that Lucretius and St. Paul are at opposite ends of the spectrum of materialism and that Frost found them consonant in their emphasis on change.

93. Thompson notes that Frost referred to Lucretius in an aside while giving a reading of "West-Running Brook" (*Robert Frost*, 624). See my discussion of "West-Running Brook" in chapter 4.

94. Thompson, *Robert Frost*, 381–82. Thompson says that Frost read and reread the English translation of Bergson's *Creative Evolution* when it was published in English in 1911. My own examination of Frost's copy of Bergson, which is in the Fales Collection at New York University, shows that Frost's marginal annotations to Bergson stop after ninety pages of the four-hundred page work. Not all of those annotations indicate enthusiasm for Bergson (see my discussion of "A White-Tailed Hornet" in chap. 2). The most in-depth treatment of Frost's reading of Bergson is John F. Sears, "William James, Henri Bergson, and the Poetics of Robert Frost," *New England Quarterly* 48 (1975): 341–61. Bergson's metaphors are employed by Frost most prominently in "West-Running Brook," though Frost departs from them in significant ways (see my discussion in chap. 6).

95. Elaine Barry, ed., *Robert Frost on Writing* (New Brunswick: Rutgers University Press, 1973), 18.

96. Royce, *Spirit of Modern Philosophy*, 321–22.

97. Ibid., 338.

98. Ibid., 338–39.

99. Cook, *Robert Frost*, 212.

100. Darwin, *Voyage of the* Beagle, 319.

101. In a letter to Susan Ward in 1895 Frost writes "I am botanizing will I nill I ... I am overwhelmed with books on the subject" (*Selected Letters of Robert Frost* [New York: Holt, Rinehart and Winston, 1964], 28). Orchids figure prominently in Frost's poetry, particularly in the somewhat neglected dramatic poem "The Self-Seeker," which is discussed in chapter 4 of this study.

102. See Nicolete Scourse, *The Victorians and Their Flowers* (Beaverton, Oreg.: Timber Press, 1983), esp. chap. 8, "The Passion for Detail," and chap. 9, "Scientific Controversies." Scourse notes in her discussions of Darwin's botanical researches and work on orchids: "Darwin looked in detail at the incident of color and scent and found that white flowers are by far the most favored in nature in wealth of perfume" (179).

103. Richard Poirier, *Poetry and Pragmatism* (Cambridge: Harvard University Press, 1992), 88.

104. *The Faerie Queene* 7:8, in Edmund Spenser, *Poetical Works*, ed. J. C. Smith and E. de Selincourt (Oxford: Oxford University Press, 1979), 406.

105. Grant Allen, *Colin Clout's Calendar: A Record of a Summer, April–October* (London: Chatto and Windus, 1883), 107.

106. Ibid.

107. Ralph Waldo Emerson, *Essays and Lectures*, ed. Joel Porte (New York: Library of America, 1983), 554.

108. Nicholas Berdayev, *The Meaning of History*, trans. George Reavey (London: Centenary Press, 1936), 115.

109. Ibid., 117.

110. I. A. Richards, *Science and Poetry* (New York: W. W. Norton, 1926), 54.

111. Dartmouth College Library, Ms. Frost 001714.

TYLER HOFFMAN

The Sense of Sound
and the Silent Text

As we have seen, despite Frost's confident claims that he can reproduce intonation contours on the printed page without the assistance of graphetic cues, his poetry demonstrates his reliance on a range of devices meant to clarify utterance. Notably, though, these devices do not rule out ambiguity altogether, even if they do help to delimit the range of potential vocal contours. Indeed, Frost often tries to capitalize on the intonational deprivation of the written word in his poems. As Eric Griffiths finds, "The intonational ambiguity of a written text may create a mute polyphony through which we see rather than hear alternatively possible voicings, and are led by such vision to reflect on the inter-resonance of those voicings."[97] Frost's slighting of the faculty of vision in his theory of form suggests a lack of concern for such indeterminacies, but our experience with his poetry suggests their absolute importance. On the silent page, we are offered opportunities not available through the spoken word; we are able to try out a range of tones that would satisfy the conditions established by a text, to turn lines in different expressive directions, without ruling out all but one. Although one Frost critic has claimed that "There is no poet of whose voice we are surer than Frost's, no poet whom we hear more distinctly as we read," tonal indecision often thwarts such certainties, productively opening up the

From *Robert Frost and the Politics of Poetry* by Tyler Hoffman. © 2001 by Tyler Hoffman.

text to the reader's imagination as it opens up questions about the politics of his poetry.[98]

Only on the rarest of occasions did Frost admit the open-endedness of voice in black and white. As Sidney Cox recalled, in a 1916 lecture he "admitted there were cases of ambiguity about the sound images, but convinced us that they were not more numerous than those of ambiguity about visual images."[99] Here Frost insists that while ambiguity might not be averted fully; it is kept to a minimum and so does not get in the way of his ability to convey his meanings; he does not acknowledge that tonal ambiguity is the foundation on which many of his most complicated and rewarding poems rest. A few years later, Frost is taken aback by those who believe he rules out ambiguity in poetry, and in the privacy of his notebook he mentions more positively the persistence of ambiguity in life and art: "The Buffalo papers said I made an attack on ambiguity. The Syracuse papers said I was suffering from hasty recognition. (false recognition.) I had tried to show how unavoidably ambiguous we are most of the time in word, phrase, sentence, tone, deed and even situation" ("Notebook" 156). Of course, this claim undercuts his many statements about "sentence sounds" up to this point and is far more tenable than the extreme statements found elsewhere: we *are* unavoidably ambiguous most of the time in word, phrase, sentence, tone, deed, and situation. It is surprising that Frost felt his position had been misrepresented by the papers, since his avowal in his notebook does not bear any resemblance to his public polemic (as he told a Harvard audience in 1936, "A poem should be read as written").[100] The fact is, though, that some of Frost's most successful—and most challenging—poems do not secure proper voicing, leaving it to readers to construct divergent meanings out of his ambivalent speech rhythms.

The ambiguity of the printed word should have been brought home to Frost in 1915. After watching a theatrical production of "The Death of the Hired Man" by "The Am. Dram. Soc. (Ink.)" in Boston that year, Frost complained of the actors' interpretation of character through tone of voice, especially that of the husband: "The thing about that, the danger, is that you shall make the man too hard. That spoils it. That's the error the people made: they made the man too hard. And all our thinking turns on that" (*LU* 16; *CPPP* 763). As these remarks indicate, Frost believes that there is only one way to "hear" Warren in the poem, and that to hear him otherwise constitutes an "error." However, there is nothing on the page that mandates the degree or quality of the husband's hardness. The tone of voice to be assigned the following two sentences spoken by him is far from fully resolved: "'When was I ever anything but kind to him? / But I'll not have the fellow back,' he said." With the minimal marker, "he said," we are left with much to imagine. His question could be heard as indignant, peremptory, or beseeching, while still satisfying metrical conditions. But what does it matter, one might ask, whether we construe the man's statements as more "hard" or more "soft"? Frost's contention that "all our thinking turns on" our "correct" interpretation of tone makes clear his sense that our perception of the meaning of the poem is strongly affected by the answer to that question. And, indeed, much does turn on our interpretation of tone, but Frost has made it so that we can hear a statement as spoken in various ways. Again, there are limits to the range of possible intonation contours; we do not hear Warren as joyful in the passage quoted above. But to admit these limits is not to admit that there is one and only one way—and that way authorized by Frost—to construe "voice" in his poems. Griffiths explains the impact of such tonal ambiguities: "when a reader faces and tries to voice an intonationally ambiguous line, he is asked to reflect on the pull one reading rather than another exerts on him, and to ask why it does so. He comes to know himself in the act of becoming convinced that he knows the fictional speaker."[101] Frost's ambiguous lines and sentences incite such self-knowledge, requiring us to come to terms with our own attitudes as we draw toward or away from a speaker based on our soundings of tone.

The silent drama of "The Death of the Hired Man" bears out Griffiths's remarks. Mark Richardson has dismissed the poem for its "formulaic" treatment of gender, pointing to a correlation Frost makes between sentiment and tone in the poem and his personal political views:[102]

> They think I'm no New Dealer. But really and truly I'm not, you know, all that clear on it. In *The Death of the Hired Man* that I wrote long, long ago, long before the New Deal, I put it two ways about home. One would be the manly way: "Home is the place where, when you have to go there, / They have to take you in." That's the man's feeling about it. And then the wife says, "I should have called it / Something you somehow hadn't to deserve." That's the New Deal, the mother's love. You have to deserve your father's. He's more particular. One's a republican, one's a Democrat. The father is always a Republican toward his son, the mother's always a Democrat. Very few have noticed that second thing; they've always noticed the sarcasm, the hardness of the male. (*CPPP* 885)

In this 1960 discussion Frost revises himself, suggesting that "the sarcasm, the hardness of the male" has crowded out appreciation of the tone of feminine kindness, not that the man has been misheard as "hard." Evidently, Frost, like his readers, is susceptible to hearing his poem differently in light of changes in attitude. Here he fixes tone in order to define more clearly the ideological poles in his construing of the poem as a political allegory. Ironically, though, it is this sharp distinction between the tones of husband and wife that Frost criticizes the Boston actors for making. While Richardson is correct to point out that Frost stereotypes gender in these remarks about the poem, the negotiation of gender in the play of tone in the poem itself is more nuanced than Frost's retrospective account suggests. Citing that account, Karen Kilcup finds that Frost reveals "a strikingly politicized sense of gender relations" in the poem and ultimately embraces the feminine perspective.[103] I would agree that Frost politicizes gender in the poem, but it is less clear that the empathic feminine voice wins out; as Frost himself insists, both the manly and feminine perspectives assert claims on our sympathies, and it is for us to weigh them in turn.

How we hear the sentences by husband and wife that we read on the page determines in large part what we think of the characters and the sentiments they express, and some of Frost's most astute critics disagree about what precisely they hear. Richard Poirier finds the wife's statement, "'I should have called it [home] / Something you somehow haven't to deserve,'" annoyingly "sententious."[104] Reuben Brower, on the other hand, hears a tone of "gentle plainness" in that last line.[105] I can imagine the statement as moralizing and as tender in various readings of it, and in different expressive turnings of the line I reflect on the pull one reading rather than another exerts and consider why it does so. Does the woman sound as if she is correcting her husband, teaching him how to temper his justice with mercy? Or is she offering up an alternative definition of "home" that is not meant so much as a reproof of her husband's as it is an affective supplement to it? To what extent is she preaching and to what extent gently coaxing? The quality of the relationship between husband and wife is revealed in the answers to such questions.

Sidney Cox says that Frost spoke of "The Death of the Hired Man" as "a little drama in which the gradual change in Warren is shown," but readers (who are also imaginative hearers) are divided about just how much Warren evolves in the course of the dialogue.[106] Katherine Kearns notes his emotional progress when she finds that at first "Warren's concerns are economical and his attitude is juridical, and it is only when he is brought to remember that Silas could impose a small but perfect order in building a load of (usable, marketable) hay that he begins to be deterred from anger."[107] Here are the lines to which she refers:

"I know, that's Silas' one accomplishment.
He bundles every forkful in its place,
And tags and numbers it for future reference,
So he can find and easily dislodge it
In the unloading. Silas does that well.
He takes it out in bunches like big birds' nests.
You never see him standing on the hay
He's trying to lift, straining to lift himself."

                                        (*CPPP* 43)

In contrast to Kearns's interpretation of this speech, Brower refers to it as a "slightly acid tribute," suggesting his belief that Warren's sarcastic tone in these lines is consistent with the "juridical" tone apparent in earlier exchanges.[108] One of these exchanges also prompts Brower to remark on the man's "hard"ness:

"What did he say? Did he say anything?"
"But little."
        "Anything? Mary, confess
He said he'd come to ditch the meadow for me"
"Warren!"
        "But did he? I just want to know."

As he finds, "Her tone is begging and explanatory, her 'Warren' here and later pressing the personal is very unlike his stern 'Mary,' calling the defendant to the bar."[109] Brower's interpretation of Warren's tone is not unwarranted, but it is certainly possible to imagine his voice as not "stern" but teasing—a tone that is meant to call the hired man to the bar more than his wife.

Based on his reading, Brower comes to the opinion that "Mary's character like her husband's grows more distinct as she builds out the picture of Silas," with one pitted against the other in this drama of tone. He specifically refers to the "harsher turns" of Warren's concluding speech, believing that the "wife's voice is entirely different" from the husband's—a difference maintained throughout the poem: "But though their feelings converge [in the end], their last words are thoroughly characteristic, hers questioning, his brief, hard, and final, though much is unsaid."[110] Kearns, on the other hand, contends that whereas early on in the poem Warren "thinks legalistically, in terms of imperatives whose violation would result in some punishment," his tone softens as Mary continues to talk; ultimately, she credits "Mary's great power to move Warren toward empathy," and finds that "Such yielding as Mary would awaken in her husband is nonetheless a form of unmanning, almost a kind of bewitchment, as if she would bring Warren to be as ineffectual in worldly terms as the 'son' Silas whose case she pleads."[111] Brower's and Kearns's divergent interpretations point to the ambiguity of these "sentence-sounds" and reveal the pull between the values of justice and mercy in the poem and in the world.

In "Home Burial," another dramatic dialogue in *North of Boston*, scripted utterances similarly can be turned in different ways, and these co-existent tonal possibilities profoundly affect our interpretations of character and gender politics in the poem. Since Frost rarely consented to read "Home Burial" in public, most of those who would seek to pin tones to his own reading of it are left with nothing to go on but the printed page. Ambiguity of voice not only exists in the poem; it is thematized there as well: Amy's accusation, "There you go sneering now!" prompts her husband's denial, "I'm not, I'm not!" an exchange that suggests that tone of voice can be mistaken even in speech, especially at heated moments. Although attitudinal markers in a poem (for example, "mocked gently") may enforce a particular tone, such markers are infrequent in Frost's dramatic verse, and, consequently, ambiguities proliferate. With this in mind, we would be wise to scrutinize Frost's statement about the emotionally charged sentence that ends "Home Burial": "I am not bothered by the question whether anyone will be able to hear or say those three words ('If—you—do!') as I mean them to be said or heard. I should say that they were sufficiently self-expressive" (*SL* 130). While it may be clear that the words are said in a fit of desperation, just how much fury is entangled in them is in question, and that undecidability of tone presides over the action of the entire poem.

Other statements in the poem betray the same ambivalence, a condition that complicates our laying of sympathies. To the husband's plea, "'Don't—don't go. / Don't carry it to someone else this time,'" Richard Poirier responds, "if he [the husband] is insensitive, he is at least not without gentleness," and further finds that "he is less peremptory than is she: 'Don't, don't, don't, don't,' she cried."[112] As Poirier believes, the husband's "reasonable beseeching" is pitted against the wife's "physical and spiritual lack of outgoingness, forthcomingness."[113] While I would agree with the view of the husband as "beseeching" and the wife as non-forthcoming, I can imagine hearing these words by husband and wife differently. In the two sentences that Poirier defines as "less peremptory" than the wife's speech, I also can hear peremptoriness, frustration, pique (*not again!*). In the wife's concatenation of "don't"s I can pick up a highly pathetic beseeching; in fact, I am able to hear each "don't" in a different tone as each registers a different agony. Frost once remarked that "the four 'don't's were the supreme thing" in the poem, and they are if by that he means the height of ambiguity of expression.[114]

Through this tonal ambivalence Frost explores cultural attitudes about gender and bereavement and forces us to come to terms with our own. Although he identifies "The Death of the Hired Man" as the "elegy" in *North of Boston*, "Home Burial" more fully stages the work of mourning the dead (*RFW* 82). As we have seen, the different responses of husband and wife to the death of their child, and, consequently, to each other, provoke different attitudes in readers. Do we understand the bereft woman as engaged in what Freud calls "normal mourning," or is she enacting the work of "melancholic" mourning, as she resists solace, lashing out at her husband and wishing for her own death.[115] In other words, do we feel that she is going through a stage on her way to surpassing her grief, or that she is mired in a grief that is not to be consoled, that is bound to destroy herself and her marriage? To the extent that we feel she is normative, we tend to extend sympathy to her, to upbraid the husband for his callous remarks. To the extent that we feel she is "psychotic," we probably take the side of the husband, who we imagine is trying to save her from her own extreme condition.[116] Confronting the ambiguous tones of the poem, we come to our own conclusions about what constitutes reasonable reaction to loss, or whether reason is a thing to be considered in the face of loss, as we identify with one or the other (or both) speakers.

Moments of vocal indecision shape other dramatic narratives in *North of Boston* as well and compound the (political) meanings that they convey. One such poem is "Mending Wall." During a public reading of that poem, Frost remarked on the aphorism that is twice spoken by the neighbor: "You know, I've read that so often I've sort of lost the right way to say, 'Good fences make good neighbors.' See. There's a special way to say [it] I used to have in my imagination, and it seems to have gone down. You say it in two different ways there."[117] Frost's confession that he has not been able to retain the intonation that he originally had in mind suggests the inability of the printed page to record unambiguously tones of voice; here he reveals that he has lost his own intention. Nevertheless, he continues to believe that there is a "right way" to say the sentence, when in fact there are several possible ways. The first appearance of the famous aphorism comes in reply to the narrator's taunt:

> My apple trees will never get across
> And eat the cones under his pines, I tell him.
> He only says, 'Good fences make good neighbors.'
>   (*CPPP* 39)

In 1915, when the tone is fresher in his mind, Frost advises that this instance should be heard as expressing "Incredulity of the other's dictum" (*CPPP* 689). But how much sarcasm is entangled in the speaker's quotation of his neighbor's statement? The tone is held in suspension, allowing us to imagine it as said with either a shrug or a sneer. The second inscription of the maxim comes at the end of the poem and is introduced by the narrator's description of the relationship between neighbor and cliché:

> He will not go behind his father's saying,
> And he likes having thought of it so well
> He says again, "Good fences make good neighbors."

We might hear this second voicing of the aphorism differently from the first, as Frost says we should, perhaps imbuing it with a self-satisfied tone, but no tone is perfectly clear. Of course, none of the imaginable tones is flattering to the neighbor: when we hear it one way, we condemn him as smug and self-congratulatory; when we hear it another way, we write him off as a blockhead ("an old-stone savage armed").

However, there is wisdom in the sentence, as Frost himself acknowledged on more than one occasion, and his identification with both speakers ("Maybe I was both fellows in the poem")—his refusal to take sides ("I make it a rule not to take any 'character's' side in anything I write")—further complicates our interpretation of tone (*I* 257; *SL* 138). The narrator is, after all, the one who proposes mending the wall *and* the one who questions the need to do so. The tone is tricky here, as is the situation. How are we to take the speaker's criticism of his neighbor if he himself is in some way behind the expression? How light-hearted is his criticism or how heavy-handed? Reginald Cook has said that in a reading of "Mending Wall," Frost stressed the sentence, "I'd rather he said it for himself," in the following lines, which speculate humorously on the forces that topple the wall:[118]

> I could say 'Elves' to him,
> But it's not elves exactly; and I'd rather
> He said it for himself.

Nothing on the page indicates that we should emphasize this remark, but if we do, certain meanings come to hand, for instance, that it is not so much the content of the phrase, as it is the neighbor's uncritical absorption and echoing of it, that galls. Stanley Burnshaw describes the situation of the poem in the following way: "Two 'contradictory' speakers, both of them 'right' up to a point, and only when they are joined is the poem resolved— and then in an 'open-endedness.'"[119] But to see this confluence one must hold to a certain interpretation of tone in the poem. It would be just as easy to reject fully the position of the neighbor, since the printed page does not reveal definitely the speaker's sympathy with the essence of the aphorism. Frost grants us leave to accept or reject the neighbor's message based on the tones of voice we project onto the lines and, in doing so, forces us to probe our often conflicted attitudes about personality and inter-personality, and, on a political level, about nationalists (those who want walls) and "One-worlders" (those who want none), a tension that Frost claimed in 1955 the poem was about.[120] The "open-endedness" of tone requires us to judge for ourselves where the point of intersection between the positions of the two speakers lies, and our inflection of the lines no doubt will depend upon our feelings about political conditions at the time we read, or reread, the poem.

Despite such ambiguous tones, critics are quick to fix attitudes to statements in Frost's poetry and pin their interpretations of meaning in the poem on them. The final quatrain of "Come In" is a case in point, as the tone of the speaker's refusal of the thrush's call asking him to "come into the woods and lament" resists easy classification:

> But no, I was out for stars,
> I would not come in.
> I meant not even if asked,
> And I hadn't been.
>
> (*CPPP* 304)

Of these lines, Marie Borroff writes: "In a dramatically expressive reading, there will be a slight rise of pitch on *I* and *stars* in the first line and on *meant* and *asked* in the third. The most striking sentence sound comes in the elliptical phrasing of the last line: 'I hadn't been,' a reduction of 'I hadn't been asked.' The last chief syllable of the poem, *been*, must be read with weak stress and a corresponding drop in pitch. Both the contracted form 'hadn't' and the expression 'out for stars' have the distinctive ring of everyday speech."[121] Surely, Borroff's interpretation of tone in this stanza is valid, as Frost does not provide italics to assist us. However, one might hear the expression "I was out for stars" without a slight rise of pitch on *I* and *stars*, and instead as "I was *out* for *stars*." In Borroff's version, the utterance assumes a defiant tone, with the speaker boldly asserting himself when confronted by an invitation to self-extinction. In the other version, the line takes on a more jaunty tone, as if to suggest that it takes no special effort not to succumb. The title itself predicts this ambivalence, as we cannot be sure whether the phrase is to be heard in a casual colloquial voice (Come *In*), or as full-throated and ominous (*Come In*).

Assigning tone of voice in the last stanza of "Come In" is difficult because the tenor of the metaphor is unclear. Is the poem about the speaker's refusal to bow to grief? (In the period leading up to the first publication of the poem in February 1941, Frost had lost a daughter, son, and wife.) Is it about his refusal to join with other modernist poets in their "difficult" poetics? Is it about his rejection of political leftists who lament social conditions in America? The tonal ambiguities at the end of the poem thwart resolution of these questions. If we read it as a refusal to wallow in loss, we might hear the sentence in the way Borroff does, as the speaker attempts to safeguard his ego in the face of a potentially all-consuming grief. If we read it as a rebuke to unpatriotic forces, we might hear it otherwise, with the speaker rather blithely turning his back on them as holding no special interest: "But no I was out for stars." By enforcing neither of these interpretations, Frost lets us hear the sentence on the page variously and imagine the range of contexts that could give rise to such utterance.

Such shiftiness of speech rhythm has occasioned a great deal of critical wrangling, and the controversy that erupted when the renowned literary critic Lionel Trilling announced at Frost's eighty-fifth birthday party that he is "a terrifying poet" owes much to the "problem" of tone in Frost's work.[122] The two poems that Trilling cites—"Neither Out Far Nor In Deep" and "Design"—exemplify both the ambiguity of tone and the opportunities that that ambiguity afforded Frost. "Neither Out Far Nor In Deep" narrates an epistemological crisis, but it is not immediately clear what the poem is in fact about and, thus, how it should be heard:

> The people along the sand
> All turn and look one way
> They turn their back on the land.
> They look at the sea all day.
>
> As long as it takes to pass
> A ship keeps raising its hull;

The wetter ground like glass
Reflects a standing gull.

The land may vary more;
But wherever the truth may be—
The water comes ashore,
And the people look at the sea.

They cannot look out far.
They cannot look in deep.
But when was that ever a bar
To any watch they keep?
                    (*CPPP* 274)

One is left to wonder whether that final stanza is optimistic or pessimistic. Is it a cheering statement of Frost's "attitude and belief that man will never conquer nature but that he will never cease trying" or rather a sneering at the masses, who are visually and critically impaired, but who refuse to acknowledge that fact, foolish in their futile quest (*CR* 115). Is the word *they* in that stanza pronounced with "deadpanned contempt" or are the final lines spoken with a rouse?[123] One critic has noted that in the poem Frost recognizes "the essential limitations of man, without denial or protest or rhetoric or palliation," but that he "doesn't say it [the last stanza] unpleasantly—he says it with flat ease, takes everything with something harder than contempt, more passive than acceptance.... The tone of the last lines—or, rather, their careful suspension between several tones, as a piece of iron can be held in the air between powerful enough magnets—allows for this too."[124] This condition of tonal indecision points up a complexity of attitude and meaning at the heart of the poem, and compels us to search out our attitudes about our fellow man, our sense of our capabilities in an often inscrutable world—a world that will not yield up its mysteries to either telescope or microscope (the two instruments that Frost says he alludes to in the lines "They cannot look out far. / They cannot look in deep").[125]

Like "Neither Out Far Nor In Deep," "Design" is about our ambivalent relation to the universe—a relation figured through ambivalent speech contours—and our sense of purpose in it. In the final lines of the poem—the sestet of the sonnet—we find a series of questions and a final statement that confound interpretation of the speaker's mood:

What had that flower to do with being white,
The wayside blue and innocent heal-all?

> What brought the kindred spider to that height,
> Then steered the white moth thither in the night?
> What but design of darkness to appall?—
> If design govern in a thing so small.
>
> (*CPPP* 275)

Does the first question sound like "ordinary annoyance at a fact that doesn't fit in," or does it sound honestly quizzical?[126] Is the next question ("What brought the kindred spider ... ") heard as in "a voice of lost innocence," or does it mark the speaker simply as dumbfounded.[127] At issue is whether the speaker has been touched by the "darkness" of the world or whether he remains unknowing—and at sea—in his grappling with the mysteries of his surroundings. The cadence of the final question—"What but design of darkness to appall?"—is as elusive, leaving us to decide for ourselves whether the speaker expresses sheer incomprehension or rather deep suspicion at the shape of things. One critic has referred to "the soothingly humorous hesitation" of the last line of the poem, a "hesitation that points to something many readers may find less agreeable than design of darkness, to no order whatever," but it, too, is ambiguous, and could be taken as more serious than humorous, a frightening reminder of the possibility of teleological breakdown.[128] Frost's claim that "Design" is "very undramatic in the speech entirely," that "It's a kind of poker-face piece," suggests some of the problems that the poem's hearers are up against.[129] But that description of it is also misleading, since it is not that the poem is tone dead, but rather that its elusive tones keep us guessing, just as we are left unsure whether a higher force shapes our ends.

The tonal inter-resonance of "The Road Not Taken"—another case in which Frost plays it close to the vest—similarly has perplexed readers, and no wholly adequate account of the auditory dynamics at the end of the poem has been forthcoming, despite much work on the part of critics to lay bare the irony involved in those lines. Here is what the speaker of the poem declares:

> I shall be telling this with a sigh
> Somewhere ages and ages hence:
> Two roads diverged in a wood, and I—
> I took the road less traveled by,
> And that has made all the difference.
>
> (*CPPP* 103)

Frost himself revealed that in the first line of the last stanza tone is difficult to ascertain, cautioning, "See, the tone of that is absolutely saving. You've got to look out for it, though. See."[130] William Pritchard comments on the discrepancy between Frost's poetics and the intonational ambiguity at work in the poem, mapping its biographical coordinates:

> Yet Frost had written Untermeyer two years previously [in 1915] that "I'll bet not half a dozen people can tell who was hit and where he was hit in my Road Not Taken," and he characterized himself in that poem particularly as "fooling my way along." He also said that it was really about his friend Edward Thomas, who when they walked together always castigated himself for not having taken another path than the one they took. When Frost sent "The Road Not Taken" to Thomas he was disappointed that Thomas failed to understand it as a poem about himself; but Thomas in return insisted to Frost that "I doubt if you can get anybody to see the fun of the thing without showing them and advising them which kind of laugh they are to turn on." And though this kind of advice went exactly contrary to Frost's notion of how poetry should work, he did on occasion warn his audiences and other readers that it was a tricky poem.[131]

Which kind of laugh are we to turn on when we see that the speaker has falsified the record, pretending in his old age that he took the road less traveled, despite the fact that earlier in the poem we learn that "both [roads] that morning equally lay / In leaves no step had trodden black"? Do we laugh with derision when the speaker stands exposed as a revisionist, or is the laugh we turn on gentler—one directed as much at ourselves as at the speaker of the final lines? If we hear the final statement as heartfelt, absent a moralizing strain, we probably regard the speaker with some sympathy, as symbolic of the human propensity to construct fictions to justify choices made in clouded circumstances. But if it strikes our ear as sententious, we are more likely to laugh at his expense, to mock his pretentiousness. Frost permits us to hear the final statement in at least these two ways, perhaps at different stages of our life, even as we register its irony, and so encourages us to come to terms with our vexed attitudes about what it means to fashion a personal history, to represent life as worth living.

As such poems testify, moments of epistemological and eschatological crisis often are shaped by tonal ambiguity in Frost's poetry, which is keenly aware of the limits (and possibilities) of our comprehension of our world. Frost is not a "spiritual drifter," as Yvor Winters alleged, but a poet committed to undermining easy confidences about our moral position.[132] In

"For Once, Then, Something" Frost depicts someone who tries to find a way to know (and know he has known) such a moral absolute as Truth. The speaker seems to be an object of ridicule for pursuing absolutes without a proper faith—a person blinded by egotistical concerns ("Others taunt me with having knelt at well-curbs"). But that figure is not fully imagined; we do not receive a profile that would help us determine with certainty the attitudes and emotions behind his utterances. It is unclear how he feels about the taunting that he receives and how his search for "Something more of the depths" is shaped by it. The questions leading up to the phrase in its final appearance only muddy the water: "What was that whiteness? / Truth? A pebble of quartz?" How are we to hear these questions? Does he ask them in an agitated tone? Is he profoundly disturbed or gently quizzical? The disparity between "Truth" and "A pebble of quartz" suggests that he has glimpsed either something essential or something wholly inconsequential. Does his tone reflect the crushing distance that lies between them? Is he exasperated by the refusal of his world to yield full meaning to him, or excited by what he has been shown? The epistemological problem that the poem presents—"How can we know Truth if at all?" and "How do we know if we have known Truth?"—is never finally resolved. Originally, the poem was titled "Wrong to the Light"; Frost changes it to the polyvocal "For Once, Then, Something" in order to highlight the uncertainty of vision and stimulate the reader to face the perplexities of his relationship to nature and God.

The same suspension of tone shapes the conclusion of Frost's lyric "The Most of It," a title that is clipped from a colloquial utterance (the poem was originally called "Making the Most of It") and that we can hear in at least two ways—as much or little, as cheery or deflated—as we measure our expectations against the realities of our world. When we say in life we will "make the most of it," we either express through our tone a weary resignation to our fate (we will do the best we can with meager resources) or an enthusiastic acceptance of matters as they lie. In the poem a man's quest for "counter-love, original response" from the universe ends in an ambiguously coded buck ("nothing ever came from what he cried / Unless ... ") that crashes through the water in front of him. The final phrase of the poem compounds this ambiguity, as we are told that the buck

> landed pouring like a waterfall,
> And stumbled through the rocks with horny tread,
> And forced the underbrush—and that was all.
> (*CPPP* 307)

It is not quite clear here how we are to regard the speaker's attitude toward the response he gets to his call and, therefore, how we should say "—and that was all": does the pitch fall on "all" to suggest disappointment or does it rise in signal of wonderment? The intonation is not indicated by the "notation" of the sentence and, consequently, the meaning of the buck's crash remains uncertain. It either represents an "original response," even if not human, in which the speaker can take satisfaction, or mocks his wish for "counter-love," thwarting his desire for human colloquy. William Empson argues that the word "all" is "as suited to absolute love and self-sacrifice as to insane self-assertion," and Frost's use of the word here invokes that range of attitudes.[133] Ultimately, there is not a "right" way to speak the final phrase, because there is not a simple solution to the speaker's dilemma: the buck is something and nothing; it comes in the wake of the man's appeal, but it may or may not betoken the thing for which he is searching. Richard Poirier has argued that in the poem "to be told 'that was all,' does not, needless to say, mean that 'all' is nothing," that the final words "are addressed not to the inadequacy of the buck to live up to the spectator's sentimental expectations but to the incapacity of the spectator, and of us, to find any way to account for the buck, its power and fantastic indifference."[134] I would say rather that Frost's tonal play allows us to weigh the significance of the buck for ourselves—to see it both as something and nothing—in our various soundings of the phrase that the mute polyphony of "all" allows.

Like "The Most of It," the title of Frost's thanatopsis "Away!" represents a segment of a larger statement, this one derived from a song—the chorus of the old chantey *Shenandoah* ("I'm—bound—away!"). Abstracted from that phrase, however, its tone becomes highly ambivalent and, as such, provides an ironic counterpoint to the poem that it introduces. The exclamatory expression from the song appears in full in the penultimate stanza:

> Unless I'm wrong
> I but obey
> The urge of a song:
> I'm—bound—away!
>   (*CPPP* 427)

The same sentence appears in Frost's *A Masque of Mercy* (1947) with the helpful stage direction that Jonah *"quotes it to the tune"* of the song (*CPPP* 396). But "Away!" is not a theatrical script, and Frost does not include such a cue. Despite this fact, one is likely to conjure up a wistful air with that song in mind when the sentence is met with in the poem, as that mood is in keeping with the sentiments expressed by the speaker, who, happy with this world, simply chooses to explore the (not so) final frontier:

> And I may return
> If dissatisfied
> With what I learn
> From having died.

But if, as I have suggested, the full line "I'm—bound—away!" would seem to indicate a particular intonation contour, the mere title "Away!" does not. In remarks about the poem at a reading at the Bread Loaf Writers' Conference (June 30, 1958), Frost lets on that the intonation of the title is not fixed in his mind, but wonderfully suggestive of a range of attitudes: "[H]ere's a little death [poem]—just for the fun of it. This is a real death poem. It's called—I guess I call it 'Away'—'Away'—'Away.' [Giving the word different intonations] That would make you suspicious to begin with."[135] The transcript does not tell what tones of voice he tried out, only that he turned the word in three different expressive directions. If said wistfully, it would make one suspicious of the poem as about death, since we usually do not think of our demise in terms of that emotion. But one can imagine other turnings, for instance, toward fear (*Stay away!*) and pleasurable excitement (*Up and away!*), whose coexistence also makes one suspicious, disturbing our stereotyped notion of death. Rereading the title in light of the poem, we find that the ambivalent tone expresses an ambivalent view of mortality, for the speaker, who is given to imagine death as reversible.

The title of Frost's poem "'Out, Out—'" calls attention more obviously to its status as borrowed text, alluding to the famous soliloquy by the title character of Shakespeare's drama *Macbeth* upon learning of the death of his queen, and its probing of the political issue of child labor calls on us to measure our own political natures in turn. As with the two poems just discussed, important questions are raised even before reaching the body of the lyric as to how to hear the words on the page. An actor on the stage would be forced to choose how to say these words ("Out, out, brief candle!"), invoking the sting of death either through a clipped, bitter pronunciation, a drawn-out melancholy one, or some other tone on the spectrum between these two poles. In any event, the expression serves as an ironic comment on what follows: Macbeth's metaphorical and philosophical turn ("Life's but a walking shadow, ... ") is foreign to Frost's poem, which is set in a place where such consideration is a luxury that the characters cannot afford. The indeterminacy of the initial vocal contour is matched by the final tone of voice displayed in the poem: "No more to build on there. And they, since they / Were not the one dead, turned to their affairs" (*CPPP* 131). Are these final lines contemptuously said, "a bitter comment on the callous indifference to human suffering"?[136] Or is there poignancy entailed in the flat remark? How we hear the end of "'Out, Out—'" ultimately depends on our personal sympathies and attitudes, as Sidney Cox discovered: "Some of my optimistic acquaintances think the close [of "'Out, Out—'"] uncomfortable. In other words it is too sincere for them, and they fail to sense the tender sympathy."[137] Here he suggests that some who want the world better than it is cringe at the conclusion, but those, including himself, who take the world as it is, find in those same lines a current of "sympathy" for the conditions that give rise to the boy's untimely death. In defense of the poem to his friend Alice Ray, who had expressed qualms about it, Cox further remarked, "I know how you feel about the last line. But that isn't Mr. Frost. That's life. I don't know anyone who has more of the right sort of tenderness than Mr. Frost. It shows in the [tenth] line 'Call it a day I wish they might have said.' You say 'I like it and still I don't.' That's exactly how I feel about life."[138] How Cox feels about life conditions his hearing of "tenderness" in the poem, and he is right to say that when we read the poem we cannot help but reflect our own political response to the world and suffering in it.

Indeed, in several of Frost's poems that exhibit tonal ambivalence he represents an elusive public politics through them, registering his ideological ambivalence and compelling us to search out our own sympathies when we come into contact with them. Sometimes, irony in Frost's political verse is hard to see, and there often are no clues (unlike in "The Road Not Taken") to go by. For instance, in his early poem "My Giving" that he sent in 1911 to Susan Hayes Ward, he plays both sides of the political question. On the face of it, the poem asserts a solidarity with industrial workers that the speaker of "Good Relief" (a poem of the same period that I address in the first chapter) cannot muster—one that would have pleased Ward; on the other hand, the speaker in the poem could be heard as mocking the idea of full-blown sympathy for the dispossessed:

> Here I shall sit, the fire out, and croon
> All the dismal and joy-forsaken airs,
> Sole alone, and thirsty with them that thirst,
> Hungry with them that hunger and are accurst.

No storm that night can be too untamed for me;
If it is woe on earth, woe let it be!

(CPPP 518–19)

Is this an ironic expression or does the plaint come across as sincerely felt? Probably its tonal resonance depends on the politics of the hearer, on how far one believes caring should go.

Later during the Depression Frost again writes poems in which we may or may not hear the voice on the page as ironic, and that ambivalent condition holds his politics in abeyance. In "Provide, Provide" in *A Further Range* it may be clear that the speaker is exhorting self-protection, but his precise attitude to the problem of our security is not immediately apparent:

The witch that came (the withered hag)
To wash the steps with pail and rag
Was once the beauty Abishag,

The picture pride of Hollywood.
Too many fall from great to good
For you to doubt the likelihood.

Die early and avoid the fate.
Or if predestined to die late,
Make up your mind to die in state.

Make the whole stock exchange your own!
If need be occupy a throne,
Where nobody can call *you* crone.

Some have relied on what they knew;
Others on being simply true.
What worked for them might work for you.

No memory of having starred
Atones for later disregard,
Or keeps the end from being hard.

Better to go down dignified
With boughten friendship by your side
Than none at all. Provide, provide!

(CPPP 280)

Stanley Burnshaw points to this poem as one that bothers our notion of Frost's conservatism, as it "confounds oversimple judgments" by virtue of the fact that "though [the poem is] 'sung' by a single speaker, the contradictory voice is heard through implications that cannot be missed."[139] I would argue, however, that the tonal implications may well be missed and that Frost invokes a reticence on the written page to figure his political openness and to make room for our own political involvement. Randall Jarrell has said that for him the poem "is full of the deepest, and most touching, moral wisdom— and it is full, too, of the life we have to try to be wise about and moral in."[140] But is the speaking voice purely poignant, or do we find in it a "bitterly sarcastic" note?[141] Does it mock the striking scrubwomen at Harvard that Frost said the poem is about, or rather does the speaker mock himself by exhorting Americans to provide for the future at a time when for many merely providing for the moment is in question? Although Jarrell claims that the poem has a "conclusiveness" about it, it is ultimately inconclusive in its political posture, not a simple screed directed at the sentimental humanitarianism of the New Deal.[142] In readings of the poem, Frost often quipped after the final line, "Or somebody else'll provide for you! ... And how'll you like that?"[143] Here Frost shows his political hand more fully, revealing in his oral performance of the poem an animus against the welfare state that the poem on the page withholds.

Before the dawn of the New Deal, in his poem "The Egg and the Machine" (1928), Frost addressed the rapidly changing economy and the political forces involved in it through a similarly ambiguous speaking voice— one that seenms so flatly expressive that we are kept guessing as to whether it is at points ironic. The title announces an opposition between the natural and the man-made, and in the poem the speaker blasts the incursion of industrial forces into the rural setting, inveighing against what Leo Marx has termed "the machine in the garden":[144]

> He gave the solid rail a hateful kick.
> From far away there came an answering tick,
> And then another tick. He knew the code:
> His hate had roused an engine up the road.
> He wished when he had had the track alone
> He had attacked it with a club or stone
> And bent some rail wide open like a switch,
> So as to wreck the engine in the ditch.
>
> (*CPPP* 248)

Here Frost activates "the trope of the interrupted idyll"—a trope that shapes the work of some important nineteenth-century American writers responding to the new industrial economy.[145] In the poem the locomotive is imagined as a steam monster reminiscent of the shrieking mill: "Then for a moment all there was was size, / Confusion, and a roar that drowned the cries / He raised against the gods in the machine." The speaker's hatred of it prompts a belated wish that he had sabotaged the rails "So as to wreck the engine in the ditch," a statement that raises questions about the man's political identity. At the time Frost wrote the poem, it was widely believed that the International Workers of the World (I.W.W.) sponsored acts of sabotage; Bill Haywood, Wobbly organizer in the 1912 textile strike in Lawrence, Massachusetts, is credited with saying, "Sabotage means to push back, pull out or break off the fangs of Capitalism."[146] In addition, the poem was entitled "The Walker" when it was first published—the same title as a poem by Arturo Giovannitti, an Italian-born writer and orator who came to Lawrence early in the strike to take charge of strike relief. Giovannitti wrote his poem in prison after being jailed for his involvement in the strike, and it was published in a pamphlet issued by the I.W.W. in 1913. It is quite possible that Frost's rail-walker is meant to be an I.W.W. itinerant worker, especially in light of the fact that "Most of them beat their way by freight car from one place to another, and railroad companies estimated that there were half a million hoboes riding the rails, walking the tracks, or waiting at railroad junctions to catch onto a train, at any one time."[147]

The climax of the poem holds in suspension Frost's attitude toward the man and his proposed act of sabotage. Following the track of a turtle (as opposed to the artificial steel track that the engine rides), the man finds a buried nest and arms himself with turtle eggs, preparing to throw them at the train engine's headlight upon its next approach:

> "You'd better not disturb me anymore,"
> He told the distance, "I am armed for war.
> The next machine that has the power to pass
> Will get this plasm in its goggle glass."

The "war" that he stands ready to wage conjures up the reality of warfare between labor and capital raging in America at the time, but his insufficient arsenal may be seen as mocking his position. Yvor Winters faults Frost for expressing in the poem his "sentimental hatred for the machine," thereby associating the poet with the title figure.[148] But just what is Frost's relation to the armed man? Does he identify with his desire to draw limits to the spread of industry? Or is he being ironic, trying to point up the futility (and hilarity) of union attempts to disrupt industry? (The landmark Railway Labor Act of 1926 emphasized collective bargaining and mediation over settlement of wage disputes by a federal board, and Frost may be suggesting that such legislation is fruitless, that each individual must measure himself against industrial forces at work in the world.) When asked about the poem, Frost denied any bias, stating that he was not "taking sides" and that whether he was leaning toward the organic or the mechanical (two political alternatives) "is for you to choose."[149] As these remarks indicate, his is no "sentimental hatred of the machine," but rather a careful weighing—and ambivalent staging—of the impact of the new industrial order through elusive tones of voice.

Elsewhere, too, undecidability of tone—or vocal latency—in Frost's poetry is implicated in class politics, as for one lower-class audience the oral performance of a poem from *A Further Range* effectively congeals its conservatism. Although it has been said of "Two Tramps in Mud Time" (1934) that "line after line speaks itself in the mouth with the turn and tone unmistakably intended; the poem reads itself," the fact is that in the poem on the page a rich ambiguity of tone requires readers to search out Frost's personal political philosophy—and, more importantly, their own—in their encounters with it (*CR* 114). It is possible to hear the ending as "rather sententious," as Malcolm Cowley does, with the narrator cautioning,[150]

> But yield who will to their separation,
> My object in living is to unite
> My avocation and my vocation
> As my two eyes make one in sight.
> Only where love and need are one,
> And the work is play for mortal stakes,
> Is the deed ever really done
> For Heaven and the future's sakes.
> (*CPPP* 252)

But in what manner is the speaker moralizing here? Is he trying to teach us a lesson or merely trying to content himself with a lesson he has learned? Our answers to these questions depend on whether we hear (and see) the narrator talking aloud to us or musing to himself. A teacher of the poem told Cowley that his students from poor families in the Alleghanies were made "vaguely uncomfortable when they heard it read aloud."[151] Their uneasiness no doubt arises from the sense they get that the narrator speaks the words in the poem, since the words are read aloud to them, that he is unsympathetically sermonizing upon sight of the displaced workers who want his job for pay. If, however, we imagine that the words are self-directed, comprising an interior monologue, or tacit text, it becomes possible to interpret the passage—and the message of the poem—differently. If unspoken, the speaker can appear less harsh, more pragmatic, his personal philosophy not foreclosing offerings of charity.

In this chapter we have observed the discrepancies between how Frost says his poetry operates and how it actually operates in a range of poems from throughout his career. Thus far, I have discussed primarily the unit of the sentence, the same unit to which Frost consistently draws our attention. In order to interrogate his formalism—and the politics of that formalism—fully, however, we must move away from that unit of discourse, turning light on the unit of the line—a unit that he is persuaded to say less, not more, about in the interest of "the sound of sense."

NOTES

97. Griffiths, *The Printed Voice*, 66.

98. Reuben Brower, *The Poetry of Robert Frost: Constellations of Intention* (Oxford: Oxford University Press, 1963), 1.

99. Evans, *Forty Years of Friendship*, 103.

100. Carlson, "Robert Frost on 'Vocal Imagination, the Merger of Form and Content,'" 520.

101. Griffiths, *The Printed Voice*, 205.

102. Richardson, *The Ordeal of Robert Frost* 49–50.

103. Kilcup, *Robert Frost and Feminine Literary Tradition*, 83.

104. Poirier, *The Work of Knowing*, 108.

105. Brower, *Constellations of Intention*, 18.

106. Evans, *Forty Years of Friendship*, 89.

107. Kearns, *Poetics of Appetite*, 18.

108. Brower, *Constellations of Intention* 160.

109. Ibid., 159.

110. Ibid., 159, 18, 158, 162.

111. Kearns, *Poetics of Appetite*, 19, 18.

112. Poirier, *The Work of Knowing*, 128.

113. Ibid., 198.

114. Evans, *Forty Years of Friendship*, 89.

115. I am drawing on Freud's terminology as set forth in his essay "Mourning and Melancholia" (1917), vol. 14 of *The Standard Edition of the Complete Psychological Works of Sigmund Freud*, ed. James Strachey (London: Hogarth, 1953–74).

116. Randall Jarrell, "To the Laodiceans," in *Robert Frost: A Collection of Critical*

Essays, ed. James M. Cox (Englewood Cliffs: Prentice-Hall, 1962), 191.

117. Cook, *A Living Voice*, 136.

118. Cook, "Robert Frost's Asides on His Poetry," 35.

119. Burnshaw, *Robert Frost Himself*, 279.

120. Cook, *A Living Voice*, 82; *Family Letters* 267.

121. Botroff, *Language and the Poet*, 136.

122. Lionel Trilling, "A Speech on Robert Frost: A Cultural Episode," in *Robert Frost: A Collection of Critical Essays*, 156.

123. Lentricchia, *Modernist Quartet*, 121.

124. Meyers, *Robert Frost: A Biography*, 216.

125. Jarrell, "To the Laodiceans," 86–87.

126. Brower, *Constellations of Intention*, 106.

127. Ibid., 106.

128. Ibid., 107.

129. Cook, *A Living Voice*, 126.

130. Ibid., 112.

131. Pritchard, *A Literary Life Reconsidered*, 127.

132. See Yvor Winters, "Robert Frost: or, the Spiritual Drifter as Poet," in *Robert Frost: A Collection of Critical Essays*, 58–82.

133. William Empson, *The Structure of Complex Words* (Totowa, New Jersey: Rowman and Littlefield, 1979), 101.

134. Poirier, *The Work of Knowing*, 164–65.

135. Cook, *A Living Voice*, 123.

136. Meyers, *Robert Frost: A Biography*, 140.

137. Evans, *Forty Years of Friendship*, 113.

138. Ibid., 109.

139. Burnshaw, *Robert Frost Himself*, 66, 279.

140. Jarrell, *Poetry and the Age*, 41.

141. Thompson, *Years of Triumph*, 437.

142. Jarrell, *Poetry and the Age*, 42.

143. Meyers, *Robert Frost: A Biography*, 215–16.

144. For the elaboration of this metaphor, see Leo Marx, *The Machine in the Garden: Technology and the Pastoral Idea in America* (Oxford: Oxford University Press, 1964).

145. Ibid., 27.

146. *Rebel Voices: An I.W.W. Anthology*, ed. Joyce L. Kornbluh (Ann Arbor: University of Michigan Press, 1965).

147. Ibid., 66.

148. Winters, "Robert Frost: or, The Spiritual Drifter as Poet," 68.

149. Cook, "Frost's Asides on His Poetry," 35; Reginald L. Cook, "Frost on Frost: The Making of Poems," in *On Frost: The Best from* American Literature, eds. Edwin H. Cady and Louis J. Budd (Durham: Duke University Press, 1991), 49.

150. Malcolm Cowley, "The Case against Mr. Frost," in *Robert Frost: A Collection of Critical Essays*, 41–42.

151. Ibid., 42.

Chronology

1874	Robert Frost is born on March 26 in San Francisco, California to William Prescott Frost, Jr., and Isabelle Moodie Frost.
1874–84	Frost spends his childhood in San Francisco.
1885	After the death of his father, Frost moves to Lawrence, Massachusetts, with his mother and sister.
1892	Graduates from Lawrence High School with his co-valedictorian and future wife, Elinor White. He attends Dartmouth College for a few months.
1893	Frost takes his first teaching job (8th grade) in Methuen, Massachusetts. He works in the Arlington Mill in Lawrence.
1894	"My Butterfly," Frost's first published poem, appears in *The Independent*.
1895	Frost marries Elinor Miriam White.
1896	Their first son, Eliot, is born.
1897–99	Frost attends Harvard as an undergraduate.
1899	Frosts's daughter Lesley is born.
1900	Eliot Frost dies. Another son, Carol, is born. The family moves to a farm in Derry, New Hampshire.
1900–10	Years of farming and teaching at the Pinkerton Academy in Derry.

1903	Daughter Irma is born.
1905	Daughter Marjorie is born.
1907	Daughter Elinor Bettina is born; dies in infancy.
1911–12	Frost teaches psychology at New Hampshire State Normal School in Plymouth.
1912–15	Resides in England with Elinor and their four children. Frost writes and farms in Buckinghamshire and Hereford-shire. Meets Ezra Pound.
1913	*A Boy's Will* is published in London. Frost meets Edward Thomas.
1914	*North of Boston* is published in London.
1915	The Frosts return from England and move to a farm in Franconia, New Hampshire. Frost's two books are published in the U.S.
1916	*Mountain Interval* is published. Frost reads as Phi Beta Kappa Poet at Harvard and is elected to the National Institute of Arts and Letters.
1917	Frost begins teaching English at Amherst College.
1919	Moves to a new farm near South Shaftsbury, Vermont.
1920	Co-founds the Breadloaf School of English at Middlebury College.
1921–23	Frost is Poet in Residence at the University of Michigan.
1923	*Selected Poems* and *New Hampshire* are published.
1923–25	Serves as Professor of English at Amherst College.
1924	Receives the Pulitzer Prize for *New Hampshire*.
1925–26	Frost is Fellow in Letters at the University of Michigan.
1926	Resumes teaching at Amherst College.
1928	*West-Running Brook* is published.
1929	*A Way Out* is published. Robert and Elinor move to Gully Farm in Bennington, Vermont.
1930	*Collected Poems* is published.
1934	Frost's daughter, Marjorie Frost Fraser, dies.
1936	A Further Range is published. Frost serves as Charles Eliot Norton Professor of Poetry at Harvard University.
1937	Receives his second Pulitzer Prize for *A Further Range*.

1938	Elinor White Frost dies. Frost resigns from Amherst College.
1939	The enlarged *Collected Poems* is published. Frost is awarded the National Institute of Arts and Letters Gold Medal for Poetry. Buys a farm in Ripton, Vermont, for a summer home.
1939–42	Serves as Ralph Waldo Emerson Fellow in Poetry at Harvard.
1940	Frost's son Carol commits suicide.
1942	*A Witness Tree* is published.
1943	Frost receives his third Pulitzer Prize for *A Witness Tree*.
1945	*A Masque of Reason* is published.
1947	*Steeple Bush* and *Masque of Mercy* are published.
1949	*Complete Poems* is published.
1950	The U.S. Senate passes a resolution commending Frost on the event of his seventy-fifth birthday.
1954	Frost celebrates his eightieth birthday with a reception at the White House. He represents the U.S. at the World Congress of Writers in Sao Paulo, Brazil.
1957	Frost travels to England, where he is honored at Oxford and Cambridge Universities and the National University of Ireland. Dines with President Eisenhower at the White House.
1958	Appointed Consultant in Poetry to the Library of Congress.
1959	Frost's eighty-fifth birthday is marked by another U.S. Senate commendation and Lionel Trilling's speech "A Cultural Episode."
1961	Frost reads "The Gift Outright" at the Inauguration of President John F. Kennedy. Lectures in Athens and Jerusalem.
1962	Frost visits Moscow as a guest of the Soviet Government. He meets privately with Premier Khrushchev; reads "Mending Wall ." *In the Clearing* is published.
1963	Frost is awarded the Bollingen prize for Poetry. He dies on January 29 in Boston.

Contributors

HAROLD BLOOM is Sterling Professor of the Humanities at Yale University and Henry W. and Albert A. Berg Professor of English at the New York University Graduate School. He is the author of over 20 books, including *Shelley's Mythmaking* (1959), *The Visionary Company* (1961), *Blake's Apocalypse* (1963), *Yeats* (1970), *A Map of Misreading* (1975), *Kabbalah and Criticism* (1975), *Agon: Toward a Theory of Revisionism* (1982), *The American Religion* (1992), *The Western Canon* (1994), and *Omens of Millennium: The Gnosis of Angels, Dreams, and Resurrection* (1996). *The Anxiety of Influence* (1973) sets forth Professor Bloom's provocative theory of the literary relationships between the great writers and their predecessors. His most recent books include *Shakespeare: The Invention of the Human* (1998), a 1998 National Book Award finalist, *How to Read and Why* (2000), and *Genius: A Mosaic of One Hundred Exemplary Creative Minds* (2002). In 1999, Professor Bloom received the prestigious American Academy of Arts and Letters Gold Medal for Criticism, and in 2002 he received the Catalonia International Prize.

RICHARD POIRIER is Professor Emeritus of English at Rutgers University. He is the Editor of *Raritan Quarterly* and in addition to *Robert Frost: The Work of Knowing* (1977), he is the author of *The Performing Self* (1971), *A World Elsewhere* (1968), *Poetry and Pragmatism* (1992), and *Trying it Out in America : Literary and Other Performances* (1999).

DAVID BROMWICH is Housum Professor of English at Yale University. His books include *Hazlitt: The Mind of the Critic* (1983), *Disowned By Memory:*

Wordsworth's Poetry of the 1790's (1998), and most recently, *Skeptical Music* (2001), a collection of essays and reviews on modern poetry.

HERBERT MARKS is Associate Professor of Comparative Literature and Religious Studies, as well as Director of the Biblical Institute, at Indiana University. He has written extensively on the Bible and on modern poetry.

CHARLES BERGER is Associate Professor of English at the University of Utah. He has co-edited a collection of essays on James Merrill and is the author of *Forms of Farewell: The Late Poetry of Wallace Stevens* (1985).

SHIRA WOLOSKY is Professor of English and American Literature at the Hebrew University of Jerusalem. She is the author of the widely acclaimed *The Art of Poetry: How to Read a Poem* (2001) and *Language Mysticism: The Negative Way of Language in Eliot, Beckett and Celan* (1995).

GEORGE F. BAGBY is Professor of English at Hampden-Sydney College and is the author of *Frost and the Book of Nature* (1993).

MARK RICHARDSON is Associate Professor of English at Western Michigan University. He is the author of *The Ordeal of Robert Frost* (1997) and co-editor, with Richard Poirier, of the Library of America edition of Robert Frost's *Collected Poems, Prose, and Plays* (1995).

KATHERINE KEARNS has taught at New York University and at Yale University. She is the author of *Robert Frost and a Poetics of Appetite* (1994), *Nineteenth-century Literary Realism* (1996), and *Psychoanalysis, Historiography, and Feminist Theory* (1997).

SEAMUS HEANEY has won the Nobel Prize and has taught at Harvard University, Oxford University, and the University of California, Berkeley. His is the author of numerous collections of poetry, including *Death of a Naturalist* (1966), *Field Work* (1979), *Seeing Things* (1991), and most recently, *Electric Light* (2001). His essays have been collected in *Preoccupations* (1980), *The Government of the Tongue* (1988), and *The Redress of Poetry* (1995).

ROBERT FAGGEN teaches English at Claremont McKenna College. He has edited the *Cambridge Companion to Robert Frost* (2001) and is the author of *Robert Frost and the Challenge of Darwin* (1997).

TYLER HOFFMAN teaches English at Rutgers University, Camden. He is the author of *Robert Frost and the Politics of Poetry* (2001) and is Associate Editor of *The Robert Frost Review*.

Bibliography

Angyal, Andrew J. "From Swedenborg to William James: The Shaping of Robert Frost's Religious Beliefs." *Robert Frost Review* (Fall 1994): 69–81.

Auden, W. H. "Robert Frost." In *The Dyer's Hand and Other Essays*, 337–353. New York: Random House, 1962.

Bacon, Helen. "For Girls: From 'Birches' to 'Wild Grapes.'" *Yale Review* 67 (1977): 13–29.

Bagby, George F. *Frost and the Book of Nature*. Knoxville: University of Tennessee Press, 1993.

Barry, Elaine. *Robert Frost*. New York: Frederick Ungar, 1973.

Berger, Harry, Jr. "Poetry and Revision: Interpreting Robert Frost." *Criticism* 10 (1968): 1–22.

Bogan, Louise. *A Poet's Alphabet*. New York: McGraw-Hill, 1970.

Borroff, Marie. *Language and the Poet: Verbal Artistry in Frost, Stevens, and Moore*. Chicago: Chicago University Press, 1979.

Brodsky, Joseph. "On Grief and Reason." *The New Yorker* (September 26, 1994): 70–5.

Bromwich, David. *A Choice of Inheritance: Self and Community from Edmund Burke to Robert Frost*. Cambridge, MA: Harvard University Press, 1989.

Brower, Reuben A. *The Poetry of Robert Frost: Constellations of Intention*. New York: Oxford University Press, 1963.

Cook, Reginald L. *Robert Frost: A Living Voice*. Amherst: University of Massachusetts Press, 1974.

Cowley, Malcolm. "Robert Frost: A Dissenting Opinion." In *A Many-Windowed House*, 201–12. Carbondale: Southern Illinois University Press, 1970.

Cox, James M., ed. *Robert Frost: A Collection of Critical Essays*. Englewood Cliffs, NJ: Prentice Hall, 1962.

Cox, Sidney. *A Swinger of Birches*. New York: New York University Press, 1960.

D'Avanzo, Mario L. *A Cloud of Other Poets: Robert Frost and the Romantics*. Lanham, MD: University Press of America, 1991.

Dawes, James R. "Masculinity and Transgression in Robert Frost." *American Literature* 65 (June 1993): 297–312.

Dickey, James. "Robert Frost." In *Babel to Byzantium: Poets and Poetry Now*, 200–9. New York: Farrar, Straus and Giroux, 1968.

Donoghue, Denis. "Robert Frost." In *Connoisseurs of Chaos: Ideas of Order in Modern American Poetry*. New York: Macmillan, 1965.

Doreski, William. "Robert Frost's 'The Census-Taker' and the Problem of the Wilderness." *Twentieth-Century Literature* 34, no. 1 (Spring 1988): 30–39.

Dowell, Peter W. "Counter-images and Their Function in the Poetry of Robert Frost." *Tennessee Studies in Literature* 14 (1969): 15–30.

Faggen, Robert. *Robert Frost and the Challenge of Darwin*. Ann Arbor: University of Michigan Press, 1997.

Gerber, Philip C. *Robert Frost*. New York: Twayne Publishers, 1966.

Hadas, Rachel. *Form, Cycle, Infinity: Landscape Imagery in the Poetry of Robert Frost*. Lewisburg, PA: Bucknell University Press, 1985.

Harris, Kathryn Gibbs, ed. *Robert Frost: Studies of the Poetry*. Boston: G. K. Hall and Co., 1979.

Haynes, Donald T. "The Narrative Unity of *A Boy's Will*." *PMLA* 137 (1972): 452–64.

Heaney, Seamus. "Above the Brim." In *Homage to Robert Frost*, 61–88. New York: Farrar, Straus and Giroux, 1996.

Hoffman, Tyler. *Robert Frost and the Politics of Poetry*. Hanover: University Press of New England, 2001.

Howe, Irving. "Robert Frost: A Momentary Stay." In *A World More Attractive*, 144–57. New York: Horizon Press, 1963.

Ingebretsen, S. J., ed. *Robert Frost's Star in a Stone Boat: A Grammar of Belief*. San Francisco: Catholic Scholars Press, 1994.

Jarrell, Randall. "The Other Frost" and "To the Laodiceans." In *Poetry and the Age*, 28–36, 37–69. New York: Alfred A. Knopf, 1953.

Kearns, Katherine. *Robert Frost and a Poetics of Appetite*. New York: Cambridge University Press, 1994.

Kemp, John C. *Robert Frost and New England: The Poet as Regionalist*. Princeton: Princeton University Press.

Kennedy, John F. "Poetry and Power." *Atlantic Monthly* 213 (February 1964): 53–54.

Lea, Sidney. "From Sublime to Rigamarole: Relations of Frost to Wordsworth." *Studies in Romanticism* 19 (1980): 83–108.

Lentricchia, Frank. *Robert Frost: Modern Poetics and the Landscapes of Self*. Durham, N.C.: Duke University Press, 1975.

———. *Modernist Quartet*. New York: Cambridge University Press, 1994.

Lynen, John F. *The Pastoral Art of Robert Frost*. New Haven: Yale University Press, 1960.

Marcus, Mordecai. *The Poems of Robert Frost: An Explication*. Boston: G.K. Hall and Co., 1991.

Marks, Herbert. "The Counter-Intelligence of Robert Frost." *Yale Review* 71 (1982): 554–78.

Maxon, H. A. *On the Sonnets of Robert Frost*. Jefferson, NC: McFarland and Co., 1997.

McGavran, Dorothy. "The Building Community: Houses and Other Structures in the Poetry of Robert Frost." *Robert Frost Review* (Fall 1994): 1–12.

Meyer, Jeffrey. *Robert Frost: A Biography*. Boston: Houghton Mifflin, 1996.

Michaels, Walter Benn. "Getting Physical." *Raritan* 2, no. 2 (Fall 1982): 103–13.

Monteiro, George. "Frost's Hired Hand." *College Literature* 14 (1987): 128–35.

———. *Robert Frost and the New England Renaissance*. Lexington: University Press of Kentucky, 1988.

Norwood, Kyle. "The Work of Not Knowing: Robert Frost and the Abject." *Southwest Review* 78 (1993): 57–75.

Oster, Judith. *Toward Robert Frost: The Reader and the Poet*. Athens: University of Georgia Press, 1991.

Pack, Robert. "Frost's Enigmatical Reserve: The Poet as Teacher and Preacher." In *Affirming Limits: Essays on Mortality, Choice and Poetic Form*, 174–88. Amherst: University of Massachusetts Press, 1985.

Parini, Jay. *Robert Frost: A Life*. New York: Holt, 1999.

Pearce, Roy Harvey. *The Continuity of American Poetry*. Princeton: Princeton University Press, 1961.

Perrine, Laurence. "Provide, Provide." *Robert Frost Review* (Fall 1992): 33–39.

Poirier, Richard. "Frost, Winnicott, Burke." *Raritan* 2, no. 2 (Fall 1982): 114–27.

———. *Robert Frost: The Work of Knowing*. New York: Oxford University Press, 1977.

Poole, Robert. "Robert Frost, William Carlos Williams, and Wallace Stevens: Reality and Poetic Vitality." *CLA Journal* 26 (1992): 12–23.

Pritchard, William. *Frost: A Literary Life Reconsidered*. New York: Oxford University Press, 1984.

Richardson, Mark. *The Ordeal of Robert Frost: The Poet and His Poetics*. Urbana: University of Illinois Press, 1997.

———. "Robert Frost and the Motives of Poetry." *Essays in Literature* 20, no. 2 (Fall 1993): 273–291.

Ridland, John. "Fourteen Ways of Looking at a Bad Man." *Southwest Review* 71, no. 2 (Spring 1986): 222–42.

Sabin, Margery. "The Fate of the Frost Speaker." *Raritan* 2, no. 2 (Fall 1982): 128–39.

Sears, John F. "The Subversive Performer in Frost's 'Snow' and 'Out, Out.'" In *The Motive for Metaphor*, ed. Francis Blessington. Boston: Northeastern University Press, 1983.

Sheehy, Donald G. "(Re)Figuring Love: Robert Frost in Crisis." *New England Quarterly* 63 (June 1990): 179–231.

Tharpe, Jack L., ed. *Frost: Centennial Essays*. Jackson: University Press of Mississippi, 1974.

Thompson, Lawrence. *Fire and Ice: The Art and Thought of Robert Frost*. New York: Holt, Rinehart, and Winston, 1942.

Trilling, Lionel. "A Speech on Robert Frost: A Cultural Episode." *Partisan Review* 26 (Summer 1959): 445–452.

Walcott, Derek. "The Road Taken." In *Homage to Robert Frost*. New York: Farrar, Straus and Giroux, 1996.

Warren, Robert Penn. "The Themes of Robert Frost." in *Selected Essays*, 118–36. New York: Random House, 1958.

Winters, Yvor. "Robert Frost: Or, The Spiritual Drifter as Poet." In *The Function of Criticism*, 157–88. Denver: Alan Swallow, 1957.

Wolosky, Shira. "The Need of Being Versed: Robert Frost and the Limits of Rhetoric." *Essays in Literature* 18, no. 1 (Spring 1991): 76–92.

Acknowledgments

"Choices" by Richard Poirier from *Robert Frost: The Work of Knowing* by Richard Poirier. © 1977 by Richard Poirier. Used by permission of Oxford University Press, Inc.

"Wordsworth, Frost, Stevens and the Poetic Vocation" by David Bromwich from *Studies in Romanticism* 21, no. 1 (Spring 1982). © 1982 by the Trustees of Boston University. Reprinted by permission.

"The Counter-Intelligence of Robert Frost" by Herbert Marks from *The Yale Review* 71, no. 4 (Summer 1982). © 1982 by Yale University. Reprinted by permission.

"Echoing Eden: Frost and Origins" by Charles Berger from *Robert Frost*, ed. Harold Bloom. © 1986 by Charles Berger. Reprinted by permission.

"The Need of Being Versed: Robert Frost and The Limits of Rhetoric" by Shira Wolosky from *Essays in Literature* 18, no. 1 (Spring 1991). © 1991 by Western Illinois University. Reprinted by permission.

"The Promethean Frost" by George F. Bagby from *Frost and the Book of Nature* by George F. Bagby. © 1993 by The University of Tennessee Press, Knoxville. Reprinted by permission.

"Robert Frost and the Motives of Poetry" by Mark Richardson from *Essays in Literature* 20, no. 2 (Fall 1993). © 1993 by Western Illinois University. Reprinted with the permission of the author.

"The Serpent's Tail" by Katherine Kearns from *Robert Frost and a Poetics of Appetite* by Katherine Kearns. © 1994 by Cambridge University Press. Reprinted with the permission of Cambridge University Press.

"Above the Brim" by Seamus Heaney from *Homage to Robert Frost* by Joseph Brodsky, Seamus Heaney and Derek Walcott. © 1996 by the Estate of Joseph Brodsky, Seamus Heaney, and Derek Walcott. Reprinted by permission of Farrar, Straus, and Giroux, LLC.

"The Fact Is the Sweetest Dream: Darwin, Pragmatism, and Poetic Knowledge" by Robert Faggen from *Robert Frost and the Challenge of Darwin* by Robert Faggen. © 1997 by the University of Michigan Press. Reprinted by permission.

"The Sense of Sound and the Silent Text" by Tyler Hoffman from *Robert Frost and the Politics of Poetry* by Tyler Hoffman. © 2001 by Tyler Hoffman. Reprinted by permission.

Index

"Acceptance," 260
Adams, Henry, 226–27
"After Apple-Picking," 259
  image of growth and decay in, 239
  metaphor in, 64
  the quest in, 5
"Aim Was Song, The"
  moral terms in, 71
  origins and echoes in, 71–72
  Wordsworthian model of nature in,
    72, 113
"Aimless," 259–60
"All Revelation"
  maternal influence in, 184
  sexuality in, 185
  vision of natural unrest in, 162
Allen, Grant, 258
  *Colin Clout's Calendar: A Record of a
    Summer*, 257
Arnold, Matthew
  influence on Frost, 34–35, 37
"Asking for Roses," 13
  impoverished dwellings in, 14–15
"At the Fishhouses" (Bishop)
  compared to "Directive," 83
"Away!"
  tone of, 285–86
"Ax-Helve, The," 205, 217

Bachelard, Gaston,
  The Poetics of Space, 150

Bagby, George, F., 300
  on the Promethean element in Frost,
    109–37
Bartlett, John, 25, 207
"Bear, The," 53
Beckett, Samuel, 216
"Before the Beginning and After the
    End of a Poem"
  intention in, 155
  lecture of "The Constant Symbol,"
    155
Bercovitch, Sacvan
  on Emerson's "philogy of nature,"
    103
  on natural theology and federal
    eschatology, 102–3
"Bereft"
  impotence in, 170
  symbolic value in, 171
Berger, Charles, 300
  on Frost's fictions of origins and
    echoes, 67–85
Bergson, 226
  Creative Evolution, 249–50
"Birches"
  image of growth and decay in, 239
  "love" and kinship in, 129, 131
  meditative poem, 110
  natural act in, 130, 209, 214
  Promethean poem, 111, 129
  visionary assertions in, 130
  writing style of, 209–10

"Birthplace, The"
  maternal influence in, 179–81
Bishop, Elizabeth, 83
Blake, William, 113–14, 122, 129–30
  "single vision" and, 117
"Black Cottage, The," 12
Bloom, Harold, 299
  introduction, 1–7
"Bond and Free"
  balance of imagination in, 131
  "love" and bondage in, 131, 167
  Promethean poem, 135
"Bonfire, The"
  desire in, 168–69, 171
  maternal influence in, 177
  metaphor in, 188
Bonner, Amy, 202
Borroff, Marie
  on "Come In," 279–80
  on Frost's use of Christian symbols,
    84
  on Frost's language, 70
Boy's Will, A, 9–10, 13, 18, 215
  landscape symbolism in, 15–16
  choices in, 11–12, 17
  drama of freedom and form in, 11–12
  harmony with seasons and sexuality
    in, 16
  metaphors in, 17
  poems in, 11–12, 15–16, 19, 34, 255
  writing style of, 5, 25, 91
Braithwaite, William Stanley, 25
Bromwich, David, 29–43, 299–300
  on the contrast between Frost and
    Stevens, 31, 37–41
  on the contrast between Frost and
    Wordsworth, 31–37, 41
  on the contrast between Stevens and
    Wordsworth, 31, 37–41
  on Wordsworth, 29–30
Brower, Reuben
  on "Death of the Hired Man,"
    274–76
Burke, Kenneth
  A Grammar of Motives, 140–41

Burnshaw, Stanley
  on "Mending Wall," 279
  on "Provide, Provide," 289

"Cabin in the Clearing, A"
  Emersonian irony in, 6
"Carpe Diem"
  dissents from the traditional
    suggestion in, 111
"Census-Taker, The"
  barren landscape in, 117, 122, 133
  defeat of human effort in, 116,
    122–23, 132
  compared to "Hyla Brook," 11
  image of growth and decay in, 240
  man and nature in, 116, 118
  meditative emblem poem, 123
  Promethean poem, 116, 118
"Choose Something Like a Star," 231,
  257
Ciardi, John
  reviews of Frost, 151–52
"Cocoon, The"
  physical presence in, 134
  visionary power in, 134
"Code, The," 217
Coleridge, Samuel Taylor, 65, 126, 134,
  236, 256, 261
"Come In"
  first-person narrative of, 58
  sounds of nature in, 23
  tone of, 279–80
Concealment themes, 45
  in "The Constant Symbol," 56
Conduct of Life, The (Emerson)
  "Circles " in, 2
  essays in, 2, 6–7
  "Experience" in, 2, 220
  "Fate" in, 2–3, 220
  "Illusions" in, 2, 6–7
"Constant Symbol, The," 150, 157
  aphorism in, 148–49
  classicism in, 148–49
  concealment in, 56

intention revealed in, 143
metaphors in, 98, 146, 239
motivation theories in, 146–47
poet's conviction in, 50
powers of control in, 162
satire and irony in, 144
self-annihilation in, 152
Shakespeare's integrity in, 144
"sincerity and intention" in, 142–43
sexuality in, 56, 162
"vocal imagination" in, 26
writing style of, 152, 154
Cook, Reginald
    on "Mending Wall," 278
"Course of a Particular, The" (Stevens)
    compared to "Resolution and
        Independence," 31, 38–40
    compared to "Two Tramps in Mud
        Time," 31, 37, 39–40
Cox, Sidney, 46–47, 64, 146, 149–51,
    272, 274, 287
Culler, Jonathan, 143
    On Deconstruction, 143
Crane, Hart, 1, 83

Darwin, Charles, 257
    "conditions of existence," 229
    concept of natural selection, 226–29,
        234–35, 241–43, 249, 253–55
    fact and metaphor in vision of,
        226–27, 231, 236
    human consciousness of, 242, 247
    influence on Frost, Emerson,
        Thoreau, and James, 219–62
    Milton's influence on, 222–24, 249,
        261
    On the Origin of Species, 224, 232, 239,
        249, 258
    and pragmatism, 226, 241–42
    science and, 247
    The Various Contrivances by Which
        Orchids Are Fertilized by Insects, 256
    view of evolution, 227, 229, 232, 240
    The Voyage of the Beagle, 232, 254, 262

"Death of the Hired Man, The," 13
    male-female relationship in, 180,
        272–76
    maternal solicitude, 179
    political views in, 273–76
    tone of, 272–77
"Demiurge's Laugh, The," 259
    sardonic nihilism in, 173
Derrida, Jacques, 155
    on moral or political responsibility,
        141–42
"Desert Places," 220, 251
    dark side of Frost in, 204
    impotence in, 170
    loneliness of nature in, 23
    compared to "Stopping by Woods on
        a Snowy Evening," 203
    writing style of, 204–7
"Design," 231, 256
    image of growth and decay in, 240
    natural emblem, 115
    terror in, 202
    tone of, 6, 280–82
Desire themes, 161–62
    in "The Bonfire," 168–69, 171
    in "For Once, Then, Something," 231
    in "Home Burial," 169
    in A Masque of Reason, 187
    in "On Going Unnoticed," 169
    in "The Silken Tent," 157, 171
    in "A Soldier," 121
    in "Stopping by Woods on a Snowy
        Evening," 171
    in "The Subverted Flower," 169
    in "There Are Roughly Zones," 121
    in "To Earthward," 168, 192, 214
    in "To a Moth Seen in Winter,"
Dewey, John, 146, 150, 155, 157
    Art as Experience, 146,155
    Art as Expression, 150
    "The Impact of Darwin on
        Philosophy," 243–44
Dickinson, Emily, 16
"Diemiurge's Laugh, The"
    mocking demonic derision at the self-
        realization in, 5

"Directive," 1, 217
  blank-verse narrative in, 62
  Christian symbols in, 45, 62–66, 84
  confusion in, 4–5, 84–85
  criticism of, 84–85
  compared to Emerson's "Illusions," 6
  compared to *Excursion*, 63
  compared to "At the Fishhouses," 83
  journey homeward in, 83
  the landscape of, 82
  origins and echoes in, 70, 81–85
  remorse in, 5
  compared to "The Snow Man," 83
  theme of the *nostos* in, 82–83, 208
  wholeness and simplicity in, 81–82
"Discovery of the Madeiras, The"
  history of his own lifelong
    engagement in, 66
"Dream Pang, A," 24
  connections between sexual love and
    poetic making, 19
  sounds of nature in, 23
  time scheme of, 23

"Education by Poetry"
  metaphors in, 98, 104, 235
  personification in, 90
"Egg and the Machine, The"
  political views in, 289–91
  tone of, 289–91
Eliot, T.S., 1, 139, 146
  compared to Frost, 21, 140, 146–51, 156
  "The Function of Criticism," 147–48
  "Shakespeare and the Stoicism of Seneca," 149
Emerson, Ralph Waldo, 22, 58, 65–66, 124, 129, 142, 237
  criticism of, 61
  "Divinity School Address," 1
  compared to Frost, 146, 219, 221, 232, 238, 246, 261–62
  influence on Frost, 1–6, 24, 50, 72, 112, 131, 245

Nature, 112–113, 219, 258
  and nature as a metaphor, 103, 120, 127, 219–20, 258
  negativity of, 4
  "Self-Reliance," 2
  "Terminus," 50
Empson, William
  on "The Most of It," 285
"Empty Threat, An," 51, 53
  first-person narrative of, 58
  metaphors in, 64
"Encounter, An," 13
Excursion (Wordsworth)
  compared to "Directive," 63

Faggen, Robert, 300
  on Darwin's long argument and nature's chaos, 226–40
  on Darwin and the rise of pragmatism, 240–49
  on the modern Lucretius, 249–62
  on the "philosophical" Frost, 219–69
"Figure a Poem Makes, The," 19
  emergence into consciousness in, 10–11
  mysterious workings of choice in, 10–11
  poetic practice in, 55, 156, 210
"Flood, The"
  vision of natural unrest, 162
"Flower Boat, The," 13
"Flower Gathering"
  young poet's escape in, 16
"For Once, Then, Something"
  desire in, 231
  tone of, 284
  work of manhood in, 182
Form in Modern Poetry (Read)
  Movement poets in, 139
  romanticism and classicism in, 148
Foucault
  The History of Sexuality, 165
"Fragmentary Blue"
  blue of "heaven" in, 134

sexuality in, 187
Frazer, James
  The Golden Bough, 247–48
Freud, Sigmund, 277
  influence on Frost, 224
  The Interpretation of Dreams, 224
Frost, Elinor White (wife), 15, 280
  death of, 81
  in "Never Again Would Bird's Song
    Be the Same," 81
  relationship with Frost, 16–18
Frost-Francis, Lesley (daughter), 140,
    146, 154, 280
  lecture on "New Movement' poetry,
    139
Frost, Robert
  ambiguity of tone and, 271–92
  Arnold's influence on, 34–35, 37
  associations with pastoralism, 69
  choices of, 9–27, 143–47, 155
  chronology of, 295–98
  criticism of, 21,46, 87, 109, 118,
    150–51, 201, 271, 273, 278–82
  Darwin's influence on, 221, 224, 226,
    232, 233, 239–40, 243, 246, 261
  compared to Eliot, 21, 140, 146–51,
    156
  and Emerson, 1–6, 24, 50, 131, 146,
    219, 221, 232, 238, 245–46, 261–62
  as a farmer poet, 217
  Freud's influence on, 224
  gnosticism and, 4–5
  human narcissism and, 224
  compared to James, 219, 234, 238
  compared to D.H. Lawrence, 11
  Lucretius' influence on, 250
  metaphor use, 166, 233, 237–38, 246,
    249
  Milton's influence on, 80
  as a Movement poet, 139
  as nature poet, 5, 16, 26–27, 161, 166,
    233, 236, 238, 245, 250
  origins and echoes of, 67–85
  philosophy of, 241, 292

political views of, 272–76, 287–92
  religion and, 3, 45–46, 237, 240, 244,
    246
  science and, 240, 244, 248
  self criticism of, 201–18
  "sentence-sounds" of, 25, 69–70, 208
  and sexuality, 161–92, 246
  and "sincerity," 141–44
  compared to Stevens, 1, 31, 37–41, 67
  theories of, 24, 139–41, 144–46,
    148–49, 151, 207
  compared to Thoreau, 115, 130,
    219–21, 233
  compared to Wordsworth, 31–37, 41,
    54, 110–11, 124–25, 255
  writing styles of, 46, 87, 153–54, 244
  and Yeats, 21, 74, 201, 215
  Yeats influence on, 74
Further Range, A
  poems in, 288, 291
"Future of Man, The"
  motivation theories in, 147
  "sincerity" in, 142
  unpublished essay, 142

"Generations of Men, The"
  "Eve" symbolism in, 61
  metaphors in, 249
"Ghost House"
  barren landscapes in, 15
"Good Relief," 287
Griffiths, Eric
  on "Death of the Hired Man," 273
  on Frost, 271, 273
Grossman, Allen
  on Hart Crane and the question of
    origins, 83

Hamilton, Ian, 202
Hawthorne, Nathaniel, 61
Heaney, Seamus, 300
  on Frost's sense of his own faults,
    201–18

"Hill Wife, The," 59
Hoffman, Tyler, 301
  on the relation of Frost's poetic
    formalism and poetry politics,
    271–93
Hollander, John, 69
  The Figure of Echo, 69
"Home Burial," 59
  desire and in, 169, 175, 181
  "Eve" symbolism in, 61, 211
  grieving mother in, 171, 176, 179,
    210, 277
  tone of, 276-77
  writing style of, 210–11, 213
"Housekeeper, The," 12, 59
  domestic life in, 176
  maternal influence in, 178
"How Hard it is to Keep from Being
    King When It's in You and in the
    Situation"
  freedom in, 189
  love and the poetic act in, 165
  male-female bonds in, 177
  sexuality in, 185
  wife's infidelity in, 176
Hulme, T.E., 148, 250
"Hundred Collars, A"
  man's alienation in, 188
"Hyla Brook," 13, 231
  compared to "The Census-Taker,"
    117
  metaphors in, 249
  nature in, 262
  native speech in, 70

"I Could Give All to Time"
  Promethean poem, 122
  untimeliness in, 122
"In a Vale"
  connections between sexual love and
    poetic making, 19
  criticism of, 21
  time scheme of, 22–23

"In Equal Sacrifice," 13
In the Clearing, 6
"Into My Own"
  barren landscapes in, 15
  first-person narrative of, 58
Irigaray, Luce, 161
  Speculum of the Other Woman, 161

James, Henry, 61
James, William
  Darwin and, 242–44
  compared to Frost, 219, 234, 238
  human consciousness, 242, 249
  pluralism and confusion of, 241
  Principles of Psychology, 241–42
Jarrell, Randall
  on "Provide, Provide," 289
Jehlen, Myra, 103
Joyce, James, 54

Kearns, Katherine, 300
  on "Death of the Hired Man,"
    274–76
  on the nihilism of Frost's sexuality,
    161–99
Keats, John, 18–19, 51, 75, 85, 128, 172
  "A Song About Myself," 51
Kermode, Frank
  The Genesis of Secrecy, 84
Kilcup, Karen
  on "Death of the Hired Man," 274
King Jasper, 153
"Kitty Hawk"
  dream of "easy gold" in, 52
  Elinor White Frost in, 112
  echoes of Emerson in, 112
  freedom and power in, 119
  imaginative dominance in, 117
  man and nature in, 120
  metaphors in, 64, 114, 127
  parallel between poetics and
    Christology in, 50

Promethean poem, 114, 116, 131
  compared to "There Are Roughly
    Zones," 121
  Wright Brothers in, 112
  writing style of, 112

"Last Mowing, The"
  dream of "easy gold" in, 52
  Faraway Meadow in, 51–52, 60
"Late Walk, A
  faint signal of a new vitality in, 15–16
Lawrence, D.H.
  Frost compared to, 11
"Leaf Trader, A"
  sounds of nature in, 23
Lentricchia, Frank
  on Darwin, 231
  on Frost limits on imagination and
    irony, 101–2
  on Frost's winter landscapes, 150
"Lesson for Today, The" (Frost)
  fragmentary style of, 64
  sexuality in, 185, 188
"Line-Gang, The, " 13
"Line-Storm Song, A"
  passion in, 167
"Locked Out"
  maternal influence in, 177
"Loneliness," 13
Longfellow, Henry Wadsworth, 259
"Love and a Question," 15
  compared to "Two Tramps in Mud
    Time," 34
Lowell, Robert, 217–18
  History, 217–18
Lucretius, 249, 253, 262
  influence on Frost, 250

Man, Paul de
  theory of verbal irony, 98
Marks, Herbert, 300
  on displacement and loss in Frost's
    work, 45–66

  on Eve symbolism in Frost's female
    characters, 53–62
  on the fall from Eden symbolism in
    "Directive," 62–66
  on Frost's theological themes, 45–53
Marx, Leo, 103, 246, 289
Masque of Mercy, A, 45–46, 285
  God in, 3, 178
  sexuality in, 185
  theological themes in, 45
Masque of Reason, A
  desire in, 187
  Emerson's influence in, 2
  God in, 3, 178, 253
  Job in, 2–3, 47, 65, 176–78, 183, 237
  male-female bonds in, 177
  nihilism in, 3, 162, 173, 185, 187
  wife's infidelity in, 176
Meditative emblem poems, 110
  "Birches," 110
  "The Census-Taker," 123
  "On the Heart's Beginning to Cloud
    the Mind," 110, 132
  "Spring Pools," 75
  "To a Moth Seen in Winter," 110,
    115, 122
  "West-running Brook," 110, 118
  "Wild Grapes," 110, 126
"Meeting and Passing"
  mutuality in, 216
Mellville, Herman
  Pierre, 103
Memoirs of the Notorious Stephen
    Burroughs
  theological themes in, 45–46
"Mending Wall," 231
  tone of, 277–79
"Men Improve with the Years" (Yeats)
  compared to "To Earthward," 215
Mertins, Louis
  on Frost, 150–51
Milton, John, 55, 57–58, 60, 113, 142,
    211
  influence on Darwin, 222-24, 249

influence on Frost, 80
Paradise Lost, 56–58, 60 222
Paradise Regained, 50
"Missive Missile, A"
  sexuality in, 185
Monroe, Harriet, 13
"Moon Compasses"
  triumphant vision of, 134
"Most of It, The," 217, 220
  American Adam in, 77–79
  brutish indifference in, 24
  erotic fulfillment in, 78
  "garden of Eden" poem, 54–55, 77,
    79
  laughing voice of Eve in, 80
  man and nature in, 24
  origins and echoes in, 77–79
  tone of, 284-85
Motives of "conformity" and "formity,"
  141–42, 144, 147
  in " The Silken Tent," 144–45
Motivation theories
  in "The Constant Symbol," 146–47
"Mountain, The"
  metaphors in, 249
Mountain Interval A, 5
  poems in, 13, 131
  shattering of human ties and humans
    in, 6
"Mowing," 12, 256–57, 259, 261
  chain reaction of rapture in, 215–16,
    255
  image of growth and movement, 239
Munson, Gorham
  on Frost, 148
"My Butterfly," 18
"My Giving"
  political views in, 287–88
  tone of, 287–88
"My November Guest"
  barren landscapes in, 15

Nature themes
  in "The Aim Was Song," 72, 113

in "Birches," 130, 209, 214
in "The Census-Taker," 116, 118
in "Come In," 23
in "Desert Places," 23
in "A Dream Pang," 23
in "Hyla Brook," 262
in "Kitty Hawk," 120
in "A Leaf Trader," 23
in "The Most of It," 24
in "The Need of Being Versed in
  Country Things, " 26–27, 88–89,
  95–97, 100–1
in "Never Again Would Bird's Song
  be the Same," 24
in "On a Tree Fallen Across the
  Road," 123–24, 131
in "On the Heart's Beginning to
  Cloud the Mind, 132, 135"
in "Once by the Pacific," 118–19
in "A Soldier," 119
in "The Subverted Flower," 24
in "There Are Roughly Zones,"
  122–123
in "To Earthward," 171
in "To a Moths Seen in Winter,"
  115–16, 118
in "The Vantage Point," 24
in "West-running Brook," 117–18
in "Wild Grapes," 124, 125, 130
"Need of Being Versed in Country
  Things, The"
anthropomorphism in, 89
imagery in, 89, 91, 211
intentionality in, 90, 92, 94, 96, 101
irony in, 88, 97–98, 102, 104
the language of, 88, 95–96, 98, 101,
  105
man and nature in, 26–27, 88–89,
  95–97, 100–1
moral lessons of, 89
personification in, 89–90, 92–96,
  98–99, 102
writing style of, 91, 93, 102, 211
"Neither Out Far No In Deep"
  tone of, 280–81

"Never Again Would Bird's Song Be the Same," 256
    American Adam in, 81, 213
    elegy to Elinor Frost, 81
    the fall of "Eve" in, 55, 81, 212–13
    "garden of Eden" poem, 54, 79–81, 212–13
    man and nature in, 24
    Milton's influence on, 80
    origins and echoes in, 80–81
    shadows the succession of generations in, 56
"New Hampshire"
    blank-verse narrative in, 62
    male-female bonds in, 176–77
Nietzsche, 104, 226
    The Will to Power, 104
"Nothing Gold Can Stay," 174
    "Eve" symbolism in, 80
    myths of the garden and the golden age in, 74
    origins and echoes in, 74–76
    compared to "The Snow Man," 75
    Yeats influence on, 74
North of Boston, 5, 13
    poems in, 12, 256, 259, 276–77
    review of, 216
Nuttall, A.D.
    on Wordsworth, 41
"Nutting" (Wordsworth)
    human assault, 125
    ravishment of nature in, 125
    sense of blessedness in, 124
    compared to "Wild Grapes," 124–26

"Of Ceasing to Question What Doesn't Concern Us," 250
"Old Cumberland Beggar, The" (Wordsworth)
    compared to "Resolution and Independence," 41
"Old Man's Winter Night, An," 13
    compared to "There Are Roughly Zones," 121

universal solitude in, 216
"On Going Unnoticed"
    desire in, 169
"On a Tree Fallen Across the Road"
    double vision in, 123
    human yearning in, 124
    natural obstruction in, 123–24, 131
    Promethean poem, 112, 124, 128, 135
"On the Heart's Beginning to Cloud the Mind"
    man and nature in, 132, 135
    meditative emblem poem, 110, 132
    processiveness in, 132–33
"Once by the Pacific"
    God in, 3
    man and nature in, 118–19
    Promethean poem, 118–19
"One or Two"
    "garden of Eden" poem, 54
    history of his own lifelong engagement in, 66
"Out, Out—," 217
    maternal influence in, 178
    political views in, 6, 287
    tone of, 84, 286–87
"Oven Bird, The," 13, 231, 256
    irony in, 170
    lyric voice in, 170, 211

"Palladium" (Arnold)
    compared to "The Trial by Existence," 34
    compared to "Two Tramps in Mud Time," 35
"Pan With Us," 259–60
    theme of, 21
Parini, Jay
    on Frost, 219
Pater, Walter
    Plato and Platonism, 247
"Paul's Wife," 57, 61, 163
    metamorphic landscape in, 174
    necessity of concealment in, 47–48

symbols and mythical echoes in, 47
"Pea Brush," 13
"Poet's Next of Kin in College, The"
  "constant symbol" in, 157
"Poetry and School," 155
Poirier, Richard, 299
  on the affinity between Frost and
    Emerson, 2
  on "Death of the Hired Man," 274
  on "Directive" and confusion, 84–85
  on Frost, 53, 70, 131, 150, 152–3,
    166, 172
  on Frost compared to Lawrence, 11
  on Frost's early choices, 9–27, 35, 67
  on Frost's "negative designation," 51
  on "Home Burial," 276
  on "The Most of It," 285
Pound, Ezra, 139–40, 146
  Frost admirer, 13
  link to Whitman, 1
  review of A Boy's Will, 13
  review of North of Boston, 216
Porter, David
  on Frost, 219
"Power" (Emerson)
  in The Conduct of Life, 2
  law of Compensation in, 2
  savage of strength in, 5
Pragmatism
  significance of Darwin and, 226,
    241–42, 248
"Prayer in Spring, A" (Frost)
  in A Boy's Will, 16
  young poet's escape in, 16
Prelude, The (Wordsworth) meditative
    process in, 111, 126, 129
"Prerequisites, The" (Frost)
  fragmentary style of, 64
Pritchard, William
  on Frost, 151, 202, 208
  on "The Road Not Taken," 283
  Robert Frost: A Literary Portrait, 208
Prometheus, 109–137
Promethean impulses, 109, 135

in "Birches," 111, 129
in "Bond and Free," 135
in "The Census-Taker," 116, 118
in "I Could Give All to Time," 122
in "Kitty Hawk," 114, 116, 131
in "On a Tree Fallen Across the
    Road," 112, 124, 128, 135
in "Once by the Pacific," 118–19
in "The Silken Tent," 131
in "A Soldier," 112, 121, 128, 131
in "There Are Roughly Zones," 121,
    123, 128
in "To a Moth Seen in Winter," 110,
    122, 132
in "West-running Brook," 110–11,
    135
in "Wild Grapes," 124, 126–28, 135
"Provide, Provide" (Frost)
  in A Further Range, 288
  political views in, 287–88
  terror in, 202
  tone of, 288–89
"Putting in the Seed" (Frost)
  in A Mountain Interval, 13
  sexual metaphor in, 171–72

"Range Finding" (Frost)
  in A Mountain Interval, 13
Ray, Alice
  on "Out, Out—," 287
Read, Herbert, 139–40, 146, 148
Reichert, Victor, 54
"Reluctance" (Frost)
  Promethean poem, 122, 131
  untimeliness in, 122
"Resolution and Independence"
    (Wordsworth)
  compared to "The Course of a
    Particular," 31, 38–40
  criticism of, 30
  compared to "The Old Cumberland
    Beggar," 41
  compared to "Two Tramps in Mud
    Time," 31–37, 39–40

Richards, I.A., 139–40
    Science and Poetry, 261
Richardson, Mark, 300
    on "Death of the Hired Man,"
        273–74
    on T.S. Eliot's influence on Frost's
        metaphor, 139–159
Richardson, Robert
    on *Walden*, 220–21
"Road Not Taken, The" (Frost), 287
    tone of, 282–83
Robinson,
    Frost on, 153
"Rock, The" (Stevens), 1
Roethke
    link to Whitman, 1
"Romantic Chasm, A" (Frost)
    the necessity of concealment in, 62
"Rose Pogonias" (Frost)
    confusion in, 65
    in *North of Boston*, 16, 256–57
    young poet's escape in, 16
Rossetti, 18
Royce, Josiah
    "Nature and Evolution: The Outer
        World and Its Paradox," 241
    "Nature and the Paradox of
        Evolution," 251
    "The Rise of the Doctrine of
        Evolution," 241
    The Spirit of Modern Philosophy,
        251–53
    survey of modern philosophy, 241
Russell, Bertrand, 226

Sabin, Majorie
    on Frost's vitality of speech, 208
"Sad Strains of Gay Waltz" (Stevens), 39
"Sand Dunes" (Frost)
    dead external coverings in, 129
    defeat of human effort in, 120
    man and nature in, 118, 120, 124
    metaphors in, 127

Promethean poem, 112, 118, 129–30,
    132
Schopenhauer, 225, 243
"Self-Seeker, The" (Frost), 259
"Semi-Revolution, A" (Frost)
    sexuality in, 187
Sentence-sounds, 11, 25, 69–70, 208
"Servant to Servants, A," 59, 61, 163
    correspondence between masking and
        metaphor in, 48
    freedom and restraint in, 48
    love and the poetic act in, 164
Shakespeare, William, 156, 286
    Eliot on, 149
    Frost on integrity of, 144
    Macbeth, 286
Shelley, Percy Bysshe, 18, 124, 128, 130
    "Epopsychidion," 18
    "Ode to the West Wind," 37
Sidney, 18
    Astrophel and Stella, 257
"Signature Event Context," 155
"Silken Tent, The"
    "blending of answerabilities" in, 145
    "formity and conformity" motivation
        in, 144–45
    freedom and restraint in, 48–49, 145
    imagery of the tent in, 49–50
    inner desire in, 157, 171
    "love" in, 131
    natural fact in, 131
    poetic voice in, 166–67
    Promethean poem, 131
    seeds of nihilism in, 172
    structure of, 49, 145
    symbols in, 172
    unparalleled harmonic balance in,
        166, 216
"Sitting by a Bush in Broad Sunlight"
    bringing the sacred into the social
        realm in, 73
    Emerson's influence on, 72
    origins and echoes in, 72–74, 80
    persistence in, 80

subject of entropy in, 72
two creation stories in, 73–74
Slotkin, Richard, 103
"Snow Man, The" (Stevens), 37–39
  compared to "Directive," 83
  force of "misery" in, 75
  compared to "Nothing Gold Can
    Stay," 75
"Soldier, A"
  capable imagination in, 119
  death in, 120, 214
  desire in, 121
  double vision in, 123
  man and nature in, 119
  natural obstruction of human desire
    in, 131
  Promethean poem, 112, 121, 128, 131
"Sound of Trees, The"
  first person narrative of, 58
"Spoils of the Dead," 13
"Spring Pools,"
  chilly narcissism in, 76
  emblematic focus of meditation in, 75
  limits of reflective consciousness in,
    225
  "logic" of, 11
  origins and echoes in, 75–76
"Star in a Stoneboat, A," 249, 258
  life's emptiness in, 6
"Stars"
  accent of Emily Dickinson in, 16
  landscape in, 16
Steeple Bush, 55
Stevens, Wallace, 51, 58, 63, 75, 113–14,
    119, 153, 223
  "The Auroras of Autumn," 1
  "The Emperor of Ice Cream," 153
  "Esthétique du Mal," 39
  compared to Frost, 1, 31, 37–41, 67,
    82–83
  "The Idea of Order at Key West," 80
  link to Whitman, 1, 37
  "Mozart, 1935," 39
  "Notes toward a Supreme Fiction,"
    39–40, 63, 75

"An Ordinary Evening in New
    Haven," 67
  Promethean impulses in, 110
  compared to Wordsworth, 31, 37–41
  unfettered imagination in, 131
"Sunday Morning," 223
"Stopping by Woods on a Snowy
    Evening," 21, 157
  desire and self-annihilation in, 171
  compared to "Desert Places," 203
  first-person narrative of, 58
  theories of motivation in, 153
  writing style of, 154
"Storm Fears"
  compared to "There Are Roughly
    Zones," 121
  young man's fear in, 16
"Subverted Flower, The," 13
  autobiographical nature of, 15
  desire in, 169
  failure of love in, 24
  the fall of "Eve" in, 55–56, 59
  'frigidity in women' in, 15–16
  imagery in, 14
  man and nature in, 24
  theory of personality and motive in
    poetry, 151
  sexuality between flowers and poetry
    in, 14–15, 192
  writing style of, 14–15
Swinger of Birches, A (Cox)
  relaxed irony of Frost in, 146

"Taking Something Like a Star," 187
"Telephone, The," 13
Tennyson, Alfred Lord, 18, 261
"Thatch, The"
  symbolic value in, 171
Theory of sound and poetic form, 24,
    207
Theory of motive in poetry, 139–41,
    144–46, 149, 151
  in "The Future of Man," 147

in "Stopping by Woods on a Snowy
    Evening," 153
in "The Subverted Flower," 151
Theory of personality in poetry, 139–40,
    148, 151
in "Subverted Flower, The," 151
"There Are Roughly Zones"
    desire in, 121
    compared to "Kitty Hawk," 121
    man and nature in, 122–23
    compared to "An Old Man's Winter
        Night," 121
    obstinacy of "soul or mind," 121
    Promethean poem, 121, 123, 128
    compared to "Storm Fear," 121
    threatening external forces in, 121
Thomas, Edward, 119, 283
Thompson, Lawrence, 48, 249
    biographer of Frost, 9, 15
    on Frost's letters, 46
    on Frost's publications, 12–13, 55
Thoreau, Henry David, 51, 111, 119,
    255
    "Autumnal Tints," 221
    Cap Cod, 220
    Darwin influence on, 221, 233
    "Dispersion of Seeds, The," 221
    on Frost, 26
    compared to Frost, 115, 130, 219–21
    "Ktaadn," 223
    The Maine Woods, 220–21
    nature and, 220
    "Old Marlborough Road, The," 51
    "The Succession of Forest Trees,"
        221
    "Wild Apples," 221
    "Wild Fruits," 221
"Three Voices of Poetry" (Eliot)
    the poet's burden in, 149
    poet's personal motives in, 149
"Time Out"
    theory of vision in, 111
"To Autumn" (Keats)
    compared to "Waiting," 19

"To Earthward"
    desire in, 168, 192, 214
    earthly love in, 167, 213–14
    man and nature in, 171
    compared to "Men Improve with the
        Years," 215
"To a Moth Seen in Winter"
    defeat of human effort in, 132
    isolation of, 133
    limitless trait in, 122
    man and nature in, 115–16, 118
    meditative poem, 110, 115, 122
    Promethean poem, 110, 122, 132
    wintry state of the imagination's life,
        117, 132
"To the Thawing Wind"
    young poet's escape in, 16
"Too Anxious for Rivers," 250–51, 253
"Tradition and the Individual Talent,"
    147, 156
"Tree at My Window"
    impotence in, 170
"Trial by Existence, The"
    compared to "Palladium," 34
    description of the soul's birth in, 50
    relish of self-exposure in, 9–11
Trilling, Lionel
    on Frost, 204
    on "Neither Out far Nor In Deep"
        and "Design," 280
"Tuft of Flowers, The," 12
    chain reaction of rapture in, 215
Twilight
    first collection of poetry, 18
"Two Look at Two," 217
"Two Tramps in Mud Time," 1
    compared to "The Course of a
        Particular," 31, 37, 39–40
    compared to "Love and a Question,"
        34
    negative theology in, 3–4
    compared to "Palladium," 35
    compared to "Resolution and
        Independence," 31–37, 39–40

political views in, 291–92
tone of, 291–92

"Uriel" (Emerson), 2, 237
    Frost on, 1
    mode of irony in, 1
    poetic speech of, 50
    confusion in, 4, 65–66

"Valley's Singing Day, The"
    comedy of disproportion in, 68–69
    the subject of beginnings in, 68–69
"Vantage Point The"
    man and nature in, 24

Walden (Thoreau), 221
    nature in, 220
    self-exile in, 220
"Waiting," 19–20
    connections between sexual love and
        poetic making in, 19
    evocations of natural sounds in, 20–21
    compared to Keats ode "To Autumn,"
        19
    time scheme of, 22–23
"Waiting for Godot"
    furious assertions in, 175
Warren, Robert Penn
    on Frost and nature, 101
Weiner, Philip
    Evolution and the Founders of
        Pragmatism, 241
"West-running Brook"
    "Eve" symbolism in, 61
    human community in, 135, 162
    meditative poem, 110, 118
    metaphors in, 249
    natural fact in, 117–18
    Promethean poem, 110–11, 135
"White-Tailed Hornet, The"
    blank-verse narrative in, 62

sexuality in, 188, 191
Whitman, Walt, 241
    other poets linked to, 1, 4, 37
Wilbur, Richard
    on "Wild Grapes," 130
"Wild Colonial Boy, The"
    maternal influence in, 178
"Wild Grapes"
    heroine of, 124, 126
    human will and aspiration in, 131,
        133, 135
    man and nature in, 124, 126, 130
    meditative poems, 110, 126
    compared to "Nutting," 124–26
    a Promethean poem, 124, 126–28,
        135
    visionary assertions in, 110, 124, 130
Wilson, Daniel
    Science, Community, and the
        Transformation of American
        Philosophy, 1869-1930, 241
Williams, W.C., 1
    "Beautiful Thing," 54
"Wind and Window Flower"
    male/ female relationship in, 16
"Winter Eden, A"
    animated, playful poem, 76
    cold pastoral in, 76
    language of innocence in, 77
    origins and echoes in, 76–77
Winters, Yvor
    on Frost, 283, 290
"Witch of Coös, The," 217
    male-female bonds in, 177
    maternal influence in, 177, 179–80
Witness Tree, A
    poems in, 12, 54–55
Wolosky, Shira, 300
    on Frost's rhetorical limitations in
        "The Need of Being Versed in
        Country Things, 87–107
"Wood-Pile, The," 2, 23
    image of growth and decay in, 240
Wordsworth, William, 16, 124, 126,
    128–29, 131, 261

criticism of, 29–30
"Elegiac Stanzas Suggested by a
    Picture of Peele Castle in a Storm,"
    30
first lyric allegorist, 30
compared to Frost, 31–37, 41, 54,
    110–11, 124, 255
"Immortality," 30
"Lines Composed a Few Miles Above
    Tintern Abbey," 30, 40, 111
meditative vision of, 110, 134
nature model of, 72, 236

"Ode to Duty," 30
sense of vocation, 29–30
"Solitary Reaper," 255
compared to Stevens, 31, 37–41
theory of composition of, 110

Yeats, William Butler, 30
    "Dialogue of Self and Soul," 201
    compared to Frost, 21, 201, 215
    influence on Frost, 74
    Promethean impulses of, 110